Merry Christmas, James P.   2013
Hope you get the
       chance to play here again
                        someday!
       ♡ Love, Mary to, "the wife"

D1552368

Pebble Beach:
The Official Golf History

Neal Hotelling

Photography by Joann Dost

TRIUMPH
BOOKS

Copyright © 2009 by Pebble Beach Company

Pebble Beach®, Pebble Beach Golf Links®, The Lodge at Pebble Beach™, Pebble Beach Concours
D'Elegance®, Spyglass Hill® Golf Course, The Links at Spanish Bay™, The Inn at Spanish Bay™,
Casa Palmero®, 17-Mile Drive®, Del Monte™ Golf Course, The Lone Cypress™, The Heritage Logo,
and their respective images are trademarks, service marks, and trade dress of Pebble Beach Company.
Used under license.

No part of this publication may be reproduced, stored in a retrieval system, or transmitted in any form
by any means, electronic, mechanical, photocopying, or otherwise, without the prior written permission
of the publisher, Triumph Books, 542 South Dearborn Street, Suite 750, Chicago, Illinois 60605.

Triumph Books and colophon are registered trademarks of Random House, Inc.

Library of Congress Cataloging-in-Publication Data
Hotelling, Neal.
  Pebble Beach : the official golf history / Neal Hotelling ; photography by Joann Dost.
    p. cm.
  ISBN 978-1-60078-300-5
  1. Pebble Beach Golf Links (Pebble Beach, Calif.)--History. I. Title.
  GV969.P43H69 2009
  796.35206'879476—dc22
                              2009035825

Published by:

Triumph Books
542 South Dearborn Street
Suite 750
Chicago, Illinois 60605
(312) 939–3330
Fax (312) 663–3557
www.triumphbooks.com

Printed in U.S.A.
ISBN: 978-1-60078-300-5
Design by Wagner Donovan Design

Contents

FOREWORD BY ARNOLD PALMER

*P*ebble Beach has been called "America's Course"—as iconic as St. Andrews in Scotland. Like St. Andrews, Pebble Beach has one course that stands out under its name, and a small group of courses that claim the name as their locale. The quality of the courses at Pebble Beach, however, is unequalled—with four of the courses ranked among the Top 100 in America. This book tells their story and that of championships contested on them. Nearly every famous golfer—professional and amateur, male and female, young and old—of the past century has played this celebrated venue. No place in the nation with such a small population has hosted so many USGA Championships—the 2010 U.S. Open marks the 16th—let alone one of the longest running PGA Tour events (over 60 years and counting) and hundreds of state and regional amateur championships.

I have known Pebble Beach for quite a few years. In doing his research for this book Neal Hotelling discovered I was the only professional to compete at Pebble Beach in each of the last six decades. Even before I visited Pebble Beach for the first time, it was already legendary as a championship venue. It became the first golf course west of St. Louis to host a U.S. Amateur in 1929, the year I was born.

My first invitation to play came from Bing Crosby for the 1958 Pro-Am. I made it a regular part of my schedule for several years—missing only one cut in my first 14 years. My closest shot at victory came in 1966, where despite starting the final round with a double-bogey, I stayed in contention and made three birdies on the last four holes. Unfortunately for me, Don Massengale also got hot, and after an early eagle on hole 2 and a front nine 32, he beat me by a single stroke, sinking a birdie putt on 18.

The next year I finished third behind Jack Nicklaus and Billy Casper—this despite my remarkable 9 strokes on the par-5 14th hole in the final round. Nicklaus had taken the lead with a birdie on 12, so I pressed a 3 wood in an attempt to reach the green in 2 and keep the pressure on Nicklaus. Not once, but twice I hit that 3 wood, both times hitting a tree on the right and ricocheting out of bounds. There is no doubt I should have heeded the age-old advice of my father Deacon Palmer—"Play your own game and mind your own business and you'll do much better."

Many people have heard the legend that the night after my quadruple-bogey in 1967 a storm came through and felled the tree. I can tell you that story is true! As my agent and frequent playing partner Mark McCormack recorded, it left many wondering "How big is Arnie's Army?" Of course that was just one of many trees that have gone down on Pebble Beach Golf Links since I started playing there. Now that I have a direct role with the course, I have actively been involved with replacing some key trees—most notably the large cypress at the 18th green—but also a few along the 14th fairway where my nemesis once stood.

I finished second again in 1971, losing by two strokes to Tom Shaw. What made the Crosby, today's AT&T Pebble Beach National Pro-Am, unique was not just Bing's special involvement; it was the combination of using three great courses and pairing professionals with interesting amateur partners. Mark McCormack became my regular partner in 1963, but before and after Mark, I

had some wonderful partners. My first was Dr. Frank Taylor, a dentist that had twice won the California Amateur at Pebble Beach and was a member of the 1957 Walker Cup team. Other partners included singer Gordon MacRae, Phil Harris, and in 1961 Bing paired me with Dick Groat, the MVP shortstop for the 1960 World Series Champion Pittsburgh Pirates. I knew Dick in my high school days as a sports star from nearby Swissvale High, less than 30 miles from Latrobe. We remain good friends and he has owned and operated a good public course not far from Latrobe for around 40 years.

In 1977, after having not played in the Crosby for a few years, I returned and played the first round at Cypress Point without a partner; he was busy with a function in Washington D.C. The next day, President Gerald Ford joined me on the 3rd hole of Monterey Peninsula Country Club—just hours after having turned the White House over to Jimmy Carter. We paired up three more times at Pebble Beach, but only came within two strokes of making the cut as a team. In 1994, I was in the foursome with President George Herbert Walker Bush and Hale Irwin. I paired with my friend Russ Meyer, then chairman and CEO of Cessna, whom I've known since 1963 when he was a law partner with Mark McCormack and handled some of my business early in my association with Mark and all of my aviation activities.

In addition to a couple of dozen Pro-Am's, I competed in the first two U.S. Opens at Pebble Beach (finishing third to Jack Nicklaus in 1972), the PGA Championship in 1977, and even filmed one of my televised *Challenge Golf* matches—in it Gary Player and I lost our 1964 match to the team of Byron Nelson and Ken Venturi. In 2004 I helped launch the Champions Tour's Walmart First Tee Open at Pebble Beach, coming out of competitive retirement to pair with junior golfers for the first two years of the event. I've also enjoyed many casual rounds at Pebble Beach.

In my fifty-five years of professional golf, I accumulated many wonderful memories in a very successful career. While that career has included over 60 victories, the success can better be measured by the many friends I made both on and off the golf course. In 1999 I joined forces with three of those friends—Peter Ueberroth, Dick Ferris, and Clint Eastwood—to purchase Pebble Beach Resorts, returning it to American ownership just before it hosted the 1999 U.S. Amateur and 2000 U.S. Open. Ten years later, we are still friends and partners, having secured the most stable ownership group since Samuel F.B. Morse died in 1969 after fifty years of leadership. Clint and I played here long enough to count both Mr. Morse and Bing Crosby among our friends. Peter and Dick have played Pebble Beach only slightly less long. As did Morse and Crosby, we share a passion for the history and tradition of great golf that makes Pebble Beach one of the icons of the sport and the vision to assure it continues as a great venue for future generations.

We hope you enjoy this look at the great championship history of golf at Pebble Beach, and take the opportunity to come and make your own history on these storied links.

All the best,
Arnie

INTRODUCTION

*I*t has been more than ten years since I first sat down to record the official history of Pebble Beach Golf Links, and what a decade transpired:

- a new ownership group led by Peter Ueberroth, Richard Ferris, Arnold Palmer, and Clint Eastwood
- a wonderful U.S. Amateur won by David Gossett, who two years later recorded his first PGA TOUR victory
- an incredible U.S. Open won by Tiger Woods, who parlayed it into what became known as the "Tiger Slam"
- the launch of a new Champions Tour event, the Walmart First Tee Open, which pairs the senior players with junior golfers from the First Tee initiative
- agreement with the USGA to bring back the U.S. Open in 2010 and
- the decision to change the rotation in the Annual AT&T Pebble Beach National Pro-Am—replacing Poppy Hills Golf Course (a tournament venue since 1991) with the redesigned Shore Course at Monterey Peninsula Country Club effective 2010

Of course, Pebble Beach has also played 10 more AT&T Pebble Beach National Pro-Ams, and considering the weather we had when I was writing the prior history in the late 1990s, it is remarkable to note that in the last decade, there has been only one tournament day lost to weather. Another remarkable note is that in 2006, Kathryn Crosby, the widow of Bing Crosby who initiated the Pro-Am, returned to the event for the first time in the twenty years since the Crosby name was dropped from the tournament. I had the pleasure of walking a few holes at Spyglass Hill with her and her grandson as her two sons, Harry and Nathaniel, played together as amateurs in the time-honored event. I also walked 18 holes with her at Pebble Beach in 2008 following Harry. Any animus seems to have left, and many of us can again dream of the day when the Crosby name may return to the event that continues the tradition the incredible entertainer envisioned seven decades earlier.

One never-ending truth at Pebble Beach is that no book will ever hold the entire history. The good news is that history never changes, but it does expand, and our understanding of the past continues to evolve. One of the fears of writing a history, especially of such a unique place as Pebble Beach, is that you will get something terribly wrong. I am happy to report that the first edition has stood the test of time, was honored as Book of the Year by the International Network of Golf, and was described by noted golf writer Mark Soltau, who has covered numerous events here, as "The Bible on Pebble Beach."

Continuing in the Biblical vein, if the first book was equivalent to Chronicles, then don't think of this new edition as Second Chronicles, but rather as the books of Kings—some of the same history, but with a slightly different take, featuring other key players in the history, and for the first time ever compiling the history of many of the national and regional championships that have been played at Pebble Beach, and of course continuing the story with more recent events.

Because no ongoing records exist for many of the past tournaments, this effort required culling through thousands of newspapers and magazines to piece together records, occasionally interpreting conflicting reports based on the best data available. Amazingly, even where ongoing data existed, errors were found and information was missing—in most cases just scores, but in a couple of cases errors were identified on perpetual trophies. Errors happen and sometimes become part of history. An appendix with the compiled data (apologies for a few holes that remain) is provided in the back of the book. But names and numbers don't tell the story of the great players—men, women, and children—who have played these courses, so some of their stories are here, as well.

The Monterey Peninsula is geographically a small area of only a few square miles and, even combing the population of the surrounding communities, has a population of less than 100,000 people—and that is today. It was significantly smaller when the story began, so it is all the more amazing how much history of national and international interest has occurred along these shores. It truly is the golf capital of America (if not the world) not just because of one great golf course, but for the multitude of great courses—four of which are ranked in the Top 100—and the great golfers and championships that have played out on its storied links.

The sad news in the past decade is that our volunteer archival team of Elmer and Elena Lagorio, now both in their nineties, officially retired shortly after the 2000 U.S. Open. They will always be missed, but their organization of materials continues to be a helpful resource. That resource, now called the Pebble Beach Company Lagorio Archive was greatly expanded in 2003 when Pebble Beach Company recovered and began scanning nearly 50,000 original negatives from prior company photographers Julian P. Graham and William C. Brooks. Many of these images were not available or even known to exsist when I wrote the first history.

Graham began shooting for the company in 1924 and continued as the official photographer until his death in 1963. Brooks began working with Graham in 1953 and continued the legacy until he retired in 1986. Pebble Beach has been fortunate to have many great photographers, notably Joann Dost since 1982, preserve Pebble Beach on film, but there has not been a full-time photographer on-site since 1986. The legacy of these two early photographers, and the new availability of these early images, contributes greatly to our understanding of, and ability to interpret, the history with a fresh eye.

We therefore hope you will enjoy this new volume on the history of golf at Pebble Beach as much as many of you enjoyed the earlier history of Pebble Beach Golf Links.

Neal Hotelling
September 2009

CHAPTER *One*
GENERAL HISTORY

Pebble Beach Golf Links. (PBC–J.P. Graham)

(PBC – J.P. Graham)

THE BEGINNING

It was February 22, 1919. Everything had taken shape, and Samuel Finley Brown Morse was ready to host the elite of the San Francisco Bay area at the new lodge and golf course at Pebble Beach. Morse had been working toward this day for more than three years through numerous challenges and with an ever-growing vision. Festivities began with the ceremonial planting of a cherry tree in honor of George Washington's Birthday. The group then gathered around so that Russell R. Flint, a rancher and trustee from Sacramento, could administer the golfer's oath:

We pledge ourselves by our faith in the cherry tree to turn in honest scorecards.

The preliminary promotion for the two-day golf tournament assured both the Men's and Women's California Amateur champions would play. Douglas Grant won the 1918 Men's Amateur at Del Monte. But the report that it was Miss Josephine Moore who "won the title at the tournament here [Del Monte] last September," is just wrong. Moore actually finished as runner-up to Miss Edith S. Chesebrough as the Del Monte Women's Champion in 1918, there was no Women's State Amateur Championship that year. Nevertheless, in addition to Miss Moore, Miss Chesebrough did play, as did M.A. McLaughlin, the former (and future) Colorado Amateur Champion and, of course, Jack Neville, co-designer with Douglas Grant of Pebble Beach Golf Links and a two-time State Amateur himself.

The nature of the tournament was more social than competitive. Its goal was to attract the elite of society, and as such it was successful. Morse had visualized that if he provided the proper enticement, he could not only get them here, but convince them to buy property. The response to the gala weekend promised a prosperous future for Morse and the property. This was especially important to Morse, who was completing plans to purchase the holdings from his employer, Pacific Improvement Company.

The 1919 opening of The Lodge and Pebble Beach Golf Links made headlines in San Francisco as many of the elite from that area were in attendance. (PBC-Archives)

Hotel Del Monte was the primary resort facility when Pebble Beach opened in 1919. (PBC-Archives)

Charles Crocker (1822–88). (PBC-Archives)

Collis P. Huntington (1821–1900). (PBC-Archives)

Leland Stanford (1824–93). (PBC-Archives)

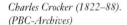

Mark Hopkins (1813–78). (PBC-Archives)

PACIFIC IMPROVEMENT COMPANY

Business partners Charles Crocker, Collis Huntington, Leland Stanford, and Mark Hopkins came to California as part of the Gold Rush of 1849. They were known as "The Big Four" and found their "gold" not in the hills but in serving the needs of the thousands of hopeful miners who needed supplies for the mine fields. Based in Sacramento, the nearest port to the gold-filled dreams of the Sierra foothills, the visionary merchants quickly became wealthy merchants. Stanford took an active role in shaping the future of the young state by making his initial mark as a justice of the peace. He served as Governor of California from 1861–63 and later as a U.S. Senator (1885–93). His influence was felt throughout the state but was especially significant in helping focus the efforts of his partners' profitable development in the Far West.

In 1863, the team began building a railroad extending eastward from San Francisco. Six years later, they arrived at Promontory Point, Utah. There, on May 10, 1869, Charles Crocker, who led the construction efforts, drove the golden spike, merging their rails with those of the Union Pacific Railroad to complete the trans-continental railroad. Huntington had spent most of that time in Washington D.C. lobbying for federal funds to complete the work and assure the future of rail transportation. At times the personal fortunes of the partners were at great risk as they borrowed against every asset to meet the large construction payroll and cost of materials. But the successful completion of the railroad made them each multi-millionaires, and they continued to advance the development of the West.

As their success seemed assured, in 1868 they formed the Pacific Improvement Company essentially as a real estate holding company to support the plans of the railroad—or more accurately, railroads.

Robert Louis Stevenson (1850–94), author of several books including Treasure Island, *spent a few months at Monterey in 1879 writing and courting his wife, Fanny Osbourne. (PBC-Archives)*

The Lone Cypress stands strong against the waves in a storm. (PBC-J.P. Graham)

An artist's rendering of the original Del Monte in its setting near Monterey Bay and the old Pacific Capitol. (PBC-Archives)

Shortly after completing the east-west Central Pacific Railroad, they acquired and began expanding the Southern Pacific Railroad, connecting southern California with the Pacific Northwest and eventually Texas. As their development needs grew, they bought the lands needed for such development. Acres of forestland were purchased and mills were built to produce lumber. They bought and developed coal mines, developed and controlled ports, and built shipping lines. Resort properties and small towns were built along the railway. They created ranches and even built a coffee plantation in Guatemala (where they built another railroad) to provide food for both the railroads and resorts. With each new development came more profits and more needs.

In 1878, the Southern Pacific Railroad acquired the narrow-gauge Salinas Valley Railroad that moved supplies back and forth from the port at Monterey and the farmlands of the Salinas Valley. Activity at Monterey had slowed significantly following the discovery of gold. From being the capital city of Alta (or upper) California in the Spanish and Mexican eras, the once-important city had become a somewhat forgotten relic in the 30 years that followed the United States occupation and statehood. Scottish writer Robert Louis Stevenson was in Monterey in 1879 courting his future wife, Fanny Osborne. In a letter to a friend that September, he wrote, "The population of Monterey is about that of a dissenting chapel on a wet Sunday in a strong church neighborhood. They are mostly Mexican and Indian—mixed." [1]

Charles Crocker believed the railroad would make a difference. The Southern Pacific replaced the narrow-gauge track of the Salinas Valley Railroad with full-size tracks, and Crocker announced plans to build a luxury

resort on Monterey Bay. Most people called the endeavor "Crocker's Folly" and it was not universally admired. By the time the hotel opened, Stevenson had married Fanny Osborne in San Francisco and was honeymooning near St. Helena in Napa County. Of the new hotel he wrote:

A huge hotel has sprung up in the desert by the railway. Three sets of diners sit down successively to table. Invaluable toilettes figure along the beach and between the live oaks; and Monterey is advertised in the newspapers, and posted in the waiting rooms at railway stations, as a resort for wealth and fashion. Alas for the little town! It is not strong enough to resist the influence of the flaunting caravanserai, and the poor, quaint, penniless native gentlemen of Monterey must perish, like a lower race, before the millionaire vulgarians of the Big Bonanza. [2]

Crocker called it Hotel Del Monte—"hotel of the grove"—for the oak grove in which it was built. It opened on June 3, 1880, and the public quickly proved Crocker's vision correct as the facility prospered. Among the early guests bringing acclaim to the hotel was President Rutherford B. Hayes, who in September 1880 became the first United States president to visit California—a visit that included a stay at Hotel Del Monte and a drive along the partially constructed 17-Mile Drive. Other guests included royalty from Europe such as Princess Louise, the popular fourth daughter of Queen Victoria, and the Marquis of Queensbury, the latter of whom said of Del Monte, "There is no place in the world so beautiful." [3]

Hotel Del Monte boasted overnight accommodations for 400, and on many nights it was full. The hotel grounds included more than 100 acres of manicured gardens. The initial facilities featured billiards, bowling,

and, of course, fine dining. For additional pleasure, Del Monte soon added an elaborate bathhouse at the beach, a short "eight-minute walk" (as it was advertised) from the hotel. The bathing pavilion was 70 feet wide and 170 feet long and featured four tanks, each about 50' x 36' and heated to differing temperatures by the steam plant. The addition of stables, a race track, and polo fields followed in short order.

The fabulous Hotel Del Monte, with its acres of manicured gardens, opened for business in June 1880 and quickly attracted the elite of society from around the world. (PBC-C.T. Watkins)

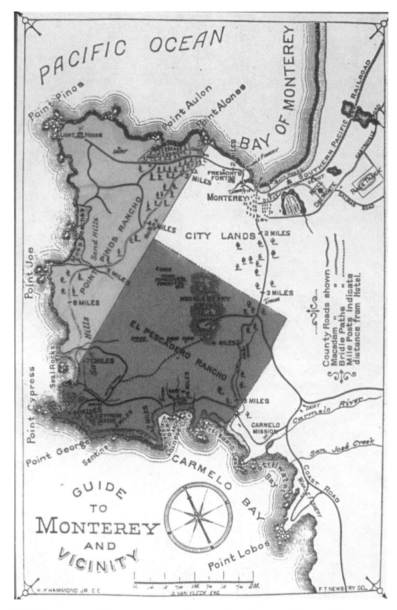

Pacific Improvement Company purchased the two ranchos that comprised most of the 7,000-acre Monterey Peninsula in May 1880, but an ownership dispute over El Pescadero Rancho delayed development for more than 20 years. (PBC-Archives)

DEL MONTE FOREST

The construction of the hotel provided local land baron David Jacks with an opportunity to unload two of his large ranchos that were bringing him grief. The 2,666-acre Point Pinos Rancho, where a church retreat began in 1875, had become a financial failure but was still active and creating challenges to the development of the area. To its immediate south, the 4,426-acre El Pescadero Rancho had been embroiled in litigation over ownership for more than a decade. The well-funded Pacific Improvement Company was in a much better position to address the challenges and agreed to buy the two ranchos that comprised most of the actual Monterey Peninsula for roughly $5 per acre—$35,000. The deed from Jacks to Pacific Improvement Company was completed on May 3, 1880.

The first move with the new property was to build a scenic drive from Hotel Del Monte around the spectacular coastline of the peninsula and back to the hotel. Completed in 1881, the route became known for its distance as the 17-Mile Drive. Although early references indicate it was once called the 16-Mile Drive and even the 18-Mile Drive, by 1883 the name 17-Mile Drive was clearly established. It became a popular attraction of the resort, with guests enjoying an all-day event that often included an elaborate picnic in the cypress grove or along the meadowland at Pebble Beach. The company continued a land lease for a Chinese fishing village at Stillwater Cove that Jacks had allowed, but other development of El Pescadero Rancho would have to wait for a clear title to the land. Instead, the company focused on the development of Pacific Grove as a supplement to its resort on Monterey Bay.

Jacks had helped a Methodist minister begin a retreat at Pacific Grove by donating 100 acres to the Pacific Grove Retreat Association in 1875 and loaned them $30,000 to create the infrastructure, including roads, surveys, and lot development. The plan was to repay the loan from the sale of hundreds of small lots. While the retreat in the woods attracted several seasonal guests, few lots were sold and the Association defaulted on the loan. Except for the sold lots, the 100-acre retreat land reverted back to Jacks in 1878 and was included in the sale to the Pacific Improvement Company. On the coastline at the eastern edge of the rancho, Jacks had leased a site to another Chinese fishing village; the company continued that lease, as well.

The Jung San Choy family lived and worked at this fishing village for many years (1868–1912). It was located near today's Beach Club on land the family first leased from David Jacks and later from the Pacific Improvement Company. The road was part of the 17-Mile Drive, and the field in the background became the 4th fairway. (PBC-Archives)

On the 1875 Retreat map, Jacks highlighted the few lots that had been sold before incorporating the unsold retreat lands into the acreage sold to the Pacific Improvement Company in 1880. (PBC-Archives)

EARLY PROPERTY DEVELOPMENT

The company was content to continue relationships and looked to enhance the area around the Methodist Retreat. While the company took over economic development, it continued the commitment Jacks had made that allowed the Pacific Grove Retreat Association to maintain moral and prudential control in the area "extend[ing] to the distance of one mile from the geographical center of the original survey." [4]

To assist the retreat, the company built a large but simple structure in 1881 to store tents in the off-season. In the summer, when not full of tents, it became a meeting hall. Now known as Chautauqua Hall, the historic building remains a popular meeting place. The company replaced the old bathhouse at the retreat with a new one in 1882—22 dressing rooms and eight private salt baths—managed by Mrs. Annie McDougall; [5] in 1883, provided land and a small octagonal building to house Pacific Grove's first museum—the scientific specimens of Professor Josiah Keep. In 1902, the land and original structures were donated for the current museum.

More significantly, the company piped in water from Carmel Valley and built a large water reservoir at Point Pinos Rancho in 1883 to service Hotel Del Monte and its development efforts at Pacific Grove. Demand quickly grew, and in 1888 the company risked building a second reservoir, Forest Lake, in the still-disputed El Pescadero Rancho. A newspaper article described the project still under construction as utilizing "thirteen hundred men—twelve hundred and fifty of whom are Chinamen—three or four hundred horses, and maybe two hundred carts. All are continually in motion, and a casual glance from an elevated position gives one an impression similar to the restless, undulated motion of the sea." The article went on to state they would create, "A body of water thirty acres in extent and from 35 to 40 feet in depth will make quite a respectable lake." It held 100 million gallons of water. [6]

These two reservoirs built in the 1880s remained in service for more than a century. After a decade of being empty, the Forest Lake reservoir in El Pescadero Rancho was retrofitted and put back in service in 2006 as part of the reclaimed water system that services all of the golf courses in Del Monte Forest. The Point Pinos reservoir remains dry.

A Pilsbury panoramic photo from 1906 of the Pacific Improvement Company's hotel in Pacific Grove. Originally known as El Carmelo, the name was changed when guests began looking for it in the emerging development at Carmel. (Hotelling)

The bathhouse above the beach at Lovers Point in Pacific Grove (1892) was where visitors to the Methodist Retreat bathed and also where they changed for a brisk dip in Monterey Bay. (PBC-Archives)

A construction crew—largely Chinese workers—builds Forest Lake Reservoir in 1888 to expand the community water system. (PBC-Archives)

Only the chimneys stood after a devastating fire destroyed the original Hotel Del Monte in 1887. (PBC-C.W.J. Johnson)

The company also installed a much-needed system of sewers and storm drains, so that "no fears could be reasonably entertained of malaria or 'the thousand natural shocks that flesh is heir to.'" [7]

Whether it was the water, the improved rail service to the Monterey Peninsula, or the added influx of wealthy guests at Hotel Del Monte, the little lots in Pacific Grove began selling. With no reason to stay within the bounds of the original retreat, the company began developing above Lighthouse Road, as well.

In 1887, the company made one of its most noticeable impacts on Pacific Grove. On May 20, 1887, it opened El Carmelo Hotel. The hotel provided 114 guest rooms in a modern three-story structure. It featured water from the company's water system, extending service into every guest room. It also included gas lighting with an on-site power plant and an elevator. With a frontage of about 200 feet on Lighthouse Avenue, El Carmelo became a focal point of the town, which had grown dramatically in just seven years of company ownership.

While El Carmelo was nearing completion, on the night of April 1, 1887, Hotel Del Monte was destroyed by fire. Company officials pled for leniency from the retreat association on the alcohol ban, at least until they could rebuild Del Monte. The retreat officials refused to budge, and if guests of El Carmelo desired a glass of wine, they were obliged to travel to Monterey. Company officials therefore put full effort into rebuilding Hotel Del Monte, creating an even larger hostelry in just a year's time.

Crocker personally saw to the reconstruction of Hotel Del Monte. The new and improved Hotel Del Monte was ready to receive guests in March

1888. Five months later, on August 14, 1888, while staying at Hotel Del Monte, Crocker had a heart attack and ended an era of corporate passion for the area. This is not to say the company abandoned the peninsula, but for the rest of the board, "The Del Monte Unit" (as it was known) was just one of its many land holdings.

Crocker's eldest son, Charles Frederick Crocker, took over the primary management of Pacific Improvement and was named second vice president in 1890 when Stanford stepped down and Huntington was named president. Mark Hopkins had died in 1878, and his widow remarried. In 1891, after less than four years of marriage, Mary Hopkins Searles died, leaving her entire estate to her significantly younger husband, Edward. Searles took a much more active role in the company. When C.F. Crocker died in 1897, Searles arranged for the appointment of General Thomas H. Hubbard as first vice president in charge of operations under Huntington. Hubbard had been a Civil War hero and returned to his New England legal practice after the war. Hubbard was a partner in the law firm that looked after the Hopkins-Searles holdings while Mary was still alive and became a trusted advisor to Edward Searles.

Following the death of Huntington, Hubbard was elected president of the company and in 1901 sold the railroad interests to a group controlled by Edward H. Harriman that also controlled the Union Pacific Railroad. It took years to unweave the railroad holdings from the other holdings of the Pacific Improvement Company, and without the railroads, the Pacific Improvement Company lost much of its power. The remaining large property holdings had heavy tax burdens with minimal income production.

When the original Hotel Del Monte burned to the ground in 1887, Charles Crocker (on horseback) personally oversaw its rapid reconstruction into an enlarged version of its initial design. (PBC-Archives)

The train station at Hotel Del Monte was a hub of activity. (PBC-Archives)

Charles Crocker leads a group of millionaire family and friends in a walking line on the grounds of Hotel Del Monte. (PBC-Archives)

The second version of Hotel Del Monte, similar in design to the original, opened in December 1887, less than a year after the original hotel burned to the ground. (PBC-Archives)

This early five-some at Del Monte Golf Course has been identified as L.H.P. Lamb, Jack Neville, Charles Templeton Crocker, A.S. Lillie, and Vincent Whitney. (PBC-R.J. Arnold)

Del Monte Golf Course opened on May 1, 1897, just a short walk from Hotel Del Monte. (PBC-Archives)

THE DEL MONTE UNIT

During the corporate transitions of the 1890s, Hotel Del Monte continued to run profitably. Following the 1887 fire, George Schöenwald, who had served as manager of the luxury hotel from it initial opening until April 1886, returned to help oversee the reconstruction and re-opening, and served another four years, adding needed stability. In June 1892, the company sent him to open their new resort at Castle Craggs, but he was back at Del Monte the next April and continued until the end of 1894.

The architecture of the rebuilt hotel was similar to the original, although slightly larger, and of course the setting remained incomparable. The rich and powerful visitors quickly returned. President Benjamin Harrison set up the hotel's east wing as his western White House for an extended stay in 1891, even having it wired for direct communication with Washington D.C. Other early visitors included business magnates Joseph Pulitzer and Dale Carnegie.

A combination of positive factors came together in the 1890s, including a strong economy, a more mobile society with a growing group of wealthy individuals having increased leisure time, and an influx of Scots and Brits coming to America, including California. The result was golf coming to California, although when and where it began is still debated. While various individuals argue for earlier recognition, it is generally conceded that the first course in America was a three-holer built in 1888 near Yonkers, New York.

As for golf in the West, there is a similar lack of the definite. Most believe the first course in the Far West was built in 1891 near Riverside in Southern California, but even that is open to debate. Regardless, as golf gained popularity, room needed to be made for it at Del Monte.

George Arnold took on management duties of Hotel Del Monte on January 1, 1895, and he was challenged with where they could put a real golf course. David Jacks had land nearby but was not willing to sell it. Eventually, Arnold arranged a lease of the Jacks land and began construction. Del Monte Golf Course officially opened on May 1, 1897, with what was then considered the best nine-hole course in California. A month later, Schöenwald returned as Del Monte's manager, hired James Melville as the golf professional, and helped establish golf and the

The Log Lodge at Pebble Beach stood from 1909 through 1917 and saw the preferred mode of transportation move from the horse and buggy to the horseless carriage. (PBC-Archives)

Del Monte Cup tournament as part of the annual late summer sports gathering.

Schöenwald was strict, organized, and trusted by the management. While he left Del Monte again in September 1899, he was brought back in December 1901 to lend his expertise during the large transition of running the hotel separate from the railroad and under the new leadership of General Hubbard.

While Schöenwald was in charge of Hotel Del Monte, General Hubbard recruited A.D. Shepard from the Southern Pacific team and appointed him General Manager of the Pacific Improvement Company in 1901. Shepard had been a railroad man for years, beginning with the Erie Railroad in 1868. By 1898, he rose to general freight agent for the Southern Pacific at its San Francisco headquarters.

As manager of Pacific Improvement Company, his first job was to analyze the holdings and maximize revenue opportunities. The Del Monte Unit was doing well, so he gave it little attention. Some assets he liquidated, such as a coffee plantation in Guatemala and its associated rail system. Others he developed for greater profitability, including the Carbon Hill Coal Mine in the state of Washington. Adding to Shepard's opportunities was the 1905 U.S. Supreme Court action finally resolving ownership of

The interior of The Log Lodge offered an austere alternative to the elegance of Hotel Del Monte, but it had large stone fireplaces for heat and electric-powered log chandeliers accented with abalone shells around the lights. (PBC-Lagorio Archives)

Omnibuses like this shuttled guests between Hotel Del Monte and The Lodge in the early 20th century. (PBC-Archives)

Chris Jorgensen built this elaborate log home in 1910. The first home in the new Pebble Beach Estates stood near today's post office. (PBC-Archives)

Louis Hill, president of the Great Northern Railway, built one of the early log homes at Pebble Beach around 1910. It burned to the ground in 1937, but the Hills rebuilt and descendants remain at Pebble Beach to this day. (J.P. Graham)

IN 1900, EXHIBITING THE RAPID GROWTH OF GOLF IN CALIFORNIA, *OUTING* MAGAZINE PUBLISHED AN EXTENSIVE ARTICLE IDENTIFYING 19 COURSES THAT EXISTED IN CALIFORNIA AT THAT TIME:

COURSES OF SOUTHERN CALIFORNIA
Riverside Golf & Polo Club (9 holes)*
Pasadena Country Club (9 holes)*
Redlands Golf Club (9 holes)*
Los Angeles Country Club (18 holes)*
Pachappa Golf Club (Riverside) (9 holes)*
Coronado Golf Club (9 holes)
Santa Catalina Island (9 holes)
Santa Monica Golf and Polo Club (9 holes)
North Shore Golf Club (Santa Monica) (9 holes)
Rubidoux Golf Club (Riverside) (9 holes)
Casa Loma Hotel (Redlands) (9 holes)
Hotel Green (Pasadena) (9 holes)
Pintaresca (Pasadena) (6 holes)
Hotel Redondo (Santa Monica) (9 holes)

COURSES OF NORTHERN CALIFORNIA
San Francisco Golf Club (Presidio) (9 holes)
Oakland Golf Club (9 holes)+
Del Monte Golf Course (9 holes)+
Burlingame Golf Club (9 holes)
San Rafel Club (9 holes)

Initial courses of the Southern California Golf Association (established August 1899)
+ Two courses identified as the exception with grass greens, rather than oil and sand

the El Pescadero Rancho in the company's favor. This provided clear title and the ability to plan a new development. Before much progress could be made on plans there, however, disaster struck the west coast.

On April 18, 1906, one of the largest earthquakes ever to hit California devastated San Francisco. It was felt from Los Angeles to Oregon and as far east as Nevada. Damage in San Francisco was compounded when broken gas lines caused the eruption of multiple fires. The ongoing damage worsened over several days, and it took many months to recover. The company had extensive holdings in the San Francisco area, which required much of Shepard's focus.

As the rebuilding of San Francisco balanced out, Shepard returned his focus to other properties. He promoted Holden R. Warner as the new manager of Hotel Del Monte in July 1907. Shepard had visions for a large

This Chinese family operated the first retail operation at Pebble Beach, selling abalone shells and other treasures from the sea from this location on what is today's 18th fairway. Among the customers was President Benjamin Harrision in 1891, who attempted to pay with a $10 bill and was reportedly told, "No good. You pay me real money." (PBC-Archives)

Property Manager A.D. Shepard published this promotional book in 1909 to help promote real estate sales at Pebble Beach. The cover featured an artist's rendering of the Log Lodge. (PBC-Archives)

Samuel F.B. Morse was only 29 when Crocker put him in charge of the Pacific Improvement Company's holdings, including the 18,000-acre Del Monte Unit. (PBC-Archives)

(left) William H. Crocker and his wife, Ethel, at Del Monte Golf Course (1930). (PBC-J.P. Graham)
(right) The log mansion of A. Kingsley Macomber was built in 1917 on the hill overlooking Carmel Bay. (PBC-J.P. Graham)

This 1913 aerial drawing emphasizes the significance of Del Monte. Note that Pebble Beach is barely mentioned near the top of the drawing. A planned casino (never built) is identified on Del Monte Beach. (PBC-Archives)

development on the company's property at Hope Ranch, just north of Santa Barbara. For that he built a large rustic lodge of wood and stone that was completed in November 1908. He built a similar large log lodge above the popular picnic area at Pebble Beach. The Lodge was a centerpiece for an elaborate plan for lot sales at Rancho El Pescadero, which he called "Pebble Beach Estates."

Pebble Beach Lodge officially opened on August 28, 1909, and Shepard threw a gala party with a virtual who's who of San Francisco society. The Lodge was completely constructed of native pine logs. It featured a full kitchen under the direction of the hotel staff, and the main assembly hall was 30' x 60' with massive stone fireplaces on either side. Even the lighting was constructed of native materials, with log chandeliers featuring finely polished abalone shells as reflectors for the electric bulbs powered by an on-site electric power plant.

Also utilizing the power plant were the electric omnibuses that shuttled guests from Hotel Del Monte and back. Carriage rides remained an option, but modern transportation was preferred, especially as many guests now showed up with their own motor cars to enjoy not only the world-famous 17-Mile Drive but the new scenic 40-Mile Drive that wove

through the forest climbing from sea level to scenic vistas as high as 800 feet.

The first to buy and build in the Pebble Beach Estates was artist Chris Jorgensen, who moved from his home in Carmel to a home near the new lodge. Jorgensen also built his home of native logs. Following soon after was Louis Hill, son and heir of James J. Hill who built the Great Northern Railway. Louis Hill had become president of the railway in 1907 and did nothing in a small way. Living up to his name, he bought several lots that comprised the hill west of The Lodge at Pescadero Point and built the Hill estate on the "hill." It too was built of native logs, yet was very elaborate.

With a jump start to initial sales, Shepard created the first addition to Pebble Beach Estates. It filled the coastal meadow between the Chinese fishing village and the village of Carmel. Here Shepard laid out hundreds of small lots similar to the plan that had worked so well in Pacific Grove. With this expansion, the time came to end the lease with the Pescadero fishing village. By then the village had declined to just a few members of the Jung San Choy family, and fishing had become secondary. On the 1900 census, Jung was listed as a fisherman; on the 1910 census, he and his son were listed as "abalone shell sellers." Their lease ended in 1912, and the village was dismantled, ending more than 40 years of Chinese occupation on the site.

Unfortunately, land sales did not go as well as planned. Shepard's efforts also failed to attract major buyers for the company's landholdings. With the property continuing to cost more in taxes than Shepard was able to generate in revenue, his days were numbered.

At the Crocker-Huffman Land and Water Company in the Merced area, Samuel Finley Brown Morse was proving himself a capable manager of a major property. William H. Crocker became the patriarch of the Crocker family following the death of his older brothers Charles Frederick and George in 1897 and 1909, respectively. His younger sister Hattie (Mrs. Charles B. Alexander) also survived, but she spent most of her time in New York and abroad. William ran the bank and business affairs and had hired Sam Morse in 1910 to manage their ranches. This was in part on the recommendation of Crocker's nephew, Templeton, who had met Morse at Yale. Morse was a natural leader and had been captain of the national champion 1906 Yale football team and a member of the elite and secretive Skull and Bones for the class of 1907. Templeton was a year behind but encouraged Morse, a native of the Boston area, to come to California after graduation.

For the Crockers, Morse managed their 45,000 acres of ranch land in the vast central valley of California and also one of the largest privately owned irrigation systems in the state, with some 400 miles of canals and the water system that serviced the city of Merced. Morse sold off operations that did not fit and bought land that would benefit the

Carlos Stanley joined Morse's team at Del Monte in 1915. Next to Morse, no other individual had as much influence over the resort's operation during the next 30 years. (PBC-Archives)

A row of cottages extended above the coastline at Pebble Beach for nearly 50 years and from 1916 until after World War II provided most of the resort lodging at Pebble Beach. (PBC-Archives)

Only one section of the log pergola, propped up on its posts, and the stone fireplaces survived the fire that started on the morning of December 26, 1917. (PBC-Archives)

Between 1910 and 1915 Douglas Grant lived in England and became quite familiar with its courses and players. He put his knowledge to use in designing Pebble Beach Golf Links. Here he enjoys a round with 5-time British Open Champion James Braid at the Walton Heath Golf Club in 1914. (Elspeth Bobbs)

operations. In 1914, he developed a plan to sell the irrigation system to a district yet to be created that would be managed by all the ranches in the area.

Such vision coupled with successes and profits impressed Crocker, and he put forward Morse to the board of the Pacific Improvement Company as the man who could do what they had wanted Shepard to do. Over the objections of General Hubbard, the board hired Morse, then not quite 30, and released Shepard. Hubbard, age 76, died a month after Morse's appointment, but before he died Hubbard appointed Andrew Hammond, head of the Hammond Lumber Company, as his successor with orders to get rid of Morse. Hammond asked for Morse's resignation, and Morse resisted, stating, "I had been appointed by action of the board of directors, and when the directors ask me to resign, I will do so." [8] The board held firmly behind Morse, and eventually Morse and Hammond became friends.

As the new manager of Pacific Improvement Company, Morse reviewed the Del Monte Unit with H.R. Warner, the on-site manager since 1907. At every turn, Morse sought Warner's suggestions for improvement. Warner consistently replied that he felt the operation was being run well, they just weren't getting enough business. That Warner didn't get the connection greatly disturbed Morse. Warner was promptly asked to resign. Morse replaced him with Carl Stanley. Another 30-year-old powerhouse, Stanley had already made his mark managing a number of fine California hotels.

Together, Morse and Stanley made notes on the property and persuaded Pacific Improvement Company that to get the best price it would need to fix up the holdings and make them attractive to a younger clientele. They started with the hotel and golf course, seeking perfection before the upcoming 1916 Western Amateur Championship. To the log lodge at Pebble Beach a row of cottages was added to provide overnight accommodations.

The California Golf Association had helped attract the Western Golf Association (based in Chicago) to hold its amateur championship in California for the first time as an opportunity to show off California's golf. Morse saw it as an opportunity to showcase the property. Amateur golfers in those days were often wealthy and well connected.

Seeing little value to the company's alcohol-free and unprofitable hotel in Pacific Grove, Morse met with city officials and told them they could have the hotel; they could even set the price. The city thought he was joking and when they declined to make an offer, Morse had it dismantled and stored the useable lumber.

Morse held an auction to sell off all the company's small lots in Pacific Grove and reserved the northwest area of Pacific Grove for future development on a different model. At Pebble Beach, Morse looked for residential buyers to purchase multiple lots and acreage. William Beatty, a business executive from Chicago, purchased a 5.5-acre parcel on a bluff above Stillwater Cove encompassing more than 20 of Shepard's small lots. A. Kingsley Macomber purchased 80 acres on the hill overlooking Carmel

Herbert Fleishhacker, President of San Francisco's Anglo Bank, brought the financial muscle to make Morse's plan work. (PBC-Archives)

Bay above the lot development. Macomber was a millionaire, banker, adventurer, and horse breeder. While Beatty delayed building, Macomber immediately set to building a huge log retreat on the hill in the fledgling enclave.

Morse worked out of the company's headquarters in San Francisco, a city that was abuzz in 1915 with the Panama Pacific International Exposition, which attracted millions of people from around the world at a time when world travel was still an ordeal. Morse successfully convinced many of these visitors to spend time at Del Monte. Morse had picked up on the idea of possibly building another golf course and believed a course on the shore at Pebble Beach would increase interest in development of that area. He actively solicited the opinions of visiting golfers, all of whom encouraged building a course on the site. Many even offered suggestions for hole and course designs. In early 1916, Morse convinced the board to build Pebble Beach Golf Links by assuring them it could be done inexpensively designed by amateur golfers Jack Neville and Douglas Grant and would help attract a buyer.

In the early morning hours of December 26, 1917, the log lodge at Pebble Beach burned to the ground. The golf course was still under construction, and Morse had not yet found the right buyer for the Del

Monte Unit. Morse, however, remained confident and persuaded the board that with the insurance proceeds and the lumber they had from the old Pacific Grove hotel, they could build a grand new lodge that, with the soon-to-be-finished golf course, would certainly attract the right buyer.

The original plan had been to have the new course ready to open on Washington's Birthday 1918, and Morse invited a wealthy friend to come out to California and view the opportunities. The friend was Gustave Maurice Heckscher, another classmate from Yale (1906) and the son of multi-millionaire August Heckscher. He was a German immigrant who, after making millions in zinc mining, made millions more in New York real estate. The father's contributions to New York are immortalized by his role in the development of Central Park.

G.M. Heckscher was an avid club man who excelled in polo and tennis, while his wife, the former Miss F. Louise Vanderhoef, was a champion golfer. The Heckschers enjoyed California. While the opening of Pebble Beach Golf Links was delayed, Heckscher found plenty to keep himself busy. He bought the San Mateo Polo Club that winter, and after touring Del Monte and hearing Morse's pitch, he made an offer to buy the Del Monte Unit on the condition that Morse remain as manager of the property. The offer was lower than the asking price, and Morse, seeing the potential, was not sure he wanted to stay with Del Monte as just a manager; Heckscher was not offering him an ownership position. Morse presented the offer to the board, and when it was not accepted, he made an offer of his own. If they would give him one year to pull together the financing, he would pay the full asking price of nearly $1.4 million. The board accepted Morse's offer. Morse broke the news to Heckscher, and then introduced him to the company's Hope Ranch property near Santa Barbara. Heckscher liked what he saw and bought that holding.

Morse confidently walked into the offices of William H. Crocker to discuss financing his purchase of Del Monte. To Morse's surprise, Crocker refused to help with the financing. Crocker explained that it would be a conflict of interest to loan Morse money to buy a property in which Crocker was a principal owner. Morse was stunned but not defeated. He believed in the project and arranged a meeting with another bank president, Herbert Fleishhacker.

Fleishhacker headed the Anglo Bank in San Francisco. He was intrigued by Morse's enthusiasm and asked Morse to give him a tour of the property. Upon seeing the property and hearing Morse's plan, Fleishhacker indicated that although the bank would not loan young Morse the required money, he would help Morse create a corporation in which Morse would be president and Fleishhacker would be a major stockholder. Anglo Bank could then loan money to the corporation to complete the purchase. Morse saw the advantages of this scenario, and the two immediately set about forming Del Monte Properties Company.

The new Lodge at Pebble Beach in 1919 was somewhat smaller than it is today—an open patio on the west end in 1919 currently houses the Library and Card Room. (PBC-Archives)

DEL MONTE PROPERTIES COMPANY—A NEW BEGINNING

With renewed fervor, Morse oversaw the completion of the new Lodge and golf course, which opened on February 22, 1919, under the ownership of Pacific Improvement Company. He and Fleishhacker quickly finished up the paperwork, and Del Monte Properties Company was officially formed on February 27, 1919. Less than a week after the opening festivities, the purchase of the Del Monte Unit was consummated. The final price of $1,363,930.70 provided a massive holding. Morse described it in a stock-offer letter to a friend:

The properties include 18,000 acres of land on the Monterey Peninsula, all of the Pacific Grove and Pebble Beach areas, Del Monte Forest lands (which are traversed by the 17-Mile Drive), the Los Laureles Rancho (more commonly called the Del Monte Rancho), Hotel Del Monte and all improvements, Pebble Beach Lodge and all improvements, and the capital stock of The Monterey County Water Works, which supplies water to the towns of Monterey, Pacific Grove, and Carmel. In a word, the entire holdings of the Pacific Improvement Company in Monterey County. [9]

The fledgling company attracted a number of interested parties with their stock offering, which included $1 million in 6-percent bonds, $1 million in 8-percent preferred stock, and $3 million in common stock. Thus, Morse was quickly out of his commitments to Anglo Bank and had sufficient working capital to properly develop the real estate. The initial Board of Directors, in addition to Morse and Fleishhacker, consisted of Jack Beaumont, K.R. Kingsbury, John Barenson, Wellington Gregg, Henry T. Scott, Hugh Goodfellow, Charles W. Clark, and G.M. Heckscher, Morse's friend from New York who made the initial offer to buy Del Monte. Heckscher bought into a position Morse intended for William Crocker. Crocker declined, still lacking confidence in the holding.

Vision and timing are essential to success. There is no substitute for vision, which throughout the years proved Morse's chief strength. Timing, however, is dependent on a variety of factors and the ability to rise above some and adjust to others. Morse learned this lesson early and well. The first adjustments came in the golf courses. The California Golf Association was not willing to accept Pebble Beach for the 1919 State Amateur, preferring to stay at Del Monte. Morse charged Carl Stanley and golf professional Harold Sampson with improving the course.

S.F.B. Morse revitalized the equestrian center at Del Monte and reintroduced polo, a sport he preferred to play over golf. (PBC-J.P. Graham)

S.F.B. Morse incorporated Del Monte Properties Company in February 1919 and headed the company for the next 50 years. (PBC-Archives)

Horse racing at Del Monte. (PBC-J.P. Graham)

Several elaborate mansions were built in the 1920s along the rocky coast between Cypress Point and Pescadero Point. (J.P. Graham)

Explosives were used to limit damage from the 1924 fire at Hotel Del Monte to the loss of the main building. (San Francisco Public Library)

The courtyard of the Crocker-Irwin mansion near Pescadero Point. (PBC-J.P. Graham)

So Sampson could focus on Pebble Beach, the big Scotsman, Peter Hay, was hired as the head instructor at the Del Monte course.

In addition to golf, polo and horse racing were also important aspects of life at the revitalized resort, as was tennis. The resorts and sporting empire were meant to attract quality people to the peninsula so they could be enticed into buying their own slice of paradise. With real estate sales going well and golf becoming ever more popular, creation of a private country club was inevitable. The questions were how, where, and to what maximum advantage to the company. To Morse's good fortune, he was approached on two fronts, and he had the vision to grab them both. This is perhaps all the more amazing given the timing.

On the night of September 27, 1924, Hotel Del Monte suffered a major fire. The main building burned to the ground, but utilizing dynamite as planned for such an emergency, they saved the wings that housed most of the guest rooms. The hotel stayed open with the aid of a tented dining room. Within a year, Del Monte was underway on construction of not only an elaborate new hotel, but also two new country clubs along the coastline of Del Monte Forest—Cypress Point Club and Monterey Peninsula Country Club.

The 1920s saw many elaborate mansions added to the peninsula. Gone were the days of log buildings. Morse controlled development and required approval on all structures within Del Monte Forest. He actively encouraged the Mediterranean style. In 1924, Morse himself built his home at Pebble Beach and moved his primary office to Hotel Del Monte, yet also maintained an office suite in San Francisco for the rest of his life.

Marion Hollins walking in the dunes at Cypress Point in 1925 envisioning the new course. (PBC-J.P. Graham)

THE COUNTRY CLUB DEVELOPMENTS

Marion Hollins came from a wealthy Eastern family and began making annual treks to Del Monte in her mid-twenties. Even before winning the 1921 U.S. Women's Amateur, she began considering Pebble Beach as her future home. Her fiery spirit impressed Morse, and the possibilities with the property electrified Hollins. She briefly accepted a role as sports director and immediately began playing an instrumental role in Del Monte's development.

Hollins provided Morse with a concept for an elite private club in 1924. If successful, it would be a profitable land sale for Morse and an attraction for lot sales, not a club he would need to manage. He reserved 150 acres at Cypress Point for the course and put Hollins in charge of developing a plan and seeing it through.

Concurrently, Morse was examining possibilities in another area of the Forest encouraged by local military officers. This setup would be quite different than the Cypress Point Club. With Morse leading the charge and opening the company's checkbook to see it through, Monterey Peninsula Country Club happened much more quickly than Hollins' effort at Cypress Point. The Dunes Course and Clubhouse officially opened on July 2, 1926.

The reconstructed Hotel Del Monte had its grand opening a month earlier in May 1926. It was redesigned by Clarence Tantau (who also designed The Lodge) to meld with Morse's preference for Mediterranean-style architecture. Del Monte was again the place to be and be seen. World leaders, business leaders, and Hollywood stars—often on the peninsula to make movies—all came to spend time at Del Monte.

With the resorts and real estate all thriving and the clubs on the rise, Morse also invested in the sand operation. When he first toured the property, a small operation gathered sand with a mule team and generated about $5,000 per year in revenue for the company. In the 1920s, the company greatly expanded the operation, adding processing equipment that allowed the separation of the unwanted iron particles from the pure

Heavy equipment was brought in to move rocks to shape the ocean holes of the Dunes Course near Point Joe. (PBC-J.P. Graham)

white sand that was most desirable for creation of glass and dinnerware. The unprocessed sand was used for sand-blasting on playgrounds, in golf course bunkers, and for a variety of other purposes. With the new equipment the capacity of the sand plant increased, as did the revenues from sand. It seemed everything Morse touched was a success.

The one thing evading Morse was a national golf championship. He was hopeful to host the National Amateur as early as 1923. Still, the USGA was slow to come west. Two things happened in 1926 to help the USGA come around. The first was that a Western golfer broke into the major ranks that autumn when George Von Elm, winner of the 1925 California Amateur at Pebble Beach, dramatically won the 1926 U.S. Amateur at Baltusrol. The win was a 2&1 final match victory over the seemingly unbeatable Bobby Jones, who was attempting to win his third straight U.S. Amateur. Jones had already won the U.S. and British Opens in 1926, so Von Elm's win over the defending champion was a major upset.

Adding to this, Morse decided to promote his own championship tournament for the top golfers of the country—the 1926 Monterey Peninsula Open. A fledgling group of professional golfers had started a winter tour, playing courses between California and Texas when many of the courses in the north and east were closed. In January 1926, the Los Angeles Open put the tour on the map by offering a record $10,000

Seth Raynor designed the Dunes Course at Monterey Peninsula Country Club, and Clarence Tantau designed the elegant clubhouse. Both opened in 1926. (PBC-J.P. Graham)

Hotel Del Monte reopened in 1926 with a new design. (J.P. Graham)

Cypress Point, with its magnificent ocean holes, opened for play in 1928. (PBC-J.P. Graham)

Pacific Improvement Company had begun a sand mining operation at Spanish Bay that harvested raw sand from the vast dunes located there. (PBC-Archives)

Morse expanded the sand operation at Spanish Bay in the 1920s. (J.P. Graham)

purse. For the winter 1926–27 tour, Morse arranged for the tour to begin with a $5,000 championship on the Pebble Beach course in December.

California had finally grabbed the USGA's attention and, after a year of negotiating, the USGA announced in December 1927 that they would hold the 1929 U.S. Amateur on Del Monte Golf & Country Club's Pebble Beach course.

Soon after actual work started on Cypress Point, Marion Hollins was struck with a debilitating illness that forced her to turn the final stages of membership and opening details to another of Morse's salesmen, Harrison Godwin. Godwin failed to completely fill the needed subscriptions—nevertheless, the club was completed and held its inaugural tournament on August 11, 1928.

Morse had achieved the perfect backdrop for the USGA's first foray into tournament play in California. The golf world was centered on Pebble Beach in September 1929, celebrating not only the USGA's first trip to California, but also the first trip of Bobby Jones—the clear favorite to win, as he was in every championship in which he played.

Remarkably Jones, after tying for medalist honors in qualifying, lost his first match of the tournament to a young Johnny Goodman and was out of the competition. It made headlines around the world and took a lot of the excitement out of the tournament. After the match he told Morse, "The next time I am in an 18-hole match of importance, I am going to feel mentally that I am starting two down." It worked; he never lost a significant match again. The next year he won what sportswriter George Trevor dubbed "the impregnable quadrilateral of golf." O.B. Keeler adapted the more popular baseball term "Grand Slam" for winning the four majors of the era—the British Open and Amateur and the U.S. Open and Amateur. No golfer since has matched that feat, and it is very unlikely anyone ever will.

Southern California's George Von Elm alerted the rest of the country that California was serious about golf by winning the 1925 California Amateur and then defeating Bobby Jones for the 1926 U.S. Amateur crown. Seen here, VonElm returned to Pebble Beach in December 1926 and finished as low amateur in the inaugural Monterey Peninsula Open. (J.P. Graham)

(above) Polo was a popular sport for local players and visitors. Here Hollywood superstar Clark Gable (left) joins Eric Tyrell-Martin, who ran the stables at Del Monte in 1931. (PBC-J.P. Graham)

(right) Jones was well known by the USGA officials when he arrived at Pebble Beach. (left to right) Bobby Jones, USGA Vice President Roger Lapham, and USGA Secretary Prescott Bush. (PBC-J.P. Graham)

Johnny Goodman (left) knew his odds of making it past his first-round match against Bobby Jones were not good, but he jumped to an early lead and held on for a major upset. Goodman lost in the afternoon to Lawson Little. (PBC-J.P. Graham)

Art Bell, veteran of several Masters Championships and three-time California Open Champion, served as head professional at Pebble Beach from 1966–78. (W.C. Brooks)

Marvin Davis (1925–2004) acquired Pebble Beach Company in 1981 when he purchased 20th Century-Fox. In the decade he owned it, he built The Inn and Links at Spanish Bay. (PBC-Archives)

Shortly after the 1972 U.S. Open, California voters passed Proposition 20, the Coastal Zone Conservation Act creating the powerful California Coastal Commission. Almost immediately, restrictions were put on discharges within 1,000 yards of the ocean, and the sand operation at Spanish Bay and Sawmill Gulch was prohibited from processing on-site. Remote mining operations continued to do well, but the company reevaluated all operations on the peninsula.

A Chicago real estate analyst examined the company operations and advised that holding on to tax-burdened land did not make sense; they should sell all land that was not needed for the operation. They changed the focus from ground leases to land sales, and in the 1970s sold significant acreage, including the expanded Holt Ranch property that was then developed into Carmel Valley Ranch Resort and 164 acres to the Northern California Golf Association, which was to be developed into Poppy Hills Golf Course.

Golf professional Art Bell, who was hired in 1966 following the death of Cam Puget, had full run of the golf pro shop at Pebble Beach, which

included risks and profits from retail sales—still standard practice in most pro shops across the country. "When Gawthrop saw I made more than he did during the U.S. Open," recalled Bell, "he didn't like it." They agreed to a phase out of Bell's contract, and the company established its own Retail Division for the sale of resort wear and other goods.

The company looked at alternatives for the land at Spanish Bay. Quickly eliminating any thought of bringing the prior-approved marina idea before the Coastal Commission, they asked Roger Larson manager of golf operations to develop plans for a golf course. He created his own design and also got designs from Jack Neville and golf professional Jack Nicklaus, who was just beginning his golf course design activities.

On March 30, 1977, Del Monte Properties Company reincorporated as Pebble Beach Corporation. In 1978, many large companies began looking at the profitable record of Pebble Beach. Among those interested were United Airlines, Marriott, and Twentieth Century-Fox. Accordingly, the share price began to climb. Amid wide speculation, trading of Pebble Beach stock was suspended on the morning of August 24, 1978, with a closing

Pebble Beach Company vice president Bob Grace meets with the design team for The Links at Spanish Bay (left to right): Frank "Sandy" Tatum, Tom Watson, and Robert Trent Jones, II. (W.C. Brooks)

price the previous afternoon of $33.75, more than double that of six months earlier. A few days later, the intended acquisition was announced. Twentieth Century-Fox would use profits from its film, *Star Wars*, to buy Pebble Beach Corporation. The acquisition was completed in May 1979 when Fox paid $42.50 per share for all outstanding stock, bringing the total acquisition cost to approximately $81.5 million.

Pebble Beach had come a long way from the initial real-estate vision of Samuel F.B. Morse. Fox reorganized the company as a wholly owned subsidiary called Pebble Beach Company and refined the focus to resorts and real estate, selling off the mining operation to Martin-Marietta. The focus then turned to getting ready for the 1982 U.S. Open, but before that could happen, in June 1981, Denver-based oil tycoon Marvin Davis purchased Twentieth Century-Fox and brought in some high-profile board members including former president Gerald Ford and his secretary of state, Henry Kissinger. Ford was a frequent visitor to Pebble Beach.

Marvin Davis began breaking up Fox and selling off the pieces. He later restructured the company, bringing in three close business associates. MKDG I and II became the new official partners of the company. The initials stood for the new "Big Four" in charge of Pebble Beach—Myron Miller, Thomas Klutznick, Marvin Davis, and Gary Gray.

Following the 1982 U.S. Open, the corporate focus shifted away from Pebble Beach Golf Links to see through the development of The Inn and Links at Spanish Bay. The team of Robert Trent Jones II, Tom Watson, and Frank "Sandy" Tatum designed the golf course, adapting it slightly as it wound through the approval process. By 1985, the plans received the last of the necessary approvals, and the company broke ground on the new project. While most of the land was degraded from years of mining, a few untouched sand dunes remained. As prescribed in the approved

Stringy Kikuyu grass took over most of the fairways of Pebble Beach during the drought of the 1980s. (PBC-Archives)

plans, the development protected the native dunes habitat and recreated dune forms throughout the areas surrounding the course. The dunes areas would be used to restore native plant communities in one of the most extensive programs designed to blend public access, recreation, and environmental habitat restoration. The Inn and Links at Spanish Bay opened to the public in November 1987.

The U.S. Open was returning in 1992, and there was a lot to accomplish. In addition to the issues with a young course at Spanish Bay, the peninsula was in the midst of another drought and water rationing was taking its

Heads of Pebble Beach under the Taiheiyo Golf Club ownership were rightfully honored for a successful 1992 U.S. Open (left-right): Daisuke Saji, Masatsugu Takabayashi, PBC president Thomas Oliver, Hiroshi Watanabe, and PBC vice president Paul Spengler. (PBC-P. Lester)

toll on Pebble Beach Golf Links. The golf management team had gone through several changes under Davis, and the courses were not being well maintained. The golf operation needed a new strong leader. In April 1990, Paul J. Spengler Jr. became the new Vice President of Pebble Beach Company's Golf Division. Spengler had a passion for the game, a tremendous circle of associates, and he knew how to build a team; he was a perfect solution.

Despite a few political skirmishes, Marvin Davis enjoyed owning Pebble Beach Company. From most accounts, he had little desire to sell the property, but he was a businessman. Minuro Isutani, headman of Japan's Cosmo World and a golf fanatic, had recently acquired Ben Hogan Properties Company to complement his Japanese golf properties. In Japan, Isutani controlled a number of private clubs with pricey memberships. Isutani wanted to own Pebble Beach in the worst way— which is often a bad time to buy. Actual negotiations are disputed, but the general story is that Davis repeatedly rebuffed Isutani's overtures. As Isutani pressed for any price, Davis, in an effort to force him to give up, finally offered to sell for $1.2 billion—far more than the $81.5 million Fox paid a decade earlier. Instead of going away, Isutani saw it as the beginning of real negotiations. Soon, and to everyone's surprise, they agreed to a price estimated at about $830 million. Isutani took possession in September 1990.

Isutani was excited about the purchase and the upcoming U.S. Open. His first directive was to hire Jack Nicklaus to consult on preparing Pebble Beach for the Open, and he committed $1 million to its restoration. Regrettably,

the Japanese purchase angered many around the nation. Isutani was ill-equipped to overcome America's unhealthy anger. A very private individual, Isutani's motives were questioned by many outside the company, causing a public relations nightmare. His goals were split. His golf mind focused on the complete restoration of Pebble Beach. His business mind needed to retire much of the debt from his purchase. Rising interest rates in Japan were making this latter concern more important. His two options to retire the debt were 1) selling planned housing lots, which were subject to a lengthy development process, and 2) selling memberships to a new Pebble Beach National Club.

Spurred by speculative media coverage around the country, the proposed club further inflamed hostility of the nation's golfers fearing Pebble Beach would become private. The uproar created numerous hurdles for the membership plan, which was much smaller than anyone was willing to believe. The plan amounted to setting aside a preferred two-hour block of tee times each day and was far from the feared privatization. Fees were never determined, but internal discussions on pricing were a mere fraction of media speculation.

Course renovation proceeded on schedule. The same was not true for Isutani's membership plan. Despite approval at the county level, at the state level, an attorney for the Coastal Commission speculated that if not controlled, the proposed membership could absorb all the tee times at Pebble Beach and perhaps those of all the courses in the Pebble Beach stable. An incredulous ownership group watched as the commission, ignoring basic principles of business, rejected the plan by a vote of 10-to-1.

Isutani's attorneys prepared an appeal of the decision, but an incident that could only happen in the movies happened in real life. Attorneys worked on the appeal right up to the filing deadline and then sent it by courier to the courthouse. The courier failed to get good directions and got lost along the way. When he finally found the right directions, he arrived 15 minutes after the court closed. They missed the deadline for appeal.

With the membership plan officially terminated, Isutani's empire was in turmoil beyond his control. Japanese banks moved swiftly to assemble an effective acquisition plan to stabilize the Pebble Beach holding. Taiheiyo Club, Inc. operates a number of golf courses in Japan. Its then-president, Masatsugu Takabayashi, was a former Sumitomo banker and the best choice to head a new organization. Taiheiyo and Sumitomo formed The Lone Cypress Company for the express purpose of buying Pebble Beach Company for something closer to $500 million. Isutani was left to deal with a loss of more than $300 million, but Pebble Beach was secured and assured of whatever was necessary to host the 1992 U.S. Open.

The official change occurred in March 1992, just months before the U.S. Open. Takabayashi, along with his key staff, went out of their way to be public, provide interviews, and meet with government officials. They were determined to avoid the pitfalls that plagued Isutani. A successful U.S. Open was the first priority, and that effort exceeded all expectations.

POLISHING THE JEWEL

Following the successful 1992 U.S. Open, management and ownership evaluated many long-term operational issues, which first led to major investments in coastal stabilization and development of a reclaimed water system. Priorities were determined based on a number of factors and work soon began. It wouldn't all happen at once, but it would all happen. The first priority was to assure no major damage occurred before the next U.S. Open, which had been determined—the 100th U.S. Open would be played at Pebble Beach in 2000, preceded by the 1999 U.S. Amateur. At the same time, the company was finally able to buy back the 5-acre lot sold to Beatty in 1915 and build a new 5th hole on the coastline.

While work progressed on the golf course, other projects were going on nearby. In 1995, the company also bought a former estate near The Lodge known as Casa Palmero. It was the one parcel on the right-hand side of the first two holes of Pebble Beach Golf Links not owned by the company. Plans were developed to refurbish and expand the main house and add a cluster of 24 luxury guest rooms laid out in a Mediterranean-style village setting complete with flowers, fountains, and elevated walkways. Adjacent to that the company built a 22,000-square-foot full-service luxury spa. Adjacent to that they built a three-level underground parking structure. Casa Palmero opened in 1999, together with the parking structure. The Spa at Pebble Beach was completed and opened in 2000.

(top) Casa Palmero, with 24 luxury guest rooms, opened near The Lodge in 1999. (PBC-Gary Geiger)

(bottom) The Pebble Beach coastline has been battered by the sea over the years. Much of the 18th tee and a large portion of the 17th green area was washed away in the winter of 1982 and 1983. Constant repairs led the golf team to prepare a complete engineering study and stabilization plan in the 1990s. (PBC-W.C. Brooks)

CHANGES AT THE TOP

As efforts progressed toward final preparations for the 1999 U.S. Amateur, rumors spread in late May that Pebble Beach Company was for sale. The Taiheiyo-Sumitomo Japanese ownership group tried to keep discussions confidential, but more and more information leaked out. To clear the air, Arnold Palmer agreed to conduct an interview on The Golf Channel, a cable-television station he partially owned and helped launch in 1995. The rumors were true, and he was involved with Peter Ueberroth and others in an effort to complete the purchase—more details would follow.

The Taiheiyo-Sumitomo group took great care to improve the property during its ownership and to heal the wounds of distrust with the community brought on by prior ownership groups. The group retained Paul Leach, a former investment banker, to be its primary U.S. advisor on Pebble Beach and followed his advice on how to restore that trust by reinvesting in the company and the community. But by 1999, it was ready to sell and wanted an equally reputable buyer who was interested in long-term ownership, not someone looking to flip the company to make a quick profit. Leach led the discussions with four potential buyers: Marriott Hotels, Club Corp (already the owner of Pinehurst Resort and several other top properties), KSL (the golf and hotel division of Kohlberg, Kravitz & Roberts), and a group of investors led by Peter Ueberroth. The key was not just price (something north of $800 million), but the total package that each interested bidder would bring to the table.

For many reasons, the group led by Peter Ueberroth quickly became the front-runner to acquire Pebble Beach Company. The world remembers

Peter Ueberroth as *Time* magazine's 1984 Man of the Year and for making the 1984 Olympic Games all they could be—most notably, profitable. He later served as Commissioner of Major League Baseball (1984–88). While those high-profile roles made headlines, his primary business background was in the travel and hospitality industry. Prior to heading the Olympics, Ueberroth founded First Travel Corporation in 1962 as a reservations agency for hotels, airlines, and ships. He grew the company into reportedly the second-largest travel services company in the country, acquiring the Colony Hotel resort chain and Ask Mr. Foster travel agencies along the way. In 1980, Ueberroth sold his company to avoid any conflicts with running the Olympics.

After the Olympics and baseball, Ueberroth jumped back into the hospitality business with partner Richard "Dick" Ferris. Ferris was also a savvy businessman with a hotel and travel background. After graduating from Cornell with a degree in hospitality, Ferris joined Western International Hotels, Inc. (later Westin) in management, where he quickly rose through the ranks. He moved to United Airlines when the growing UAL conglomerate acquired the Western chain in 1970. He was selected as president of United in 1975, rose to president and CEO of UAL in 1979, and ultimately became chairman of UAL in 1982, a role he held until June 1987. During this era, UAL owned and operated the airline, the Westin and Hilton hotels, and even the Hertz car rental agency. In 1987, Ferris left UAL, which soon after sold off most of its non-airline businesses.

In 1992, Ueberroth and Ferris teamed up and bought a small chain of hotels, Guest Quarters Hotels. Together, they built Guest Quarters into a major chain, acquiring Doubletree Hotels in 1994 and Red Lion Hotels

(top) In the summer of 1999, the new "Big Four" gathered at Casa Palmero to close the deal on their purchase of Pebble Beach Company (l to r) Arnold Palmer, Richard Ferris, Peter Ueberroth and Clint Eastwood. (PBC – T.G.O'Neal)

(left) Richard MacDonald, produced a large bronze work of art, "Momentum," to celebrate the 100th playing of the U.S. Open in 2000. (PBC-Archives)

in 1996, and then merging with the Promus Hotel Corporation (the owner of the Embassy Suite and Hampton Inn brands) in 1997. Working side-by-side with them from 1992 to 1998 was a young executive they had recruited from General Electric—William "Bill" Perocchi. Perocchi became their Chief Financial Officer and the main guy they relied on to handle the financial affairs and due diligence for their various business ventures during this period.

When the opportunity to buy Pebble Beach Company came up in 1999, Ueberroth quickly pulled together his two trusted partners from the Doubletree years. Both Ferris and Perocchi immediately agreed to become involved, both as investors and as participants in putting the deal together. Perocchi agreed to lead the group's due diligence efforts during the negotiations. Ferris worked with Ueberroth in lining up additional partners interested in investing in this once-in-a-lifetime opportunity.

Ferris, as chairman of the PGA Tour's policy board, was well connected in the golf world and good friends with Arnold Palmer. Palmer's presence as part of the ownership team would emphasize the group's respect of the game. As one commentator put it, "Like having the king in Camelot." Palmer needed no convincing from Ferris and signed on immediately. Finally, they wanted someone close to the Monterey Peninsula with an equally strong reputation. Ueberroth contacted fellow Cypress Point Club member Clint Eastwood, the former mayor of Carmel, and offered him a role with the lead group—it made his day. The final piece of the puzzle came from the General Electric Pension Trust, which agreed to invest in the deal and to include its president, John Myers, on the new

Board of Directors. Together, the newest Big Four—Eastwood, Ferris, Palmer, and Ueberroth—along with Perocchi and GE Pension, would form the nucleus of an ownership group that insiders immediately dubbed the Dream Team.

With the key ownership team set, the group's final plan to assure the long-term future of the company was to offer limited partnership interests to a diverse group of wealthy, golf-loving individuals. They quickly had more than 130 partners who invested primarily for pride of ownership and their love of Pebble Beach, all with the understanding that the plan was to never again sell the Pebble Beach Company to another ownership group. The formal closing occurred on July 30, 1999.

As part of the new management structure, Perocchi became the CEO and Ferris and Ueberroth co-chairmen of the Board of Directors. In addition to Ferris and Ueberroth, the Board included Eastwood, Leach, Myers, Palmer, and Perocchi—as business-savvy and influential a board as might be found in America.

Just weeks later, Pebble Beach hosted the 1999 U.S. Amateur. Despite the distraction of a national event, the new leaders were digging in to understand all of the company's plans and operations—including the Del Monte Forest Plan that had been winding its way through the approval process since 1992. After several meetings with various local groups, the new owners revised the plans to eliminate nearly all new residential sites, dedicate the majority of undeveloped land to permanent open space, and focus instead on a new golf course and expansion of the resorts. They

A bust of company founder Samuel Finley Brown Morse (1885-1969) near the putting green was unveiled on July 18, 1999. (PBC-Archives)

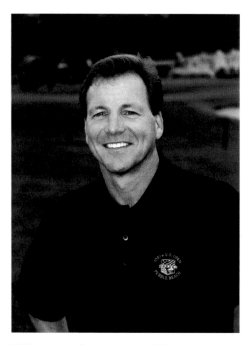

RJ Harper came from Tennessee to Pebble Beach on vacation in 1986 and decided to stay. Starting as a marshal at Pebble Beach while coaching college sports at MPCC, he quickly rose through the ranks to golf professional, then director of golf, and now serves as senior vice president. (PBC)

Arnold Palmer competed in the first two years of the Walmart First Tee Open at Pebble Beach in 2004 and 2005. Here he embraces two of the junior golfers. (Monterey Peninsula Foundation)

even sold the company-owned brokerage, Del Monte Realty, to Coldwell Banker. Pebble Beach Company was now primarily focused on resort operations—and, of course, getting ready for the 2000 U.S. Open.

Hosting a successful U.S. Open literally takes a village—including a company of great employees and a sea of volunteers. The U.S. Open Village filled the nine-hole Peter Hay Golf Course. A highlight at the Village was the unveiling of the gigantic new U.S. Open sculpture by Richard MacDonald, a noted local artist who, just a year earlier, had been commissioned by the Japanese owners to do a bust of Samuel F.B. Morse. MacDonald's U.S. Open sculpture, titled *Momentum*, presents a larger-than-life golfer swinging within a circle from take-away to finish. Pebble Beach Company unveiled *Momentum* at the public entrance to the U.S. Open Village at the beginning of U.S. Open week. On its base, the names of the prior 99 winners of the U.S. Open were engraved, and a space was left for a brass medallion that would bear the name of the 100th champion. The smart money was on Tiger Woods, but no one imagined he would win in such dramatic fashion. Nor that he would use it to launch his Tiger Slam, winning the U.S. Open, British Open, and PGA Championship in 2000 and the Masters in 2001, to become the only golfer ever to hold all four modern majors simultaneously, even if not winning them in the same calendar year for the elusive Grand Slam of golf.

With the Open in the history books, the Del Monte Forest Plan became the top priority. The new development plan required a zoning change to some of the acreage, and in a rather unique move, the company took the matter to a vote of the people of Monterey County in the form of an initiative. The company wanted to know if its proposal had public support before moving forward with its plans. Measure A was placed on the ballot in November 2000. The voters showed strong support for the company's plan with more than 63.5 percent of the public voting in favor of it (and an even higher number among Del Monte Forest residents who had the most at stake in the plan).

The company then went through a lengthy public hearing process with Monterey County, including preparation of an environmental impact report. With a positive environmental report, and the strong approval of county voters, the Monterey County Board of Supervisors approved the project by a unanimous vote on March 15, 2005. But because the project lay within the boundaries of the California Coastal Act, the company also needed to get the approval of the California Coastal Commission, which some regard as the most powerful land-use agency in the country, if not the world.

The company took the plan to the Coastal Commission on June 13, 2007. The specific question before the Commission was whether to uphold the measure approved by the voters of Monterey County as consistent with the California Coastal Act. The staff report recommended denial, but the company remained hopeful that the Commission would see the overall merits of the plan and the validity of the voters' will. After hours of public comment—both in favor of and opposed to the plan—the Commission deliberated and, at the end of an 11-hour public hearing, voted 8–4 to reject Measure A as inconsistent with the Coastal Act.

It was a major setback at the time, and the next chapter is yet to be written. All sides agree a compromise can be reached, but that is for the future, not for the history.

While the Del Monte Forest Plan was a dominant factor in the first decade of the new ownership, there were other priorities, not the least of which was negotiating the return of the U.S. Open. RJ Harper was promoted to senior vice president of golf, overseeing that entire operation. Harper helped negotiate the return of the USGA for the 2010 U.S. Open, an event for which he is the general chairman.

There was also the creation of a new golf tournament. In addition to being new owners of Pebble Beach Company, Ueberroth and Eastwood have been for many years on the Board of the Monterey Peninsula Foundation, the non-profit group that was created by Bing Crosby to run the Pro-Am. Like Crosby, Ueberroth and Eastwood have a passion for youth programs. The Foundation took an active role in establishing the First Tee of Monterey County, which led to an exciting opportunity to host a first-of-its-kind pro-am on the Champions Tour. The Walmart First Tee Open at Pebble Beach began in 2004 and has become a favorite stop on the Champions Tour. The pro-am event pairs an over-50 professional golfer with a top-rated junior amateur selected from First Tee chapters from around the country. The tournament has enjoyed tremendous success thus far while supporting the First Tee youth golf program throughout the nation.

The new owners have made improvements to many aspects of the resort during their ownership tenure. Palmer obviously focused on golf course improvements, but all facilities received attention from the board of directors. Every room on the property has been extensively refurbished, including the addition of wireless Internet and high-definition televisions. Fire pits and an outside bar were added to the popular patio at Spanish Bay where a bagpiper closes the course each evening. These and many other improvements have kept Pebble Beach Resorts at the top of the great golf resorts of the world.

Additionally, the company continues to invest significantly in recycling and environmental programs at every level. The company financially guaranteed a $67 million publicly owned water reclamation facility that provides 100 percent recycled water to meet the irrigation needs of the golf courses of the Del Monte Forest. In addition, the Pebble Beach Company's golf courses have all been certified by Audubon International as "cooperative sanctuaries." Finally, the entire resort is now "green-certified" by the Monterey Bay Area Green Business Program. In sum, Pebble Beach Resorts have never looked better, nor been more environmentally friendly, than under the watchful eyes of the current ownership group.

With history as a guide, many good things surely lie ahead for Pebble Beach. With the current ownership now in place for longer than any owner since S.F.B. Morse, the foundation for a long and stable future for Pebble Beach Company is in place. ■

CHAPTER *Two*
THE GOLF COURSES

Del Monte Golf Course from a 1941 aerial survey. The equestrian center with its polo fields and racetrack are at the left. The edge of the hotel grounds are the wooded area below the golf course in this image. (The Fairchild Aerial Photography Collection at Whittier College, 22-Nov-1941, C-7254, 40)

This colorized photo shows golfers on the 5th hole of Del Monte Golf Course during a tournament in 1902. (PBC-Archives)

Del Monte Golf Course quickly became one of the most popular courses throughout the Far West and remained the most heavily played course on the Monterey Peninsula until after golf's post-World War II resurgence. (Monterey Public Library)

A putting green was developed near the Del Monte clubhouse on the hotel grounds as early as 1893. It had 12 holes set around the perimeter and was often called the Clock Putting Green. (courtesy Ted Throndson)

The golf courses at Pebble Beach are among the best known in the world. In 1997, *Golf Digest* used an aerial image of the Monterey Peninsula in their Top 100 issue as it was the one photograph that included four top 100 golf courses in America at the time—Cypress Point Club (No. 3), Pebble Beach Golf Links (No. 4), Spyglass Hill Golf Course (No. 27), and The Links at Spanish Bay (No. 99). In addition, the photograph included other golf courses—Monterey Peninsula Country Club Dunes Course and Shore Course, Poppy Hills Golf Course, and Peter Hay Golf Course. And just outside the image borders are the Pacific Grove Municipal Course and Del Monte Golf Course where it all began—10 golf courses all built within the property development plans of Samuel Finley Brown Morse. In the 2009 rankings, four of the 10 were again in the Top 100. Although Spanish Bay is just out of the running (still ranked No. 70 among public courses), Michael Strantz's 2004 redesign of the Shore course earned it an entry onto the list in 2007, and in 2009 it is ranked at No. 72. While today the Pebble Beach Company owns only five of the ten courses, they are all part of the story.

Unknown golfers are served by young brothers on the new 11th green at Del Monte Golf Course in 1911. The brothers grew up to become professional golfers Olin (back) and Mortie Dutra then ages 9 and 11, respectively. (PBC-Archives)

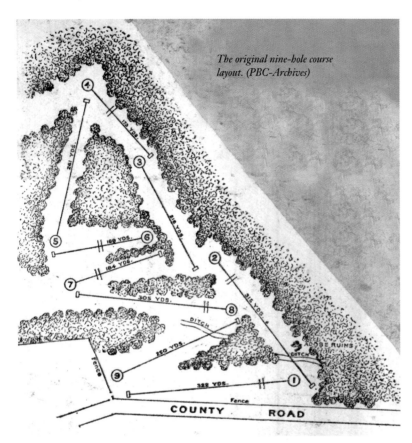

The original nine-hole course layout. (PBC-Archives)

DEL MONTE GOLF COURSE— ESTABLISHED 1897

This is where the golfing empire began, and for half a century it remained the most popular golf course in California. Even after other courses on the peninsula were opened, Del Monte continued as the home course of the resort and the hub of activity. Among my favorite quotes on this score is the lament of Alister Mackenzie, where in his manuscript of 1932 he wrote,

"The fourth course on the Monterey Peninsula is the Del Monte Course. It has always been a complete mystery to me, and is so contrary to my experience in other countries, that it should enjoy such great popularity, which cannot be entirely due to its proximity to the Del Monte Hotel, there being a greater amount of play on it than all the other courses put together."

Mackenzie, of course, had a role in the other three.

Del Monte remains a popular golf course to this day and perhaps one vital aspect of the course missed by Mackenzie was the character described by Johnny Miller as "sneaky-hard." It looks easy on paper but can provide a challenge for the top professionals without beating up the average duffer. Through a century of evolution, it has maintained its beloved charm as a course that can be played by anyone and enjoyed by everyone.

There is no conclusive evidence that Charles E. Maud was the original architect of Del Monte Golf Course, and while S.F.B. Morse was still in school at Andover when Del Monte opened, he knew Maud later and has given him that credit, so it stands. There is no question that Maud, a British immigrant, was a frequent visitor to Del Monte from southern California and an avid promoter of golf and polo in the 1890s. Regardless, little of the original nine-hole course remains, and many hands have had a role in its changes.

A core challenge in building a course near the hotel was space. The hotel grounds did not have the room for more than a putting green, and David Jacks, who held the adjacent property, was not interested in selling. Eventually a lease was arranged, and the relatively simple nine-hole Del Monte Golf Course was built on leased land. It opened on May 1, 1897, under the care of the Scottish-born golf professional T.W. Tetley. The original nine holes measured 2,241 yards.

Tetley did not stay long, and in the summer of 1898, William Robertson took a leave of absence from San Francisco Golf Club, which had lost its golf course, at least temporarily, due to the Spanish-American War. That course was on the Presidio grounds, which were needed to drill soldiers in preparation for duty. At Del Monte, Robertson introduced many new players to golf, and he re-measured the course and named the holes. Before Robertson left Del Monte in September 1898, he staked out modifications to lengthen the course over the winter.

HOLE	NAME	YARDS	BOGEY
1	Morro	344	5
2	Pines	343	5
3	The Oak	223	4
4	Fence	189	3
5	Alameda	263	4
6	The Hill	215	4
7	Monte	146	3
8	Guilty	277	5
9	Home	219	4
	Totals	**2,219**	**37**

James Melville, a 35-year-old Scot who learned the game on the Earl's Ferry Links near St. Andrews, served as Del Monte's next pro. Melville was a first-rate teacher of the game. Melville taught and encouraged everyone he met—man, woman, and child. Melville invited the neighborhood boys of Monterey to become caddies and learn the game. He selected 10-year-old Abe Espinosa as his personal caddie; in exchange, Abe received free lessons. Soon Abe's four younger brothers followed him into the caddie ranks, and eventually, they all became golf professionals. Melville did much to develop golf in California and served as Del Monte's golf professional until he died in 1909.

Under Melville, in the winter of 1902–03, Del Monte was further expanded to become one of the first 18-hole golf courses in California.

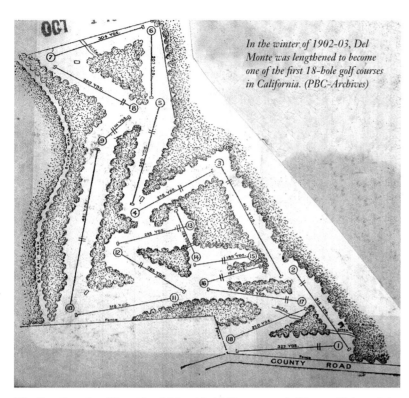

In the winter of 1902-03, Del Monte was lengthened to become one of the first 18-hole golf courses in California. (PBC-Archives)

James Melville (1872–1909) learned the game on the Earl's Ferry Links near St. Andrews and served as Del Monte's golf professional from 1898–1909. (courtesy Eleanor Curtice)

The San Francisco Chronicle of May 17, 1902, reported, "Ernest Folger, J.A. Folger, and T.P. Gower went down to Del Monte last Sunday and put in the day laying out the new course, which will be more than 6,000 yards long, as compared with the old one of 2,400 yards, and will be constructed on the most scientific golf lines without regard to expense."

The plan used much of the existing course, expanding some holes and cutting out new ones as well. The length of the new 18-hole course came in short of their goal, measuring only 4,934 yards, but had a bogey rating of 72. In those days bogey was akin to today's par—a good goal. The USGA officially adopted "par" nomenclature in 1911, but bogey did not come to mean "1 over par" until much later. The Royal and Ancient did not adopt par until after World War I.

The arrangement of the new course was:

HOLE	YARDS	BOGEY	HOLE	YARDS	BOGEY
1	322	5	10	491	6
2	315	4	11	318	4
3	410	5	12	265	4
4	278	4	13	225	4
5	360	4	14	125	3
6	202	3	15	189	4
7	304	4	16	184	3
8	280	4	17	305	4
9	111	3	18	250	4
Totals	2,582	36	Totals	2,352	36
			Grand Totals	**4,934**	**72**

Numerous championships were played under this configuration, which even S.F.B. Morse criticized from his first visit to Del Monte, before he had any direct affiliation with the company. Of that early configuration, he wrote:

"One type of hazard then was the 'chocolate drop'—little molded hills exactly the shape of chocolate drops, about 3 feet in height, and standing like wooden soldiers by the side of the fairway, all in perfect rows. The traps were all laid off as if by a ruler, the bunkers the same way—perfectly straight and of a fixed height. The greens were round and flat on the ground. The fairways were not watered, and in the summertime, even though the balls were then of gutta-percha, a well-hit drive would roll as far as it would carry." [By 1908, when Morse first visited Del Monte, the gutta percha ball had given way to the "Bounding Billy," a hard-core, wound-rubber ball that added to the roll.]

Following the highly successful 1911 Del Monte Championships, everyone in the state agreed that Del Monte was the ideal place for contesting statewide tournaments, but a better course was needed. There was some discussion of another location on the peninsula, but the company expanded its lease with the Jacks estate (David Jacks had died in 1909) and changed the course yet again, using many of the same greens but completely changing the routing, even reversing the direction. While the old 1st hole played south from the clubhouse, the new 1st hole played north. What had been the 10th green became the 1st green and what had been the 1st green became the 15th green. Other holes were entirely new creations. One of the new holes that became an instant favorite was the short par-3 17th with a green surrounded by a moat-like bunker. It was dubbed The Punch Bowl.

The new course measured more than 6,200 yards and identified its "par" rating in line with the new USGA course rating system. However, as many golfers were still more comfortable with the old concept of "bogey," the course also had ratings for men's and women's bogey. The new card read:

HOLE	YARDS	MEN'S PAR	MEN'S BOGEY	WOMEN'S BOGEY
1	396	4	5	5
2	500	5	5	6
3	153	3	3	3
4	323	4	4	4
5	575	5	6	7
6	490	5	5	6
7	192	3	4	4
8	225	3	4	4
9	460	5	5	5
Totals	**3,314**	**37**	**41**	**44**
10	473	5	5	6
11	299	4	4	4
12	385	4	5	6
13	201	3	4	4
14	381	4	5	5
15	277	4	4	4
16	432	4	5	5
17	145	3	3	4
18	386	4	5	5
Totals	**2,979**	**35**	**40**	**43**
Grand Total	**6,293**	**72**	**81**	**87**

The new course came with a new club—Del Monte Golf and Country Club incorporated on January 17, 1912. Although it was wholly owned by Pacific Improvement Company, it did have a membership. The new club's primary purpose was to attract a national championship to California, and it did just that a few years later—the 1916 Western Amateur. For the Western, the 11th hole was shortened to 233 yards, but the rest of the card remained unchanged.

In April 1915, S.F.B. Morse took on the management and liquidation of the Pacific Improvement Company, including the Del Monte holdings. He initially convinced his board to make enhancements to Hotel Del Monte and then build a new golf course and lodge at Pebble Beach. In February 1919, he bought the unit from his employer. As the owner, he remained dissatisfied with the Del Monte golf course. In 1920, he

British golf architect William Herbert Fowler reworked the Del Monte golf course in 1920–22 and also did some work on the course at Pebble Beach. (courtesy Ron Whitten)

THE FAMOUS
DEL MONTE GOLF COURSE
DEL MONTE, CALIFORNIA

Del Monte Golf course was further expanded in 1912. (PBC-Archives)

retained British golf course architect William Herbert Fowler to revamp the Del Monte golf course yet again. Fowler ended up doing work on both golf courses, but his 1920–22 revamp of Del Monte was nearly total, leaving only the popular Punch Bowl untouched. Much of his general design remains, although some routing has been further altered. The Fowler layout measured:

HOLE	YARDS	PAR		HOLE	YARDS	PAR
1	390	4		10	420	4
2	420	4		11	210	3
3	330	4		12	370	4
4	380	4		13	510	5
5	180	3		14	135	3
6	530	5		15	340	4
7	305	4		16	395	4
8	300	4		17	150	3
9	455	4		18	380	4
Totals	3,290	36		Totals	2,910	34
				Grand Total	**6,200**	**70**

In 1937, Morse was offered the opportunity he awaited. The Jacks heirs were finally ready to sell the land under Del Monte Golf Course. Morse made the purchase and created a housing development, widening the Sylvan Walk that used to go around the course into Sylvan Lane, a road that allowed access to new golf-course lots in the Del Monte Fairways Tract. To make room for the lots, the golf course layout was tightened up a bit, but the general course design remained.

Things went fine at Del Monte until World War II. Even though the Great Depression hit the overall resort, Del Monte Golf Course remained popular with golfers, and the Monterey economy did better than much of the country on the strength of its fishing and agriculture industries. The war, however, took away both golfers and workers who enlisted in large numbers. Morse weighed his options, and in 1943 announced that he was closing the Del Monte Golf Course. With its closure, Peter Hay moved over to take the headship of Pebble Beach Golf Links, but as city councilman, Hay led an effort to keep Del Monte open. The city quickly struck a deal, and Morse left some of the crew there to become city employees, including Harry Clemens, who oversaw not just the greenskeeping but managed the entire operation for the city.

In 1948, the company took back management of the course, and Bill Kynoch, who had come with Morse from the Crocker ranch operation, returned from the army and was put in charge of the Del Monte course. Morse sold a bit of land on the southwest corner of the course to his friend Mark Thomas, who built The Mark Thomas Inn in 1955, requiring a slight modification to the course layout in the 1950s, including a loss of the Punch Bowl. That year, Morse also built a new clubhouse and grill for the course, and with Kynoch's retirement, Morse enlisted Frank Thacker, an avid amateur golfer then working at the sand plant, to become the new course pro. The grill was operated on a lease to Gene Lambert.

The clubhouse on the old 18th green and 1st tee was dwarfed by The Mark Thomas Inn—both were built on Del Monte Golf Course in 1955. (PBC-J.P. Graham)

The four golf professionals serving Pebble Beach in 1948 (left to right): Peter Hay–Pebble Beach; Cam Puget–MPCC; Henry Puget–Cypress Point; and Bill Kynoch–Del Monte. (PBC-J.P. Graham)

With the new highway completed, and The Mark Thomas Inn (far point of course) already operating, Hyatt constructed its hotel requiring a further realignment of Del Monte Golf Course, as well as moving the pro shop and grill in 1967. (PBC-W.C. Brooks)

Nick Lombardo is caricatured on the mower in the upper left of this mural that once hung in Del Monte Grill featuring many of the "regulars," including Joe Di Maggio and S.F.B. Morse (upper left side) and Peter Hay (far right). (PBC-W.C. Brooks)

Thacker stayed at Del Monte for most of a decade when the popular pro was tapped to become the first head professional at Spyglass Hill, which began construction in 1964. In late 1964, well before the new course was ready, Morse leased Del Monte to Nick Lombardo, a young golf professional operating a course in Fresno. Thacker took a year-long vacation while Lombardo took over the operation of the Del Monte course.

Lombardo's lease was initially a three-year contract with a five-year performance-based renewal option. The contract required Lombardo to manage the course on site. He would have all hiring and firing responsibility for the golf operation. Lombardo began management in November 1964 and was allotted $900 per month for the wages of himself and two employees. All other staff was paid out of the operation, with a guarantee to the company of $72,000 net in year one, rising to $90,000 net in year three. He kept any net income over that. Lombardo found there were many little deals going on, and by tightening the operation the net in year one exceeded $100,000. He made the targets easily and in 1967 exercised his five-year option.

During this period, the state built the new highway through Monterey, and Morse leased a part of the golf course for Hyatt to build a new hotel. The loss of land for the hotel and highway required some further re-alignment of the course. The pro shop and grill buildings built in 1955 were moved north to their current location in 1967, and what had been the 2nd hole became the 1st hole. The old 1st and other holes in the southwest corner of the course were lost for the hotel and highway, forcing some further creative shifts in the course's hole placements.

Lombardo's hope had been to prove himself at Del Monte and then get the management contract for all of the Pebble Beach courses. In Lombardo's view, a personality conflict with Tim Michaud, who served as company president under Morse beginning in 1964, prevented that from happening. Things were going so well at Del Monte that Lombardo expanded on his own, taking out a 30-year lease to operate Pajaro Valley Golf Club near Watsonville. He negotiated to manage Laguna Seca Golf Ranch, then under construction, and put together his own land-lease deal to develop Rancho Cañada near the mouth of Carmel Valley. Al Gawthrop, who took over as chairman of the board after Morse's death in 1969, was not happy that Lombardo's profit share

was so large, and as the management contract required Lombardo to be on duty at Del Monte, the company challenged him over the additional courses. Lombardo gave up the last three years of his Del Monte contract in exchange for the right to not have to stay on property and left Del Monte at the end of 1969, giving management back to the company.

Roger Larson, who had been hired as head superintendent of Spyglass Hill and oversaw its construction, had grown within the company and had earned the responsibility for managing all of the company's courses. Larson's first move at Del Monte was to design and build proper new holes and create the current alignment of Del Monte. The current 6th, 7th, and 8th holes opened for play in 1970. Larson also hired Bill Henry as the new course professional. In the last 40 years, the course has received many enhancements, but the layout has remained constant since Larson's realignment

Del Monte celebrated its centennial in 1997 with an international gathering of other centennial golf clubs and continues to be a popular venue for golfers of every level.

Roger Larson (left) plays the new par-3 4th hole at Del Monte Golf Course in 1970 with course professional Bill Henry. (PBC-W.C. Brooks)

Pebble Beach Golf Links. (The Fairchild Aerial Photography Collection at Whittier College, 22-Nov-1941, C-7254, 12)

The original greenskeepers at Pebble Beach were these sheep grazing along the 14th tee at Pebble Beach Golf Links. Their employ did not last long after Morse took ownership of the property. (PBC-Archives)

PEBBLE BEACH GOLF LINKS— ESTABLISHED 1919

The official opening of Pebble Beach Golf Links occurred on February 22, 1919, but its conception began much earlier. Shortly after Morse took on management of the Pacific Improvement Company in April 1915, the idea for a golf course at Pebble Beach took hold. Morse sought opinions and ideas from many of the eastern golfers that came to San Francisco for the Panama Pacific International Exposition in 1915 as well as the California golf community. He convinced the board that a course could be built inexpensively, designed by amateur golfers for free, and maintained by sheep at nearly no cost. More importantly, the idea was so universally popular with all to whom he had shown the property that it would surely improve lot sales and also attract the right buyer for the whole operation. On that basis, the plan was approved.

Morse bought back most of the few lots that had been sold and retained Jack Neville and Douglas Grant to finalize a design plan for the course. Several ideas had been supplied to Morse from those who had visited the property in 1915, and Neville and Grant were challenged to decide on the optimal routing. Grant had recently returned from five years in England, where he made notes on many of the courses of the British Isles. The more-natural, less-refined links turf was an aspect of golf not known by many California golfers. The goal at Pebble Beach was to create a links-style course with as many holes as possible on the coastline. The natural-turf concept fit with Morse's plan to maintain the course with sheep. The pair's first challenge was to work around the one 5.5-acre parcel on the coast that Morse could not buy back.

The routing was defined in April 1916, and construction started shortly thereafter at a relatively slow pace as cost remained an issue. They designed it as a challenging course with very small greens, even by that day's standard. Neville, twice the California champion, believed the ability to hit a long iron shot into a small green was one of the best tests of a golfer's skill. With golf course technology improving and only a short rainy season on the peninsula, the team experimented with underground irrigation at the Del Monte golf course and then convinced the company's board that building the new course with underground irrigation would be a cost savings in the long run. It was without a doubt the most expensive aspect of the course construction, and Pebble Beach Golf Links is believed to be the first course built tee-to-green with such an irrigation system. It featured 450 sprinkler heads in the original configuration.

The course was originally planned for an opening on George Washington's birthday 1918 but was delayed while they awaited custom-made irrigation parts from the east. A field of more than a dozen golfers gathered for an "opening event," which began with a four-ball exposition on March 31, 1918 followed by a 36-hole April Fool's Day tournament. The critiques on the opening day prompted an embarrassed Neville to immediately offer that "the course is in an early state of development and it will be many months before all the fairways and greens are in condition for real tournament play." The golfers were not receptive to the natural and thin coastal turf. Evidence of minimal grading effort was apparent in the rocks and stones that peeked up through the fairways. The rock-strewn fairways were just one of the factors contributing to a very challenging competition, but the tournament went on just the same.

The early course, despite its par-72 rating, proved quite a challenge to the group. The top four-ball score was 71, leading to speculation and many wagers that no one would break 160 using just their own ball over 36 holes. This nearly proved true. In a field that included many top golfers, only one golfer achieved the feat. Mike Brady, the reigning Massachusetts Open Champion, showed a steady hand and head under the less-than-favorable conditions. Brady grabbed a narrow lead after the first 18 with a 79 and then waxed the field with a 75 on the final 18. His nearest competition finished 13 strokes back with a 167.

Given the results, the course was immediately closed down for further refinement. Harold Sampson, the course professional who had served Del Monte since 1915, assisted Neville and Grant. The general layout was not changed, but the course conditions were improved and the course was softened. Alternative routes were created for some of the holes, and natural areas were converted into bunkers to strategically catch balls that might otherwise be lost in deep or wooded barrancas. Conditions were improved sufficiently so that prior to the official opening, while the course was still rated at par 72, Harold Sampson had established a course record of 70 as the target for golfers to try and beat. The delay in the official opening until George Washington's birthday 1919 may have been to await completion of the new Lodge; the earlier Log Lodge burned to the ground in 1917.

Regardless of the cause, The Lodge and "Del Monte's Second Course" officially opened on February 22, 1919, with a gala affair and tournament.

Still the reviews were mixed. More work was needed on the course. In the week following the opening, Morse moved from being the manager in charge of liquidation for Pacific Improvement Company to president of the newly formed Del Monte Properties Company in charge of developing the property. While some early reports declared the new course at Pebble Beach the best and most scenic course in the country, other reports were less glowing. In particular, the California Golf Association declined Morse's offer to use Pebble Beach for the 1919 State Amateur that summer, preferring to stay at Del Monte's "Number One" golf course.

Morse put Hotel Del Monte manager Carl Stanley in charge of the entire resort operation, including further improvements to the new course. While Stanley knew little about golf, he knew how to get things done. He increased the labor on the course to fourteen men. In April 1919, the crew raked all the remaining rocks from the fairways and began a program to weed and re-seed all of the greens. Stanley also ordered that the sheep be kept off the softer turf of the fairways and greens and informed Morse that the sheep would, at best, be worthwhile two months out of the year. The idea of using sheep at all was soon abandoned.

In obvious frustration, Stanley wrote to Morse at the end of April. Morse applauded Stanley's concern but also understood the challenges Neville had faced in building the course on a limited budget and respected his ability. In June, Morse tactfully set Stanley on the proper course of action:

I had a long talk with Templeton Crocker today regarding the Pebble Beach golf course. He said he, and several others who played over the course were very much pleased with the lay of the course and the condition of the fairway, but stated that the greens were a disgrace and that we would suffer a great deal if we didn't take immediate and active

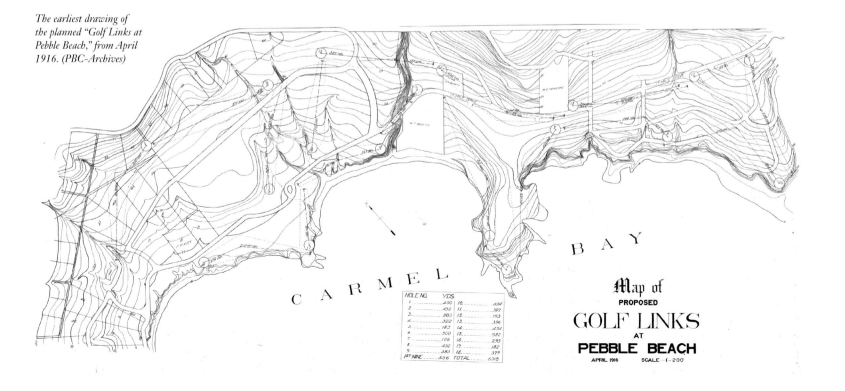

The earliest drawing of the planned "Golf Links at Pebble Beach," from April 1916. (PBC-Archives)

Bunkers were nearly non-existent on the early 8th green as designed by Neville and Grant. (PBC-J.P. Graham)

Mike Brady of Boston led all contenders in the inaugural April Fool's Day tournament at Pebble Beach. With a 79-75—154, he bested the rest of the field by 13 strokes. (PBC-J.P. Graham)

steps to have the greens in condition by the time the golf tournament starts.… Templeton Crocker also stated that in one instance he saw a dozen sprinklers running on one green, which was simply saturated with water and had a regular torrent of water running off it to one side. This does not sound as though our greenkeeper had much sense or ability. Would it not be economy in the long run to employ a good greenkeeper such as the one who used to take care of Lakeside? I believe he is now available.

Morse always believed in hiring the best people for the job, as did Carl Stanley. This was Morse's direct message to get Stanley back on track. Mr. Lee was foreman of the greens crew at Pebble Beach and Harold Sampson was the pro, but Morse and Stanley knew that neither possessed the skills necessary to transform Pebble Beach from good to great.

The Lakeside greenkeeper was apparently unavailable, but Fleishhacker arranged for Mr. Ed Lydon, manager of the Beresford club, to visit Del Monte in September 1919. Lydon's suggestions were well received, but getting him back to supervise the changes proved difficult. Course professional Harold Sampson was on the front end of all of the complaints. And while Pebble Beach was not used for the State Amateur Championship that September, many of the visiting clubmen toured Pebble Beach during their trip and offered opinions. As the winter season approached, and with improvements still being delayed, Sampson dashed off a letter to Morse:

Just to remind you to get after Lydon concerning the Pebble Beach golf course. I am going to go right ahead with the work as best I can but would say that now is the time to finish that course up in general so as to get the advantages of rains and also to have it in playable condition for the winter season. There is work besides the greens that has to be done. There is no one here that understands that work except the foreman at Pebble Beach and myself.… Mr. Lee could do the greens alright but he does not know the other work. If you brought a new man in to take charge it would take some months before he would get his bearings and then our winter season would already be started. Anyway I do not believe you could find a good man out here and an eastern man would be worse because he would not understand conditions out here.… I am going to assume full charge until you nix it; so that I will get the credit or kicks that I deserve. Heretofore I have received the kicks for other men's mistakes but I am going to stick and want the credit for putting it over right; so please get after Lydon. [November 10, 1919]

Sampson's entrepreneurial aggressiveness clearly impressed Morse. It also tells us that all was not well during the beginnings of the golf course. Lydon made it to Pebble Beach in December and indicated his pleasure with Sampson's efforts. In January, Sampson was put in charge of the company's entire golf operation—both courses—agronomically and professionally. In exchange for a higher manager's salary, he gave up revenue from sale of golf-related goods and had to give up most of his teaching.

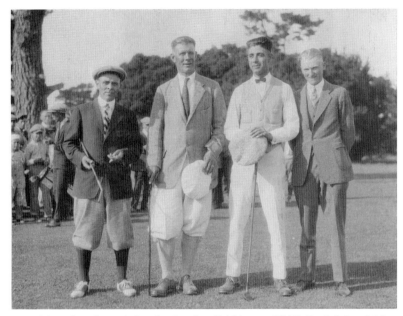

Four of the early professionals that played a role at Del Monte and Pebble Beach (left to right): Abe Espinosa, Peter Hay, Mortie Dutra, and Harold Sampson. (PBC-Archives)

This 1923 aerial shows the ruggedness of Pebble Beach Golf Links, even after refinements by architect Herb Fowler. That is not an early cart path running through the course. It is the remains of the early 17-Mile Drive. (PBC-Archives)

The putting green with The Lodge in the background is in the same location as the current putting green. (PBC-J.P. Graham)

Under the new guidance, the crew removed the surface rocks that still remained. They overseeded the entire course with a fine fescue grass to create more even playing conditions and adapted the underground irrigation to create a more consistent watering pattern. With the surface modifications underway, Pebble Beach Golf Links really took shape. By spring, the CGA agreed to move the State Amateur Championship, scheduled for September, to Pebble Beach. The popularity of the venue decision forced another innovation. Nearly 300 golfers enrolled in the tournament. For the first time, the State Amateur used two courses. To accommodate the sign-ups, qualifying rounds consisted of eighteen holes at Del Monte and eighteen holes at the new Pebble Beach links. Following the championship, the Association was still dissatisfied. More work was needed.

Arthur Hill "Bunker" Vincent, who had come to California from Michigan on lumber business in 1910 and stayed, agreed to manage improvement projects outlined at both courses by British architect William Herbert Fowler. Vincent, an avid golfer, quickly fit into San Francisco society and played in many championships out of the Burlingame Club. He was just a couple of months older than Morse, and they became good friends. Vincent's first big project at Pebble Beach was moving the 18th tee back to a rocky promontory. This tee was used in the 1921 State Amateur, but still a par-4, golfers continued to find the last hole unsatisfactory. The next summer, Fowler and Vincent dramatically lengthened The Finisher, by culverting the creek, backfilling the area as fairway, and moving the green 170 yards up the coast. By January 1922, work on the new green was well underway. Work was completed on the hole in late spring.

Mark Daniels was the man responsible for the agronomic work on the golf course for most of 1921 and 1922. His first task was to create conditions that would grow turf. Daniels led the effort to eliminate the rocks from the fairways and began bringing in fertilizer for the turf. The soil along the coast was very hard and of high salinity. To sweeten the grounds, he began mixing in compost mulch primarily comprised of the manure from the company's stables. It was soon apparent that they would need much more to make the fairways green. In 1922, Del Monte won the contract to dispose of the waste from the Presidio of Monterey's cavalry unit. This new supply of compost material was enough to treat the entire acreage of the golf links and provide additional mulch for the residents who were beginning to landscape their estates. Soon the grass was growing well throughout the course.

That summer the CGA expressed their pleasure with the golf course and especially the new 535-yard par-5 18th hole. Satisfied with the success,

Morse began negotiating with the USGA to bring the 1923 U.S. Amateur to Pebble Beach. The USGA knew that it would need to compete in the Far West someday, but 1923 was still too soon.

Intent on proving to the USGA that they needed to come sooner rather than later, Morse created headlines promoting the championship quality of Pebble Beach at every turn. The State Amateur was one means, but he needed more top golfers. In December 1922, reigning British Open champion and two-time U.S. Open champion Walter Hagen and Australian golf expert Joe Kirkwood came to Del Monte and played a well-publicized 36-hole exhibition match at Del Monte against local professionals Peter Hay and Mortie Dutra—18 holes at Del Monte and 18 holes at Pebble Beach. The match was won 6-up and four-to play by the visitors, punctuated by Hagen's eagle 3 on the 6th hole at Pebble Beach. Morse also solicited Hagen for ideas on enticing the USGA to California. Hagen praised the course and expressed confidence that the National Amateur would soon be played at Pebble Beach.

The USGA awarded the 1929 U.S. Amateur to Del Monte Golf and Country Club's Pebble Beach course. The acceptance included a requirement that San Francisco's Roger Lapham, a vice president with the USGA and founding member of the Cypress Point Club, be allowed to create a committee to prepare Pebble Beach for the championship. Lapham selected H. Chandler Egan and Robert Hunter. Egan was a former U.S. Amateur champion who had moved from Chicago and was then living in Portland, Oregon. Hunter was also originally from Chicago and was living at Pebble Beach, working with Alister Mackenzie on the Cypress Point Club.

Significantly more trees grew near the 18th green after the hole was lengthened to a par-5 in 1922. (PBC-J.P. Graham)

The U.S. Cavalry, stationed at the Presidio of Monterey, enjoyed access to the coastline and dunes at Spanish Bay as part of their deal with the company. (PBC-J.P. Graham)

Egan is generally given credit for the work done on Pebble Beach Golf Links in 1928, but it was a team effort and likely also included suggestions from Alister Mackenzie, who had rebuilt the 8th and 13th green complexes in 1926 shortly before the Lapham team went to work. Another key member of the team was Joe Mayo, the greens superintendent who oversaw the agronomics of all of the company's courses.

On December 24, 1922, Walter Hagen made a stop at Del Monte and Pebble Beach as a part of his national promotional tour that followed his British Open victory. Hagen and traveling companion Joe Kirkwood defeated local pros Mortie Dutra and Peter Hay 6&4 in a 36-hole match that included 18 holes at Pebble Beach in the morning and concluded at Del Monte in the afternoon. (PBC-Archives)

Course architects and champion golfers were often hard to tell apart at Pebble Beach. Celebrating the selection of Pebble Beach as the site of the 1929 U.S. Amateur are (left to right): Bobby Cruickshank, Al Espinosa, H. Chandler Egan, Tommy Armour, Robert Hunter Jr., Jack Neville, and Robert Hunter Sr. (PBC-J.P. Graham)

Before the current seawall was completed in 1997, the earlier seawall had been patched and expanded several times and lacked structural integrity. (PBC-W.C. Brooks)

A gallery surrounds the early 9th green before it was extended in 1928 to sit directly on the bluffs above Carmel Bay. (PBC-J.P. Graham)

In 1928, they added 300 yards in length to the course and added numerous bunkers to create a much more dunes-like links feeling. While they avoided any major routing changes, they rebuilt nearly every green complex, which improved the playability of the golf course for the good golfer and added significant challenge for the average golfer. Chief among their goals was to provide alternative strategies for playing most holes—a shorter, difficult route, and a longer, safer route. The most momentous change was on holes 9 and 10, where they moved the 9th green further out and directly at the cliff's edge over Carmel Beach. The 10th tee had been on the cliff playing a slight dogleg back into the fairway. With the 9th green moved to that position, the 10th tee had to be moved inland so that hole played as a straightway par-4 but with a deep sloping fairway that became hard to hold.

Between the 1929 U.S. Amateur and the 1972 U.S. Open, the changes to the course were mostly a function of aging and maintenance. The bunkers became less dunes-like, and a few disappeared completely. The coastline continued to erode and the seawall on hole 18 was repaired and extended several times. With an average life span of 90-100 years, many of the more mature Monterey Pine trees were lost to age, while others were lost to storms. In general, however, Pebble Beach Golf Links remained unaltered.

Prior to the 1972 U.S. Open, the USGA put Frank "Sandy" Tatum in charge of preparing Pebble Beach. He worked with Jack Neville to strategize the original shot values and balance the course design with the current-day technology. Similarly, Tatum led a team to prepare the course for the 1982 U.S. Open. During both occasions, some new tees were built to lengthen the course, and a few strategic bunkers were added to modernize it.

The next modification was made by nature. In the winter of 1982–83, an El Niño storm hit Pebble Beach with heavy rain and high seas. In the middle of the night, a large piece of Pebble Beach Golf Links, including part of the 17th green and much of the 18th tee, broke away and washed into the Pacific

(top) Following storms in the winter of 1982/83, fabriform bags were used to secure the coastline from further erosion along the 17th hole. (PBC-Archives); (middle) From the turf level can be seen how near the 17th green the erosion damage came. (PBC-Archives)

Roger Larson (kneeling), head of golf at Pebble Beach, P.J. Boatwright (left), executive director of the USGA, and Sandy Tatum, inspect the turf around the 5th tee prior to the 1972 U.S. Open. (PBC-W.C. Brooks)

Ocean—this included that actual spot where Watson made his miraculous chip in the 1982 U.S. Open. Emergency repairs were made with fabriform bags to secure the coastline and backfill the area of the 17th green, but the 18th tee area could not be readily restored, and for the next several years, the teeing grounds were smaller and not as far back.

In 1990, after an extended drought, the fairways had been overrun with invasive kikuyu grass with thick stems that created a dense, gnarly thatch. Joe Mayo had initially introduced the African grass to stabilize the coastal bluffs at Pebble Beach in the 1920s. For that, its deep roots and density worked well, but it is not a good turf grass, although it is extremely drought-tolerant. Paul Spengler was hired in 1990 to take charge of the golf division and to get Pebble Beach ready for the 1992 U.S. Open. A few months later in September 1990, Isutani purchased the company and allotted $1 million to prepare Pebble Beach for the Open. Ed Miller, a top graduate of Penn State's school of agronomy, was hired to manage the turf operation of all of the courses, and Jack Nicklaus was retained as a consultant on the course preparation. Tim Morghan of the USGA provided further consulting assistance, especially to ensure the course setup conformed to the USGA's standards for the 1992 U.S. Open. Fairways were literally killed to get rid of the kikuyu grass but in a manner that play could continue. The fairways, reseeded with rye, filled in quickly. The 4th, 5th, and 7th greens were rebuilt from the sub-ground up to USGA specifications. Early course photographs were reviewed, and long missing bunkers and chipping areas were restored. And tees were leveled and extended to add some length to the course.

Following the 1992 U.S. Open, the company renewed earlier studies on the coastal erosion issue and in 1995 commissioned a three-dimensional aerial photographic survey that could be compared to a similar survey from 1945. Calculations determined the average loss of coastline was three inches per year. Some areas, like the 7th green, were naturally fortified by the offshore rocks. The 18th had lost its beach, but erosion had been minimized by the seawall.

The seawall, however, was very degraded. No record exists of its initial construction, the earliest recorded repair occurred in 1936. The belief is that the original construction occurred in 1922 with the lengthening of the 18th hole by Fowler. Construction of a new seawall on 18 occurred during the spring and summer of 1997. In addition to the wall near the green, the company received permission from the California Coastal Commission to recover the land at the tee lost in the 1982–83 storm. An artificial rock revetment wall was constructed to repel the waves and provide the extended teeing area. Additional artificial rock was used to create a more natural appearance to the face of the wall below the 17th green. Stabilization work was also completed on the banks below holes 9 and 10. As part of the overall erosion control, extensive new drainage was added to manage the subsurface flow of water.

The original 5ᵗʰ hole is concealed by trees in this early aerial. In 1995, the company was able to buy back this 5.5-acre parcel—the only lot developed on the oceanside of Pebble Beach Golf Links. (PBC-J.P. Graham)

A NEW FIFTH HOLE

While work progressed on the coastline, Pebble Beach Company got the opportunity to buy the property between holes 4 and 6 that had eluded Morse. William Beatty bought the property in 1915 and commissioned Julia Morgan to design and build a home on the site. The Beattys moved there full time in 1931 after he retired from his business in Chicago. Beatty died in 1933, but his widow, Valerie, stayed on until her death in 1941. Having gone through the Great Depression and with World War II on the horizon, Morse was not in a position to purchase the property.

Matt Jenkins bought the property in 1944 and moved in with his wife, Mimi. They became good friends with Morse and together established the Stillwater Yacht Club as an adjunct to The Beach Club. The Julia Morgan–designed home on the Beatty-Jenkins property was destroyed in a 1953 fire, but the Jenkins rebuilt and remained residents until their deaths—Matt in 1982, Mimi in 1995. The Jenkins heirs, faced with taxes and other concerns, opted to put the property up for sale. For the first time, the company was in a position to consider purchasing this missing link—the only segment of coast between the 10ᵗʰ and 18ᵗʰ greens that was not part of Pebble Beach Golf Links. Accordingly, Pebble Beach Company's management conferred with Lone Cypress Company executives and agreed to the purchase.

The 18th hole during the 2000 U.S. Open. (PBC-P. Lester)

The original 5th tee played through a narrow shoot to an elevated green and was occasionally referred to as the only dogleg par-3 in golf. (PBC-J.P. Graham)

The 5-plus acre lot was subdivided with the company keeping the oceanside parcel for constructing the new 5th hole and selling two good-sized parcels inland of the hole for home sites. Jack Nicklaus was retained to design and build the new hole. It officially opened on November 18, 1998, just in time for the Callaway Golf Pebble Beach Invitational but was then taken out of service until January when it reopened for the 1999 AT&T Pebble Beach National Pro-Am. During the 1999 Pro-Am, the new 5th played a little longer than the old 5th—187 yards versus the 166 yards of the old hole—and when the winds came up, the real difference was apparent. While 76 percent of the professional golfers playing the hole on Thursday and Friday made par or better, less than half (28-of-60) did so on a blustery Saturday. Eight of Saturday's pros made double-bogey or worse, when only two total did so over the first two days.

Beyond the new hole and the coastal stabilization, there was not a lot of additional work needed to prepare the course for the 1999 U.S. Amateur and 2000 U.S. Open. The biggest difference, other than the new 5th hole, was that the USGA chose to play the 2nd hole as a long par-4 (484 yards), rather than a short par-5 (502 yards).

Having a recognized golf legend who also designs courses as one of your owners has been a decided advantage since Arnold Palmer joined Peter Ueberroth's team that purchased Pebble Beach Company in 1999. Palmer has directed a number of course improvements to Pebble Beach since the 2000 U.S. Open—nearly all designed to tighten up the golf course for the long-hitters while maintaining the intrinsic character of the course. Working closely with RJ Harper, senior vice president of golf, who had previously

The fairway bunkers on the 6th hole have been moved in toward the fairway and the fairway has shifted neared the water, adding to the challenge of this long par 5 hole. (J. Dost)

served as the professional at Pebble Beach Golf Links, the first of two changes were implemented on hole 18. A new fairway bunker was added forward of the original bunker to the right of the fairway in the landing area off the tee, and a large tree was dramatically moved in to replace the Monterey Pine that had long guarded the right front of the green.

The old Monterey Pine at the front right of the 18th green had been hit first with pitch canker and then with lightning. It was dead and had to go. The 2001 AT&T Pebble Beach National Pro-Am was played without a tree, and nearly all the players took advantage of the opening to take the ocean largely out of play.

The solution was dramatic. An 85-foot cypress tree was identified on the 1st hole and moved to the 18th. The principal move was completed by a quick-moving team in the late afternoon of May 16, 2002—creating little impact to play, except for a few dazzled golfers finishing late rounds. They began down the 1st fairway at 4:00 in the afternoon and reached the 18th green at 7:00 that evening. The tree was set in place the next day and secured with wire supports for the first year and a half. It immediately put the ocean back into play and looks like it has always been there. The cypress also offers a longer life span by a few hundred years. It is expected to stay for a long time. The pines in the landing zone off the 18th tee had been replaced multiple times with poor results, so they too were replaced with younger cypress and will likely be there for the long haul. Trees were also added near the barranca on the 2nd hole to tighten up the second shot into that green for the long hitters.

Palmer turned his focus to other strategies:
- On the 15th where the loss of a tree opened up the tee shot in 1998, Palmer designed a series of bunkers on the left side to tighten up the landing area for the long hitters, but that will not effect the more typical golfer.
- The 2nd green was rebuilt to USGA standards with the hope that improved hybrid seeds would allow a new bent grass variety to out compete the poa annua on the greens.
- The verdict was not clear, and additional testing was done by rebuilding the 15th green.
- The 3rd green was also rebuilt; and while the poa annua prevails, the greens are nicely improved.
- The 1st green was rebuilt with a bunker added to the left.
- Bunkers were added all along the left side of the 2nd fairway, and bunkers were added on the right side of the 3rd fairway.
- The one long fairway bunker to the left of the 6th fairway has been broken into a string of bunkers with the ones farthest out angling ever closer to the fairway.
- The fairway bunkers were shifted right on the 4th hole.
- And new tees were built to lengthen the course to just over 7,000 yards for the first time.

With the fairways cut tighter and closer to the coastline to put the most dramatic lateral hazard in golf more clearly into play, Pebble Beach Company and the USGA will again be looking for par to be a very good score at the 2010 U.S. Open.

Workers on the Monterey Peninsula Country Club had to cut through a rugged pine forest and trench in irrigation lines to create playable turf. (PBC-J.P. Graham)

MONTEREY PENINSULA COUNTRY CLUB—ESTABLISHED 1926

In a November 1924 press release, the company reported:

"The club will take in an area of 1,600 acres along the world-famous seventeen-mile scenic drive. It will extend for two miles along the shoreland from Moss Beach to Bird Rock and two miles into Del Monte Forest. The 18-hole golf course, six tennis courts, a trapshooting grounds, a bathing pavilion, a $100,000 clubhouse, and many miles of automobile roads and numerous parks will be developed.... Work of surveying the land and roads is now going on and will be open for inspection about March 1, when invitations for membership will be issued."

Monterey Peninsula Country Club would encourage property ownership as a condition of membership. In the new Country Club Tract, Morse would establish quarter-acre lots wrapping around two championship courses, strategically placed green belts and a large clubhouse. The goal was to appeal to people of more moderate means.

To make the plan work, the big challenge for the company was overcoming the weaknesses of the desired site for the country club and real estate development. Of the site Morse wrote:

This aerial survey from 1941 shows not only the Dunes Course of the Monterey Peninsula Country Club, it also verifies that some of the Hunter-Mackenzie designed holes of the Shore Course were built in the late 1920s, even though the full course was not completed until 1960-61 by Robert Baldock. (The Fairchild Aerial Photography Collection at Whittier College, 22-Nov-1941, C-7254, 14)

"One can hardly realize, looking at that area today, that it was a complete wilderness when we began. It was dense, thick growth. Much of it was damp and soggy underfoot. It was impossible to ride a horse through much of it, and it certainly didn't look possible to develop."

Morse convinced his board to agree to invest up to $1,250,000 to make the club and development work. This was almost as much as they had paid for the entire holding just six years earlier. It was no easy sale, but Morse was no ordinary salesman when he believed in his vision. They quickly got to work clearing the land. Clarence Tantau took charge of the large and elaborate clubhouse. Mark Daniels, an engineer with the company,

was in charge of surveying and laying out the lots, roads, and greenbelt park lands within the development in conjunction with the course to be designed by golf architects Charles Blair Macdonald with Seth Raynor.

Macdonald was one of the best-known golf architects working in America at the time, and Raynor, his frequent partner, was then working on constructing a golf course at Yale. While the Yale connection would have helped impress Morse, the pair was most likely commissioned due to their prior relationship with Marion Hollins. They had assisted Devereaux Emmet in the design and construction of Hollins' Women's National Club on Long Island. Early records clearly indicate Macdonald

The Dunes Course and this large clubhouse building officially opened on July 2, 1926. (PBC-J.P. Graham)

was intended to be the lead architect, but there was also frustration expressed in corporate minutes in trying to get Macdonald on site. Few golf historians give Macdonald credit for an assist, and most simply credit Raynor with the initial design. The Dunes Course starts out by stretching back into the forest and then runs out to the ocean near Point Joe. Holes 10 through 15 lay exposed to the ocean, hole 14, the gem of a par-3 on the oceanside of 17-Mile Drive, and then holes 16 through 18 go back inland to the clubhouse.

The method of operation was that the company would own and operate the club with anticipated membership of more than 1,000. For $1,500 one could buy a lot and become a member of the club, as the price of the lot included the $100 membership fee. A few non-property owners joined, and active military living outside of the enclave were allowed membership for $50—but one had to be a member to buy a lot. Once a member, the chief responsibility was to pay the $5 monthly dues and enjoy.

Initial sales were strong. The club was established on January 19, 1925, and by February, well ahead of schedule, the company announced membership was "now half complete." That July, Seth Raynor returned to take personal charge of construction of the original course, The Dunes, and lay out a second course, The Shore, for the new club. At the same time, he created an initial routing design for the course envisioned at Cypress Point.

The Dunes Course and Clubhouse officially opened on July 2, 1926, but Seth Raynor died of pneumonia on January 26, 1926, and did not see his

Eliot Callender, the first golf professional at Monterey Peninsula Country Club, was proud of his athletic daughters Mary (left) and Clara (right). Seen here at age 12, Clara had already won the MPCC Women's Club Championship. (PBC-J.P. Graham)

courses through to completion. Charles Banks, a key member of Raynor's design team, reportedly finished the course construction.

Monterey's Archie Sanchez defeated G.B. Jordan of San Francisco, 4&3 in the opening tournament for men and Mrs. C.F. Jarvis visiting from the Sequoya Country Club, defeated Mrs. Eliot Callender, wife of the club professional, 2&1 in the women's event.

Cam Puget moved from Pebble Beach Golf Links to MPCC when Callender died in 1939. Clara Callender preferred Puget's instruction even when her father was alive. (PBC-J.P. Graham)

The spacious large lobby of the Tantau-designed Clubhouse for Monterey Peninsula Country Club. (PBC-J.P. Graham)

This beach house for the use of members of MPCC was the only building Morse allowed to be built along the beach on the oceanside of 17-Mile Drive. It has been remodeled and weatherized over the years and remains a popular venue for club members. (PBC-J.P. Graham)

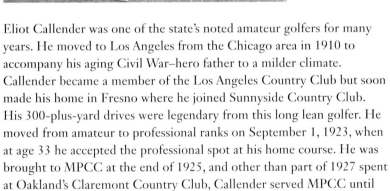

At the 1956 Tran-Miss Championship played at the Montery Peninsula Country Club.

Eliot Callender was one of the state's noted amateur golfers for many years. He moved to Los Angeles from the Chicago area in 1910 to accompany his aging Civil War–hero father to a milder climate. Callender became a member of the Los Angeles Country Club but soon made his home in Fresno where he joined Sunnyside Country Club. His 300-plus-yard drives were legendary from this long lean golfer. He moved from amateur to professional ranks on September 1, 1923, when at age 33 he accepted the professional spot at his home course. He was brought to MPCC at the end of 1925, and other than part of 1927 spent at Oakland's Claremont Country Club, Callender served MPCC until his death in 1939.

Cam Puget, who filled the gap in 1927, returned upon Callender's death and served as the club's golf professional until 1960. Puget headed to Pebble Beach Golf Links shortly after the company sold the club to the members as ailing Peter Hay could no longer continue day-to-day management. Jules Platt served briefly as the club pro in 1960, but he soon left and in November 1960 came John Geertsen Jr., a 31-year-old Brigham Young graduate. Geertsen grew up with golf. His father had been a golf pro since the 1930s and counted Tour pros Tony Lema and Johnny Miller among his students. It was therefore a natural fit for Geertsen Sr., to assist with golf instruction at the club. After more than 20 years, Geertsen retired in 1983. David Vivolo has been the head pro since 1994.

The large, spacious clubhouse was designed by Clarence Tantau, who also designed The Lodge at Pebble Beach in 1919 and the final incarnation

Jack Neville (hand raised) heads the New Course Committee and leads a tour with Robert Baldock around the new Shore Course in 1961. (PBC-J.P. Graham)

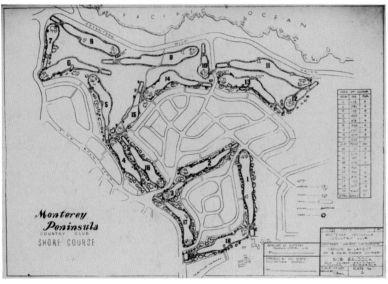

Baldock's routing plan for the original Shore Course, using some of the holes produces in the late 1920s. (PBC-J.P. Graham)

of Hotel Del Monte in 1926. It was enlarged in the 1960s and again a few years ago but retains much of its 1920s aura. While there is not a formal pool, for many years it had "The Old Swimming Hole," an old rock quarry with a sandy beach that has since been filled in. Additionally, there is a beach house near Point Joe on Spanish Bay that was built as a changing room for members that chose to go ocean bathing. The club still has the beach house that has been enlarged and winterized and is now used for private meetings rather than as a changing room.

Before the club reached the membership size that would trigger the construction of the second course, the Great Depression hit. New property sales stopped to allow members in financial trouble to sell their sites. Nevertheless, some of the holes of the second course were built by Mackenzie, Hunter, and Egan. Mackenzie pressed Morse hard in the early 1930s to allow him to finish the second course. Correspondence from

Mackenzie indicates his belief that Morse was not allowing him to finish due to friction between Mackenzie and Joe Mayo. The reality is that it did not make business sense to build the second course at MPCC when the other courses weren't busy and finances were tight. Mackenzie died in 1934, and completion of the course by Mackenzie was no longer an option.

After World War II, life at MPCC was revitalized, aided by its use in the Crosby National Pro-Am. In 1956, the members petitioned Morse to sell the Club to the members. Following years of dialogue, the Club had a special meeting on June 8, 1959, and voted overwhelmingly to accept the terms negotiated and take over ownership. The terms were very favorable to the Club with little actually paid to the company—only a commitment to modernize the clubhouse and to complete the Shore Course within seven years. It would not take that long.

The Second Course Committee, which included Jack Neville, was formed right away to develop the plan for building and financing the course. Robert Baldock was hired to build the course based on a straight-forward and inexpensive design. By the end of 1960, all construction was completed, and the course was seeded at a total cost of about $164,000. The Shore Course opened in early 1961, less than two years after members took over the club.

They hired John Zoller from Eugene Country Club in Oregon as their golf course superintendent in 1974, and when Pebble Beach Company "stole" him away for their organization, the club hired Zoller's son, Bob, who has held the position since 1978.

In 1998, the club hired Rees Jones to refurbish the Dunes Course, making it almost new again. Many of the features were redefined, but the essential routing remained the same. Things were very different when they hired Michael Strantz in 2003 to go over the Shore Course. The routing of the opening and closing holes remained similar due to houses lining those holes nearer the clubhouse, but nothing in between was left untouched. Holes 5–14 are where the land spreads out open to the ocean, and houses sit only in the background on the inland side of the course. Strantz, who worked with Tom Fazio before striking out on his own, was no slave to tradition. The Shore Course is a par-72 course with five par-3s and five par-5s in the mix.

"I wanted to shape the course to sweep with the natural terrain—the rocks, the trees and grasses, the ocean," Strantz said. "I dreamed that the course would appear to dance among the cypress trees on this coastline forever." [11]

Strantz's redesign was his last. The course reopened in June 2004 and on June 10, 2005, Strantz lost his battle with cancer that had waged through all of his work on the Shore Course. But he left a great legacy that leapt onto the *Golf Digest* list of America's 100 Greatest Golf Courses in 2007 at number 77 and moved up to 72 in 2009. Selected to replace Poppy Hills for the 2010 AT&T Pebble Beach National Pro-Am, a few new tees have been added to lenghten the course for the pros. If the wind comes up, look for this course to play extremely difficult.

The sweeping vistas of the Shore Course, as redesigned by Michael Strantz, was selected to replace the inland Poppy Hills Course for the 2010 AT&T Pebble Beach National Pro-Am. (J. Dost)

The par-3 16th hole (left) and the par 4 17th hole (right) at Cypress Point Club require each require a significant carry over water from the tee. The Del Monte Forest stretches into the background from this ocean and dunes masterpiece. (J. Dost)

CYPRESS POINT CLUB—ESTABLISHED 1927

In 1924, just before the Hotel Del Monte fire, Marion Hollins approached Morse with the idea for creating an elite private club. Morse saw it as an opportunity to extend open-space protection to another area of coastline and attract new residents. The pair agreed on a 150-acre site at Cypress Point for the course and clubhouse. Hollins approached it much as she had the creation of the Women's National Club that she was opening on Long Island that summer. She arranged an option to purchase the site for a price of $1,000 an acre and began meeting with individuals that could help create a successful club.

An initial meeting with Roger Lapham and William C. VanAntwerp adjusted Hollins' original thinking. She had drafted a plan for as many as 500 members subscribing for $1,000 to $1,200 each. The two men convinced her that it would be better and easier to create a smaller group of individuals "say, 200, representing an individual stock subscription of $2,500." So with plans in place for a first-class golf course, a comfortable clubhouse with eight to ten sleeping rooms, and a limited membership, she began gathering names and meeting with prospective members.

Seth Raynor prepared an initial routing plan for a course at Cypress Point in the summer of 1925 while working on MPCC. While $100 memberships were grabbed up and work progressed at MPCC, the more pricey memberships at Cypress Point were not selling well.

At the time, Pebble Beach resident Robert Hunter was working on *The Links*, the first book on golf course architecture published in America in 1926. Hunter had taught sociology and written books on that subject. Golf was a sideline that had his special interest. He was a very good amateur golfer and made a couple of trips to Great Britain to play and study the courses there. On one of those trips, he met Alister Mackenzie.

Hunter invited Mackenzie to come to California, which he did in the fall of 1925, to discuss some possible work on the Claremont course and explore other opportunities—one of which was the Meadow Club in Marin County just north across the bay from San Francisco (there was no bridge in 1925). His 1925 visit was relatively brief as he had business back in Scotland, but he returned to California on January 28, 1926, to follow up with the Meadow Club. The timing was fortuitous as word reached Hollins that Raynor had died of pneumonia on January 26, 1926, while working in Florida. Hunter introduced Hollins to Mackenzie, and it was quickly agreed that Mackenzie would take over the Cypress Point course project. Hunter became Mackenzie's partner in California, managing properties on-site while Mackenzie traveled and designed courses around the world, stopping in to oversee certain details.

In early 1927, Hollins called together her Executive Committee: William W. Crocker, Fred W. Flint Jr., Harry H. Hunt, Roger Lapham, Kenneth R. Kingsbury, and Edith Van Antwerp. From correspondence it is clear

Cypress Point Club. (The Fairchild Aerial Photography Collection at Whittier College, 22-Nov-1941, C-7254, 21)

they wanted to move forward but were still hesitant about finances and looking for a back door before exercising the option. There was no question that the site was exceptional and worth considerably more than the $150,000 purchase price—but the option required that the land be used only for the operating of a club. The committee wanted the right to subdivide and sell off lots if they exercised the option and could not make the club work.

Morse was emphatic that it must be a club with a golf course; any other use would cause the ownership to revert back to the company. As a compromise, he offered some long-term options, one of which was the financing of the purchase price. With an initial payment of $25,000, the club would get the deed to the property, the balance would be carried on a 6-percent note with another $25,000 to be due five years after purchase, and the remaining $100,000 would be due within ten years of the purchase. This would allow the club to get up and running and make the sale of future memberships less challenging.

During the summer of 1927, Mackenzie was on-site determining tee placements and finalizing the construction plans, and the Committee was busy working out articles of incorporation and final deal points for the purchase. As it had at Pebble Beach, 17-Mile Drive went right through the proposed golf course site and some rerouting of the Drive would be necessary but still with a right-of-way through the course. The roadway hugged the coastline as much as possible. At Cypress Point, "the loop" had been a popular feature of 17-Mile Drive since it opened in 1881. The

A gallery follows a 1929 exhibition match up the 11th hole of Cypress Point. The players are Jack Neville (looking back) Glenna Collett, Leona Pressler, and Frank C. Stevens Jr. (PBC-J.P. Graham)

This early routing plan for the Cypress Point course shows the 16th as a par-4 and the 18th being played from a tee on a large rock just off shore. (PBC-Archives)

loop was the round-about at the tip of the peninsula where Mackenzie designed placement of the 16th green and 17th tee, but that was not the problem. Mackenzie designed the 14th green to be so near the coastline that it would impact the safe design of the new routing of 17-Mile Drive. There was also a minor issue to be resolved as to road access in the area of the 18th tee, an area now accessed at the Cypress Point Lookout.

To move the project forward, the Club and Company executed the deed with an understanding that they would work out impacts to the routings of the course and roadway. Construction started at the end of October. Hunter's son, Robert Hunter Jr., started a construction company to build the Cypress Point course. The inland pines in fairway routings were felled with dynamite to allow clearing of roots with the trees. This work took longer than expected, and rather than have the grading crew stand by, Hunter Jr. put them to work on grading the treeless ocean holes—prematurely closing 17-Mile Drive and doing so without notifying the company.

Responding to a stern letter from Morse (dated November 3, 1927), Hunter Sr. apologized, explaining that he was out of town and had directed Hunter Jr. as to what work was to be done, but not what work was not to be done. He also offered, "For all our sakes, we are trying to rush the work and I hope if we make a slip now and then, you will be merciful."

Rush was putting it mildly. While organization of the club took nearly three years, once they committed, the Hunters built Cypress Point in record time. They worked out the road issues and completed all major grading and construction in six months, moving to seeding in April 1928 and an opening tournament on August 11, 1928. Less than 10 months from start to finish and unlike Pebble Beach Golf Links, where initial criticisms resulted in a decade of changes, Cypress Point met with raves from the beginning.

The initial card released on the new course showed it to be a par-73 course of 6,776 yards from the back tees. Perhaps the most interesting aspect to this card is that it showed the 16th hole as a 350-yard par-4. This hole was soon reestablished as one of the most dramatic par-3s in all of golf, but the initial card serves to emphasize Mackenzie's resistance to that concept.

HOLE	YARDS	PAR	HOLE	YARDS	PAR
1	430	4	10	475	5
2	565	5	11	450	4
3	160	3	12	420	4
4	410	4	13	380	4
5	476	5	14	410	4
6	515	5	15	130	3
7	170	3	16	350	4
8	360	4	17	420	4
9	290	4	18	365	4
Totals	**3,376**	**37**		**3,400**	**36**
				6,776	**73**

Mackenzie fully credits Marion Hollins with the 16th in his 1932 manuscript on golf that was finally published in 1995 as *The Spirit of St. Andrews*. He acknowledges that she had to convince both Raynor and him to build the hole. Elsewhere in the book he records:

Course designer Alister Mackenzie tees it up from his preferred tee on the "par-4" 16th hole at Cypress Point—hitting a shorter carry from the tee to a landing area, and then across to the green. (PBC-J.P. Graham)

"Being a Scotsman, I am naturally opposed to water in its undiluted state. I am also opposed to a hazard involving the risk of a lost ball. On the other hand, I am very much in favor of utilizing water where it exists as a natural feature…. Players also get such a tremendous thrill driving over the ocean at the spectacular 16th and 17th holes at Cypress Point that this is also well worth the risk of losing a ball or two." [12]

Given the early yardage, it is clear he came to that belief only after the hole received raves as an unequalled par-3 hole.

When Bobby Jones was at Pebble Beach for the 1929 U.S. Amateur, he had the opportunity to play Cypress Point, as well. Asked which he preferred, he diplomatically responded, "that Pebble Beach, as a championship test, was excelled by no other course, but that Cypress Point was the one that he would like to have in his backyard." [13] With that, he hired Mackenzie to join him in Georgia to build the Augusta National course.

The club would have no doubt taken off in great fashion had it not opened on the cusp of the Great Depression. Membership declined to a few dozen, and play was minimal. The club went through three professionals in the first three years. It was in 1931 that Morse asked Peter Hay for advice. Hay offered his assistant, Henry Puget, who had been working with him at Del Monte since Cam Puget had been swept up for MPCC and then Pebble Beach. Henry Puget wanted nothing to do

with it—all the action was at Del Monte. Hay insisted he at least give it a try. The trial run lasted 40 years. He became a great club maker, which filled the down time, he loved the members, and they loved him.

Puget retired in 1971, and the club hired Jim Langley. Puget was a hard man to follow, but Langley was up to the challenge; a patient teacher and as likeable a man as was ever born. While traveling on tournament business in 1988, the car he and club member Bill Borland shared stalled, and while they were off the road, another car slammed into them, sending them both to the hospital. Both men recovered, but the accident left Langley without use of his right arm. It challenged his golf game but not his spirit, and he was soon back working at the club. He remained the club's pro until he retired in 2006 with more than 35 years of service. Casey Reamer, who earlier had served as an assistant at Pebble Beach Golf Links, is the current golf professional at Cypress Point and also plans on a long run. It is amazing to think that he is only the third professional to take charge of the course since Herbert Hoover was the U.S. President.

They have had similar good fortune with their superintendent of greens. Jeff Marco, one of the top agronomists in the country, has been on the job since 1993, tackling the challenges of both coastal stabilization and restoring many of the Mackenzie bunkers that went out of vogue in the 1960s. His predecessors, Manuel Cardoza and Tony Layton, combined for more than 60 years of service.

Only the original nine holes of Pacific Grove Golf Course existed when this 1941 aerial survey was completed. (The Fairchild Aerial Photography Collection at Whittier College, 22-Nov-1941, C-7254, 15)

PACIFIC GROVE GOLF COURSE— ESTABLISHED 1932

Morse envisioned a golf course at Pacific Grove at a time his other courses were doing little business because of the Great Depression. The Monterey Peninsula economy was actually doing better than most in the country as Monterey's fishing and canning industry was providing good-paying jobs, even though it was seasonal work. While that did not help his resort business and real estate sales within Del Monte Forest remained slow, Pacific Grove real estate continued to sell.

Morse did not like the small lots his predecessors had laid out in Pacific Grove. He believed society needed greenbelts and knew from experience that golf courses helped sell real estate. He approached the city leaders of Pacific Grove and offered to provide the land and construct a nine-hole course designed by H. Chandler Egan that he would sell to the city for $10,000. The course would provide open space and a place for healthful exercise for city residents, and all that the city needed to do was to run and maintain the turn-key operation.

City leaders quickly saw the benefits and agreed. The Pacific Grove Municipal Golf Course opened in 1932. While never a championship quality course, it served its purpose well. In the original design, the course began and ended at the end nearest downtown, right next to the railroad turntable. The course continued as a nine-hole course for nearly 30 years

H. Chandler Egan (1884-1936) won many championships throughout his long amateur career. He won the U.S. Amateur, the Western Amateur, the California Amateur, and the Pacific Northwest Amateur in addition to numerous club championships. He was also an effective course designer. (PBC-J.P. Graham)

with little room to expand. In the late 1950s, Jack Neville was asked for his opinion on expanding with nine holes on the 25-acre government reserve surrounding the lighthouse. He examined the possibilities, came up with a workable design, and helped lead the effort to get the expansion built. The effort first needed city concurrence followed by approval from the federal government—approval that required negotiating a lease. Everything progressed swiftly, and the ocean nine opened in 1962. To tie the two nines together, a new clubhouse was built near the lighthouse between the two nines, and the numbering of the inland nine was adjusted to allow the 1st tee to leave from the new clubhouse, head toward town, and then come back before crossing the street and playing the ocean nine.

Over the years the nines have switched, with play sometimes starting on the ocean holes and sometimes on the inland holes; either way, it has remained one of the most popular municipal courses on the West coast and another golf property indebted to Morse's vision.

PETER HAY GOLF COURSE— ESTABLISHED 1957

In the mid-1950s, golf professional Peter Hay and S.F.B. Morse discussed the concept for a small nine-hole course where golfers could work on their short game or just enjoy a short round when they did not have time for a full round on Pebble Beach Golf Links. They identified a hillside between the primary course and the equestrian center where they could build such a course. Even with a rerouting of Stevenson Road, the site was less than 10 acres—barely enough space. Hay conferred with friends Jack Neville and General Robert McClure as to how they could put together nine holes in such a small area.

Hay is credited with the final design of the small course where the longest hole was 108 yards, and Pebble Beach superintendent Leonard Feliciano and his team performed the construction work. Tons of manure were worked into the soil to enrich it for the grow-in of turf. The greens and tees were both small to conform to the available space. The original design had only a couple of bunkers and was built without sprinklers—simply a waterline that allowed manual watering or use of free-standing sprinklers.

Named in honor of the longtime pro and official designer, the Peter Hay Golf Course opened in October 1957 and became popular not only for practice but also for some special events and fundraisers. The course remained unchanged for 30 years but was closed in the late 1980s due to water rationing.

The course was allowed to essentially die to allow incrementally more water for Pebble Beach Golf Links. Rationing ended in 1991, and the Peter Hay course was revitalized. The irrigation system was modernized to include pop-up sprinklers, and additional bunkers were added to provide greater opportunity for practice and golf clinics. The course reopened in September 1991 and was enjoyed again by golfers of all ages.

RJ Harper, then the head pro at Pebble Beach, renewed the Peter Hay tournament for boys and girls at the Peter Hay Course. Hay had started the tournament on the Del Monte Golf Course in 1938 and moved it to Pebble Beach when he moved to Pebble Beach during World War II, but it ceased shortly after Hay's death in 1961. As a junior tournament it is again thriving on the smaller course.

During the wet years of the 1990s, the Peter Hay Course was even used a couple of times to host the professional and celebrity shoot-outs preceding the AT&T Pebble Beach National Pro-Am. More often in recent years, the Peter Hay Course becomes a tent village during special events, and in 2000 a convenient walking path was made through the middle of the course, and it was at the entrance to that path that "Momentum"—the enormous statue created by Richard MacDonald—was placed.

Still, other than during special events, Peter Hay Golf Course hosts golfers of every skill level every day.

Peter Hay and S.F.B. Morse, both in their 70s, were proud of the new Peter Hay Golf Course when it opened in October 1957. (PBC-J.P. Graham)

Phil Harris takes the tee in the hole-in-one contest. Francis Brown and Buddy Rogers are among those awaiting their turn. (PBC-J.P. Graham)

SPYGLASS HILL GOLF COURSE— ESTABLISHED 1966

By the early 1960s, the Northern California Golf Association had grown into one of the largest regional golf associations in the country. Executive Director Bob Hanna had responsibility for setting up tournaments, and there were many. This included not only lining up referees, scorers, and other officials, but the especially difficult task of locating golf courses willing to make their facilities available. Looking for a better solution, he dreamed of having a championship course that the association could use for all of its tournaments.

Knowing that dreams are only the first step to a new reality, Hanna shared his idea with others. Robert Trent Jones Sr. agreed to build a course at a very reasonable cost if the association could get the land. Some association members were encouraging, but the cost of land, especially ideal land, seemed destined to keep the dream unfulfilled. In 1963, Hanna decided to speak with S.F.B. Morse, who had long been supportive of golf in northern California. Hanna made an offer that appealed to Morse. If the company would put up the land, the NCGA would put together the funding to build a new golf course. The company would own the course and could sell tee times, except for 30 days each year that would be reserved for NCGA tournaments and a few tee times each day that would be reserved for The Founders—the actual group of NCGA members putting up the funds.

Hanna sold the concept well and arranged for Jones to come down and select a site. They looked over a site between the Indian Village and Cypress Point where the company had done a little sand mining. After giving up the shooting range facilities near Hotel Del Monte, the resort's rifle range was moved to these dunes. Other than that, Morse had set the site apart for a housing development, laid in a couple of roads, but had done little else with it. Near the ocean, the terrain was sand dunes; inland was a pine forest. There was acreage of dunes land that extended toward Bird Rock the company had previously sold that included an artist's cottage that was built in the 1940s, known as the Gingerbread House. When asked what he thought of the site, Jones expressed to Morse that with the site discussed he could build a good course. And if Morse could add that other section of dunes, he could build a great site. Morse bought back the other land and told Jones to build a great course. He did.

Design and construction for the course and clubhouse, including Jones' fee, was $650,000. Hanna sought out 260 Founders who would each put in $2,500. He filled his roster in no time, and construction started as soon as the plans were approved.

While the Jones team was constructing the course, the Hanna team worked on a name for the course. The earlier courses had required little naming imagination. They were named for where they were built. There was no "there" for the new course. The early leader for choice of names

was Pebble Pines Golf Course; Morse had veto power and used it. Still the committeemen persisted in using it on some correspondence for awhile. Morse had a passion for the local history and knew well the legend that Robert Louis Stevenson's inspiration for *Treasure Island* stemmed from his time on the Monterey Peninsula. No one can recall exactly who came up with the name Spyglass Hill, but once Morse agreed to it, Hanna

Robert Hanna, Executive Director of the Northern California Golf Association, gave the push to create Spyglass Hill. (PBC-W.C. Brooks)

The rifle range at Pebble Beach was located above what became the second fairway of Spyglass Hill Golf Course. (PBC-J.P. Graham)

came up with names for each hole based on the theme of Stevenson's pirate book.

It was a different time, and the clearing was completed as inexpensively as possible. Trees were felled in the fairways and burned on site. In retrospect, the practice was counterproductive to creating ideal conditions for turf and drainage, an ongoing challenge to the greens crews for many years.

The course officially opened on March 11, 1966. It was a beast—but a beautiful beast. Bing Crosby visited the course in August and said, "Let's use it." The course was less than a year old when it replaced the Monterey Peninsula Country Club in the Crosby rotation. It also immediately came into use for the NCGA championships, several NCGA Zone tournaments, and medal play in the California Amateur. In 1971, it hosted the Men's Trans-Mississippi Championship, and later it became part of the rotation in the Callaway Golf Pebble Beach Invitational. Spyglass Hill was also used with Pebble Beach Golf Links for the medal rounds of the 1999 U.S. Amateur.

Spyglass Hill Golf Course became loved, especially by the golfers of Northern California for its challenge and scenic beauty. Spyglass Hill has been ranked among the Top 100 courses in America and the world for more than 40 years. Among golfers of Northern California it often out polls Pebble Beach Golf Links as their favorite course.

Despite the acclaim, playability became an issue almost immediately. The pros playing in the 1967 Crosby howled with complaints as many could not come close to making par. Some of the greens were regraded in the early years, but the big challenge year to year was drainage. In 1977, because the course was so wet, the Crosby opted to use the Monterey Peninsula Shore Course. The issue of poor drainage came to a head in 1996 when poor drainage and wet conditions at Spyglass Hill resulted in a decision by tour officials to cancel the AT&T Pebble Beach National Pro-Am. The company responded with a $2 million investment to implement a complete rebuild of the drainage system that was completed in September 1996.

Lesser problems were addressed by revamping the cart paths to a concrete system with curbs to gather surface water and control its run-off through controlled drains. To handle the flow of subsurface water, curtain drains were added to assure it moved through proper channels and did not back up. Drainage has not been a problem in the years since the improvements.

The man-made ponds were addressed at the same time. The pond that had been on the 11th hole was a problem in that its position forced even the long hitters to lay up short of the pond before hitting up to the blind green. Further, it did not hold water well, creating a water seepage problem that added to ground water. It was removed and replaced with a number of bunkers stretching up the hillside to the green. Aeration was added to the other ponds to keep them clean. In recent years some tees have been added for length, and some strategic tree re-plantings have begun, but the routing of the course has remained unchanged.

S.F.B. Morse hit the first drive at Spyglass Hill on opening day—March 11, 1966. Aime Michaud (left) and course designer Robert Trent Jones (right) stand behind. (PBC-W.C. Brooks)

Proud "Founders" Bill Power (left) and Fran Watson (right) place the first sign in the fall of 1963 that there will be a new golf course coming soon—the name of the planned course would not stay "Pebble Pines" for very long. (PBC-W.C. Brooks)

Until 1996, the 11th hole at Spyglass Hill had a manmade lake. It was removed as part of the massive reworking of the course's drainage system following the 1996 cancellation of the AT&T Pebble Beach National Pro-Am. (PBC-Archives)

The Men's Trans Mississippi tournament was played on Spyglass Hill in July 1971. Allen Miller (center) of Pensacola, Florida, won the championship, here flanked by tournament officials Jimmy Vickers (right) and Bob Roos.

POPPY HILLS GOLF COURSE— ESTABLISHED 1986

In the mid-1970s, the leaders of Pebble Beach Company evaluated their land holdings and determined that the tax burden on undeveloped land made the selling of large parcels the most practical solution. Most of this land was outside Del Monte Forest, but two large parcels were within the gated community. One was the 80-acre former Macomber Estate. The other was 164 acres just below a rock quarry near the top of the hill—inland, well above sea level, with lots of hills and gullies and few ocean views.

Spyglass Hill had become so popular with NCGA members that by 1973 board members began considering the feasibility of creating a course that they would own outright. This was unheard of among golf associations, but the NCGA had grown to more than 90,000 members and was one of the largest, most financially flush of all regional golf associations. After considering other locations throughout Northern California, they determined the Monterey Peninsula area was still the best place to be. The serendipity of their timing and the Company's desire to sell property came together in 1977. The NCGA, under the presidency of Richard Ghent, bought the 164-acre site in the middle of Del Monte Forest as the future home of a golf course, tentatively called Hilltop, which would also become the new headquarters of the NCGA.

There were no immediate construction plans—in 1977, the peninsula was in the midst of a drought, and before anything could be built they had to have a secure source of water. There was also the matter of the California Coastal Commission. Established in 1973 to regulate development along the entire coast of California, for the first time the commission would be ruling on the creation of a golf course on the Monterey Peninsula. Even though the site was not directly on the ocean, it was within the Coastal Zone and within the commission's purview. Not long after Pebble Beach Company "stole" John Zoller from MPCC, the NCGA "stole" him from the company, making him their chief executive to lead the approval process and construction of the new course.

In mid-1979, the NCGA selected Robert Trent Jones Jr., who had worked with his father on Spyglass Hill, to design Hilltop as a championship-caliber course that would be fair for players of all skill levels. The change of the Land Use Plan for the site was approved in 1982. The County Planning Commission approved the project in 1983 with 44 strenuous conditions, and once plans for those conditions were met, the Coastal Commission approved the project on July 10, 1984, on a narrow 7-to-5 vote. Finally, construction began on the course that was renamed Poppy Hills—the name submitted by NCGA member Chuck Twichell of Santa Rosa.

John Zoller was hired by the NCGA to replace Bob Hanna as Executive Director of the Northern California Golf Association and oversee the construction of its new course. (PBC-W.C. Brooks)

In early 1977, Richard Ghent (left), president of the Northern California Golf Association, goes over the recently purchased Hilltop golf course site with Robert Hanna, NCGA's Executive Director. (PBC-W.C. Brooks)

In the Founders Room at the NCGA headquarters at Spyglass Hill, Robert Trent Jones Jr., receives congratulations for his appointment in August 1979 as architect of the new course. Chuck Van Linge (left) and NCGA director Joseph Zablocki I (right) were co-chairs of the NCGA golf course committee. (PBC-W.C. Brooks)

Robert Trent Jones Jr, carefully carved Poppy Hills Golf Course into the hills of Del Monte Forest. On the coastline beyond the hills juts Arrowhead Point on Pebble Beach Golf Links and in the distance Point Lobos wraps around Carmel Bay. (J. Dost)

Very different from construction of 20 years earlier, trees were selectively removed and others planted during construction. All removal was done with a methodology that minimized soil disturbance as part of an overall Erosion Control and Drainage Plan. The course was designed to rely on reclaimed water, initially through the retention ponds built on-site and to be supplemented by an off-site reclamation project then in the planning phase that came online in 1996. On-site construction altered routing slightly from initial plans that called for a course that would play 6,150 yards from the forward tees and 6,949 yards from the back.

In preparing to begin construction, Jones noted, "Design is not something that is finished prior to construction…it is virtually impossible to foresee and anticipate in all cases the 'best' solution in advance. Many design decisions can be best made (in some cases, can only be made) in the field during the construction process." [14]

Trees were cleared, fairways were shaped, and drainage and irrigation were installed throughout 1985. By early 1986, they had reached the seeding and grow-in phase to prepare for the official opening on June 1, 1986. The original golf course offered four sets of tees: Blue 6,850; White 6,215; Red 5,554; and Gold 5,331.

While the course was under construction, the NCGA also built a large clubhouse with adjoining offices for the NCGA, which were relocated from smaller offices at Spyglass Hill in April 1986, shortly before the course opened. Perhaps in line with an amateur organization, Poppy Hills opened without a PGA Class "A" golf professional on staff. Early complaints were less about the course than the customer experience. There were complaints about the course as well, with charges that it opened too soon before the grow-in was complete. Given the difficult conditions, eight-minute intervals in tee times led to long rounds and lots of waiting on the course. These early problems were handled promptly and soon forgotten when Jack Guio was hired as the course's first professional in March 1987 to oversee the day-to-day operation with a focus on customer service.

Today's course measures similarly to the original card, but with Black, Blue, White and Gold tees; with Black at the back playing 6,857 yards and no hole being more than 12 yards variant from the original Blue ratings (Hole 2 plus-12; Hole 14 minus-12) and Gold measuring 5,421 yards. This is not to say the course has not changed.

In January 1991, Poppy Hills replaced Cypress Point in the AT&T Pebble Beach National Pro-Am rotation and received its first critique from the pros. In the summer of 1991, the NCGA removed several bunkers—notably a pair of deep pot bunkers in the 3rd fairway and a fairway bunker on the 4th—and refined some of the greens, taking out some of the deep slopes. When the wet years of the late-1990s hit, Poppy Hills also took criticism for being too wet and, like Spyglass Hill, it underwent a renovation to its drainage, and in the summer of 1999, Jones completed a redesign of the par-5 9th hole.

THE LINKS AT SPANISH BAY— ESTABLISHED 1987

The Inn and Links at Spanish Bay were planned to utilize the acreage once occupied by the company's sand mining operation. By definition, the Scottish term "links" is a sandy wasteland along the ocean that links the coast with the more arable soil inland. The acreage available was a vast sandy wasteland ideally suited for creating a true linksland-style course.

Robert Trent Jones Jr., was working on Poppy Hills in the early 1980s and was called on for a design for Spanish Bay. Tom Watson and Sandy Tatum, both fans of British links golf, were called in to work with him on the project. With a rough course designed, MKDG's planners began laying out the development that would include a first-class hotel and an adjoining condominium cluster to be known as The Residences at Spanish Bay.

By 1985, the plans finally received the last of the necessary approvals, and the company broke ground on the new project. While most of the land was degraded from years of mining, a few untouched sand dunes remained. As prescribed in the approved plans, the development would protect the native dunes habitat and re-create dune forms throughout the areas surrounding the course. The dunes areas would be used to restore native plant communities in one of the most extensive programs designed to blend public access, recreation, and environmental habitat restoration. To facilitate the propagation of native plants, the company established a nursery for native stock. In the early seasons, additional nurseries were used to allow for the planting of more than 100,000 native plants each year.

On November 5, 1987, The Links at Spanish Bay had its opening ceremony. In the inaugural round, Tom Watson shot a 67, which still stands as the official course record. Watson came off the course declaring, "It's so much like Scotland, you can almost hear the bagpipes playing." Almost immediately a tradition was born, and today you can hear the bagpipes play each evening as a piper closes the course shortly before sunset.

Though named among the top new courses of 1988, Spanish Bay evolved. The grow-in of the Environmentally Sensitive Habitat (ESH) areas amid the course took longer than expected. The drought-tolerant fescue grasses were no match for invasive poa-annua on the greens. On the fairways the fescue took on a brownish, unkempt look which was not well received with visiting golfers and was eventually replaced with a rye-blend more like the other peninsula course. Golfers were also critical of the pot bunkers in the middle of the fairways—a common site on Scottish links but rare on American courses; these were left as designed.

In 1991, it was ranked No. 95 on *Golf Digest's* list of America's Top 100 courses and was briefly considered as a replacement for Cypress Point in the AT&T Pro-Am rotation. The ESH areas limited the gallery to an approved 5,000—too small for a PGA Tour event. Nevertheless, it hosts many smaller tournaments each year. Without the television coverage, it has failed to achieve the acclaim of its more famous neighbors, yet remains one of the top-ranked courses in California and offers a unique golfing experience—a links-style course with top-quality conditioning and ocean views from nearly every hole. ■

The par 3 16ᵗʰ hole of The Links at Spanish Bay nestles tightly in among the coastal dunes. (J. Dost)

CHAPTER *Three*
TOURNAMENT GOLF
THROUGH WORLD WAR II

Dubbed "The Finisher" when the course was still young, the 18th hole at Pebble Beach Golf Links can look docile on a calm day, but when the wind is up, it has challenged many of the greatest golfers in the world. It is considered by most the finest finishing hole in golf. (J. Dost)

Great tournament golf is synonymous with Pebble Beach. In the modern era, we tend to think of the magnificent U.S. Opens and the always-entertaining AT&T Pebble Beach National Pro-Ams. However, the courses at Pebble Beach Resorts have hosted thousands of tournaments during the past 100-plus years in a tradition that goes back to the early days of the first course at the resort—Del Monte Golf Course.

No book could capture all the tournaments and golfers that have won competitions at these courses, yet this book represents the first attempt to record the majority of the more significant championships played on these courses. The galleried tournaments draw top professional and amateur golfers to Pebble Beach Resorts. Of the numerous tournaments put on by corporate groups—from the Automobile Dealers Association, which held its annual gatherings at Del Monte in the early half of the last century to the Lexus Champions for Charity that holds its national championship at Pebble Beach in the current century—there simply isn't room or time to tell all of their stories.

When Del Monte Golf Course opened in 1897, there was little that could be called organized golf in California. The United States Golf Association was barely two years old and located a continent away in New Jersey. The Western Golf Association didn't organize until two years later and, as it still is today, was based in Chicago—then considered the West. California was the Far West and was left to its own devices.

At Del Monte, the annual Carnival of Sports had encouraged sports men and women from across the state to compete in various events each August from the early days of the resort. Hundreds of people came to participate and spectate the best players at tennis, badminton, pigeon shooting, racing, polo, billiards, and swimming. Putting on the green near the hotel's Clubhouse was added as an exhibition by 1893 and migrated to the new nine-hole course in 1897.

EARLY CHAMPIONSHIPS

Records from the early days of golf in California are scarce, especially for a non-club course like Del Monte. In 1898, J. Downey Harvey, the socialite nephew of former California Governor John G. Downey (1860–62) and founding member of the San Francisco Golf Club, won the silver cup at Del Monte, defeating C.R. Scudder of St. Louis two holes up with one to go in the championship match. Harvey beat Joseph Grant, a founder of Burlingame Country Club and the father of Douglas Grant, in the first round and Captain Payson in the second. Scudder, who won the handicap medal tournament with a 53-63—116 (25) 91 defeated R.M. Tobin and F.F. Ryer in the earlier matches. Scudder's wife was the low gross in the women's event with a 75 for once around the nine-hole course. Downey's wife was low net with an 80 (13) 67. Visiting professional William Robertson from the San Francisco Golf Club provided instruction in the new sport to many of the competitors.

Charles E. Maud (standing in the "on-deck box" at Del Monte hole 15 in 1912), was one of California's great champions as both a golfer and early promoter of the sport. He is credited as the original designer of Del Monte Golf Course in 1897 and was the founding president of the Southern California Golf Association in 1899. (PBC-Archives)

THE DEL MONTE CUP

James Melville took over at Del Monte when Robertson left and introduced several tournaments for men and women to encourage the fun of competition. He also traveled around the state, giving lessons and teaching clinics to introduce new players to the joys of the game. A handful of new clubs hosted local tournaments and a few had inter-club championships, but with the 1899 Sports Carnival, Melville introduced the Del Monte Cup, and it quickly became one of the most sought after early claims to golfing prowess in the state. Initially a cup for the men's championship, other sportsmen put up cups to encourage the ladies to compete—George Crocker, eldest living son of the patriarch, put up the women's cup in 1899, and it was grander than the men's cup.

One of the earliest documented champions in California, and winner of the first Del Monte Cup, was Charles Maud. The English immigrant credited with building the Del Monte Golf Course won the Del Monte championship in 1899, defeating Edward Tufts 5&2. Maud, a founding member of the Riverside Club in 1891, continued to be a force in California tournament golf for the next twenty years.

Professionally, Maud was involved with developing orchards and irrigation in southern California. As a sportsman and a confirmed bachelor, he was devoted to promoting both golf and polo. Maud led the

Gallery and golfers leave the 14ᵗʰ green at Del Monte after the ladies ended a match. In the early days it was not easy to know if players were dressed for sport or an afternoon tea. (PBC-R.J. Arnold)

effort throughout California. After developing the Riverside Golf and Country Club in the south and Del Monte Golf Course at Monterey, he continued to encourage other courses in California.

By 1899, a need for order was apparent, and Maud was elected as the first president of the Southern California Golf Association (SCGA) that year. About the same time, a growing golf community in Washington and Oregon established the Pacific Northwest Golf Association (PNGA). A third organization encompassing the other two developed in 1900—the Pacific Coast Golf Association (PCGA)—and immediately held its first professional championship on January 13, 1900, at the Oakland Country Club. Not to be left out, five clubs of the San Francisco Bay region got together and formed the Northern California Golf Association (NCGA) in 1901; it also joined the PCGA.

With the new associations, the opportunities for competition increased. The PCGA rotated its championships between the regional groups, while the component associations also held their own championships. The Del Monte sports tournaments continued each year in late August or early September and continually pulled in more golfers each year than any of the association championships. The primary association championships in the West were for men, whereas the Del Monte Cup provided competitions for both men and women.

The PCGA Men's Amateur was played in the spring. The PCGA briefly ran a women's championship as part of the Del Monte games. With minimal participation in 1901 and 1902, the women played their third and final tournament at the Los Angeles Country Club in May 1903.

The Del Monte Cup tournaments continued and regularly attracted the top golfers in the West. On the men's side, Charles Maud won the cup again in 1901 and 1905. California's wealthy class comprised the early golfing stars at Del Monte. Other winners of the Del Monte Cup included the coffee tycoon Folger brothers, Ernest (1900) and James (1902). Seventeen-year-old Douglas Grant, whose grandfather Adam Grant made his millions as a San Francisco merchant and land speculator during the heat of California's gold rush and whose father helped found the Burlingame Club, made it to the final match in 1904. Grant reached his full potential later. Grant lost the 1904 contest 11-down and 10-to-play (11&10) to Chapin F. Tubbs, heir to Napa County's 275-acre Chateau Montelena, one of the first great wine producers in California. Chapin's grandfather imported plants from Bordeaux in 1880, and Chapin took charge of the wine estate in 1919 upon the death of his father. Charles Templeton Crocker won the Cup in 1906 while home for the summer from his studies at Yale.

Among the top women golfers who won the cup were Miss Edith Chesebrough (1903 and 1908), daughter of a wealthy San Francisco shipping magnate, and Mrs. R. Gilman Brown of the Burlingame Club, who won the 1902 PCGA championship at Del Monte and was runner-up for the Del Monte Cup in 1904 and 1905—losing to Mrs. Herbert (Charlotte P.) Munn of Coronado, San Francisco, and New York (in an 18-hole playoff) and Mrs. Walter S. (Mary) Martin of Burlingame, respectively.

In 1905, Mrs. Brown organized the California Women Golfers' Association (CWGA) to create a California Amateur for women and try to fill the gap left by the PCGA. That group held a few regional tournaments in addition to an annual CWGA championship beginning in 1906. Mrs. Brown won the first annual tournament in 1906 at San Francisco; Mrs. Edmund T. Perkins won it in 1907 at Los Angeles. The new championship utilized the same perpetual trophy created for the earlier PCGA Women's Amateur.

The California Women's Amateur championship rotated between northern and southern courses, but the Del Monte Women's Amateur continued to rival it for prestige. To compete in the State Amateur, a golfer had to be a member of an NCGA or SCGA member club, while the Del Monte Championships continued to be open to all comers. The same top women golfers repeatedly rose to the top of both championships—Edith Van Antwerp (nee Chesebrough), Alice Law (nee Warner), Josephine Milton (nee Johnson), Doreen Campbell (nee Kavanagh), Isabella Kennett (nee Smith), Helen Shepherd (nee Lawson), and Clara Sherman (nee Callender)—were regularly in the finals of each.

The PCGA Amateur for men continued, and Charles E. Maud won that tournament twice as well; in 1903 at the San Francisco Presidio course and in 1907 at Del Monte. The southern California contingent, which hosted the championship at Los Angeles Country Club in 1902 and 1904, had no courses with grass greens and deferred to Del Monte as its preferred course, which then hosted the PCGA Amateur in 1907 and 1910.

THE PACIFIC COAST GOLF ASSOCIATION OPEN

Because of the large gathering of clubs and golfers at Del Monte each August, most of the state's golf professionals also attended. The PCGA therefore viewed it as the best time to hold an Open championship. The August 1901 event was won by Robert Johnstone, a professional in San Francisco with a 146 for 36 holes (four times around the nine-hole course). Charles Maud finished second and as low amateur with a 150. Johnstone received $100 and Maud a silver medal, while Del Monte's Melville and George Smith (younger brother of 1899 U.S. Open champion Willie Smith) split the third-place money for their 153s. Maud was runner-up again in 1902. In 1904, Maud bested all of the professionals to win the PCGA Open championship.

The PCGA Open continued at Del Monte through 1911, and George Smith became the dominant player, particularly after Del Monte was expanded to a full 18 holes and he moved north from Coronado to become the pro at Oakland's Claremont Country Club in 1905. Smith won in 1906, 1909, and 1912. He was runner-up in 1910, losing by two stokes to his younger brother MacDonald Smith, then the professional at Menlo Country Club. For 1911, the Open championship was adapted to match play, and George Smith reached the semifinals where he met a surprising defeat to a young Abe Espinosa, a former Del Monte caddie.

THE DEL MONTE CHAMPIONSHIPS

In the fall of 1909, recognizing how the annual play at Del Monte continually drew the largest groups of golfers, the company created the Del Monte Championships for men and women amateurs with a perpetual trophy—a silver shield from Shreve and Company with crossed clubs on which the winners' names were engraved. The Del Monte Cup was relegated to the winner of the second flight. The first men's amateur attracted 81 golfers, which marked a record even for Del Monte. Robin Y. Hayne returned the best medal score: 74-69—143. San Francisco's John Lawson won a playoff for the 16th spot over Arthur J. Owen who tied at 161 in the medal rounds. Lawson lost his opening match to J.A. Folger, who lost to Douglas Grant, who lost to Frank Newton of Claremont in the semifinal. In the final match, Newton faced Santa Barbara's F.D. Frazier, who had beaten Austin White, a 16-year-old two-time (1907, 1908) Hawaiian champion from Oahu, in the semifinal round. Newton, a two-time PCGA champion (1906, 1908), won the inaugural Men's Del Monte Championship with a 5&3 victory over Frazier.

For the Women's Del Monte Championship, more than 30 women competed with eight qualifying for the championship matches. Again, the championship came down to a north-south challenge; Miss Alice Hager of San Francisco defeated Mrs. T.W. Bishop of Los Angeles 6&4.

Four of northern California's top golfers in its early years (left to right): Robert Coleman, Robin Y. Hayne, Douglas Grant, and Vincent Whitney. (anonymous)

In 1910, the PCGA Amateur returned to Del Monte and was held at the end of August, the week following the Del Monte Championships. Douglas Grant was the medalist in each, but lost in the semifinals of the Del Monte Championship to Austin White. Austin White lost to Campbell Whyte of San Francisco 3&2 in a hard-fought 36-hole final. A week later, Austin White was again in the finals of the Pacific Coast Amateur and again fell 3&2 in the final match, that time to Vincent Whitney of San Francisco.

A record 130 men and 65 women entered the 1911 championships. Among the amateurs, three northern players—Robin Hayne, Dr. D.P. Fredericks, and Frank Newton—tied for low score at 144, with Newton winning a playoff on Sunday to win the medal. Defending champion Campbell Whyte also made a good showing with a 71-74—145 missing the playoff by a single stroke despite taking a 9 on the par-5 2nd hole in the afternoon. Most of the favorites, including Norman Macbeth (newly arrived from England) and Ervin S. "Scotty" Armstrong finished in the top 16.

In the quarterfinals, with eight top players in contention, excitement took center stage. Armstrong, Fredericks, and Judge William

Frederickson of Los Angeles continued to the semifinals as expected, but in the match of the day, Macbeth, a club champion at his former home course of Royal Lytham and St. Anne's, came up against a wily youngster in the person of John Francis "Jack" Neville. Neville was barely 20, but had grown up learning golf on the Claremont links, playing casual rounds with course professional George Smith and then superintendent Jim Barnes. He was young enough to believe he was capable of anything and would not be intimidated by the more seasoned golfer. The match went back and forth with the edge leaning toward Macbeth who led 1-up as they reached the 16th tee. There Neville hit his tee shot within 12 feet of the pin and sank the putt to square the match with a birdie. Neville saved par and won the 17th hole to take a 1-up lead and sealed the deal on 18 by again hitting his tee shot tight and winning the hole with a 5-foot birdie. Neville's surprise victory evened the odds as to whether the championship would be won by the north or south with Neville facing Armstrong and Fredericks facing Frederickson in the semifinal matches.

In what was deemed the best match of the tournament, Armstrong's play was nearly perfect against a very scrappy Neville. The match went back and forth for 17 holes until Neville missed a 3-foot putt, giving Armstrong a 2&1 victory.

The Fredericks-Frederickson match was not as well played but every bit as close. They reached the 18th with the doctor still 1-up. The Judge had a 6-foot putt to win the hole, but it lipped out, ending the match and setting up a 36-hole final pitting North against South.

The final round for the men's championship proved anti-climatic given the stellar play seen up until that time. Dr. Fredericks got off to a bad start and never recovered, while Armstrong continued to play calm, steady golf. Fredericks was down-6 when they broke for lunch, and Armstrong needed only nine more holes to finish the match 10&9.

In the women's final, Edith Chesebrough defeated southern California's Mrs. John V. Eliot 3& 2 in the final match—splitting the major trophies between the North and South.

Norman Macbeth, a member of Royal Lytham and St. Anne's in England, moved to Los Angeles and first played at Del Monte in the 1911 Championships. He continued to be a top competitor in the state for many years. (PBC-Archives)

BIRTH OF THE CALIFORNIA AMATEUR CHAMPIONSHIP

The success of the 1911 championships led to an increased interest in creating a California Golf Association with a middle ground like Del Monte to encourage full participation. The rotated tournaments of the PCGA and the State Women's Amateur had not been nearly as well attended. As Ed Tufts reflected at the end of the 1911 championships, "This meeting of the North and South has done a lot for the game, and for the good feeling between the two sections. It is impossible when a lot of good sportsmen meet on the same links and under the same roof, not to feel much better toward each other permanently."[15] In regular club tournaments, golfers went their own way after each day's play—the camaraderie at Del Monte was part of the event.

The SCGA and NCGA withdrew their affiliation with the PCGA and continued their discussions to develop a California Golf Association. In the meantime, Del Monte worked on the first major revamp of the course to address criticisms as to length, hazards, and trees discussed at the 1911 championships. When golfers gathered in September 1912 for the Del Monte Championships, NCGA and SCGA leaders met and officially created the California Golf Association (CGA). The key debate centered on whether to use the Del Monte Championship as the State Championship.

The Del Monte Championship was again well attended by the best golfers from both the North and South. Young Jack Neville of Claremont, who lost in the semifinals of the 1911 Championship, started strong, winning the medal with a score of 149 and continuing to the finals where he beat "Scotty" Armstrong of the SCGA's Annadale club. Armstrong, the defending champion, was the heavy favorite and played Neville to a 3-up lead in the morning round. Neville came back strong in the afternoon, taking a 1-up lead after the 6th hole and closed the match out 2&1 on the 17th. Given the tightness of the North-South match, the southern contingent was reluctant to allow it to stand as the State Championship, and it was agreed to hold the first State Amateur the next week.

Robin Hayne of the San Francisco Golf Club won the medal in the State Amateur with a score of 152, the smaller field was pared to 16 of the best players in the state—all 16 had been in the 32-player championship flight of the prior week's Del Monte Championship.

Neville again reached the finals but this time faced his fellow Claremont member, Dr. D.P. Fredericks, who had defeated Armstrong in the quarterfinals. Fredericks regularly beat Neville in practice matches at Claremont, but the two had never faced off in an important championship, let alone the inaugural State Championship. The lead changed several times with Neville 2-up after the morning round. Neville got to 3-up on the 7th in the afternoon, but Fredericks got

Ervin S. "Scotty" Armstrong of the Annandale Club near Pasadena, was one of the state's top golfers; twice an SCGA champion, he won at Del Monte in 1911 before it was officially the state championship and again in 1915 when it was. He reached the semifinals eight times. (Green Book of Golf 1923-1924)

Jack Neville moved to Oakland in his youth and grew up on the Claremont Clubs links, honing his skills in casual rounds with George Smith and Jim Barnes, two of the legendary British players in early American golf. (PBC-J.P. Graham)

back to within one by the 10th hole. Both made good recoveries to save halves coming in on the next five holes, but a short approach and soft putt cost Fredericks the 16th, and a half on the 17th gave Neville the 2&1 victory.

With Neville having won both championships, it was agreed that going forward the two championships were unnecessary. The Del Monte Championship became the State Amateur and continued annually as part of the yearly meet at Del Monte. As Del Monte had only recently instituted the perpetual trophy listing the men and women champions, they continued to list the State Amateur champion on the original shield and the later shields that were created to record the men and women winners.

Neville continued to be one of the top competitors in the state and easily the favorite among the Northern California contingent to win nearly every year thereafter. Southern California had its own favorites. Top among them was Scotty Armstrong. In the early years of the championship, a handful of old stalwarts and a few impressive newcomers

were often in the competition. Neville beat Armstrong in the final match of the 1913 contest. Neville was defeated in the semifinals of 1914 by eventual winner Harry Davis. In 1915, Armstrong rose to the top defeating Heinrich Schmidt in the final match, which he nearly missed. Eye-witness Sam Morse offered the following account:

In the early days of the State Championship, the event was a great deal of fun… one of the most amusing events happened one of the years that "Scotty" Armstrong, who, by the way, everybody loved, won the championship.

Prohibition was in the offing and there was a lot of talk about it. The tournament went down to the finals and in the finals Scotty was opposed by Heine Schmidt. Scotty was a bon vivant and a happy-go-lucky individual who enjoyed life to the fullest. Heine was a total abstainer and he took his golf—and everything else—very seriously.

The event was just before the First World War. I think it was perhaps the first year that Peter Hay went to work for us. Anyway, he was presiding in the matter of starting off the players. On the day of the finals there was a goodly gallery—in those days that meant a few hundred people at the most. No gallery was expected to go 18 holes without a drink, and for that matter, most of the players felt in need of something at about the 9th hole, so we had a gay pavilion at the 9th hole where drinks were dispensed to the needy.

Everybody waited anxiously for Scotty to show up. Heine had been on the putting green for an hour before he was slated to play. He was getting more and more anxious. Finally it got to be twenty minutes after starting time and Peter, with his Scotch brogue, announced that he was afraid he would have to award the championship to Heine by default. Just as he was about to do so, Scotty showed up—in his dinner coat! He hadn't been to bed!

He yelled out to wait a few minutes. He rushed into the caddy house and took off his dinner jacket, put a belt around his dinner trousers, put on his golf shoes, rolled up his sleeves, had a gin fizz, and appeared on the 1st tee.

They both played brilliant golf. They reached the 9th hole and Scotty felt very much in need of another gin fizz. Heine could hardly contain his annoyance, but he had to wait, to be a good sportsman.

To make a long story short, Scotty won [6&5]. I walked out to congratulate him, and he said with a wide grin, "The wets win."

In 1916, Schmidt won the more serious Western Amateur at Del Monte, but never the State Amateur. A stalwart who retuned to Del Monte in time for the Western Amateur and did have good fortune in the State Championship was Douglas Grant, who returned to California in 1916 after several years in England, where he played a lot of golf and married Elsie, the daughter of the Lord-Mayor of Liverpool. Grant brought his new wife to California to escape the hazards of World War I. In this four-year visit, Grant left his mark on California golf. He was the medalist in the State Amateur three straight years; 1917, 1918, and 1919. In 1917, he beat Neville 6&4 in the semifinals, but lost down-1 to Dr. Charles H. Walter in the final. In 1918, Grant was dominant, defeating Arthur Vincent in the semifinal and J.K. Wadley in the final. In 1919, he won the opening tournament at Pebble Beach Golf Links (which he and Neville designed), but surprisingly failed to make the semifinals in the State Amateur. Instead, his rival, Jack Neville, ascended to the winner's circle with a tough semifinal win over Fred Wright and an 11&9 shellacking of Robert Hunter in the final. Shortly after the championship, Grant returned to England where he continued to be a top golfer in that country.

Alice Warner was the daughter of H.R. Warner and just 16 when her father became the manager of Hotel Del Monte. She quickly became one of the best golfers in the state and regularly disappointed male hotel guests—twice—first for being paired with a girl, then for being beaten by her. (courtesy Edward Throndson)

Alice Warner continued to be competitive as Mrs. Hubert E. Law, winning the State Amateur championship for a third straight time in 1919 and doing so at the course on which she grew up. (courtesy Edward Throndson)

DEL MONTE CHAMPIONSHIP FOR WOMEN—THE EARLY YEARS

The Del Monte Championship for Women continued to be a top draw in the state. Sixty-nine women played in the qualifying round for the 1912 Del Monte Championship. Among the sixteen ladies who qualified for the championship flight, the top three came from San Francisco: Mrs. A.R. (Alice) Pommer (87), defending champion Edith Chesebrough (90), and 1909 champion Alice Hager (91). The opening round was fairly predictable with the favorites winning easily, although Hager needed 20 holes to defeat Mrs. Walter S. Martin of Burlingame.

Edith Chesebrough VanAntwerp won her sixth Del Monte Championship in 1923. (anonymous)

In addition to winning three State Amateurs and two Del Monte Championships, Alice Warner-Law won the San Francisco Golf Club Championship three times. (courtesy Edward Throndson)

In the final for 1912, Chesebrough repeated as champion, defeating Pommer 4&3, proving herself an ever-present dominant force who, already age 31, remained a significant competitor for the next several years.

Another dominant force in this era was Alice Warner. She lost badly to Chesebrough in the 1911 quarterfinals but emerged victorious in 1913, defeating Chesebrough 4&3 in the finals. In 1914, Chesebrough defeated Warner in the State Amateur played on their home course at San Francisco (Ingleside) in April, but Warner repeated as the Del Monte Champion in 1914. H.R. Warner left his management position at Del Monte in 1915, and Alice was absent from the Del Monte Championship until 1919. She continued competing in the Women's State Amateur, defeating Edith Chesebrough in the final matches of both 1916 and 1917—playing since late 1915 under her new married name of Mrs. Hubert E. Law.

Chesebrough also missed a couple of years but returned to Del Monte in 1918. With World War I limiting resources, the Women's State Amateur

was not played, and the Del Monte Championship served as the defining championship. Instead of silver cups, golfers received certificates. The funds from the tournament that would have bought trophies were instead donated to the Red Cross. Many of the top golfers failed to attend and, as expected, Chesebrough was both the medalist and the champion.

In 1919, the championship season was again run for the benefit of the Red Cross, and the field promised to be much stronger. The ladies had not liked having to give up their State Amateur. So for 1919, it was decided that the scheduled women's match play event at Del Monte would be the Woman's State Amateur. The women gathered a bit earlier and played the Del Monte Championship as a 36-hole stroke-play event in advance of the other scheduled tournaments in August.

Forty-nine ladies signed on for the new format and headed out on a pleasant though overcast day for the Del Monte Championship. Only 41 returned cards and of them only a dozen finished in less than 100 strokes. Chesebrough and Law were paired up for the first day's play and finished near the top of the scoring—Edith with a 49-40—89, and Alice with a 44-48—92. The only golfer to score better was Mrs. Charles F. Ford, the reigning Northern California champion with a 46-40—86. This put Ford in the final pairing with Chesebrough and Law one group ahead for the final round the next day.

With five groups still on the course, Doreen Kavanagh became leader in the clubhouse, posting a 93, to go with her 98 for a 191. That only held for a couple of groups as Mrs. Thomas S. Baker posted an 86 for a 181 total, but she knew she wasn't safe. Alice Law had improved over her previous day, and it looked as though she would finish with an 88 for a 180 total. In a careless moment on the final hole, thinking she was in a match with her playing partner Alice Hanchett and out of contention on the hole, Law failed to putt out, bringing about her disqualification. Baker still settled for third, as Ford came in with a 94—180 and Chesebrough won the championship with an 89-88—177.

A few days later, the ladies faced off in the State Amateur with every bit as much competitive spirit. In the qualifying round, Law and Chesebrough tied for the medal with 87s. Given the amount of golf being played, it was agreed to playoff for the medal at a later date, and so the ladies proceeded to match play. Chesebrough and Law easily made it the semifinals, and it looked like it would be yet another classic battle in the finals, but first they had to win their current matches. Law faced Doreen Kavanagh, a young up-and-comer who had yet to make her mark. The match was well contested and went the full 18 holes before Law could claim a 1-up victory. In the other match, Chesebrough was challenged by another newcomer, Mrs. Robert A. Roos, who was making her first appearance in any championship flight. Roos played a tough match, much tougher than Chesebrough and the stress occasionally showed, such as when Edith uncharacteristically missed three putts on the 13th hole. They finished the 18th all-square, and Mrs. Roos won on the first extra hole; Chesebrough was out.

Then considered second only to the U.S. Amateur, Del Monte Golf Course hosted the 1916 Western Amateur—the first time the Chicago-based organization had traveled west of Colorado. (PBC-J.P. Graham)

Mrs. Roos entered the final match against Mrs. Law full of confidence and with a very steady game. Roos went 1-up on the second when Law double-bogeyed, and 2-up on the fifth with another double by Law. Reversing the tide, however, Law won the next three holes with fine play and halved the ninth. Law was 1-up at the turn. Law took an eight on the 10th, and the match was again even. Law won the 13th and 14th holes and halved the next two; Law was 2-up and two to play. Roos reached for something extra and won the 17th and then the 18th. The gallery increased with the excitement of extra holes in the championship match. They halved the 19th, and both played the 20th in textbook style. Roos had a 12-footer for birdie and missed by inches, leaving an opening Law embraced. Law sunk her 8-foot putt with a sigh of relief.

This marked Alice Warner Law's third and final State Amateur championship. Having won the State Amateur three times in a row, she was awarded permanent possession of the perpetual trophy. The one final competition recorded between Chesebrough and Law was the playoff for the medal in the 1919 Women's Amateur, and it was finally contested six weeks later at the San Francisco Golf and Country Club. It was won my Mrs. Law. The legendary rivalry between this pair did much to build women's golf in California. Sadly, most record books do not include their many victories. Whether it was because the Women's Golf Association of California reorganized in 1920 or because Alice Law had the trophy that recorded the previous winners is unclear, but later record books only record California Women's Amateur winners beginning in 1920, and while between them Chesebrough and Law had five wins in the State Amateur, neither won that Championship again.

In 1920, at age 38, Edith Chesebrough married William Clarkson Van Antwerp and came back to defend her title at Del Monte. For the first and only time, the women's Championship was played over the new

Pebble Beach Golf Links. Chesebrough was the medalist with an 82. Alice Law also played, but lost in the first-round match to Kathleen Wright in the longest 18-hole match in the history of the event. It went 26 holes, ending when, following a perfect tee shot, Law topped her second shot which fell into the ocean at the 8th hole chasm. Annadale's Miss Margaret Cameron, a relative newcomer, defeated Wright in the semifinals and Chesebrough in the final match to win the championship. Still not finished, Chesebrough came back the next year and beat Cameron for the championship, adding her name to the perpetual shield for a fifth time. She won the Del Monte Championship a record sixth time in 1923, that time beating Mary K. Browne, the former national tennis champion, who in 1924 was runner-up in the U.S. Women's Amateur. In 1924, Edith helped Marion Hollins successfully launch the Cypress Point Club.

Warner-Law was never again competitive at Del Monte, but in 1930 she won possession of another perpetual trophy after winning the club championship at San Francisco Golf & Country Club three years in a row.

THE 1916 WESTERN AMATEUR CHAMPIONSHIP

The Western Golf Association accepted offers from both Del Monte for the course to host the 1916 Western Amateur Championship and the CGA for a train ride to shuttle amateurs from Chicago to Del Monte. It was clearly a win-win opportunity for the WGA, which already had 232 member clubs spread across most of the United States and all of Canada. This tournament would provide more interest among California clubs, of which only sixteen had currently joined the WGA. The added support would strengthen its efforts against the dominance of the USGA.

The plan for renewed strength backfired when the WGA Board of Directors stood down to a USGA challenge that the free train ride was "payment" for golfers to play. The USGA announced it would revoke the amateur status of any golfer accepting free transportation to Del Monte. The WGA membership urged the board to hold strong against the challenge. They did not believe the USGA would follow through, and even if they did, the golfers would still be able to compete as amateurs in WGA events. The WGA Board was likely influenced by the USGA's recent revocation of the amateur status of the popular Francis Ouimet simply because he was selling sporting goods. Whatever the reason, the WGA Board reversed its decision on the train transportation, and the USGA was firmly established as the ruling body of golf in the United States.

The tournament still went on. Despite a limited field from the East and central states, there was representation from Texas, Illinois, Utah, and even England among a field of 146 starters. After two days of qualifying, Oakland's Heinrich Schmidt took medalist honors at 73-72—145, 1 over par. The high score among the 32 qualifiers was H. Warner Sherwood at 88-80—168. He was quickly eliminated in the first match 9&7. One of the more interesting matches of the competition came in the second round when two old friends were paired up. Jack Neville faced Douglas Grant. The match went the scheduled 18 holes with Grant winning 1-up. Grant won his next two matches with relative ease and proceeded to a 36-hole final against Schmidt.

Grant got off to a terrible start, plagued by his putter. After nine holes, Grant had only managed a half on the 6th hole and was down eight. On the back nine, Grant made up one hole and was still down seven halfway through the match. Grant played the next nine in 3-under-par, making back two more holes. Still, losing eight of the first nine left him down-5 in the match, and he was running out of time. They halved the 10th. A misplayed niblick, followed by three putts cost Grant the 11th hole—down-6 with seven to go. On the 12th, a 385-yard par-4, Schmidt hooked badly, and Grant countered with a slice. Both recovered and were on in three. Grant's three-putt double-bogey cost him the hole and the match. Schmidt played consistently throughout the tournament and was appropriately crowned champion.

The tournament was judged a success despite the controversy. The WGA came out a little the worse, but Del Monte received some wonderful media coverage in the Eastern magazines that wrote about not only the competition but also of the quality of the course and the beauty of the surroundings. Other courses in California also benefited from the exposure, and California was now on the map of golf's hierarchy.

Young Dalton Henderson of San Francisco was a regular competitor in the California Junior championship in his youth—even as a pre-teen in 1925. He won the championship in 1931. (PBC-J.P. Graham)

Don Edwards was a semifinalist in the 1929 and 1930 California Junior Championships, and runner-up in 1931. He went on to become the NCGA president in 1947-48. (PBC-J.P. Graham)

THE CALIFORNIA JUNIOR CHAMPIONSHIP

As golf became a family affair, especially with young boys taking up the game, the California Golf Association decided to hold a junior championship for boys and girls age 16 or younger. The first was played at Del Monte over Thanksgiving weekend 1919. Don Carlos Hines, a fine 15-year-old player from San Jose, won the medal with a 91 and was favored to go all the way, but in the final round he missed several short putts, and lost 5&4 to young Ashton Stanley, the 13-year-old son of Hotel Del Monte's manager, Carlos Stanley. The event was a hit enjoyed by both the youth and their parents. The competition moved to July in 1920 but only as a boy's championship.

The California Junior Championship was open to boys who belonged to any club affiliated with the NCGA or SCGA. Occasionally an invitation was offered to a top municipal player, but clearly the event was intended as an interclub championship where the boys, in addition to playing for a personal victory, were playing for club pride, as well as the constant rivalry between the North and the South.

Only 12 boys signed up for the 1920 event, and while descriptions show some of the boys were no taller than their clubs, the competition was terrific. Ashton Stanly, hoping to defend his title, fired a 90 in the medal round but was overtaken by E.B. "Togo" Osborne who closed with an 87. The top eight went on to the first flight. The bottom four, including investor Herbert Fleishhacker's 12-year-old son, Herbert Jr., played in a second flight. Baron Long, partial owner of San Diego's U.S. Grant Hotel and later of the Agua Caliente Racetrack, paid the expenses to get 13-year-old Don Davin, one of San Diego's top youngsters, into the event. Davin used 111 strokes to navigate the Del Monte course in the qualifying round, unaccustomed as he was to playing on grass greens. It was just good enough to make the top eight. In the first round of match play, Davin pulled off a major upset, defeating San Francisco's Martin Minney 4&3. Osborne, however, playing out of San Francisco's California Golf Club, proved to be the class of the field, defeating Davin in the semifinals and Stanley in the finals without going past the 14th hole in any of his three matches. The depth of his game was shown in the final, where despite his drives being off his earlier standard and finding five bunkers, Osborne was only 3-over par on the front nine, which included playing over a well-placed stymie for a win on the 4th hole.

Ashton Stanley made it to the finals again in 1921, his final year of eligibility, but lost to Bobby Ross of Los Angeles in the most tightly contested match in the history of the championship. The match went back-and-forth, with Stanley 1-up as they reached the par-3 17th hole. Both players sliced badly, but Stanley's ball landed in leaves at the base of a tree, virtually unplayable. He attempted to hit out with a left-handed shot but lost the hole. They halved the 18th and went to extra holes. Stanley broke his mashie getting out of a bunker on the 2nd hole, but still managed a half. On the dog-leg 3rd (today's 2nd hole), Stanley attempted to cut the corner and ended out of bounds. Trying again, he was out again, and Ross played out for the victory.

Ross, just shy of 16 in 1921, returned to defend his title in 1922 but had turned 17 days before the tournament and was not allowed to play. Instead, another pair of southern California youngsters reached the final; Jimmy Wade of Los Angeles defeated San Diego's Don Davin 2-up.

The State Junior Championship continued to be played at Del Monte through 1937, honing the skills, values, and competitiveness of many young golfers, some of whom, like Ernest Coombs, Ernie Pieper, Mat Palacio, Don Edwards, Warner Keeley, and Robert Roos, became top adult golfers in the state. In 1925, they raised the age limit of competitors to 17 and under and added a father-son event. It is unclear why the event ended, but was likely due to the extended Great Depression of the 1930s.

Ernest Coombs (left) won the 1928 Junior Championship and finished runner-up to Ernie Pieper (right) in 1929. (PBC-J.P. Graham)

Norman Macbeth Jr., of Los Angeles (right) faced Sacramento's Justin W. Esberg in the semifinals of the 1925 California Junior Championship. Macbeth went on to win the championship, defeating Esberg and then Leslie Hensley in the final. (PBC-J.P. Graham)

In a father-son tournament in conjunction with the Junior Championship at Del Monte, Northern stars Roger Lapham Jr. and Sr. flank the Southern father-and-son team of Norman MacBeth Jr. and Sr. (PBC-J.P. Graham)

THE GOLD VASE

With the opening of Pebble Beach Golf Links in 1919, Morse sought to build interest in the new course. The opening tournament at Pebble Beach Golf Links was a stroke-play event on Washington's Birthday. It was won by course co-designer Douglas Grant. It was not actually played for the Gold Vase, but was the beginning of the tradition of a Washington's Birthday tournament. The Gold Vase originated with the playing of the tournament in 1920. It was an elaborate gold-plated silver cup put up by the company that would record the winner of each year's event. The understanding was that if anyone won the event three times, they would receive permanent possession of the cup. It seemed like a safe bet. In 20 years of Del Monte tournaments, only one man had won three times—Jack Neville—and that took eight years.

The contest for the Gold Vase was an 18-hole stroke event with the vase going to the low gross score. The championship served as a qualifying round for seeding in a match play event that followed it—the Washington's Birthday tournament; essentially two tournaments in one. The combined event attracted contenders from across the country.

The winner in 1920 was a visitor from Colorado, M.A. "Mac" McLaughlin. Mac was the reigning two-time Colorado Amateur champion and founding president of the Colorado Golf Association in 1915. There was a three-way tie at 85 with McLaughlin, Kenneth Monteagle of San Francisco, and R. Walker Salisbury of Salt Lake City, a four-time Utah Amateur Champion. An 18-hole playoff was required after the match play was finished. After the first 18-hole playoff Mac and Salisbury were still tied—each with 86. Only after a third 18-hole playoff did Mac emerge the winner with an 84 to Salisbury's 91. In match play, Claremont's A.E. deArmond drew the tough route, having to defeat Salisbury in the morning round 1-up to face McLaughlin in the afternoon. The second match went 24 holes before deArmond won—only to lose in the semifinals to J.A. Rithert of Victoria, British Columbia. Rithert then lost to Portland's D. Kerr, a Scotsman by birth.

Mac successfully defended his title in 1921, edging out Fred LaBlond Jr., a student at Berkeley, 80 to 81 for the Gold Vase. Because of wet conditions, the match play was moved to the Del Monte course where Fowler had recently completed his re-design work. A.E. deArmond faced Mac in the semifinals in 1921 and won a hard-fought 1-up victory. He then won the Washington's Birthday tournament in a victory over Fred LaBlond Jr., by the same margin.

McLaughlin again returned in 1922, hoping to make a clean sweep of three victories and whisk the trophy back to Colorado permanently. He ran into trouble early, however, and took a nine on the second hole, virtually knocking him out of the running. The Vase instead went to Robert Hunter, an author and native of Chicago with significant experience in national championships when he lived in the East. He had moved to Berkeley in 1917 to teach Sociology and moved to Monterey in 1922. In the Washington's Birthday Tournament that followed, Mac made it to the final match where he lost in a 3&2 upset to Clinton LaMontagne, the stepson of Charles E. Maud, who was able to claim his first tournament victory.

The fourth time was the charm for McLaughlin. In 1923, he fired a 79 to win by a 3-stroke margin and take permanent possession of the Gold Vase. Stuart Haldorn of San Francisco won the match play event but left Morse with a dilemma—what to do about the trophy. The tournament was popular and drawing great competition. The company was flush with real estate sales. Morse did what any ostentatious resort manager would do; he created a new Gold Vase—this one solid gold. The same rule applied—three wins and you got permanent possession, but to lessen the odds of another three-peat, the stroke-play event was extended to 36 holes in 1924.

The match play records are incomplete, but the Gold Vase tournament records are complete. The event continued through 1932, after which interest waned due to the Great Depression and it was discontinued. Never again did any golfer win more than once. Future champions in the event included Jack Neville (1928); A.G. Sato (1929), a Japanese golfer from San Francisco; and H. Chandler Egan (1930). The 1930 contest was especially interesting, as the experienced and past National Champion Egan, then well into his 40s, won the Gold Vase by a single stroke over W. Lawson Little Jr., not yet 20. Little's brilliance in match play surfaced as he marched through his series of matches unscathed, defeating New York's John Ryerson 4&3 in the final of the Washington's Birthday tournament that followed.

Writer and future golf architect Robert Hunter (left) won the 1922 Gold Vase tournament and later in the year reached the finals of the California Amateur. Here he is paired at Pebble Beach with Max Behr, another writer (editor of Golf Illustrated *1914–18) who also became a golf course architect. (PBC-J.P. Graham)*

(Left to right): Leon Keller, John de Paolo, Charles Fererra, and W. Lawson Little II. Little won the Washington's Birthday Tournament in 1930; de Paolo had done so in 1926. (PBC-J.P. Graham)

THE CALIFORNIA OPEN CHAMPIONSHIP

The California Open is one of the many tournaments in California that has a poorly documented beginning. The tournament continues to be played annually, today under the direction of the Southern California PGA. A glance at the reported tournament history lists 1899 U.S. Open Champion Willie Smith as the 1900 California Open champion and Walter Hagen as the 1915 Champion, but it doesn't show annual winners until 1919.

Willie Smith, Midlothian pro from Chicago, did come to California to visit his brother Alex, the pro at Coronado, but he did not arrive until January 1901. Smith played in some hastily arranged events in 1901, including an Open at Del Monte in February that he won. Walter Hagen actually won the 1915 Open at the Panama Pacific Exposition in San Francisco. Reports of the day show Charlie Thom, the professional at Burlingame, was the 1915 California Open Champion—an event he won at Del Monte.

While records were inconsistent, the Opens held in conjunction with Del Monte Championships, such as the PCGA Open through 1911, were generally considered the California Open. The program for the 1944 California Open published a list of past champions that began with John Black's 1919 victory at Del Monte. This matches 1919 newspaper reports that show the California Open was first officially "revived"

Claremont professional John Black won the first official California Open Championship at Del Monte in 1919. Unverified records show he also won in 1920. (PBC – J.P. Graham)

by the California Golf Association in conjunction with the California Amateur Championship at Del Monte in 1919 and won by John Black, the Claremont pro, with a score of 284 for 72 holes, for which he received $150. Amateur Douglas Grant finished second with a 287. Abe Espinosa came in third at 289 but received the $100 second-place prize money because as an amateur, Grant could not accept it. The status of the 1920 Championship is unclear. Records indicate John Black won it, although when and where is not known. It was not held in conjunction with the State Amateur at Del Monte, but was delayed in the hope that British stars Ted Ray and Harry Vardon might be able to play. Thereafter, the California Open was played in the first part of the year and traveled to various courses across the state. The 1921 Open was played in March 1921 at San Francisco's Olympic Club and won by Eddie Loos. Jim Barnes won it in January 1922 at Wilshire, and so forth. It struggled with leadership and missed being played in 1928 and 1929. In 1930 it resumed as a September event. Scheduling caused it to be missed by the pros in 1931, although Leo Diegel is given credit as the 1931 champion, perhaps for his win at Agua Caliente.

In 1935, with the Depression hitting the pro ranks hard, the California Golf Association resumed management of the tournament and brought it to Pebble Beach that August, the week before the State Amateur. It attracted one of the largest fields in years as 120 golfers teed off on Tuesday. After two rounds, the cut line was at 19-over par with 63 golfers continuing to a 36-hole final on Thursday. Only three golfers were under par at the cut day: Willie Hunter of Culver City (72-71—143); Ted Longworth of Portland, Oregon (71-71—142); and Pebble Beach pro Cam Puget (70-72—142).

On Thursday's morning round, Puget and Longworth were both 3 over par, giving Hunter, who shot even par, a 2-stroke lead. Hunter went out in par-36 on the final front nine; Puget managed a birdie on the second hole to pull within 1, but he gave it back with a bogey on 12. Finally, Puget's putter got hot and he birdied 14 and 15, sinking a 20-footer on 15. On 16, he pushed his tee shot left. With what he later reported as his greatest shot in any tournament, he hit a low 2 iron with a slight hook that cleared the front bunker, bounced on the collar, and rolled to within 10 feet of the pin. He made a third straight birdie, pared the last two holes, and closed with a 69—286 for a 4-stroke victory over Willie Hunter, who finished with a 75—290. Mike DeMassey of Modesto finished third at 294, and Longworth tied for fourth with Annandale pro Fred Morrison. Two amateurs finished in the top 10: Ernie Pieper finished in sixth place with a 297, and Jack Finger tied for seventh place at 298. The top 10 pros split a $1,000 purse with Puget's first-place pay day providing $300.

The California Open returned to Pebble Beach in 1936, and the big news was Olin Dutra, who had grown up as a caddy on the local courses and went on to win the 1932 PGA Championship and the 1934 U.S. Open. The stocky 35-year-old was certainly the hometown favorite, leaving defending champion Cam Puget feeling a bit abandoned. Both stars let their local fans down, Dutra with a 76 and Puget with a 79 in the opening round. Dutra

Olin Dutra returned to the Monterey Peninsula in 1936 to compete in the California Open. The golfer who grew up as a caddie on Del Monte Golf Course had already won the 1932 PGA Championship and the 1934 U.S. Open. (PBC-J.P. Graham)

Cam Puget (left), seen here with his mentor Peter Hay, made a great showing on his home course during the 1935 California Open. (PBC-J.P. Graham)

actually started great, shooting 33 on the first nine, but 2 strokes to get out of a bunker and three putts on the 11th green brought him back to even par for the round, and he gave back 3 more strokes on the inbound nine, including 2 on the 18th where he pulled his drive into the ocean.

The first-round leaders were Roger Kelly, an amateur, and Fay Coleman, pro at the California Country Club, who both shot 71. Kelly, a 20-year-old student at Loyola, took the lead in round two with a 72, while the other leaders' scores ballooned. Annandale's Fred Morrison moved into second with a 73-72—145, 2 strokes behind Kelly. Mark Fry was third with a 74-73—147. Dutra came back with a 72 and was in a three-way tie for fifth at 149. The three leaders played together on the final day's 36 holes, and the lead changed five times. At the end of 54 holes, Morrison and Kelly were tied; the amateur missing several greens and shooting 77. Fry, with a 75 after hitting his tee shot on 18 into the ocean, was 2 strokes back in a three-way tie for third with Benny Coltrin and Olin Dura, who was closing the gap.

Dutra took himself out of it with an 80 in the final round. Kelly continued to struggle with his irons, but his putter saved him on many holes. He went out in 36; Morrison took 37. Morrison sunk a 12-footer for birdie on the 10th, and again the leaders were tied. Kelly left his par-putt on 12 just short; advantage Morrison. Mark Fry was playing steady par-golf, but was

unable to move up on the leaders. Morrison and Fry made pars through the next five holes, while Kelly's open-faced irons put him in a couple of troublesome bunkers on the home holes, costing him two more bogeys.

As they stood on the 18th tee, Morrison held a 2-stroke lead over Fry and three over Kelly. Morrison put his drive in the fairway. Fry hit next and watched his ball again head for the ocean. As it came down, however, it hit a rock and bounced back into the fairway—short but remarkably safe. Kelly also hit it down the fairway, and he and Morrison closed with pars. Fry managed a bogey-6 and ended in a tie for second with Kelly and Ben Coltrin, who finished with a 73—295. Tied for fifth at 299 were Art Bell, then of Pasadena, and Santa Barbara's Joe Hunter. Another amateur, Don Edwards, came in seventh at 301 with Olin Dutra in eighth at 302. Cam Puget, with 79-74-77-75—305, ended in a tie for 11th place, 1 stroke ahead of first-round co-leader Fay Coleman.

Firmly back to a strong start, the California Open again traveled to other courses, and Morrison won for a record third time in 1937 at San Bernardino. George Von Elm, the 1926 U.S. Amateur champion, won in Bakersfield in 1938, and Art Bell won his first of three California Opens in 1939. Olin Dutra won in 1940 and Mark Fry in 1941, demonstrating that the leaders at Pebble Beach continued to be top competitors and that the future of the California Open was secure.

MARION HOLLINS AND THE PEBBLE BEACH CHAMPIONSHIP FOR WOMEN

While tradition dictates that Marion Hollins (1892–1944) originated the Pebble Beach Championship for Women, the evidence is less clear in proving that fact. What is clear is that Hollins dominated the event and was instrumental in attracting great female players to play in it each year. The Pebble Beach Championship provided the ladies an opportunity to compete on the challenging seaside links. While the official tournament plaque indicates Hollins won the first event in 1922, the first Championship was actually played in 1923.

In December 1922, Hollins came to California in part to gain members for the Women's National Club she was planning on Long Island. It was during this trip that the Pebble Beach Championship for Women was born. Many top women entered. In addition to Hollins, two other Eastern stars, Mrs. Fred C. Letts Jr., (three-time Western Amateur Champion) and Miss D.L. Higbee, both of Chicago, played as did Mrs. M.L. Sayward of Victoria, British Columbia, and the best of California—Doreen Kavanagh, reigning California champion; Margaret Cameron, reigning Northern California champion; Miss Mary K. Browne, reigning Del Monte champion; and Mrs. W.C. Van Antwerp, a multiple winner of both the State and Del Monte championships.

In the medal play, six ladies broke 100, led by Hollins with an 88 and Van Antwerp with 90. The ladies had the added challenge of playing in rain throughout the weekend—a reported downpour occurred during the semifinal match between Hollins and Letts, which was the best match of the tournament. Hollins was down-2 with four to play and ended up winning 2-up on the 18th hole. In the final, Hollins defeated Kavanagh 6&5.

Hollins headed back East at the end of February where she again played in a few tournaments and worked with her design team—Devereux Emmet, Seth Raynor, and Charles Blair Macdonald—on the Women's National Club. She spoke with other women golfers encouraging them to come to California for the winter and play in the Pebble Beach tournament. Among those playing in 1924 was 1923 U.S. Women's champion Edith Cummings, who took the medal honors with an 86 and won her first match 9&8 over reigning Southern California champion Isabel Kennett. In the quarterfinals, Cummings faced Hollins. The two battled 18 holes with Hollins winning 2-up. Hollins then beat Canada's Mrs. H.G. Hutchings (formerly Vera Ramsey of England) 2&1 in the semifinals before again trouncing a top Californian in the final, this time Mary Browne, 5&4.

After a couple of minor tournaments in southern California, Hollins headed back East to prepare for the opening of her course on Long Island. She also won the 1924 Metropolitan Championship for a third

Marion Hollins was a successful athlete in several sports, but after winning the 1921 U.S. Women's Amateur, she became known for her golfing prowess. (PBC-J.P. Graham)

time. The course work went slower than expected with only nine holes opening in 1924, and the final nine delayed until April 1925. Marion's focus was shifting to California. Her biographer, David Outerbridge, records that her niece states, "She couldn't stand the East Coast after she once discovered California." She again won the medal and Pebble Beach Championship in 1925, went back East briefly for the opening of the back nine of the Women's National, and returned to Pebble Beach to develop Cypress Point Club.

In the 1926 championship, Canada's Vera Hutchings, the Pacific Northwest champion, won the medal; Chicago's Mrs. Melvin Jones,

Mrs. Fred C. Letts of Chicago, a three-time Western Amateur Champion, fell to Marion Hollins in the semifinals of the 1923 Pebble Beach Championship for Women. (PBC-Archives)

The 1923 U.S. Women's Amateur Champion, Edith Cummings, strides confidently down the 7th hole ahead of Marion Hollins. Cummings, however, fell to Hollins in the 1924 Pebble Beach Championship. (PBC-J.P. Graham)

winner of the 1921 Western and the 1925 North-South, finished second; and Hollins tied for third with Edith Van Antwerp. Jones and Hutchings were knocked out in the quarterfinals, while Hollins and Van Antwerp marched to the finals. For the fourth time, Hollins won the championship.

Mrs. Jones decided that that would not happen the next year. In 1927, she arrived a month prior to the event to practice on the course and prepare for the championship. Despite a howling rain intermixed with hail, Jones tied Hollins for the medal with 96; no other golfer broke 100. In match play, Hollins was dominating; in three matches to get to the finals, no match went beyond the 13th hole. Jones also played well, winning her first two matches by a 5&4 margin and defeating Alice Hanchett 3&2 to reach the final. In the final, Jones was solid and Hollins uncharacteristically shaky. Jones won the 3rd, 5th, and 6th holes on the front side to stand 3-up at the turn. She went 4-up on the 14th with a 6 to Marion's 7 and closed out the match 4&3 with a half on the 15th hole.

Two of the greatest women golfers of the 1920s, Marion Hollins (1921 national champion) and Miriam Burns Horn (1927 national champion), faced off on the new Dunes course at Monterey Peninsula Country Club for the final match of the Pebble Beach Championship for Women—a match that went 20 holes before Hollins recorded her fifth victory. (PBC-J.P. Graham)

1928 California Women's Champion, Mrs. Gregg Lifur defeated Hollins in the final round of the 1930 Pebble Beach Championship. (PBC-J.P. Graham)

Petite Mildred Green (left) defeated Marion Hollins in the 1932 Championship. (PBC-J.P. Graham)

San Francisco's Dorothy Traung was runner-up in 1933 but later won the Pebble Beach Championship three times. (PBC-J.P. Graham)

Marion Hollins resumed her winning ways at the 1928 Championship, which for the first time was not contested on Pebble Beach Golf Links but rather on the company's new Dunes Course of the Monterey Peninsula Country Club. The tournament again attracted a stellar field, including reigning U.S. Women's Amateur Champion Miriam Burns Horn of Kansas City. Horn also won the Trans-Mississippi in 1927 and had previously won the Western Amateur in 1923. This was billed to be the clash of the titans, and lived up to its name as the two faced each other in the final match. The two champions went back-and-forth through the 18-hole match. Hollins, led for only one hole, and Horn held the largest lead after hole 15 at 2-up with three holes to play. Hollins won the 16th hole, and each narrowly missed birdies on 17, leaving Horn 1-up going to the final hole. Both were about 30 feet from the pin in three, but Horn's 3-putt squared the match and sent them to extra holes where, on the 20th hole, Hollins again emerged as champion.

Hollins planned to enter the 1929 Pebble Beach Championship but had to withdraw due to a polo accident. In 1930, Marion Hollins was medalist for the fourth time at Pebble Beach and fought her way into the final match where she battled against Mrs. Greg Lifur of southern California for 25 holes before recording her second loss in the history of the event.

Hollins didn't play in the Women's Championship in 1931, but in 1932 she was back at Pebble Beach and lost to her co-medalist, Mrs. Roy (Mildred) Green of southern California, in the final match.

In 1933, the Pebble Beach Championship was contested over the Cypress Point Club course. Dorothy Traung was only 19, but was establishing herself as a competitive golfer. In the Pebble Beach Championship of 1933, Dorothy lost in the final down-1 to Hollins. It is worth noting that it was a 36-hole final and after 33 holes Traung was 2-up with three to play. Appropriately, the spectacular par-3 16th hole, which Hollins was instrumental in having built, was where the match turned around. Hollins was in with par and Traung 3-putted. Traung then found water off the 17th tee, and her drive on 18 landed under a tree. Hollins played her steady game for the win.

Dorothy Traung, however, became a new dominant force at the Women's Championship. Traung won Pebble Beach in 1934, defeating Helen Lengfeld in the final after Lengfeld knocked Hollins out in a semifinal round. Then, after finishing as runner-up in 1935, Traung won again in 1936 and 1939. During the same period, Traung made it to the final match of the 1933 U.S. Amateur, won the 1936 Western Amateur, and was medalist at the 1940 U.S. Amateur when it was played at Pebble Beach. The younger set was taking over dominance of golf.

Another golfer making her first appearance at the 1933 Pebble Beach Women's Championship was 13-year-old Clara Callender, who won the Del Monte Championship the previous year. Her medal round was just 4 strokes behind Hollins' medal-winning score. In the quarterfinals, Callender fought for 25 holes against Jane Douglas before losing her match.

13-year-old Clara Callender played seven extra holes in her first round match before surrendering to southern California's Jane Douglas in the 1933 Pebble Beach Championship for Women. (PBC-J.P. Graham)

S.F.B. Morse presents the trophies for the 1941 Pebble Beach Championship to winner Clara Callendar (right) and runner-up Marion Hollins. (PBC-J.P. Graham)

Barbara Romack at the final Pebble Beach Championship for Women

But she would be back—three times winning both medalist honors and the tournament, the first and last of those victories—1937 and 1941—coming against Marion Hollins in the final match. In addition to finishing runner-up to Callender in 1937 and 1941, Hollins also made a good showing in 1940 when she finished as runner-up to Peggy Graham. Later in 1941, Hollins competed in and won the Del Monte Championship. The 1942 Pebble Beach Championship marked Hollins' final victory at Pebble Beach with a 9&8 victory over Mrs. Frederick Sheldon. With this victory, she joined Clara Callender as the only golfers to win both the Pebble Beach Championship and the Del Monte Championship, and coincidentally, each held the titles concurrently.

While the plaque in The Tap Room does not show it, there was a tournament in 1943. Because of the war, the format was modified to a two-day event of 36 holes against par with handicap. Woman's par at Pebble Beach was 83, and Hollins' 95 (2) in the opening round, left her down-10 and well back of the leader, Mrs. Frank Capps of San Francisco, whose 99 (13) put her just down-3. Capps exploded out of the competition on Day 2, and the event was won by Ellen Kieser of San Francisco, who finished down-8 to par for 36 holes. There was no tournament in 1944 due to the war.

Marion Hollins, long a power player at Pebble Beach, died on August 28, 1944. The tournament Hollins won seven times resumed after the war, with future Hall of Famer Patty Berg winning in 1946 and 1947. The next year attracted several top ladies anxious to get an early look at the

host site of the 1948 U.S. Women's Amateur. Dorothy Traung again made a good showing but finished runner-up to local favorite Mary Sargent, who also won the club championship at Monterey Peninsula Country Club in 1946, 1947, and 1948. The perpetual trophy stops with the 1949 victory of Grace DeMoss, the Oregon golfer who also won the state championships in both Oregon and Arizona that year, before winning a spot on the 1952 Curtis Cup team. However, while not on the trophy, DeMoss successfully defended her title in 1950. The tournament ended in a fizzle. A small turnout in 1951 failed to produce enough golfers to hold matches, and 18-year-old Barbara Romack defeated the small field with a 15-stroke victory over three rounds at Pebble Beach. It was a sad end for the tournament but a great final champion, as Romack went on to win the 1954 U.S. Women's Amateur and represent the U.S. on three Curtis Cup teams (1954, 1956, and 1958) before joining the LPGA Tour.

Jack Westland stayed active in golf representing the Pacific Northwest when he won the 1952 U.S. Amateur at the age of 47. From 1953 to 1965, he represented Washington as its Congressman and then "retired" to Pebble Beach. (PBC-W.C./Brooks)

THE PACIFIC COAST INTERCOLLEGIATE CHAMPIONSHIPS

With the Gold Vase and the Women's Championship keeping Pebble Beach Golf Links abuzz in the late winter, the California Intercollegiate Golf Tournament was born at the Del Monte Golf Course in February 1924. A top college athlete himself, Morse always reveled in collegiate competition. He also sponsored a Big Game weekend each fall when the football teams of University of California (UC) and Stanford met in gridiron battle. So hosting a college golf tournament was a natural for Del Monte. Intercollegiate golf had been played since 1897, and the hope was that getting intercollegiate play going on the West Coast would soon show that California golfers could compete with the best of the East.

In 1923, a Pacific Coast Intercollegiate Championship was played in Portland, Oregon, and won by Jack Westland of the University of Washington. Only a few schools in the Northwest competed. Westland was the sole representative from the Northwest to play in the inaugural California Intercollegiate at Pebble Beach in February 1924. Of the 18 golfers who played in 1924, nine came from Stanford, seven from UC, Earl Brown was from St. Ignatius College, and Westland. Two of the

Stanford golfers ended at the bottom of the qualifying and missed the cut of 16 that continued to match play. The other seven Stanford boys were eliminated in the first round of matches. This gave UC the distinct advantage—other than Jack Westland, who topped the field with a 74 in the medal round.

Jack Westland later became one of the nation's top amateur golfers, making the cut in a dozen U.S. Amateurs and a pair of U.S. Opens, becoming the oldest player (age 47) to win the U.S. Amateur when he did so in 1952. He was later elected to Congress from the State of Washington, and when he retired from the government, he and his wife, Helen, moved to Pebble Beach where they spent their final years. Golf was clearly important to this young man's life, and his championship-level play in college golf was no fluke. Westland defeated Stanford's Richard Lang 10&8 in round one and Brown in the quarterfinals, 2-up.

In the semifinals, Westland faced UC's Lauren Upson. Upson grew up in a golfing family loosely connected the Crocker family. The Westland-Upson match went the distance, both players playing great golf. Westland had a 2-up advantage through 10 holes, but after a couple of topped tee shots, the match was squared with Upson winning on the 18th.

In the 36-hole final match, Upson defeated his team captain Stanton Haight 11&12 while Westland refereed. All agreed that it would stand as the 1924 Pacific Coast Intercollegiate and that thereafter they would annually contest the Pacific Coast Intercollegiate at Pebble Beach. As the new Pacific Coast champion, Upson entered the National Intercollegiate contested that June in Greenwich, Connecticut, where he stunned the Ivy leaguers, winning the medal with a 74-71—145, 7 strokes better than the second-place golfer, William H. Taft of Dartmouth. Upson then worked his way to the semifinals and had become a Cinderella-story crowd favorite. There was some disappointment when Taft defeated Upson 2&1. Nevertheless, Upson sent a clear message; the boys in the East need to take the West Coast golfers seriously.

In 1925, Upson returned to Del Monte, successfully defended his title in the Pacific Coast Intercollegiate Championship, and collected the medal. Jack Westland skipped the Pacific Coast Championship, but he joined Upson in the National Intercollegiate that summer at Montclair, New Jersey. They both did well. Upson lost in the quarterfinals, and Westland reached the final match where he lost to G. Fred Lamprect of Cleveland.

The Pacific Coast had proven it could produce great champions. UC won again in 1926, this time it was Harold Thompson of UC's new "Southern Branch," as UCLA was initially known. Stanford's team showed up to win in 1927, with Stanford taking four of the top-five places, including the medal honors, won by Herbert Fleishhacker Jr. Defending champion Thompson finished third in the qualifying and was the only non-Stanford player in the semifinals. He survived that but fell down-2 in the final to Stanford's Eddie Meyberg.

Lauren Upson of the University of California, Berkeley showed his dominance in collegiate golf by winning the Pacific Coast Intercollegiate in 1924 and 1925. He was also the medalist in the 1924 National Intercollegiate. (PBC-J.P. Graham)

Dick Lang, of the golf team at Stanford came down early for the 1927 Pacific Coast Intercollegiate and entered and won the Gold Vase Tournament. He did not fair as well in the college tournament. (PBC-J.P. Graham)

As a freshman, Stanford's Eddie Meyberg lost in the quarterfinals to Lauren Upson in 1925, but won the Pacific Coast Intercollegiate in his junior year, 1928. (PBC-J.P. Graham)

Gibson Dunlap was a college freshman at the University of Wisconsin in 1926–27 and transferred to UCLA in the fall of 1927. The former Chicago City Amateur champion made his mark in California. He won the Los Angeles municipal golf tournament in December and came to the intercollegiate at Del Monte and fired a 73 on the rain-soaked Del Monte course, 4 strokes better than USC's Allen Moser. The two southern stars defeated Stanford players in the semifinals (defending champion Eddie Meyberg fought Moser for 23 holes), with Dunlap defeating Moser 5&4 in the 1928 final.

In 1929, the college championship moved to Pebble Beach Golf Links, recently brought into top tournament condition for the 1929 U.S. Amateur. Dunlap repeated as medalist in 1929, although scores were higher than at Del Monte. Dunlap's 80 was the low score, and Allen Moser, despite birdies on holes 3 and 6, finished eighth with an 88, hampered by a cumulative 6 penalty strokes on holes 8 and 14. Stanford again showed its depth, and with Dunlap knocked out in round one, Moser was the only non-Stanford player to reach the semifinals. Moser went on to win the championship.

Stanford's Warner Edmonds punctuated his medal-winning 73 in 1930 with a hole-in-one on the 17th. Dunlap rushed up to Pebble Beach after finishing his exams and was not up to his usual game. He had caught National attention at Pebble Beach the prior September when in the first round of qualifying he shot a 69, leading Bobby Jones by a stroke. Edmonds lost in the semifinals to USC's Russell Thompson, but Stanford pride was upheld when Richard Stevenson knocked out defending champion Moser and then won the championship with a 1-up victory over Thompson.

Throughout the 1930s, Stanford put together several great golf teams, but one of its all-time great players was William Lawson Little II. In his high school days he won the 1928 Northern California Amateur. At age 19, he reached the quarterfinals in the U.S. Amateur at Pebble Beach. Before losing to Francis Ouimet, Little defeated Johnny Goodman, who had vanquished Bobby Jones in the opening round. In the early 1930s, he played for Stanford and honed his match-play skills—including at the Intercollegiate at Pebble Beach. USC's Neil White won the California Amateur at Pebble Beach in 1932, but in February 1933 he ran into Little in the final round of the Intercollegiate and was dominated, losing 6&5.

In 1934, Little became the first player since Upson to repeat as Pacific Coast Intercollegiate Champion. While Upson followed up his wins with a national tournament, Little went international. He was selected as a member of the 1934 Walker Cup Team that trounced the Brits at St. Andrews 9-to-2. He then won the British Amateur at Prestwick, defeating Jimmy Wallace 14&13 in the 36-hole final to become only the third native-born American to win the championship. He returned to the states in time to play in the U.S. Open at Merion, and his tie for 25th in the stroke-play event gave him low-amateur honors. His next stop was Brookline, Massachusetts, for the U.S. Amateur, in which he defeated David Goldman 8&7 in the final match to claim another major title. He returned to Stanford for his senior year, and despite a car accident that sent him through the windshield on December 3, Little signed up and played in the first annual San Francisco Open Match Play championship at the Presidio course. In an upset, Little was knocked out 5&4 in a first-round match by a little-known, 22-year-old Texan named Byron Nelson.

As a youth, Allen Moser, representing Wilshire Country Club, was the 1924 medalist in the California Junior Championship. He returned in 1929, representing USC, to win the Pacific Coast Intercollegiate. (PBC-J.P. Graham)

Top Collegiate golfers (left to right): Winston Fuller (USC), Warner Edmonds (Stanford), and Edgar Lindner (UC). Edmonds was the medalist in 1930 and 1931; Fuller won the Pacific Coast title in 1932. (PBC-J.P. Graham)

Stanford's William Lawson Little II won the Pacific Coast Intercollegiate back-to-back in 1933–34. He followed that up by winning both the U.S. Amateur and British Amateur back-to-back in 1934–35. He became one of the sport's top champions. (PBC-J.P. Graham)

Little missed the Intercollegiate in 1935 but accepted an invitation to play in the second annual Masters Championship. In the warm-up team round, Little was paired with the host, Bobby Jones. They finished sixth in the better-ball competition, which was won by a pair of Californians—Olin Dutra and Jimmy Thompson. In the actual Masters, Little finished sixth and took low-amateur honors. In June, he returned to Britain and successfully defended his British Amateur crown at St Anne's and stayed around for the Open, where he finished fourth, again the low-Amateur, and set an amateur record on the Leatherhead course near London. On his way back to California, he stopped by the White House to receive congratulations from President Franklin D. Roosevelt.

In September it was off to Cleveland and the U.S. Amateur. Little made comebacks through match after match, and when he finally reached the semifinals, ready and waiting was Johnny Goodman. The two went after each other with sensational play. Lawson held a 2-up lead after the morning round, but Goodman came back inspired and used only 32 strokes on the front nine, squaring the match on the 7th hole and matching birdies on 8 and 9. Little made three more birdies on the home holes, closing out the match with a 40-foot birdie on the 15th to win 4&3. Little defeated Walter Emery 4&2 in the final to complete

THE $5,000 1926 MONTEREY PENINSULA OPEN

Future Hall of Famer Lawson Little recorded his first victory at Pebble Beach at the Washington's Birthday Tournament in 1930, narrowly missing the Gold Vase by 1 stroke. He won again as a college player in 1933 and 1934. (PBC-J.P. Graham)

In later years Lawson Little had a home on the second hole of Pebble Beach Golf Links, and in addition to playing in the Crosby for many years, he helped promote many fundraisers, including a hole-in-one tournament on the Peter Hay course in 1962 to benefit the new Community Hospital. (PBC-J.P. Graham)

the unprecedented double-double with back-to-back wins in the U.S. and British Amateurs, along with three low-amateur awards across two continents in two years—all of which were kicked off with his back-to-back wins at the Intercollegiate at Pebble Beach. Not surprisingly, Little turned professional shortly thereafter and later made his home at Pebble Beach.

The Pacific Coast Intercollegiate continued to be played at Pebble Beach through 1938, when it was decided to move it to a different course each year.

In the 1920s, the USGA and even the Western Golf Association based in Chicago, thought of anything west of Chicago as the wild frontier. In January 1926, the Los Angeles Open put up a record $10,000 purse to attract the top professionals to California. For the following winter, California's sports leaders put together an early version of the West Coast Swing. Morse put up $5,000—a handsome purse for its day—with $1,200 going to the winner and scheduled the Monterey Peninsula Open for December 9–13, 1926. It served as the launch for a series of California tournaments offering a combined purse of more than $20,000 that concluded on January 5–9, 1927, with the 2nd Annual $10,000 Los Angeles Open—then the richest tournament in the country. From there, the pros headed across the South.

No small event; the Associate Press reported it as "one of the greatest fields ever assembled outside of the National Open championships." Top professionals and amateurs came from across the country—many saw Pebble Beach for the first time, while others grew up within sight of its roots. Past and future U.S. Open champions included Cyril Walker (1924), Tommy Armour (1927), Johnny Farrell (1928), and Olin Dutra (1934). Several famous U.S. Open runners-up were also on hand for the early competition at Pebble Beach: Mike Brady (1911, 1919), Leo Diegel (1920), John Black (1922), Bobby Cruickshank (1923, 1932), Joe Turnesa (1926), Harry Cooper (1927, 1936), Al Espinosa (1929), and George Von Elm (1931). Willie Hunter, 1921 British Open Champion, was also in the field, as was Bill Melhorn, runner-up to Walter Hagen in the 1925 PGA Championship. Hagen himself was scheduled to play, but he pulled out at the last minute when offered a guarantee in an exhibition tournament at Sequoyah Country Club in Oakland that was higher than the first place money at Pebble Beach. Two other U.S. Open champions, Gene Sarazen (1922, 1932) and Jim Barnes (1921), were reported to have entered, but there is no record that either posted a score.

Strong winds blew on Friday morning as the golfers began the first 18 holes of medal play. The low score on Day 1 belonged to "Wild" Bill Melhorn, who managed a par 72 despite the wind and his reputation to be a bit wild. Al Espinosa and Hutt Martin were close behind with 73s, and 21 others were within 4 strokes of the leader. The average score along the windswept coastline that day was 81, with a few amateurs posting scores in the 90s. Only three amateurs came in under 80—George Von Elm (76), the reigning U.S. Amateur champion; Johnny Dawson (78); and E.M. Burnham (79).

Scores were much better on Day 2 with the clear majority improving over Day 1—including Bill Melhorn, who appeared to be running away with a 2-under-par 70, while Martin and Espinosa fell back with 78 and 77, respectively. Moving up by matching Melhorn's 70 were Olin Dutra, Johnny Golden, and Harry Cooper, the latter two in a three-way tie for second with

(top) *The gallery watches the action on the 8th green that sports bunkers designed and completed by Alister Mackenzie just before the playing of the 1926 Monterey Peninsula Open (PBC-J.P. Graham) (bottom) Eddie Loos putts on the 18th green. "Wild" Bill Melhorn (far left) and Joe Turnesa (center) await the result. S.F.B. Morse's stately manor can be seen in the background. (PBC-J.P. Graham)*

Former Los Angeles golf writer Darsie L. Darsie (left), as the company's PR man, helped convince champions Gene Sarazen and Eddie Loos to be part of the 1926 Monterey Peninsula Open. (PBC-J.P. Graham)

"Wee Bobby" Cruickshank stands on a tee block to gain height on Johnny Golden and Tommy Armour "The Silver Scott." (PBC-J.P. Graham)

Johnny Farrell, "Wild" Bill Melhorn, and reigning U.S. Amateur Champion George Von Elm were among the top competitors at Pebble Beach in 1926. (PBC-J.P. Graham)

The famous Espinosa brothers—Abe kneeling and Al standing—returned to their native peninsula for the 1926 Open. Their three younger brothers also played in the tournament. (PBC-J.P. Graham)

Harry Cooper enjoyed California in 1926, beginning the year with a win in the Los Angeles Open and closing out the year with a win at Pebble Beach. (Hotelling)

"Light Horse" Harry Cooper was among the fastest players on the winter tour. He grew up in Texas, where he emigrated with his parents from England. For many years he held the record for the most wins on American soil by a foreign-born player—a record finally surpassed in 2008 by Vijay Singh of Fiji. (PBC-J.P. Graham)

George Martin (74-71) and 3 strokes behind the leader. Sixty golfers made 158 or better to survive the cut for Sunday's 36-hole marathon.

Melhorn fell back into the field with a 79 in the morning round, while Harry Cooper shot par to hold a share of the lead with Johnny Farrell, who played tremendous golf and fired a 69. Equaling 69 and moving into third one shot back was Larry Nabholtz, the Ohio pro who rose from obscurity by defeating Gene Sarazen in a second-round match in the 1924 PGA Championship and who won the Ohio Open in 1925. Michigan's Al Watrous, winner of the 1926 Western Open and runner-up in the 1926 British Open, was in fourth.

"Light Horse" Harry Cooper, earning his nickname for his swift play in winning the inaugural Los Angeles Open to begin the year, started to take control in the afternoon, looking to close out the year with another West Coast victory. Cooper jumped into the lead with a 34 on the front nine, while Farrell and Nabholtz shot par to remain in second and third. But

on the back nine, fortunes began to change with Cooper losing strokes and missing putts and giving Farrell another chance. Then Farrell also began to falter, hitting it out of bounds on hole 14 and again on hole 15. Despite that, any of the three leaders remained capable of the win as each struggled against the pressure. Farrell fell back for good when he put his tee shot in the ocean. His 36-43—79 final round earned him a tie for third place with Bill Melhorn, who closed with a 75. Holding onto a 1-stroke advantage in second was Nabholtz, who closed with a 36-41—77. This left Harry Cooper alone at the top with a 2-stroke margin of victory, despite a 6-over-par 42 on the final nine holes.

As for the future of the Monterey Peninsula Open…it continued to be played annually but on a much smaller scale at Del Monte Golf Course, where its name was shortened to the Monterey Open. For many years, the tournament was run by the Monterey Elks Club. It was discontinued after the 1997 event, and in 2004, Del Monte course professional Neil Allen resumed the tournament as an annual event each fall.

Dr. Paul Hunter of Los Angeles won the 1920 California Amateur Championship—the first one played over Pebble Beach Golf Links. He won again in 1921. (PBC-Archives)

Jack Neville and Fred Wright played a hard-fought match in the semifinals of the 1922 State Amateur before Neville went on to claim his fourth victory. (PBC-J.P. Graham)

Meeting on the first tee at Pebble Beach were three generations of California golfers—Dr. Charles Walter, millionaire Chris Buckley, and Johnny J. McHugh, who would later win the State Amateur in 1923, 1927 and 1928. (PBC-J.P. Graham)

THE STATE AMATEUR AT PEBBLE BEACH

The move of the State Amateur to Pebble Beach Golf Links was not immediate. In 1919, the California Golf Association deemed Pebble Beach was not ready for Championship golf and preferred to stay at Del Monte. In 1920, the Association reluctantly agreed to use Pebble Beach, but only in conjunction with Del Monte. The golfers of the state showed their approval of the decision by coming out in record numbers. Nearly 300 golfers played in the championship. Half the field played the first round at Del Monte on the first day, the other half at Pebble Beach. The second day they switched. Claremont's Robert Hunter's 76-73—149 was good for the medal, besting "Scotty" Armstrong by 1 stroke. The low 32 golfers moved to the championship matches, which were all held on Pebble Beach Golf Links. All matches were played over 36 holes, a practice begun in 1919. The two southern California cracks reached the final match, with Dr. Paul Hunter defeating Armstrong 6&4.

Young and old, H. Chandler Egan had won the U.S. Amateur twice before George Von Elm was of school age. In 1925, Egan was the medalist and Von Elm champion in the California Amateur. The next year, Von Elm defeated Bobby Jones to win the 1926 U.S. Amateur and Egan won the California Amateur. (PBC-J.P. Graham)

Roger Lapham presents the trophy to Jack Neville in 1929 for his record fifth California State Amateur Champion title. (PBC-Archives)

The format worked and was continued in following years. Dr. Paul Hunter continued his top-level play in 1921, winning the medal and the championship. Jack Neville won the State Championship for a record fourth time in 1922 after a tough semifinal win over Fred J. Wright Jr. and a decisive 11&9 victory of Robert Hunter, who had recently moved to Monterey.

In 1923, John J. McHugh blasted on to the scene, defeating Neville in the semifinals and Wright in the final match to win his first state championship. McHugh, a municipal golfer, learned the game and honed his skills at San Francisco's Lincoln Park course, and he previously reached the third round of the State Amateur in 1921. In 1922 and 1923, he was the medalist in the Northern California Amateur, finishing as runner-up both times. Still, the 19-year-old McHugh was well down in the state rankings when he handily defeated two of the top-five golfers in the state. No one overlooked McHugh again.

In 1925, McHugh played his best golf early, defeating southern California's George Von Elm 3&2 in the North-South team matches that preceded the actual championship. Von Elm was considered by many to be the best golfer in the West, a title he redeemed by winning the State Championship. Von Elm opted not to defend his state title in 1926 as the dates conflicted with the National Championship at Baltusrol on the other side of the continent. There Von Elm proved he was not only the best in the West but the best in the nation, as he defeated Bobby Jones in the final match, robbing Jones of achieving his third-straight U.S. Amateur Championship.

In 1926, McHugh finished as runner-up in a 3&1 loss to H. Chandler Egan. The 1926 championship also welcomed the new Dunes Course at Monterey Peninsula Country Club. The qualifying rounds for more than 400 golfers were still split with 18 holes each at Del Monte and Pebble Beach, breaking the golfers into multiple flights. The top six flights played matches over Pebble Beach Golf Links. The next eight flights utilized the new MPCC course, and the remaining flights played off at Del Monte.

More changes were in store for the 1927 Championship. Golfers with a handicap of nine or less played both qualifying rounds at Pebble Beach; seven or less was required in 1928. Golfers with higher handicaps split qualifying with 18 holes at the Dunes course and 18 at Del Monte. In other words, for the true champions, all golf play would be at Pebble Beach. George Von Elm returned to state competition in 1927. In the North-South matches, McHugh again beat Von Elm 1-up. Von Elm, however, set a new course record in winning the medal honors 68-72—140 before losing in a first-round upset to 17-year-old Donald Moe of Portland, Oregon. McHugh rose to the top and won the 1927 State Championship. He did it again in 1928 when the final was a rematch with Egan.

The 1929 State Amateur was played in May because Pebble Beach would host the U.S. Amateur in September. McHugh was co-medalist with an 80-73—153 on a course that had been fortified for its national debut. McHugh was reaching for Neville's record of four victories. To get there, he would have to go through Neville himself. They met in the semifinal match and Neville showed he was still capable of playing championship golf, defeating McHugh 3&1. Neville then beat Frank C. Stevens Jr., 3&1, capping his record with a fifth victory and the honor of being paired with Bobby Jones in the qualifying rounds of the U.S. Amateur that September.

For 1930, State Amateur qualifying was again spit over two courses for all players. The low handicappers (seven and less) played one round at Pebble Beach and one at Cypress Point. The higher handicappers again used Del Monte and MPCC. The medalist was rising star W. Lawson Little Jr. In match play, the top of the coast golfers was an off-coaster—Francis Brown, a Hawaiian champion. Brown later built a home at Pebble Beach, and while he maintained Hawaii as his primary residence, the convivial millionaire became a big part of life at Pebble Beach and was a regular in the Crosby events for many years.

The California Golf Association made a big change in 1931. Patterning their decision after the British Amateur, they eliminated qualifying rounds and went straight to match play. A record 172 golfers with handicaps of seven or less were accepted, and a draw was made with 88 golfers playing first-round matches on Pebble Beach Golf Links, the others receiving a bye and entering matches in the second round. Golfers that fell in the first two rounds played for a consolation cup on Cypress Point, while the winners proceeded with championship matches on Pebble Beach Golf Links. The higher handicap golfers continued to play for a handicap championship over the Del Monte and MPCC courses.

In 1934, the Association decided the early matches lacked the pizzazz of the medal qualifying, so qualifying was resumed with the low handicaps again playing 18 holes at Cypress Point and 18 at Pebble Beach. Many of the "kids" that competed in the Junior and Intercollegiate championships began to dominate the State Amateur in the 1930s. San Jose's Ernie Pieper, the 1929 Junior Champion at Del Monte, made his first appearance in the 1931 State Amateur and reached the final match where he fell to David Martin, who had been a finalist in the 1924 Junior Championship. Pieper reached the semifinals five times in the 1930s went on to win the State Amateur twice; in 1941 and 1944. He later set the record for reaching the semifinals 10 times, his last time in 1968 at the age of 56. Other youthful champions included Neil White (1932), Stuart Hawley (1934), Mat Palacio (1936), and Roger Kelly (1937 and 1938). Jack Gaines, a 36-year-old physical education instructor from Glendale, California, was the rare exception to youthful dominance when he frustrated Stuart Hawley's defense of his title, nipping the 23-year-old 2&1 in the 1935 championship.

(above) Five-time Hawaiian Amateur Champion Francis Brown missed out of match play in the 1929 U.S. Amateur by losing a playoff for the final spot. But in 1930, he returned to Pebble Beach and won the California Amateur. (PBC-J.P. Graham)

(left) Big David Martin of Santa Barbara was a semifinalist in the 1926 California Junior Championship. As a young adult, Martin won the State Amateur in 1931. (PBC-J.P. Graham)

Another youngster who made his first of many appearances in the 1930s was "Bud" Taylor. The youngster, yet to enter USC's dental school, lost in the semifinals of 1937 after forcing eventual winner Roger Kelley to two extra holes. In 1940, Taylor lost in the semifinals to 1939 champion Jack Gage. The 24-year-old Gage was expected to repeat as champion in 1940, but he fell 7&5 to Fresno's Eddie Monaghan before literally collapsing and being rushed off the course for an emergency appendectomy.

The early 1940s were impacted by World War II, but while the National Amateur was canceled, the State Amateur continued. John Dawson, who switched from selling stocks to sporting goods in 1929, was stripped of his amateur status by the USGA just prior to the 1929 U.S. Amateur at Pebble Beach. In 1942, the ace golfer, who never played for money despite a spectacular game, was restored to amateur competition when he left the sporting goods business. In 1942 alone he won many titles, including the Crosby at Rancho Santa Fe as well as becoming the only player to win the California Open and Amateur in the same year. Who knows how many titles he would have won had he been eligible.

The 39-year-old Dawson continued in competitive golf for the next few years, losing in the semifinals to Ernie Pieper in 1944 and winning medalist honors in 1945.

Mat Palacio, a student at the University of San Francisco, fought Stanford's Bob Thompson for 37 holes before ending as runner-up in the Pacific Coast Intercollegiate. Palacio came back in the summer to win the 1936 California Amateur Championship. (PBC-J.P. Graham)

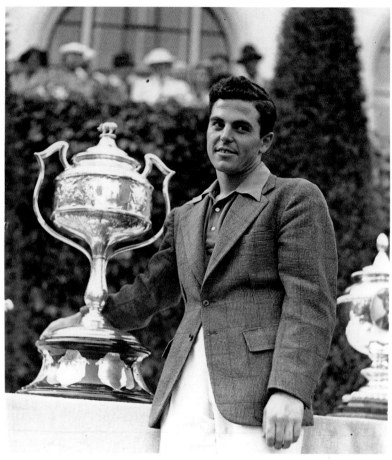

Roger Kelley won twice at Pebble Beach in 1937; in February, the junior at Loyola won the Intercollegiate. In the summer, he beat defending champion Matt Palacio 12&10 to win his first of two California Championships. In 1938, Roger Kelly joined Douglas Grant and Paul Hunter as only the third golfer to win medalist honors and the state championship in the same year. (PBC-J.P. Graham)

Dawson's amateur status was reinstated in time for him to win the 1942 California Amateur Championship—the same year he and Harry Cooper won the Crosby at Rancho Santa Fe, and also as an amateur, the 1942 California Open. (PBC-J.P. Graham)

THE DEL MONTE CHAMPIONSHIPS FOR WOMEN

Women continued to compete at Del Monte each September while the men competed in the State Amateur. Kathleen Wright, medalist and champion in 1917, remained a dominant player in the 1920s, achieving medalist honors three times. She also reached the semifinals six times in that decade, achieving back-to-back championships in 1925 and 1926.

Doreen Kavanagh was another of the top women competitors. While she won the Women's State Amateur four straight years from 1921–24, she never won a Del Monte Championship. She was twice the medalist at Del Monte, but her best finish was runner-up to Mary Browne in 1922. Browne, a former National Tennis Champion, finished runner-up to Edith Van Antwerp in the 1923 Del Monte Championship and then turned her focus to national honors. In the 1924 U.S. Women's Amateur, she defeated Glenna Collett in the semifinal before falling to Dorothy Campbell Hurd—this former Del Monte Champion was the only woman to compete in the finals of the U.S. Open in both tennis and golf.

Another of the state's ladies who was nearly always in the hunt at Del Monte was San Francisco's Mrs. Brent (Sylvia) Potter. Between 1923

and 1932 she reached the semifinals six times, continuing to the final match four times. In 1927, she lost to Helen Lawson in the final match. Potter lost to California's strongest player, Leona Pressler, twice—in the semifinals of 1929 and the finals of 1930. In 1931, Potter defeated golfing phenomenon Clara Callender in the semifinal match 2-up and recorded her only victory at Del Monte, defeating Esther Scott by a solid 9&5. In 1932, Potter faced two rematches in the closing rounds. Potter bested Helen Lawson 5&4 in the semifinal match and then lost to 12-year-old Clara Callender.

Leona Pressler did not take up golf until 1925 when she married Harry Pressler, the golf professional at the San Gabriel club in southern California, who taught her the game. She quickly became one of the best golfers in the state, then the country, and then the world. She was medalist and runner-up in the State Championship in 1927, had an off-year in 1928, and then won the State honors seven times straight between 1929 and 1934. During those same years (1927–34), she played in the U.S. Women's Amateur, reaching the quarter finals six times. She finished runner-up to Glenna Collett in 1929. She also reached the semifinals of the British Amateur in 1932. Given her busy schedule, she only competed in the Del Monte Championship twice, winning it in both 1929 and 1930.

Southern California's Mary K. Browne is famed for being the only athlete to finish in the finals of the national championship in both golf and tennis. She was the U.S. Singles Tennis champion in 1912, 1913, and 1914 in her early 20s. In her 30s, she turned to golf and in 1922 won the Del Monte Championship, defeating the reigning California champion Doreen Kavanagh in the final match. In 1924, Browne defeated Glenna Collett in the semifinal match of the U.S. Women's Amateur before finishing runner-up to Dorothy Campbell Hurd. (PBC-J.P. Graham)

Always a threat on the golf course, Sylvia Potter reached the semifinals of the Del Monte Championship six times between 1923 and 1932, winning the event in 1931. (PBC-J.P. Graham)

Even as youngsters in 1933, Mary Morse (age 13) and Clara Callender (age 14) were two of California's top golfers—both grew up at Pebble Beach. (PBC-J.P. Graham)

Youthful Ruth Tustin reached the finals in the 1936 Championship. (PBC-J.P. Graham)

Mary Hayne was the daughter of early California champion Robin Hayne and took to golf naturally. In 1940, as Mrs. Alan Pattee, Mary was the medalist in the Del Monte Women's Championship. (PBC-J.P. Graham)

Ruby Keeler (left) and Dolores Hope were two of the celebrity wives who played in the Del Monte Championships. (PBC-J.P. Graham)

As the daughter of Eliot Callender, the golf professional at Monterey Peninsula Country Club, Clara Callender was at home on the golf course from an early age. In 1933, she finished runner-up to Jane Douglas but won in 1934 and 1935. Callender was the medalist in 1936, edging out Mary Hayne by a stroke. Mary Hayne, who was runner-up to Callender in 1935, was the daughter of former champion golfer Robin Y. Hayne and Jane Selby and also lived at Pebble Beach. Hayne went out in the first round of 1936, losing to Stockton's Barbara Ransom, and Callender lost in a shocker to 16-year-old Ruth Tustin of Wilshire. At the 18th tee, the match was all square. Tustin made her par-putt. As Callender putted for the half, a camera clicked, causing her to balk and miss the putt for the loss. Tustin proved she was worthy of the win by continuing to the final match before losing to the more experienced Helen Lawson Shepherd, the 1927 Del Monte champion and veteran of two U.S. Amateurs.

Callender was back in the thick of battle in 1937. This time she faced Shepherd in the final match; Shepherd defended her title with a 2&1 victory. A few weeks later, the pair met again at Memphis, Tennessee, in the third round matches for the National Championship. It was Callender's first time at the national championship, and again experience allowed Shepherd a 2-up victory.

The Del Monte championship of 1938 attracted some of Hollywood's top ladies, including Mrs. Charles Chaplin (Paulette Goddard), Mrs. F.D. Griffin (Irene Dunne), Mrs. Phil Harris (Alice Faye), Mrs. Bob Hope (Dolores Hope), Mrs. Al Jolson (Ruby Keeler), and Mrs. Rod LaRocque (Vilma Banky). None of these ladies qualified for the Championship matches. Clara Callender, of course, reached the championship match but lost to Mrs. R.S. Morimoto in the semifinals of 1938 and fell to Morimoto again in the quarterfinals of 1939. Morimoto then fell to the champion each year—Barbara Beach Thompson in 1938 and Barbara Ransom in 1939.

Callender's father died in late 1939, and she moved to Long Beach in southern California. She returned to the peninsula in September 1940 for both the first playing of the U.S. Women's Amateur at Pebble Beach in August and the Del Monte Championship.

In the 1940 Del Monte Championship, Mary Hayne Pattee was the medalist with a strong 77, while Callender and Shepherd shot 82 and 81, respectively, to qualify. Mary Morse, 20-year-old daughter of S.F.B. Morse, scored the tournament upset by ousting Shepherd 4&3 in the second round. Morse lost to Frances Glover of Alameda in the semifinal match, and Glover fell to Callender, who secured her fourth Del Monte Championship title just a week before her 21st birthday.

Marion Hollins, six-time winner of Pebble Beach Championships, entered the 1941 Del Monte Championship for the first time, and the ladies of Hollywood were again in full presence among the 136 entrants. Long hitting Catherine Schuster Lunn recorded an 80 and won the medalist honors for a second time. Hollins qualified with an 82, and among the 16 ladies in the championship matches for the first time was Dolores Hope with an 86. Ruby Keeler just missed the low 16 with an 88. Hope lost her first match in the championship, and Keeler won all her matches to capture the second flight. Another top match player from Hollywood was Mrs. Chico Marx, who won the fourth flight. However, it was the championship that mattered, and while Hollins won her first two matches comfortably, she struggled to 1-up victories over San Francisco's Roxie Setrakian in the semifinals and Catherine Lunn in the final to record her first and only Del Monte Championship victory.

Hollins and Callender faced-off in the final match of 1942 with Callender recording her fifth Del Monte Championship victory—9&8.

Neither Hollins nor Callender returned for the 1943 Del Monte Championship, and for only the second time it was not played at the Del Monte Golf Course. Morse had turned over the Del Monte course to the City of Monterey in July 1943 after leasing Hotel Del Monte to the U.S. Navy. The women therefore played their championship on the Cypress Point course. The top golfer in the field however was not a Californian but rather a Texan, Mildred "Babe" Didrickson Zaharias. Her 79 won the medal, followed by Helen Shepherd's 81. Shepherd was upset in the first round by Mrs. Decker McAlister, and Zaharias marched through her first two 18-hole matches by the incredible margins of 8&7 and 7&6. In

Babe Didrickson Zaharias led the ladies around Cypress Point Golf course to claim the last Del Monte Championship until after the war. (PBC-J.P. Graham)

the semifinal match, she faced the cagey Peggy Rutledge of Long Beach. Zaharias hit it long; Rutledge played it safe. The pair traded wins on the first two holes, then Rutledge's strategy began to pay dividends. By the 7th, Rutledge was 3-up as the Babe's long balls found trouble. Zaharias settled down to win the next two holes but was still in the unaccustomed role of being down-1 at the turn. She finally squared the match at the 14th and birdied the 15th to take a 1-up lead. The next two holes were halved, and Zaharias won the 18th for a 2-up victory.

In the final, Zaharias faced San Francisco's Mrs. Walter McCarty. Again she traded the opening holes but then began to dominate the match, winning holes 5, 6, 7, and 8 to go 4-up. Zaharias won seven holes on the back nine, losing only the 13th and 18th with double-bogeys. In the afternoon, Zaharias won the first three holes to go 12-up. A double-bogey on the 4th gave one shot back, but she won the next two holes and closed out the match with a record score of 13&12.

It was the last time the Del Monte Championship was played until after the war.

THE UNITED STATES GOLF ASSOCIATION
THE 1929 U.S. AMATEUR

The California contingent in the 1929 U.S. Amateur included 20 young players eager to test their skills against the best in the country. Among those touted as possible threats were Fay Coleman, 1928 Southern California Amateur Champion and semifinalist in the 1929 California State Amateur; Gibson Dunlap, 1929 Southern California Junior Champion; Lawson Little, 1928 Northern California Amateur Champion; and Charles Seaver, 1927 Southern California Junior Champion, second low amateur in the 1928 Los Angeles Open and finalist in the 1929 Southern California Junior Championship.

An interesting forecast came from O.B. Keeler, a golf writer and personal friend of Bobby Jones. Most prognosticators were echoing the sentiments of Chicago's *Golfers* magazine which stated, "As has been the case for a number of years, the National Amateur simmers down to Bobby Jones against the field."

Dr. Charles H. Walter, the 1917 California Amateur Champion, gives some tips to 17-year-old Charlie Seaver who, with his father Everett Seaver, both qualified to play in the 1929 U.S. Amateur. (PBC-J.P. Graham)

Bobby Jones was the clear favorite at Pebble Beach. (PBC-J.P. Graham)

Among the golfers in this foursome on the first tee is co-medalist Eugene Homans (left); others are (left to right): H. Chandler Egan, Eustace Storey, and Phillips Finlay. (PBC-J.P. Graham)

Bobby Jones paired with course designer and reigning five-time State Champion Jack Neville in the two medalist rounds of the 1929 U.S. Amateur. (PBC-J.P. Graham)

Bucking the trend, Keeler, pointing out that Jones had never experienced golf in California before, opined, "This may be the time Bobby fails to qualify, or the first time he makes his exit in Round I. In the last two championships Bobby has been within the thinnest margin of being knocked off in one of the 18-hole matches…before he ever reached the 36-hole bouts which appear to suit him so much better. The draw will be seeded, as usual. But one hot youngster and one tepid champion compose a combination that can tip over any match-play championship."

Jones was intent on making a good showing and allowed more than a month for his first West Coast swing. He played an exhibition match in Los Angeles before leisurely making his way to the Monterey Peninsula more than a week before the championship. S.F.B. Morse and Peter Hay accompanied Jones and Cyril Tolley on an early practice round. Morse later recalled the sequence on the 555-yard uphill 14th hole:

In a practice round before the tournament opened, I was going around Pebble Beach with [Jones]. It was a foursome and Cyril Tolley, the English champion, who was the best-known amateur golfer outside of Jones. Tolley was famous for his long shots and frequently he would be out in front of Jones on tee shots. We came to the 14th hole, which is a long par 5. Bob, who had never played the course before, turned to Peter Hay and said, 'Peter, what do I do here?' And Peter, with a strong Scotch brogue said, 'Give it all you've got, Bobby.' I watched his swing and it didn't look any different to me than it had on any of the other holes—yet he was 20 yards in front of Tolley with his tee shot. He carried past the hole on his second shot, holed out, and had an eagle 3. When I questioned him about it after the round, he said, 'I never feel when I am hitting a ball that I am giving it all I have. I feel that I have at least 25 percent up my sleeve. When I feel it is necessary I put some of that extra 25 percent into the shot.' His swing was effortless and the results uncanny.

Bobby Jones shot a 70 in the first round of medal play, followed by a 75 on Day 2. This tied him for medalist honors with young Eugene V. Homans of New Jersey, who shot a steady 72-73—145. Homans had proved himself a fine junior golfer, winning the New Jersey Junior Championship five years in a row (1923–27). Still, it was a thrill for the young man to now share low qualifying score with the great Bobby Jones. Another youngster to grab attention was Gibson Dunlap, who bested Jones with an opening round 69 to take the first-day lead. He followed with a 78 to fall to 5th in the two-day qualifying.

The morning gallery was glued to Bobby Jones, who was paired against Johnny Goodman in the opening round; the latter qualified for the match with a 77-80—157. Goodman, a caddie from Omaha, Nebraska, worked his way out to California on a railroad cattle car to play in the tournament. The mere fact that the young man made the final 32 was surprising. Jones' gallery did not expect a close opening match; they just wanted to see Jones play. Imagine their surprise when after just three holes, Goodman was 3-up over the favorite. Jones worked his way back to even by the 12th but then lost the 14th. Halving the final four holes left a stunned gallery watching as a cordial Bobby Jones congratulated his victorious opponent on the 18th green.

The early loss of Jones from the competition left the gallery wondering who to follow. Some decided to leave early. One of those most disappointed by Jones' defeat was a fellow competitor. Nineteen year-old Lawson Little, fresh from his 1-up morning victory over Philip Finlay, approached Jones after the loss and expressed, "I'm very sorry you lost this morning Mr. Jones. I was so looking forward to beating you myself, this afternoon." Jones apparently took no offense, perhaps writing it off to youthful exuberance. Bravado or not, Little did defeat Goodman in the afternoon match to become the last of the young California hopefuls in the field.

The semifinal match between Harrison Johnston and George Voigt drew large galleries, partially due to the referee, Bobby Jones. Here they play the 4th hole. (PBC-J.P. Graham)

Tolley had an easy go of it defeating Fay Coleman 8&6. Chandler Egan defeated fellow Oregonian Rudie Wilhelm 7&5. Wilhelm may have been disadvantaged by his 21-hole match in the morning round. However, Jess Sweetser of New York, after going 19 holes in his morning match, defeated Indiana's John Lehman 6&4 in the afternoon. Harrison Johnston and George Voigt rounded out the eight quarterfinalists, leaving a diverse match-up even without Bobby Jones.

Tolley's strong play made him the new favorite, but he would face a West Coast gallery in his match against Oregon's Oscar Willing. Sweetser would face another Oregonian, Chandler Egan, who not only had the crowd in his favor, his course knowledge was unsurpassed. Youthful Lawson Little was to take on the experience of Francis Ouimet who had won both the U.S. Open and the U.S. Amateur before Little was old enough to swing a club.

Despite the talent in the other three matches, it was the match-up between George Voigt of New York and St. Paul, Minnesota's Harrison "Jimmy" Johnston that drew the largest gallery. Johnston had won the Minnesota Amateur annually from 1921 through 1927, and Voigt had won many championships in the East, including the 1928 Long Island Open and 1928 Long Island Amateur. The excitement of this match, however, was really centered on the referee. No longer competing for the title, Bobby Jones stayed on to help in any way he could. Voigt built a 3-up lead early but led by only 1-up when they broke for lunch. Voigt was 2-up after the 19th hole and with a little back-and forth was still 2-up after 27. Voigt bogeyed holes 10 and 11, squaring the match. They traded loses on holes 14 and 17 coming in and finished the scheduled 36 holes all-square. It took three extra holes for Johnston to secure the victory.

The Ouimet-Little match went the distance. Ouimet took the lead on the first hole, but Little came back, taking holes 3, 5, and 6 to go 2-up. Ouimet took the 9th to cut Little's lead to 1. From then on the battle seesawed back and forth with neither player ever leading by more than one. After 18 it was all square. It was again all square after 27. When Little bogeyed the 29th hole, Ouimet took the lead which held at 1-up through the conclusion of 36 holes. In the other two matches, Willing defeated Tolley 4&3, and Egan defeated Sweetser 6&5.

At age 33, Harrison Johnston was the youngster in the semifinal matches. Despite the promise of the young breed of California golfers, experience seemed to be the order for this championship. The semifinal matches each pitted a reigning state champion against a former U.S. champion. Johnston faced Francis Ouimet, who had stunned golfdom in 1913 when he defeated Harry Vardon in the U.S. Open. Ouimet won the U.S. Amateur the following year. The other match pitted two Oregonians— Oscar F. Willing who, like Johnston, had first won his state's Amateur championship in 1921, took on H. Chandler Egan, the back-to-back U.S. Amateur champion in 1904 and 1905.

Egan trailed from the beginning, taking a double on the opening hole. Following with bogeys on holes 4, 5, 7, and 9, he was quickly down-5. By the end of the first 18, he was down-8, despite Willing's only birdie coming on the 18th hole. When Egan bogeyed the first hole in the afternoon match to go down-9, an early finish was predicted. However, Egan declined to be totally embarrassed on the course he had so carefully prepared. After halving the second with pars, Egan won the next four holes, pulling out birdies on 4 and 6. He managed to win the 8th with a bogey, leaving him only down-4, but from there the match evened out.

Eight-time Minnesota Champion Harrison Johnston challenged the legendary Francis Ouimet in one semifinal match. (PBC-J.P. Graham)

Dr. Oscar Willing and H. Chandler Egan—two champions from Oregon—faced off in the other semifinal match. (PBC-J.P. Graham)

Willing won the 11th with a par. Egan got it back on 13 when Willing doubled. With pars for each on holes 14 and 15, Willing was declared the victor at 4&3.

In the other match, Johnston took the early lead with birdies on 2 and 4. Ouimet was plagued by visits to the bunkers and was down-6 by the 10th hole. Over the next 20 holes, Johnston's lead fluctuated between four and six shots. Ouimet sealed his fate with an afternoon bogey on the 13th. Johnston won 6&5.

The closest either Willing or Johnston had been in a National Championship up to this point was Willing's loss in the quarterfinals of 1928. Both carded 80 strokes for their morning round, but it was very competitive with Willing winning four holes to Johnston's three. Willing got off to an early lead and was up three holes with just six played. The gallery, however, was pulling for the likeable Johnston. Willing was 3-up after winning the 10th, but a double-bogey on 16 returned the lead to 2 strokes. Johnston then won the 17th with a solid par to cut the lead to 1.

The 18th hole, dubbed The Finisher, nearly finished Johnston. After a good drive, Johnston took out his brassie, but instead of following Willing with a perfect shot up the fairway, Johnston hooked his ball badly into Carmel Bay. As luck would have it, they were playing at low tide and Johnston's ball came to rest upon some of the pebbles situated below the rocks and seawall about 70 yards short of the green. He climbed down to examine the lie and watched as the waves lapped against his ball and then receded. He could not see the green because of the height of the seawall. Nevertheless, he called for his niblick. He watched the waves recede one more time and then moved quickly into position. With a perfectly

controlled swing, the ball sailed up over the wall and landed just short of the green. From there he chipped it close for a tap in par, changing the momentum for good. While they halved the hole, Johnston finished the morning round with a sure sense of victory.

After the first hole of the afternoon, the match was even. Johnston then jumped ahead for good, winning holes 4, 5, and 6, scoring the first and only birdie of the match on 6. Johnston missed a 5-foot birdie putt on 7 that would have put him 4-up. Instead, they halved 7 and 8, and Willing cut Johnston's lead to 2-up with a par on 9. Johnston's persistence brought him wins on 10 and 12, and when Dr. Willing's birdie putt failed to find the hole on the 15th, the tension left the match. Willing turned and greeted his challenger with a warm smile and a congratulatory handshake. Harrison "Jimmy" Johnston was the winner—4&3.

USGA president Findlay S. Douglas congratulates the finalists: Harrison "Jimmy" Johnston and Oscar Willing. (PBC-J.P. Graham)

Three-time Georgia Amateur Champion Dorothy Kirby was among the top women golfers who came to Pebble Beach for the 1940 U.S. Amateur. (PBC-J.P. Graham)

THE 1940 WOMEN'S NATIONAL AMATEUR

In hosting the ladies for the 1940 U.S. Amateur, Del Monte arranged a variety of consolation events as only 64 of the 164 top female amateurs would continue in the championship after an 18-hole qualifier on Pebble Beach. CBS sent a radio broadcast crew to the event to provide live broadcasts from the course each day. Seventeen telegraph operators were on hand to send the scores and action across the wires, and teams from each of the five major newsreel companies were on the scene.

The competitive field included a number of good golfers with a strong chance to win. While California golfers dominated the field, there were representatives from 16 other states as well as Hawaii, Mexico, and the District of Columbia. Defending champion Betty Jameson was the leading favorite. The 21-year old from San Antonio had already won the Western and Trans-Mississippi Amateurs in 1940. Kentucky's Marion Miley, who lost to Jameson in the Western finals but had previously won it twice, was another likely choice at Pebble Beach. Pacific Northwest Champion Mary Mozel Wagner was yet another top pick, as were Mrs. James Ferrie, the 1940 California champion, and past California champions including Dorothy Traung, Mrs. Gregg Lifur, and Clara Callender. Callender held the course record for women at 79. She and 18-year-old Mary Morse carried heavy local support.

Play began at 8:00AM on Monday, September 23, with 163 golfers waiting their turn to tee it up. The course was playing so tough that a few of the late starters had to finish their 18-hole qualifier the following morning. When all the cards were finally turned in, San Francisco's Dorothy Traung stood out as medalist with a score of 36-42—78, setting a new course record.

The top 10 qualifiers were:

Miss Dorothy Traung, San Francisco, CA	*36-42—78*
Mrs. Frank Russ, Burlingame, CA	*40-39—79*
Miss Elizabeth Hicks, Pasadena, CA	*40-39—79*
Miss Dorothy Kirby, Atlanta, GA	*40-41—81*
Mrs. L.D. Cheney, San Gabriel, CA	*40-41—81*
Mrs. Dan Chandler, Dallas, TX	*40-42—82*
Mrs. Willard Shepherd, Beverly Hills, CA	*40-42—82*
Miss Helen Sigel, Philadelphia, PA	*36-46—82*
Miss Thelma Carr, Glendale, CA	*40-42—82*
Miss Peggy Graham, Hollywood, CA	*41-42—83*
Miss Kathryn Pearson, Houston, TX	*41-42—83*

Amazingly, of these qualifiers only Shepherd survived the first three rounds. Six golfers finished a stroke back at 84, including Betty Jameson, Clara Callender, and Marjorie Ferrie, who would go on to comprise three-fourths of the semifinalist round. Seven golfers shot 93 and had a playoff for the two final spots.

Thirty-two matches were played on Tuesday, with Wednesday seeing 16 matches in the morning and eight in the afternoon. Of the final eight, the big surprise was little Georgia Tainter of Fargo, North Dakota. The reigning WGA Junior Women's champion was dubbed "the little giant killer" when she knocked off Dorothy Traung in the third round by a score of 2&1. Other quarterfinalists included the favorites Jameson, Callender, Ferrie, and Lifur, as well as surprise local star Mary Morse. Greenville, South Carolina's Jane Cothran, a four-time runner-up in the Carolinas Amateur, reached the fourth round with a 4&2 victory over Minnesota's Beatrice Barrett. Barrett had been a finalist in five of the last eight Minnesota championships, winning the event twice up to that time. She also set the National medalist record in 1939 with a 74. Barrett had eliminated early favorite Helen Sigel in the second round.

The eighth quarterfinalist was Mrs. Willard Shepherd (the former Helen Lawson) of Los Angeles who had tied for fifth in the medalist round. Her strong play captured the fancy of her instructor Olin Dutra, who decided watching her was certainly enough to justify a trip to Monterey that combined a visit with family. Unfortunately, she faced the popular and talented Clara Callender and fell 4&3 in her attempt to advance; Betty Jameson dispatched Mrs. Lifur, who was hobbled with a bad ankle, by a score of 6&5; and Jane Cothran managed to defeat Tainter ,"the little giant killer," 2&1. The local disappointment came in the match-up between Pasadena's Marjorie Ferrie and Del Monte's own Mary Morse. Morse came up short against the state champion, losing 5&3.

Friday's semifinal matches faced a change in the weather. Strong winds churned up the seas and added a new aspect to the challenges of Pebble Beach. Callender's local knowledge should have worked to her advantage under these adverse conditions, but Betty Jameson was able to rise to the challenge. Methodically waiting out the strongest gusts and planning her shots around the winds, Jameson raised her golf to a new level. She managed to play the first 15 holes at 1-under-par 16 complete with an eagle-three on the 15th where she closed her match, defeating Callender 5&3.

In the other match, Jane Cothran was firing her shots like a machine, and Ferrie, the California champion, was doing all she could to keep up. When they reached the 18th tee, Cothran was 1-up. Mrs. Ferrie needed to win the hole to force sudden death. Cothran's approach shot missed badly, and Ferrie momentarily saw the door crack open. But almost as quickly it slammed shut as Cothran chipped in her fourth shot from 35 feet off the green. The two Californians had been shut out. The final match would be played by two competitors with deep Southern drawls.

Conditions returned to near perfect for Saturday's 36-hole final. Jameson got off to a strong start and was leading by 3 after just five holes. On the 6th, she pushed a shot into the ocean and conceded the hole staying 2-up, a margin that held through the 9th hole. On the back side, Jameson won seven holes and halved the other two to amass a 9-up lead before they broke for lunch. Cothran was not about to give up. In the afternoon continuance, after halving the 1st hole, Cothran birdied the 2nd and then took the 4th when Jameson called a penalty on herself. The margin was now 7 with 14 to play. Jameson pushed her tee shot on the 5th hole to drop one more, and Cothran kept up the pressure by winning the 6th and 7th. Cothran was now only down-4 with 11 to play. On the 8th, Jameson got one back and then also won the 9th when Cothran missed the green and failed to sink a putt for bogey-6. That was two holes Cothran could ill afford to lose. Jameson was now 6-up. On the 10th, Cothran managed to sink a 30-foot putt to halve the hole. Jameson won the 11th, and Cothran came back with a 12-foot birdie putt to win the 12th. But she was now dormie–down-6 with six holes to play. Cothran needed to win the remaining holes just to tie. It was not to be. They halved the 13th, and Betty Jameson became the eighth Women's Champion to win back-to-back victories in the 44-year history of the event. She had put on a real show playing the 31 holes of the final match in just 6-over par. No one doubted that the best golfer had won.

Once again, things were going great. Pebble Beach Golf Links had lived up to its reputation. The gallery of about 5,000 spectators on the weekend had been good for the entire community, and everyone was looking forward to the next big tournament—the 1942 Men's National. Unfortunately, before that could happen, America was plunged into World War II. ■

(left) Mrs. Willard E. Shepherd, thrice a Del Monte champion, lost to Clara Callender in the quarterfinals of the 1940 U.S. Amateur. (PBC-J.P. Graham)

(top) Betty Jameson accepts the trophy that is almost as big as her for a second time in 1940. (PBC-J.P. Graham)

(Left to right): Jane Cothran, Mr. Cheyner of the USGA, Betty Jameson, and Peter Hay behind The Lodge prior to the final match. (PBC-J.P. Graham)

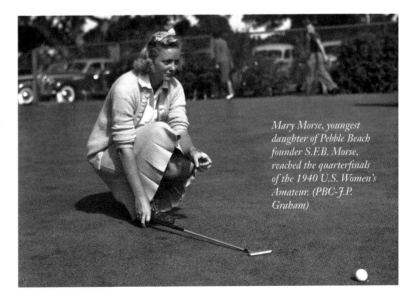

Mary Morse, youngest daughter of Pebble Beach founder S.F.B. Morse, reached the quarterfinals of the 1940 U.S. Women's Amateur. (PBC-J.P. Graham)

CHAPTER *Four*
THE GOLF CAPITAL OF
THE WORLD

Arnold Palmer played in more than 20 of Bing Crosby's clambakes. He had six top ten finishes at Pebble Beach including a second in the 1966 Crosby and a third in the 1972 U.S. Open, but amazingly, he never recorded a win at Pebble Beach. (PBC–J.P. Graham)

Bob Hope dons his make-up bib on the set at the Crocker-Irwin mansion near Pescadero Point while filming My Favorite Brunette *in the fall of 1946. His busy film career kept him out of the first few Crosby's at Pebble Beach. (PBC–J.P. Graham)*

Frank Stanahan and his partner Ben Hogan kept their distance in 1947. Here the team of Ed "Porky" Oliver and Johnny Weissmuller stand between them. (PBC–J.P. Graham)

Johnny Weissmuller, Olympic swimmer in the 1920s and film's most popular Tarzan in the 1930s and '40s, enjoyed both his character and his golf. (Durien – P. Breinig)

THE REBIRTH OF THE CROSBY

When Ted Durien first sent a letter to Bing Crosby suggesting he resume his popular Pro-Am tournament, Bing accepted the proposal through his brother, Larry, who indicated Bing thought it was a great idea and that Bing would personally cover all the expenses including the $5,000 purse. This was great, until word came back from Fred Corcoran of the PGA Tour that they had determined that beginning in 1947, the minimum purse for a sanctioned tournament would be $10,000. The local tournament committee was crushed. They passed on the bad news to Crosby to contemplate alternatives. He simply anted up and agreed to cover the larger purse.

Bing Crosby broke all the rules for a PGA Tour event. Rather than just one course, Crosby, a member at Cypress Point, wanted to use all three courses at Pebble Beach. They would play the first round at Cypress Point, the second at Monterey Peninsula Country Club, and the final round of the 54-hole affair at Pebble Beach. Using three courses was unprecedented, but Crosby countered that nowhere else offered three championship courses in such close proximity. He also wanted the amateur partners to play all three rounds. This created more anxiety for Tour director Greg Corcoran, but Bing was paying and wanted to play the entire event. The pros would still be paid-out based on their own ball. Why not at least give it a try? They did—to great success.

The mid-January weather was nearly perfect in 1947. The star-studded field of 76 pros included Ben Hogan, Sam Snead, Lloyd Mangrum, and an equal number of amateurs, including Hollywood stars Johnny Weissmuller, Richard Arlen, and Dennis O'Keefe. Crosby handpicked every invitee, and the large galleries showed their approvals. Contrary to popular belief, Crosby's constant foil Bob Hope did not play in the 1947 event. He was busy making movies. Ironically, Hope was at Pebble Beach just a few months earlier. In late 1946, he filmed *My Favorite Brunette*, a tour de force with Dorothy Lamour in which Crosby had a brief cameo.

The term "Crosby Weather" was actually coined during the Rancho Santa Fe days when the very first tournament was rain-shortened to just one round. It looked like the new venue might break the curse. Dick Metz led the 76 professionals around Cypress Point through windy conditions with sunny and rain-free skies and shot a course record, a 5-under-par 67. Closing on the 18th, Crosby landed in a deep bunker. Lofting his ball out, it never reached the green but rather lodged in the branches of a tree. This prompted the first classic line in the history of the tournament when he called out, "Where's Johnny Weissmuller?" Spotting the actor on the adjoining fairway, Crosby yelled, "Hey Tarzan, I've got a tree-climbing job for you."

For Saturday's second round, they moved to the Country Club course with the weather still clear. In the Sunday final at Pebble Beach, however, the good weather ended. Sam Snead and Newt Bassler finished early

In 1946, Bruce McCormick became only the sixth multiple winner in the first 35 years of the California Amateur Championship. (PBC-J.P. Graham)

When the troops returned from World War II, travel restrictions were lifted and the nation's economy began a strong period of growth. Leisure and disposable income returned and golf benefited. Amateur competitions continued to grow, and professional golf, which struggled through the 1930s and early 1940s, began to thrive.

Morse happily received the new economic news and positioned Pebble Beach to capitalize on the opportunities. The hub of golf activities at Pebble Beach led to its claim as the Golf Capital of the World in 1947, and while golf grew throughout the country and other locations have attempted to annex the title, Pebble Beach remains at the pinnacle of the golf world and wears the title with pride and distinction.

Bruce McCormick won his second straight California Amateur Championship in September 1946, defeating two-time champion Ernie Pieper in the final match. Eli Bariteau was the medalist with a 71. All three were looking forward to the 1947 U.S. Amateur at Pebble Beach, but another interesting tournament would come first.

with the only sub-par scores of the day. Tied at even-par 216 for the tournament, they were the leaders in the clubhouse; Team Snead with Roger Kelly was also on top. Their 64-66-66—196 had them three stokes up on the team of Bassler and Hennikin, who closed with a 68. The wind and the rain left the remaining golfers just hoping to finish. As the late afternoon rains increased, Lloyd Mangrum came off 18 with a round of 76 to tie the leaders, and George Fazio wobbled in with a 68-70-75—213 to displace them by 3 strokes. A few golfers remained on the course, but no one was going to overtake the lead from Fazio…or so they thought. As darkness descended on the first Crosby tournament, a stunned spectator rushed into The Lodge to share the news, "Furgol just got a five on the last hole for a tie!"

After a 72 at Cypress Point, Furgol had stayed in contention with a 69 at MPCC, but after falling back two against par at Pebble Beach, he, like the rest of the field, had been given little notice. Due to the weather, only a small gallery was on hand to witness his second shot on 16. In the driving rain, Furgol hit a 5 iron from the fairway for an eagle-2! Against the odds and the weather, Furgol shot par on 17 and 18 to finish tied for the win. There was no playoff. Snead and Kelly won the team victory.

Crosby committed to coming back in 1948 and so did nearly all of the stars. Everyone from the golfers to the gallery deemed it a success—not only for the players, but for charity. Bing Crosby insisted that all revenue from ticket sales would go to charity. His pet charity was the Sister Kenny Foundation, which did remarkable work with muscle rehabilitation in polio victims. The proceeds for the tournament were so far beyond expectations that he split the funds, leaving half of the money on the Monterey Peninsula to establish a youth club in Carmel. The tournament continued year after year and is now one of the longest-running events on the PGA Tour. It started the tradition of golf giving back through charity and during its 60-plus years has generated more than $80 million for charity.

Officials gather at the scorer's tent at the 1947 Amateur. Bob Jones stands in the front with S.F.B. Morse behind him. (PBC-J.P. Graham)

THE 1947 U.S. AMATEUR

As the USGA resumed tournaments after the war, it held the 1946 U.S. Amateur close to home at Baltusrol in New Jersey but quickly made arrangements to utilize Pebble Beach for the 1947 U.S. Amateur and the 1948 U.S. Women's Amateur.

A number of strong players were capable of winning the 1947 championship. Unlike the 1929 event where Bobby Jones stood as the heavy favorite, there was no clear standout in 1947. Earlier in the year, the Walker Cup matches resumed at St. Andrews for the first time since before the War. Six members of the victorious U.S. team were present, and strong possible winners among them were Ted Bishop, the 1946 U.S. Amateur winner at Baltusrol; Skee Riegel, the 1946 medalist; and two-time past U.S. Amateur champion Bud Ward.

Many of the golfers arrived early to get in practice rounds before the matches began. Unlike previous Nationals, the 1947 event was all match play; 210 golfers reached the Amateur through regional qualifying tournaments. Once into the National, they would immediately proceed to match-play competition.

Actor Randolph Scott qualified for play, and he was so confident he would be out early that he let stand a shooting schedule that called for him to be in Hollywood on Wednesday. He kept his day job when fellow southern Californian Ray Sleepy set him packing after a 7&6 first-round trouncing on Monday.

Bing Crosby reviews his list of invitees with Monterey Herald *sports editor, Ted Durien. (PBC-J.P. Graham)*

Among the few surprises on Day 1 was Washington State Amateur champion Jack Westland's loss to Ohio's Harold Paddock. Harrison Johnston, who had been victorious in 1929, went out in the first round this time. As did Walter Hagen Jr., who had his father's looks but not his game. Chicago's Charles "Chick" Evans Jr., who won both the U.S. Amateur and the U.S. Open in 1916, qualified for the 1947 event but left early with a 5&4 loss to Pennsylvania's George Rowbotham.

Local favorite Ernie Pieper, a two-time California Champion, took on Ray Sleepy in round two. Pieper got in trouble early and held on the best he could. When they reached the 17th tee, Pieper was down-2; dormie. He kept the match alive by winning the next two holes. On the first extra hole, Pieper landed in the right rough but made a beautiful recovery shot that rolled up just short of the green. Sleepy was laying two about 18 feet beyond the cup. Pieper chipped up close and it looked like they would halve with pars, but Ray Sleepy silenced the partisan crowd when he dropped the tricky downhill putt for a birdie and the win.

Another pair that drew a good-sized gallery was the 1946 California Amateur runner-up Smiley Quick against San Jose's Jack Bariteau. The Quick-Bariteau match was tight all the way. Bariteau was 1-up after nine, and the match was squared on the 13th. Bariteau won the 14th with a par and rode the 1-up margin through the remaining holes. It was the biggest upset of the day. Bariteau not only won the match, but was able to steal a little of the spotlight from his brother, Eli, who was also playing in the National and routinely defeated his younger brother.

Actor Randolph Scott takes a seat on the knee of golf professional Peter Hay. Like a child with Santa, the accomplished amateur may have been asking Hay for a near-impossible win in the 1947 U.S. Amateur. If so, the wish was not granted. (PBC-J.P. Graham)

Chicago's Charles "Chick" Evans Jr., who won both the U.S. amateur and U.S. Open in 1916, was one of a handful of golfers who competed in both the 1929 and 1947 U.S. Amateur at Pebble Beach. He left early following a 5&4 first-round loss to Pennsylvania's George Rowbotham. (PBC-J.P. Graham)

San Jose's Ernie Pieper, who had been winning at Pebble Beach since his days as a junior star, was the chief favorite among local galleryites. With him on the 7th tee is Hawaii's Francis Brown. He fought hard but lost in extra holes in the second round of the 1947 U.S. Amateur. (PBC-J.P. Graham)

Marvin Henry "Bud" Ward of Spokane, as a two-time U.S. Amateur champion and a member of the U.S. Walker Cup team, was the leading favorite from the West Coast to enter the 1947 U.S. Amateur at Pebble Beach. He reached the quarterfinals before falling to Jack Selby. (PBC-J.P. Graham)

Body-building golfer Frank Stranahan admires his tee shot on the 7th. The 1947 Walker Cup team member lost to John Dawson in the fourth round of the U.S. Amateur. The next year he won his first of two British Amateurs. (PBC-J.P. Graham)

On Wednesday, 32 matches were played in the morning, and the survivors paired off for the fourth round in the afternoon. Most of the favorites succeeded in their morning matches. The exceptions were the 4&3 ousting of 20-year-old Willie Hunter Jr., by Luke Barnes of New York and Hunter's 18-year-old brother H. McGregor "Mac" Hunter staying in the hunt with a 3&1 victory over Harold Paddock, who had earlier defeated both Jack Westland and Gene Andrews. The Hunters were the sons of Riviera Country Club golf professional "Wee" Willie Hunter, who won the British Amateur in 1921 before moving to California.

One of the best of third-round matches was between Charles Kocsis of Red Run, Michigan, and California's Bruce McCormick. Kocsis, a multiple winner in both the Michigan State Amateur and Open, barely pulled out a third-round victory over Bruce McCormick, a two-time California Amateur champion. Their nip-and-tuck match, which included McCormick's 90-yard chip in for eagle on the 14th, finished 18 all square. On the 20th hole, Kocsis put his second shot in the large barranca, while

The gallery lines the 8th hole and follows golfers around the chasm during the 1947 U.S. Amateur. (PBC-J.P. Graham)

McCormick safely cleared the trap. But from the ditch, Kocsis lofted a beautiful shot that came to rest just 6 feet from the pin. McCormick's approach was not as good and he missed the putt, allowing Kocsis to win with a birdie.

The afternoon saw some exciting matches. Six of the nine 1947 Walker Cup team members had begun the tournament, and other than Smiley Quick, each made it to the fourth round. Mac Hunter had a tough fourth-round match, losing to cupper Bud Ward 2&1. Richard Chapman defeated Jack Cole 3&1, and Robert "Skee" Riegel continued on with the only easy match of the day, ending in a 5&4 victory over Luke Barnes. The other two Walker Cup stars went no further. Ted Bishop lost 2&1 to Charles Kocsis, and Frank Stranahan lost on the 20th hole to Johnny Dawson.

Of the sixteen golfers remaining for Thursday morning's fifth round, six represented California: Dawson, Riegel, Bob Rosburg, Jack Robinson, Frank Hixon, and Jack Bariteau. Bariteau's brother, Eli, was knocked out in the fourth round. New York had four: Strafaci, Chapman, Selby, and Torza. The other six were each from a different state. Only three current Walker Cup players remained, although Michigan's Chuck Kocsis was a former cupper who had played on the 1938 team.

Frank Strafaci and Dick Chapman, frequent competitors in Eastern regional tournaments, faced off in the first match of the morning. Strafaci defeated the cupper 5&3, one-putting the last five holes. The second match ended about the same time with Johnny Dawson defeating Idaho's Otto Hofmeister 5&4.

The third match pitted John Selby against Georgia's 1941 State Amateur champion and reigning Southern champion, Thomas Barnes. This was the marathon upset of the morning. The match was close the whole way with Barnes 1-up as they reached the 18th tee. A bogey by Barnes squared the match and sent it to extra holes. Selby out-steadied the champion as they halved the next three holes with pars. On the 22nd hole, Barnes again bogeyed, and Selby was there with a par to end the match.

Washington's Marvin "Bud" Ward advanced with a 6&5 trouncing of Frank Hixon, while North Carolina's E. Harvie Ward eliminated Jack Robinson 3&2. In the sixth pairing, 27-year old Felice Torza of Connecticut defeated 1946 Colorado Amateur champion Charles "Babe" Lind 2-up on the 18th. Stanford's young Bob Rosburg surprised the experts by defeating the much more experienced Chuck Kocsis 4&3.

In the final match of the morning, Skee Riegel dueled San Jose's long shot Jack Bariteau. Skee played exceptional golf, going out in 2 under par and leading by three. With birdies on 10 and 11, Riegel extended his lead to five. Not about to quit, Bariteau won the next three holes, pulling within two, but Riegel won the 17th hole to close the match 3&1.

College entrant E. Harvie Ward of North Carolina lost to Torza in the 1947 quarterfinals. He hit his prime a few years later when he won the 1952 British Amateur and then the U.S. Amateur back-to-back in 1955–56. (PBC–J.P. Graham)

QUARTERFINALS

The opening match of the afternoon between Johnny Dawson and Frank Strafaci was expected to be a replay of the previous day's Dawson-Stranahan horse race. Dawson, however, outplayed the challenger from the start. After nine holes, Dawson's 2-under-par pace was sufficient for a 4-up lead in the match; the match ended 6&5.

The second match pitted the scrappy Jack Selby against Bud Ward, who had won three of five matches without reaching the 14th hole. Selby took a 1-up lead when Ward bogeyed the first hole. The two traded birdies on 4 and 5, and then Selby birdied 6 to go 2-up. That margin held through 9, which they both bogeyed. Selby bogeyed 10, cutting his lead. Failing to capitalize, Ward bogeyed 11 and was again 2-down. Selby opened the door with bogeys on 12 and 13, but each ended in halves. They halved the next three with pars, reaching the 17th with Selby 2-up. Selby bogeyed but with Ward unable to convert his par, the hole was halved, and Selby managed another upset 2&1.

In the third match, E. Harvie Ward fell 4&3 to Felice Torza, the 5'6" former caddie. In the fourth match, Bobby Rosburg again challenged experience. This time Riegel's slow steady pace undid the anxious Rosburg in a tight match that ended with Riegel's 2&1 victory.

Semifinalists in the 1947 vie for who will take home the Havemeyer Trophy (left to right): John Selby, Skee Riegel, Felice Torza, and Johnny Dawson. (PBC-J.P. Graham)

Despite some morning fog, the semifinalists all managed pars in negotiating the 8th hole in the 1947 U.S. Amateur. (PBC-J.P. Graham)

SEMIFINALS

On Friday, the four remaining golfers faced 36-hole matches on the fog-shrouded coastline. Selby played Dawson, and Torza took on Riegel. In both cases it was youth versus experience. As young Navy veterans, neither Selby (age 28) nor Torza (age 27) had the seasoned competitive golf experience of Dawson (age 44) and Riegel (age 32), yet each felt the confidence one can only get from winning six consecutive matches in stiff competition.

The diminutive Dawson continued with the steady golf he had played all week. His 6'1" challenger did not. Selby opened with a bogey-double-birdie and was instantly down-1. Dawson went to 2-up despite a double-bogey on five with the help of birdies on 4 and 6. Selby's bogey on 9 gave Dawson a 3-up lead after nine. Dawson's birdie on 12 followed by Selby's bogey on 13 pushed Dawson to 5-up. Selby got one back when Dawson bogeyed 15, but when Selby closed out the morning with bogeys on 17 and 18, Dawson was able to take a 6-up lead at lunch. Despite an opening bogey in the afternoon, Selby's play was much stronger than he had shown in the morning, but birdies on 3 and 6 were too little too late. Dawson ended the match on the 14th with a par victory to win the match 5&4.

The other match was much closer. Torza drew first blood when Riegel bogeyed the 1st hole, but Riegel squared it with a birdie to Torza's bogey on 2. The next 14 holes were played without a birdie. Torza bogeyed 5, 6, and 7, but as Riegel also bogeyed 6, the lead was only 2-up. Riegel bogeyed 9 to lead by 1-up at the turn. Riegel played all nine on the back in perfect par, resulting in seven halved holes. Torza bogeyed the 12th to go down-2 but got it back with a birdie on the 16th. They broke for lunch with Riegel 1-up.

They played the first six holes in the afternoon dead even, matching bogeys on 1, birdies on 2 and 4, and pars on the other three. On the short

7th, Torza squared the match with a birdie but gave it back with a bogey on 11. Riegel's 5-foot birdie putt on the 15th hole extended the lead to 2-up with just three holes to play. Pars all around on 16 and 17 gave Riegel the 2&1 victory, sending him to face Johnny Dawson in Saturday's 36-hole final.

THE FINAL

Clear, bright skies greeted the golfers as they arrived at the first tee for their final match. The pundits predicted Dawson's only chance against Riegel would be to get off to an early lead and hold on coming home. But it didn't quite work that way. After nine it was all-square and Riegel held a 2-up lead after the morning round. More than 6,000 spectators were on hand to watch the two stars from southern California battle it out for the national title. Despite predictions to the contrary, Dawson came out strong as the afternoon began. After halving the 1st afternoon hole, Dawson sank a 30-foot eagle putt on the 2nd to beat out Riegel's birdie. He won the 3rd to square the match on Riegel's bogey. It remained all-square through the 5th afternoon hole. On the 6th, Dawson was ready to take the lead with an easy birdie putt, when, from 30 feet away, Skee drained his birdie and the hole was halved.

As the fog rolled in on the coastal holes, Dawson's legs started to give out. Riegel made a 40-foot birdie putt on the 7th, and with bogeys by Dawson on 8 and 9, Riegel suddenly had a 3-up lead, his largest in the last two days. Dawson had gone out in 35 but still had a net loss of one hole to his competitor. Dawson mustered his energy and played the next five holes in perfect par. With bogeys by Riegel on holes 11 and 13, the lead was cut to just one. It was still anyone's match. A Dawson bogey on the 15th gave Riegel a 2-up lead, and after a half on 16, Dawson was dormie.

Dawson putts on the 7ᵗʰ in the finals while Riegel and his caddie (lower left) watch the effort. (PBC-J.P. Graham)

Skee Riegel accepts the trophy for his victory from USGA president Charles Littlefield. Runner-up Dawson applauds (lower left) and host professional Peter Hay (back right) smiles in broad approval. (PBC-J.P. Graham)

Smiley Quick (left) won the 1948 California Open by finishing strong. Amateur Ernie Pieper (right) led the first two rounds and held on to finish tied for third, and as the low amateur. (PBC-J.P. Graham)

With a bit of gamesmanship, Riegel deliberately hit his tee shot short on 17, landing short of the front bunker. Judging from this, Dawson over-clubbed, and his shot flew over the green. Riegel chipped to within 12 feet of the cup. Dawson's recovery left a much longer putt, and he missed. Riegel had two putts for a half that would win the match. He putted the first one close enough, and Dawson conceded the final putt giving Riegel the 2&1 victory.

At the conclusion of the round, Riegel commented, "What a man needs most on this course is to keep his head." He then reached for his to assure himself it was still there. During the presentation of the awards, USGA President Charles Littlefield proclaimed, "If I was going to be president of the United States Golf Association any longer, I'd hold 'em all here. This is the grandest place to hold a golf tournament I've ever seen."

THE 1948 CALIFORNIA OPEN

The Crosby returned in January 1948, and Lloyd Mangrum won by a remarkable 5 strokes over Stan Leonard. Ben Hogan finished third but won the team competition with amateur partner Johnny Dawson. Many of the pros returned to Pebble Beach that April for the California Open. The California Open had been played in Fresno the prior year, where temperatures soared over 100 degrees. Adding to of the other golf action, the organizers turned to cooler Pebble Beach for the 1948 California Open—its first return to the peninsula in a dozen years. Top local amateur and Monterey city councilman Warner Keeley served as tournament chairman, which kept him too busy to play. The favorite to win was 1940 U.S. Open champion W. Lawson Little II, who was then living in Monterey. But the tournament attracted more than 120 top pros and amateurs who all promised to give him a run for the title, including two of the early black professional golfers, Ted Rhodes and Bill Spiller.

An unseasonably late-spring rain dumped more than an inch of rain on the peninsula, delaying the start of play until Friday, April 30. While the sun shined on the golfers, soggy conditions impacted scores, with only three golfers besting par or better and more than half the field topping 80. Two-time state Amateur champion Ernie Pieper was the first-round leader with a 34-36—70, while rookie professional Smiley Quick was tied with Bill Nary at 71. Defending champion Art Bell and Jerry Barber, a driving range pro, were tied for fourth at 73. The favorite, Lawson Little, had a particularly bad day with a 43-40—83 to tie for 75th place.

On Saturday, Pieper held a 1-stroke lead over Smiley Quick, each with a 75. Ellsworth Vines shot a 72 to move into a tie for second with Quick. Little came back with a second round 75 for a 158. The cut was at 164 with the top 62 golfers playing a 36-hole marathon on Sunday to decide the winner. Trudging through the wet course proved too much for nearly one-third of the field, and only 43 actually finished the two-round final.

Smiley Quick took the lead with a 71 to Pieper's 73 in the morning session, then Pieper fell back further, firing a 78 in the afternoon. Quick finished with a 74 to claim the first place prize of $750 with a 3-over-par 291. Art Bell closed with the only sub-par round of the afternoon to finish second 73-76-75-71—295. Pieper and Vines finished tied for third at 296. Ted Rhodes finished fifth at 299. Bill Spiller finished 17th at 313, 1 stroke behind Lawson Little.

THE 1948 U.S. WOMEN'S AMATEUR

Women's golf began to come of age after World War II. The Pebble Beach Championship for Women resumed in 1946 with 1938 U.S. Women's Amateur champion Patty Berg winning the medal and defeating Mary Sargent in the final. In 1947, Berg repeated as medalist and champion, that year defeating Sargent in the semifinal and Beverly Hanson in the final.

The ranks of professional women golfers began to soar. In 1946, the USGA held the first U.S. Women's Open, and it was won by amateur Patty Berg. Soon, many of the top women golfers turned professional to vie for the prize money, and Berg was among them. As the 1948 National Amateur rolled around, few past champions were on hand for the competition. Louise Suggs, the 1947 Women's Amateur champion, had turned pro, as had Babe Didrickson Zaharias, the winner in 1946. Prewar champions Betty Hicks and Betty Jameson were also among the professionals. With only two former champions in contention, Glenna Collett-Vare (1922, '25, '28, '29, '30, and '35) and Estelle Lawson-Page (1937), it was anybody's tournament to win.

Most suspected the winner would come from among the successful 1948 Curtis Cup team who had defended the cup against their British rivals in May at Birkdale. It had been the first playing of that competition since 1938. Captained by Vare (of Pennsylvania), the team included Page (North Carolina), Suggs (who turned pro shortly thereafter), Dorothy Kirby (Georgia), Dorothy Kielty (California), Polly Riley (Texas), and

![Patty Berg walking up 18th hole]

Patty Berg walks triumphantly up the 18th hole while winning her second straight Pebble Beach Championship for Women in 1947. (PBC-J.P. Graham)

Glenna Collett-Vare was one of only two former Amateur champions competing at Pebble Beach in 1948. She had last won in 1935; Estelle Lawson-Page had won in 1937. The recent winners had all joined the fledgling Women's Professional Golf Tour. (PBC-J.P. Graham)

Ailene Gates, among the state's top golfers, became Mrs. Johnny Weissmuller in January 1948 when she married the popular star of many Tarzan movies. (PBC-J.P. Graham)

Grace Lenczyk (Connecticut); all but Suggs were on hand to compete at Pebble Beach.

Plenty of other top contenders were far from ready to concede defeat. Among them was Dorothy Traung, a perennial contender in the Pebble Beach Championship who finished runner-up that spring to Mary Sargent. Mrs. Gregg Lifur, the 1930 Pebble Beach Champion, was also competing as was Ailene Gates-Weissmuller, the 1946 California Amateur medalist, who with her husband, actor-athlete Johnny Weissmuller, made frequent visits to Pebble Beach. Mary Morse was also in the field. She was now entered as Mrs. Richard Osborne.

The USGA set up Pebble Beach as a 38-39 par-77 routing for the ladies. On Monday, September 13, 108 ladies competed in 18 holes of medal play to vie for the 64 openings for the first-round matches. The medalist, with a score of par-77 was Mrs. Bettye Mims White of Dallas, Texas. Grace Lenczyk finished second with an 80, and the rest of the field spread back with a 93 as the highest score among the qualifiers.

All of the favorites survived except one, who went out in a very disappointing fashion. Dorothy Kielty, the reigning Western and California Amateur champion, turned in a score of 82. On contemplation over lunch, she realized she had actually scored a nine rather than an eight on the final hole. Reporting the error to the officials herself, a clearly distraught Kielty accepted the mandatory disqualification for signing an inaccurate scorecard.

The 64 qualifiers represented 20 different states, but nearly half came from California. Weissmuller and Osborne were among the Californians to suffer first-round losses. Grace Lenczyk of Connecticut, the reigning Canadian champion, won the only extra-hole match of the round, finally defeating Mary Agnes Wall, Michigan's two-time champion on the 21st hole. The other Curtis Cup players had easier goes of it, as each defeated a Californian. Page defeated Elizabeth Elliott 6&5; Kirby won 4&3 over Mrs. Harry Winters; Vare closed out Mrs. Hedley Brown 3&2; and Riley nipped Mrs. Floyd Ratliff 2-up on the 18th. Sargent, Traung, and Lifur also won their first rounds.

During Wednesday's second-round matches, the field started to clarify. Medalist White knocked out Traung 1-up, and Lenczyk ousted Sargent 2&1. Lifur defeated her club-mate Ruth McCullah (both playing out of Riviera) 6&5 to remain California's best hope. Glenna Collett-Vare lost her second-round match to Hawaii's Jackie Pung on the 19th hole, and Page fell on the 20th hole to California's Patricia McPhee. The loss of Vare and Page assured a first-time champion would be declared at Pebble Beach.

On Thursday, eight matches were played. Helen Sigel, the two-time Pennsylvania Amateur champion, continued playing impressive golf, defeating Patricia McPhee 6&4. Grace Lenczyk advanced with an equally impressive 6&5 victory over Dorothy Workman. The other quarterfinalists were Dorothy Kirby, Polly Riley, two-time Ohio champion Peggy Kirk, four-time Tennessee champion Margaret Gunther, Beverly Hanson of North Dakota (who defeated Lifur), and California's last hope, Mrs. Jack Holmes.

Dorothy Kielty, the reigning Western and California Amateur champion, was the only Curtis Cup Player not to continue to match play. She played well enough but called a penalty on herself for signing an incorrect scorecard after her qualifying round. The infraction meant mandatory disqualification. (PBC-J.P. Graham)

Hawaiian star Jackie Pung (age 26), who won her fourth Hawaiian Amateur in 1948, defeated Glenna Collett-Vare before falling in the third round to Peggy Holmes. Pung later won the U.S. Amateur in 1952 before joining the professional tour. (PBC-J.P. Graham)

Polly Riley of San Antonio won the Trans-Miss in 1947 and 1948 and reached the quarterfinals in the 1948 U.S. Amateur. (PBC-J.P. Graham)

Finalists Grace Lenzyck (left) and Helen Sigel feign a tug-of-war with the Cox Trophy, the oldest of the USGA trophies, dating to 1896. (PBC-J.P. Graham)

Grace Lenczyk, champion of Canada and the Unites States in 1948. (PBC-J.P. Graham)

The four semifinalists in the 1948 U.S. Women's Amateur (left to right): Beverley Hanson, Peggy Holmes, Grace Lenczyk, and Helen Sigel. (PBC-J.P. Graham)

With the exception of Sigel's 5&3 ouster of Peggy Kirk, the quarterfinal matches were very close. Siegel played the first nine in a blistering 34, 4 strokes below the women's par and 2 below men's. It was reported to be perhaps the best nine ever played in the Women's National. The Holmes-Gunther match went to the 17th before the Tennessee champion fell to the Californian in an upset. Beverly Hanson also pulled off an upset, defeating Dorothy Kirby, the four-time Georgia Amateur champion and Curtis Cup star 1-up in 18. The fourth match pitted two Curtis cup teammates. The winner would be the only survivor from the team. It too went all the way to the final hole. Lenczyk defeated Riley by sinking an 8-foot putt on the 18th hole to win 1-up.

On Friday afternoon, the winners faced off to determine who would play in Saturday's final 36-hole match. Neither Hanson nor Holmes could muster one more upset. Hanson fell to Sigel 6&5, while Lenczyk defeated Holmes 4&2. The stage was set to crown a new National Amateur champion.

This was not the first meeting of the final pairing. Sigel, runner-up in the 1941 National, had defeated a 19-year old Lenczyk in the second round of 1946, the youngster's first National. Lenczyk had made it to the semifinals in 1947. By the end of the day, one of them would be the champion. Sigel's dominant play stood her as the favorite, but there are no sure things in golf. Lenczyk went out in the morning round with a rock-solid 78, just 1 over par. Sigel was the unsteady golfer, seemingly in discord with her caddie most of the way. At the break, Lenczyk led 5-up.

Sigel's game was better in the afternoon, but she was unable to shave the margin by more than one hole in the afternoon and succumbed 4&3. Lenczyk had completed a dazzling year in which the 21-year-old junior at John B. Stetson University became the amateur champion of both the United States and Canada as well as the Women's Collegiate champion. In between her studies, she also traveled to England to help defend the Curtis Cup and play through the third round of the British Amateur Championship.

THE MORSE CUP

Ever since the break-up of the Pacific Coast Golf Association brought on by the creation of the California Golf Association in 1912, there was a bit of friendly rivalry between the California Golf Association and the Pacific Northwest Golf Association. By 1949, the PNGA had grown to include clubs in Washington, Oregon, Idaho, Montana, and the Canadian provinces of British Columbia and Alberta, creating an international element to the rivalry.

Morse credited Charles W. Adams, then president of the PNGA, with the idea of creating an annual competition patterned after the Walker Cup amateur team competitions. S.F.B. Morse donated a large English sterling silver cup mounted on an ebony base that became known as The Morse Cup. The stated purpose of the competition was "promoting amateur golf and good sportsmanship between the Pacific Northwest and California."

The first Morse Cup team matches were held at Seattle Golf Club on July 9–10, 1949, just before the PNGA Championship. Representing California was a team of nine golfers, four of whom were past State Amateur champions: Ernie Pieper (1941, '44), John W. Dawson (1942), Bruce McCormick (1945, '46), Eli Bariteau (1948), Bud McKinney, Eddie Lowery, Dr. Jackson Bean, Bill Ebert, and Ralph Evans. The PNGA put up a team that included several of its own past champions: Albert "Scotty" Campbell (1933, '35), Harry Givan (1936, '37, '45, '46), Jack Westland (1938, '39, '40), Ray Weston Jr. (1947), Glenn Sheriff (1948), James Ronald Clark, Bill Mawhinney, Lou Stafford, Guy Owen, and Dave Doud. The home-field advantage left the cup in the Northwest—2$^1/_2$ to 1$^1/_2$ in the two-ball matches and 6$^1/_2$ to 1$^1/_2$ in the singles for a 9-3 overall victory for the PNGA team.

In 1950, the Morse Cup was contested over the Cypress Point Club course just before the California Amateur Championship was played. The two-ball matches were played on September 30 and ended with each side winning two matches. Dawson and McCormick faced Givan and Westland in the top match. The Californians redeemed their 1949 loss with a 4&2 win in the 1950 rematch. California's other win came from Morse Cup rookies Tal Smith, who as an amateur had won the 1946 California Open, paired up with 19-year-old Ken Venturi of San Francisco to defeat Mawhinney and Weston 3&1. To achieve one of its team victories, the Pacific Northwest used a Californian. San Diego's 20-year-old Gene Littler, semifinalist in the 1949 California Amateur and co-medalist in the 1950 U.S. Amateur, moved to Seattle that summer and paired with Spokane's Al Mengert to defeat Eli Bariteau and Bob Rosburg 3&2. Oregon's James Robert Clark and Dick Yost drubbed California's Frank Taylor and Jim Ferrie 6&5. In the next day's singles matches, the Californians showed their dominance—winning six and losing two—for an 8-4 overall taking of the Morse Cup. One of the most watched matches was between the "kids"—Venturi and Littler. Venturi, who had served part of his youth as a caddie at Cypress Point, had a real advantage and won the match 3&2.

In 1950 S.F.B. Morse donated a sterling silver cup originally for a Walker Cup–style team competition between golfers of California and those of the Pacific Northwest; it is known as The Morse Cup. (PBC-J.P. Graham)

S.F.B. Morse (right) holds the Morse Cup with Chapin Hunt, captain of the victorious 1950 California team in the second annual Morse Cup. The team (left to right): Tal Smith, Ken Venturi, Jay Sigel, John Dawson, Bruce McCormack, Bob Cardinal, Jim Ferrie, Eli Bariteau, and Dr. Frank "Bud" Taylor. (PBC-J.P. Graham)

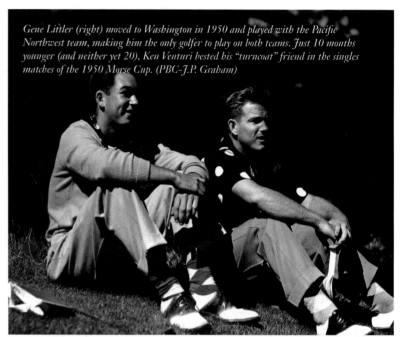

The 1950 Pacific Northwest Team (left to right): Ray Weston, Harry Givan, Dick Yost, James Clark, Bill Mawhinney, Al Mengert, Jack Westland, and non-playing captain Forest Watson. (PBC-J.P. Graham)

Gene Littler (right) moved to Washington in 1950 and played with the Pacific Northwest team, making him the only golfer to play on both teams. Just 10 months younger (and neither yet 20), Ken Venturi bested his "turncoat" friend in the singles matches of the 1950 Morse Cup. (PBC-J.P. Graham)

The 1954 Morse Cup teams gathered at Cypress Point Club. Back row (left-right): Francis Brown, Charles Adams, Ed Draper, Lyle Crawford, S.F.B. Morse, Phil Getchell, Bruce Cudd, Dick Yost, Peter Hay, Erv Parent, Ray Weston, Bob Fleming. Middle row (left-right): Jim Ferrie, John Dawson, Bud Taylor, Cy Pennell, E. Harvie Ward, Bruce McCormick, Charlie Seaver, Bob Silvestri. Front row (left-right): Chapin Hunt, Forest Watson, George E. Johnson (CGA president), J. Gordon Bowers, and Hal Booth. (PBC-J.P. Graham)

Ed Vest (left) meets with S.F.B. Morse in his Pebble Beach office to rededicate the Morse Cup for a 1967 team competition run quite differently from the earlier version of the event. (PBC – W.C. Brooks)

In 1951, the teams played in July at Spokane, and California showed no signs it was ready to give up the Cup. Dawson-McCormick again beat Givan-Westland, and Smith and Venturi were split up, Venturi paired with Ferrie and won their match, and Smith paired with Bob Cardinal and also won. Frank Taylor and Bob Gardner suffered the only California loss in Day 1 in the only match that reached the 17th hole; Mengert and Weston won 3&1. The singles matches split evenly with each side winning three and two ending in halves. California retained the cup and took a 2-to-1 lead in overall wins.

Cypress Point was again the scene for the Morse Cup action in September 1952, and the California team again took the two-ball competition three wins to one. Dawson-McCormick paired for the fourth

year and won for a third time. Still facing Jack Westland, who in 1952 was paired with Seattle's Erv Parent, the match went to the 18th hole with Dawson-McCormick winning 2-up. On the second day, the singles matches reversed the result. Ernie Pieper gave California their only match. Two matches were halved, and the Pacific Northwest team won five matches for an overall 7-5 win. Each team now had two victories, and the Cup headed north with the victors.

California retook the cup with an 8-4 win in 1953 at the Columbia-Edgewater Club in Portland, Oregon, and retained the cup after the 1954 matches at Cypress Point. Neither Dawson nor McCormick had gone to Oregon, but the pair combined again at Cypress Point for their fourth victory in five pairings. At Cypress Point, California won all four two-

The victorious Northern California team from the 1968 Morse Cup competition (left to right): Forrest Felzer (San Jose), Dick Giddings (Fresno), Robert A. Roos (San Francisco), S.F.B. Morse, Jack Bariteau (San Jose), John Miller (San Francisco), and Harry Taylor (Hayward). (PBC-W.C. Brooks)

ball matches and four of the singles matches. One of the rookies on the California team was an amateur from North Carolina who had moved to California to sell cars for Ed Lowery—E. Harvie Ward Jr.—a member of the 1953 Walker Cup Team, who had not missed qualifying for a U.S. Amateur since 1947 when he reached the quarterfinals at Pebble Beach.

Ward skipped the 1955 Morse Cup team matches at Inglewood Country Club in Kenmore, Washington, to prepare for the U.S. Amateur in Richmond, Virginia. It was worth it; he won. He won again in 1956. The California team, however, could have used him. In a near repeat of 1952, the Californians won three of the two-ball matches, but Ernie Pieper won the only singles match for California. The Pacific Northwest team won the Morse Cup with a 7-5 overall victory. In seven years, they trailed with only three wins to California's four and 39 match points to California's 45, but more importantly, the Pacific Northwest team had the cup. This possession became more significant as the matches ceased after 1955 and were nearly forgotten.

A decade later, in November 1965, several golf associations throughout the west gathered at Pebble Beach. Their goal was to create a golf championship that would better showcase the talent of Western

golfers—golfers who had largely been overlooked by the USGA for inclusion in the Walker Cup. The result was a rebirth of the Pacific Coast Amateur Championship, a championship that had not been played since 1911 when Jack Neville won it at the San Francisco Golf Club's Ingleside course. Participant associations in the first renewed playing of the championship included those of Northern California, Southern California, Washington, Oregon, Southwest, and Rocky Mountain.

The championship officially resumed at Seattle Golf Club on August 10, 1967. The new event was strictly stroke play and was open to members of any of the associations. As part of the competition, the Morse Cup was reinstituted (as part of the all-stroke play format) to honor the best team. In lieu of matches, each association instead selected a team of players, and the low scores among the team players over the first two days of play won the cup for their association. Arizona's Dr. Ed Updegraff won the Pacific Coast Amateur in 1967, and the Southern California team, with Jack Ewing (Bakersfield), Dick Runkle (Los Angeles), Bob Bouchier (El Niguel), and Jim Rheim (Chula Vista) won the Morse Cup.

The 1968 championships were played over Pebble Beach Golf Links in early August. For the Morse Cup, the associations each chose six-man

Ed Morris of San Jose accepts his medal for winning the 1968 PCGA Amateur with a score of 299 (11 over par) for 72 holes, 1 stroke better than defending champion Dr. Ed Updegraff. (PBC-W.C. Brooks)

teams, with the low four scores from each team over the first two rounds counting as the team score. Participating associations were the Pacific Northwest, Northern California, Southern California, Montana, Arizona, and Utah. After the first round, the Southern California team, which again included Runkle, Bouchier, and Rheim, held a 4-stroke lead over the Northern California team. Scores were high as afternoon fog made it harder to judge distances. Johnny Miller, who just a few weeks earlier had won the California Amateur at Pebble Beach, was the tournament favorite until his opening round 79. It made the low four scores on the Northern California team as Jack Bariteau ballooned to 85; Forrest Fezler was the NCGA's low man at 77. Among the 36 team players within the tournament, SCGA's David Barber and Arizona's Ed Updegraff were low at 75, and 23 selectees shot 80 or higher in the first round. Four golfers not in the team completion shot lower than the team leaders: Tom Culligan, 71 (San Mateo); Bill Fell, 72 (Los Angeles); Gary Davis, 73 (Portland); and Ed Morris, 73 (San Jose).

Scores improved on the second day, especially for the NCGA team. Bariteau followed his 85 with a 71, Fezler came back with a 72, and Miller a 74. With Harry Taylor's 77-75, the NCGA team's low four scores totaled 604, winning the Morse Cup by 7 strokes over the SCGA team. In the Pacific Coast Amateur Ed Morris moved into the lead with a 73-71—144; Rod Curl (Redding, California) was in second at 75-72—147; and SCGA-ace Dick Runkle, a Los Angeles attorney, moved into third at 76-72—148.

After round three, 40-year-old Runkle's 71 gave him a 2-stroke lead at 219 over 22-year-old John Schroeder of La Jolla, who shot a tournament-best 70 in round three. With an 83, Morris fell back into a tie for fifth with a large group of golfers that included Johnny Miller at 227.

Schroeder and Runkle were paired in the final round and traded bogeys. Schroeder caught Runkle twice only to fall back again. Through 15 holes, Runkle was 6 over par for the day, and Schroeder was 4 over and even for the tournament. Schroeder bogeyed hole 16 and followed it with a double-bogey on 17 to fall 3 strokes behind as Runkle played both holes in par. As they reached the 18th tee, word came that Morris had shot an even-par 72 and was in at 299; a par on 18 would still give Runkle a 2-stroke victory. He confidently laced his drive down the middle of the fairway. Assuring the ocean would not be his demise, he played his second shot to the right, but it got away from him and faded too far right—out of bounds. He topped his next shot and was laying four, still 250 yards from the green. Using his driver from the fairway, he hit it fat and found the ocean. Before he was done, Runkle tallied 10 strokes on the 18th hole and settled for a fifth place tie in the championship. Morris won, followed by defending champion Updegraff, who won a playoff for second place with Schroeder. Forrest Fezler finished fourth at 301. Johnny Miller finished just out of the top 10 with a solo 11th place finish at 304, just 5 strokes behind the winner.

The Pacific Coast Amateur and Morse Cup championships continue to be played annually. The Morse Cup team competition has been refined to three-man teams and low two scores, and the Pacific Coast Golf Association has grown to include 18 member associations around the Pacific Rim. The host sites travel throughout the West. While it has not returned to Pebble Beach Golf Links, it was played at Poppy Hills in 1996 when the NCGA team again won the Morse Cup and Scott Johnson of Kennewick, Washington, won the Pacific Coast Amateur.

Helen Lengfeld greets tournament sponsor Alvin Handmacher at the airport. Others on the trip included LPGA president Patty Berg (left) and Fred Corcoran (second from right), the LPGA's tournament manager. (PBC-J.P. Graham)

THE WEATHERVANE TRANSCONTINENTAL WOMEN'S OPEN GOLF CHAMPIONSHIP

Fred Corcoran gets the credit for coming up with the idea for a progressive tournament to create added interest in the fledgling Ladies' Professional Golf Association. He was an agent, promoter, and occasionally an irritant, but he represented and worked with the best. From 1937–48, he managed the tournaments of the PGA Tour and two Ryder Cup teams. In 1948, he lent his hand to the short-lived Women's Professional Golf Association and then helped initiate the LPGA as tournament manager for the Tour beginning with 13 ladies, some of whom were still amateurs.

The LPGA lists its founders as Alice Bauer, Patty Berg, Bettye Danoff, Helen Dettweiller, Marlene Bauer Hagge, Helen Hicks, Opal Hill, Betty Jameson, Sally Sessions, Marilyn Smith, Shirley Spork, Louise Suggs, and Babe Zaharias. Yet only seven of the founders played in each of the first two official LPGA events—the Tampa Open, played at Palma Ceia on January 19–22, 1950; and the Titleholders, played at the Augusta Country Club on March 16–19, 1950.

Sisters Alice and Marlene Bauer played in the first two events—but as amateurs to preserve their eligibility in a series of amateur tournaments. Ironically, the pretty pair from Midland, Texas, primarily delayed turning pro with plans to play in the Texas Women's Amateur Championship in April. However, just before their state championship, they announced

Peter Hay (standing) meets with tournament organizer Helen Lengfeld and sponsor Alvin Handmacher, head of the Weathervane Sports Clothing apparel company. (PBC-J.P. Graham)

they were turning professional, accepting a deal to model sports fashion for Weathervane Sports Clothing, sponsor of the next four events on the professional tour. Alvin Handmacher, head of Weathervane, saw the advantage of using the often-referenced pulchritude of the Bauer sisters to promote his apparel line and wanted them on board for the Weathervane tournament.

Handmacher put up $17,000 for the Weathervane Open, making it the richest purse on the new tour. The next biggest purse for the initial season was the U.S. Women's Open which had a $5,000 purse. However, to win the big prize in the Weathervane, a golfer must successfully compete in four tournaments over four weekends on four different courses. The first of the series was played at Pebble Beach Golf Links, and like the earlier events, it attracted seven of the thirteen founders amid a field of more than thirty mostly amateur women golfers. Among the competitors were Bettye Mims Danoff (who, as Bettye Mims White, won medalist honors at the 1948 U.S. Amateur) and the Bauer sisters, playing for the first time as professionals.

Marlene Bauer (left) withdrew with a throat infection but still encouraged her sister Alice who played in the inaugural Weathervane. (PBC-J.P. Graham)

(left) Louise Suggs battled with Patty Berg and Babe Zaharias for dominance in the early days of the LPGA Tour. (PBC-J.P. Graham)

(right) Beverly Hanson, then still an amateur, and Babe Zaharias head up the course in the inaugural Weathervane tournament. Hanson won the 1950 U.S. Amateur and then joined the professional ranks. (PBC-J.P. Graham)

Regrettably, young Marlene Bauer came down with a throat infection and had to withdraw. Betty Jameson, who won the 1940 U.S. Amateur at Pebble Beach, was playing in only her second event after breaking her knee cap in an accident and was still limping badly though game to compete. The favorites were Babe Zaharias, Patty Berg, and Louise Suggs.

Helen Lengfeld served as tournament director for the Pebble Beach leg of the Weathervane. A solid golfer in her own right when younger, the wealthy philanthropist from Hillsborough, California, had turned to promoting women's golf and publishing a magazine called *The Golfer*. She used her connections to fill the field with several top amateurs who could compete against the pros. Going into competition week, 40 women amateurs had signed up to play against the lady professionals.

Mildred "Babe" Didrickson Zaharias was at the top of her game. A star in several sports, including winning two gold medals for track and field in the 1932 Olympics (javelin and 80-meter hurdles), she did not enter

competitive golf until 1934 when she won medalist honors in her first tournament at the age of 22. The next year she won the 1935 Texas Amateur. But the USGA stripped her of her amateur status because she had played professionally in other sports. She continued to play golf exhibitions for charity, and at one such exhibition during the 1938 Los Angeles Open, she was paired with professional wrestler George Zaharias. Her heart was taken, and the two were soon married. In 1943, she was reinstated as an amateur, and one of her first victories came in the 1943 Del Monte Championship. She then proceeded to dominate the amateur circuit. From June 1946 to July 1947, she won 17 consecutive tournaments, including the 1946 U.S. Women's Amateur and the 1947 British Women's Amateur—the first American to win both. She turned professional in 1947, and in 1948 she won the U.S. Women's Open, then run by the WPGA. When it was decided to replace the WPGA with the LPGA, she signed on with enthusiasm and spent the winter in Florida refashioning her swing under the tutelage of golf legend Tommy Armour. Her first LPGA event was a little shaky, but thereafter she was on fire.

Babe Zaharias chips over the deep bunkers fronting the 16th green. (PBC-J.P. Graham)

Patty Berg tees off on the 7th hole. (PBC-J.P. Graham)

THE 1950 WEATHERVANE

In 1950, Pebble Beach Golf Links showed a ladies par of 38-39—77. In the opening day's play, Zaharias shot a stellar 36 on the front nine, but on the back she carded a 43, allowing other golfers to close the gap. Fellow professional from Texas, Betty Jameson, went out in 39 but home in 40 for a share of the lead, and equaling their score was the just-crowned California Amateur champion, Beverly Hanson, with a 38-41. Three other amateurs, Marjorie Ferrie, Grace DeMoss, and Barbara Dawson were just a stroke back at 80, and professionals Berg and Danoff were in the hunt with 81s.

The pairings had been set in advance for the 36-hole event, so play was not determined by scores. Among the leaders, DeMoss had the earliest tee time. The Oregonian amateur had already made her mark on the peninsula that spring by winning her second straight Pebble Beach Championship for Women with a 9&7 victory over Ann Pedroncelli, and the next week she won a medal play tournament at Monterey Peninsula Country Club with a 73-76-76—225 for 54 holes, beating Edean Anderson by 3 strokes. This was her third tournament in two months on the peninsula, and she played to a steady 79, posting a tough mark, 80-79—159, for the others to beat.

Jameson and Dawson were together, two groups behind DeMoss. Shooting 85 and 89 respectively, they quickly moved out of the competition. Hanson and Zaharias were together three groups behind Jameson. Hanson, perhaps intimidated by the flamboyant "Babe," also had trouble keeping up. Zaharias, however, was making her move. Again going out with a 36, she

had built a comfortable lead. But as before, trouble plagued her coming in. By the time she reached the 18th tee, she had given back 3 strokes to par but still had a comfortable 2-stroke lead on DeMoss and 4 strokes over Louise Suggs, who had closed with a strong 78, which was not enough when coupled with her 83 of the opening round.

Zaharias took a deep breath, and then near disaster. She hooked her drive off the 18th tee. In disbelief she watched as it tailed off toward rock and sea. The Finisher, as the 18th was well known, had taken its toll on another golfer. Her heart sank, and then leapt as she watched her ball carom off a rock and back on the fairway. She'd lost some distance but not her ball. She got down with a 6 and held a 1-stroke lead while waiting for the others to finish.

Danoff ballooned to an 88, but Berg was playing steady golf, a real threat most of the way. In the end, her 79 left her in third, 2 strokes behind Zaharias. The lucky break on the rocks certainly added to her success and the excitement of the tournament. Five amateurs made it into the top 10, leaving one professional back in the 11th spot. Alice Bauer, playing for the first time in a long time without Marlene in the field, may have left some of her focus on her ailing little sister. Her 90-81—171 put her at the back of the professional field but still in contention for the $5,000 pot at the end of the four-tournament rainbow. Marlene was out of the running.

The good news for the LPGA was that the tournament was building excitement, garnering headlines across the country and it was just getting under way. Pebble Beach had been a successful course from which to launch the inventive format. Each leg had its own tournament director

The gallery surrounds the 18th green in 1950 as Zaharias closes for the win after a near disaster off the tee. (PBC-J.P. Graham)

Proudly waving her check, Babe Zaharias was the first winner of an LPGA event at Pebble Beach. (PBC-J.P. Graham)

who was responsible for filling an interesting field around the lady pros, but the six professionals that played all four legs were the primary story.

From Pebble Beach they headed to Skycrest Country Club in Chicago, then Babe Zaharias' home course. Suggs won the Chicago leg by 7 strokes over Zaharias and took a 4-stroke lead after 72 holes into the third leg at Cleveland's Ridgewood Country Club.

Zaharias set two course records at Cleveland with a first-round 73 and second-round 72. Patty Berg took third place at Cleveland and moved into a solid third place in the overall still trailing Suggs by 8 strokes and Zaharias by 15.

As the group rolled into Knollwood Country Club in White Plains, New York, Zaharias was the clear favorite, but the anticipation helped draw the largest field of pros yet—11; all of the founders of the Tour played except for Helen Dettweiler and Opal Hill, the latter who, age 58, never played in an LPGA event but served as the matriarch founder, having played most of her competitive golf in the 1920s and 1930s. On a course where the ladies par was 80, Suggs knew what she needed to do and shot a 3-under-par 77, carving 4 strokes off the overall lead of Zaharias who finished second for the first round in New York with an 81. Suggs needed to do it again on Sunday to win the big prize, and she tried, carding a 78. But Zaharias tied her in the final round, giving Suggs the win in New York and $750, while Zaharias pocketed $500 for second place and $5,000 for the overall—the biggest pay day on the LPGA's 1950 tour. With two wins and two second-place finishes, Zaharias collected a total of $7,500 over the four-week event. Suggs' total came to $2,200.

Babe Zaharias led the ladies through the other three legs of the Weathervane to capture the four-course bonus of $5,000. (PBC-J.P. Graham)

Marlene Bauer was still a teenager when she joined the LPGA in 1950. Here she puts on an exhibition at the 1951 Weathervane. (PBC-J.P. Graham)

The always humorous Patty Berg demonstrates bad form. (PBC-J.P. Graham)

THE 1951 WEATHERVANE

The Weathervane had clearly struck a popular chord and helped launch the LPGA in fine style, both figuratively and with a sporty fashion line for lady golfers. The Weathervane Open continued for just four years but added a much-needed dimension to the early days of the LPGA Tour. In 1951, the LPGA schedule was much fuller, and while the Weathervane Open was still played over four courses, it was not played over consecutive weeks. The first leg was played at the Lakewood Country Club in Dallas on April 14–15. It returned to Pebble Beach for the second leg on May 5–6. The third leg was played at Meridian Hills Country Club in Indianapolis on May 19–20 and again closed out at Knollwood Country Club in New York; well, almost.

Not only had the Tour schedule grown, so had the number of competing professionals. Dallas drew 14 professionals and Pebble Beach 13. Many of the prior year's amateurs had joined the professional ranks, but the founders still dominated. Alice Bauer led the first round at Dallas with a 75 but was usurped when Babe Zaharias came back with a record-setting

66 in the second round that nullified the damage of her first round 83. Zaharias' 83-66—149 secured a 4-stroke victory over Patty Berg's 77-76—153. Polly Riley and Betty Dodd tied for low amateur honors at 160, but tied for 9th place. The amateurs were no longer a major factor in women's professional golf.

At Pebble Beach, Berg and Zaharias tied for the best cards in round one as they both shot a 76. In round two, Zaharias shot 80 while Berg fired another 76 to win the tournament and pull into a tie in the overall. Louise Suggs finished third with a 77-82—159, and in fourth place was Beverly Hanson at 161, the only amateur to finish in the top 10. In the overall, Betty Jameson was at 318, just a stroke behind Suggs; Alice Bauer was a stroke behind Jameson; and rookie pro Betsy Rawls, another Texan, was just 2 strokes further back.

With yet another one-two finish at Indianapolis, Zaharias (72-73—145) and Berg (74-73—147) were pulling away from the competition. Suggs actually managed a tie in Indianapolis with a 71-76—147, but she was down 15 strokes to Zaharias with only two rounds left to play. When

Babe Zaharias, the human machine gun, hits a series of accurate drives in rapid succession during a pre-tournament exhibition in 1951. (PBC-J.P. Graham)

Company president S.F.B. Morse dons his Weathervane cap and poses with Babe Zaharias at the 1951 Weathervane. (PBC-J.P. Graham)

the dust settled at Knollwood Country Club in New York, Berg won the event with 149, and for the first time in two years, Zaharias finished out of the top two. Suggs snuck into second with a 150, and Zaharias tied for third with rookie-pro Peggy Kirk at 151. But the significant story told by the numbers is that in four events, Berg defeated Zaharias by a mere 2 strokes twice, and Zaharias did the same to Berg. After 144 holes, the two were tied overall at 601. The tournament was not decided, and it would take a 36-hole match, at a place and time to be determined, to settle the winner and award the $5,000 over-all prize.

The playoff was set for June 16 and 17 at Scarsdale Country Club in Great Neck, New York. In the first round, both ladies shot 71. As the second round began, Berg sunk a 30-foot birdie on the 1st hole to take the lead by one, and Zaharias three-putted the 2nd hole giving Berg a 2-stroke lead. Zaharias had some opportunities but had trouble with her putter all day. On the 18th, Berg missed a putt, allowing Zaharias to get back a single stroke. The first tournament to be decided over 180 holes and five golf courses resulted in a 1-stroke victory for Patty Berg, helping her to become the leading money winner on the 1951 Tour.

THE CLASSIC COMES TO AN END

In 1952, the Weathervane was played at Miami, Houston, Seattle, and New York, with a different pro winning each leg and Betsy Rawls winning the overall 590 to Betty Jameson's 600. In 1953, they played Boca Raton, Phoenix, San Francisco, and Philadelphia with Louise Suggs winning the last three and the overall honors. With a short but amazing history, the Weathervane effectively squeezed 21 tournaments into four short years and provided a lot of excitement for the early years of the LPGA.

San Diego's Mickey Wright (center) and Martha Mumbly visit with Del Monte golf instructor Fred Sherman prior to the 1950 California Junior Girls' Championship. (PBC-J.P. Graham)

THE 1952 U.S. GIRLS' JUNIOR CHAMPIONSHIP

The USGA made its fifth venture to Pebble Beach in 1952—this time to MPCC's Dunes Course for the fourth playing of the U.S. Girls' Junior Championship. The Junior Nationals were instituted after World War II, the Boys in 1948 and the Girls in 1949. Marlene Bauer, one of the early professionals, won the initial Girls' Junior Championship, and many young ladies were starting to consider professional golf as a possibility. One such junior was Mary Kathryn "Mickey" Wright of San Diego. In 1950, at the age of 15, Wright was runner-up in the U.S. Junior. The next year she lost in the semifinals. At age 17, the trip to Pebble Beach would mark her last attempt as a junior.

The medal round was played on August 18. The women's par on the Dunes course was 75, and Mickey Wright fired a 39-37—76 to tie with

14-year-old Anne Quast (37-39—76) of Everett, Washington, for the low score. Quast won a playoff for the medal. Sixteen teenagers entered medal play for the championship. Wright marched through her first two matches, defeating Thyra Hillburn of San Gabriel, California, 7&6 in the first round and Judy Frank of Alpine, New Jersey, 5&4 in the second round. Quast also dominated her first two matches, defeating Berridge "Berri" Long of Huntington, West Virginia, 3&2 and defending champion Arlene Brooks of Pasadena, California, 7&6.

In the semifinals, the matches got much tougher as four future Hall of Famers were pitched in battle. Quast faced 17-year-old Barbara McIntire of Toledo, Ohio. This would not be the last time these two would meet in competition as each went on to have illustrious amateur golfer records. McIntire first made her mark when at age 15 she defeated Glenna Collett-Vare in the first round of the 1950 U.S. Women's Amateur. She was runner-up in the 1951 Girls' Junior. Each played on six Curtis Cup teams, as teammates in 1958, '60, '62, and '64. Quast won the U.S. Women's Amateur three times, in 1958, '61, and '63. McIntire won it twice, in 1959 and '64. Quast also won the Women's Western twice (1956 and '61), while McIntire won the British Women's Amateur in 1960. Quast also won four U.S. Women's Senior Amateur championships (1987, '89, '90, and '93) and is in the Washington and Pacific Northwest Golf Hall of Fame. McIntire is in the Golf Hall of Fame in Ohio and Colorado, and in 2000 she was honored with the USGA's Bob Jones Award. In 1952, the elder McIntire won their match 2&1. Despite playing in many of the same tournaments, they only faced off one other time in a national championship; on her way to winning the 1959 U.S. Amateur, McIntire defeated Quast in a quarterfinal match that went to the 20th hole.

Wright faced tenacious 15-year-old Judy Bell of Wichita, Kansas. Bell had reached the semifinals with a 9&7 victory over Linda Tarsky and 4&3 over Janet McIntosh. Bell had come to California early for the USGA championship and demonstrated her prowess by winning the 3rd Annual California Girls' Junior Championship. At the time, no one could have imagined these two teenagers would both end up in the World Golf Hall of Fame, Wright for winning more than 80 championships as a professional golfer, and Bell for her lifetime achievement as a golfer and golf organizer, culminating in her election to president of the USGA in 1996, the only woman ever to hold that post. In the semifinal match at MPCC, Wright defeated Bell 2&1.

Wright and McIntire were as evenly matched in the finals as any two 17-year-old girls could be. They each took 39 strokes to get around the front nine at the Dunes course and were all square. The tension rose on the final nine holes. Wright won the 10th and 11th holes and gave one back with a bogey on 13. McIntire than got hot with birdies on holes 14 and 15 to take a 1-up lead. Wright squared the match with a birdie on 16 and they halved the 17th with pars. On the 18th, McIntire put her drive in the trees and took 5 strokes to reach the green on the par-5 hole. Wright was down in five to win the championship with a par. A champion among champions, Wright had proved herself the best golfer that week, and

Judy Bell (left) defeated 1951 U.S. Girls' Junior champion Arlene Brooks to win the 1952 California championship just before the USGA championship. In the national championship, Brooks fell to Anne Quast in round two, and Bell met Mickey Wright in semifinals. (PBC-J.P. Graham)

Mickey Wright scored her first USGA trophy at the 1952 U.S. Girls' Junior Championship at MPCC. She later added four Women's U.S. Open victories during a career in which she won 82 tournaments and was the top money winner on the LPGA tour each year from 1961–64. (PBC- J.P. Graham)

Anne Quast (right) and Mickey Wright tied for the medalist honors at the Monterey Peninsula Country Club. Quast won the medal in a playoff. (PBC-J.P. Graham)

wouldn't stop there. She was runner-up to Barbara Romack in the 1954 U.S. Women's Amateur before turning professional. Between 1954 and 1972, she had 12 top 10 finishes in the U.S. Women's Open, winning it four times (1958, '59, '61, and '64) and tying Betsy Rawls for the most Open victories.

THE CALIFORNIA WOMEN'S AMATEUR

There have actually been at least three championships that are known as the California Women's Amateur, which makes it a little confusing. The longest running of the lot was that of the California Women's Golf Association. As noted earlier in this work, it was begun in 1906 and reorganized in 1920. This championship traveled around the state, and while two of its pre-1920 championships were played at Del Monte Golf Course, it did not return to the Monterey Peninsula until 1952 when Barbara Romack won it at Monterey Peninsula Country Club with a 5&3 victory over 1949 champion Ruth McCullah. This was Romack's first of four state amateur championships. Her fourth victory also came at MPCC when it returned for its last time to Pebble Beach in 1958. In 1958, Romack defeated Mrs. George Downing 5&4 in the final match.

In the mid-1960s, Helen Lengfeld, who had organized and started many women's events in California, including the California Girls' Junior, which began at Del Monte Golf Course in 1950, approached S.F.B. Morse about starting a California Women's Amateur Championship at Pebble Beach. Morse agreed, and the first of these California Amateur Championships was played on Pebble Beach Golf Links in December 1967. No one seems to know why Lengfeld saw the need for a second Women's championship, but regardless, since 1967 there have been two California Women's Amateur Championships, both contested via match play. Lengfeld's edition was played on Pebble Beach Golf Links for its first twenty years and has continued to be played annually at Quail Lodge in nearby Carmel Valley since 1987.

Barbara Romack of Sacramento won the 1950 California Girls' Junior at Del Monte Golf Course when she was 17; two years later she won the California Women's Amateur and MPCC; and continuing her biennial wins, she won the 1954 U.S. and the 1954 California Women's Amateurs. She repeated as California Champion in 1956 and 1958. (PBC-J.P. Graham)

Shelly Hamlin with her fourth straight trophy at Pebble Beach in 1970. She won the championship so often, some joked it was "The Shelly Hamlin Invitational." (PBC- W.C. Brooks)

Barbara Handley (left), runner up to Shelly Hamlin at Pebble Beach in 1970, held off future professional star and reigning U.S. Women's Amateur Champion Laura Baugh (right), then just 16, to win the 1971 California Amateur. Handley won both California Women's Amateur Championships in 1971 and 1972. (PBC- W.C. Brooks)

A bespectacled 17-year-old Amy Alcott watches as Debbie Skinner tees off in the final match of the 1973 California Women's Amateur. (PBC- W.C. Brooks)

Alcott smashes her own drive down the first fairway en route to a 2&1 victory for the championship. (PBC-W.C. Brooks)

Both championships attracted the top women golfers in the state, and as they shared winners (not always in the same year) there has often been confusion over who the state champion was. General media certainly gave the most attention to the championships at Pebble Beach, while the NCWGA and SCWGA recognized the longer-running championship.

When the California Women's Amateur began at Pebble Beach in 1967, San Rafel's Carol Bowman had recorded her third straight win in the other Women's Amateur, but there was little question that Fresno's Shelley Hamlin was the best woman golfer in the state. In 1966, at age 17, after a penalty left her runner-up in the California Junior Girl's Championship, she was low amateur in the U.S. Women's Open (tied for ninth place) and medalist in the U.S. Amateur; she lost in the U.S. Amateur to Anne Quast in a 19-hole second-round match. She also reached match play in the 1967 U.S. Amateur but suffered a first-round loss.

At Pebble Beach in 1967, Bowman didn't play, and Harriet Glanville won medalist honors. But while Glanville easily reached the finals, she was no match for Hamlin who won 5&4 to capture the championship. In 1968, Hamlin won the medal and the championship as well as the other Women's Amateur. Hamlin remained undefeated at Pebble Beach in 1969 and 1970, leading some to jokingly call it the "the Shelley Hamlin Invitational."

Hamlin lost a second-round match in the December 1971 championship to Maria Astrologes of Woodland Hills and left amateur golf for the professional circuit. Astrologes lost in the third round to medalist Laura Baugh, a 16-year-old girl from Long Beach, who was the reigning U.S. Women's Amateur Champion, Baugh continued to the finals where she met Barbara Handley. Handley was twice Baugh's age and had finished runner-up to Hamlin in 1970 at Pebble Beach. She had also won the other Women's Amateur in the spring of 1971, so it was a tough final with Handley defeating Baugh 3&2 in the final. Handley repeated as double State Amateur Champion in 1972.

Santa Monica native 17-year-old Amy Alcott, fresh from winning the 1973 U.S. Girls' Junior Championship, came to Pebble Beach in December and won the Women's Amateur. In 1974, Alcott added the other California Women's Amateur to her resume and then returned to Pebble Beach where she fired a woman's course record 70 to win the medal. She then suffered a surprising upset loss, down-1 to Mary Elizabeth Shea in the final. The next year, Amy Alcott joined the professional ranks.

Patricia Cornett (age 21) was a double champion in 1975, and though she repeated as 1976 champion in the other championship and reached the semifinals in the 1976 U.S. Amateur, Marianne Bretton won at Pebble Beach in December 1976. Bretton, a 19-year-old UCLA co-ed, narrowly defeated Barbara Handley in a 20-hole semifinal match but solidly defeated Susan Stanley 6&4 in the final. The win earned her an invitation to play in the 1977 Bing Crosby National Pro-Am. She paired with professional Eddie Merrins and was joined by 20-year-old Nancy Lopez, paired with Jose Gonzalez, in what was deemed "a novel and provocative experiment" to include women in the popular event.

Stellar amateur play earned Nancy Lopez (left of Crosby), winner of the 1976 Intercollegiate Champion for Women, and California Amateur Champion Marianne Bretton (right of Crosby) playing spots in the 1977 Bing Crosby National Pro-Am. (PBC-W.C. Brooks)

Marianne Bretton won the 1976 championship and earned a birth as an amateur in the 1977 Crosby. (PBC-W.C. Brooks)

Patty Sheehan (right) was another of the winners of both California Women's Amateurs. Her first win at Pebble Beach came in 1977, seen here with runner-up Irene Zuniga (left) and tournament founder Helen Lengfeld. (PBC-W.C. Brooks)

Patty Sheehan, a past Nevada State Champion, transferred to San Jose State and was a double California State Champion in 1977 and 1978. In 1979, Sheehan was runner-up in the U.S. Amateur and returned to Pebble Beach in December where she tied for medalist honors with Sally Voss, a San Francisco med student who had won the other Women's State Amateur that spring. Sheehan went out early in the matches, while Voss worked her way up the ladder, eking out a 1-up victory over Patricia Cornett in the semifinal before defeating Linda Maurer in the final match by the same margin to become yet another double amateur winner. The next year, after playing on the 1980 Curtis Cup team, Sheehan turned pro.

Sally Voss won the 1979 championship and remained an amateur becoming a San Francisco physician. She has often returned to play in the AT&T Pebble Beach National Pro-Am, missing team victory by only 2 strokes in 1999. (PBC-W.C. Brooks)

Juli Inkster shows her winning form in 1981 at Pebble Beach. She is one of just three women (the other two being Babe Zaharias and Patty Berg) who have won at Pebble Beach as both an amateur and a professional—all are in the World Golf Hall of Fame. She won the 1981 California Amateur and the 1990 Spalding (now the Callaway Golf Pebble Beach Invitational). (PBC-W.C. Brooks)

Another future pro, 20-year-old Juli Simpson Inkster, the 1980 U.S. Women's Amateur champion, came to Pebble Beach and won the medalist honors in 1980. Although Mary Enright won the 1980 State Amateur, Inkster returned in 1981 after winning a second U.S. Amateur championship to win both the medal and the state championship at Pebble Beach. Inkster won her third straight U.S. Women's Amateur Championship in 1982 before turning pro in 1983 and becoming one of the top all-time money winners in the history of the LPGA.

Patricia Cornett, then a physician at San Francisco's Presidio, was a semifinalist or better in all of the remaining years the championship was played at Pebble Beach. She won the championship a second time in 1983 and lost a final match to one of the great amateur players when Anne Quast Sander returned to Pebble Beach in 1985 and added the California Amateur to her list of many titles. Cindy Scholefield, a 25-year-old accountant from Malibu who played college golf at UCLA, tied the women's course record of 70 to win the medal in 1985.

Scholefield changed careers and became an assistant golf coach at UCLA. She returned to Pebble Beach in 1986 and became the final California Women's Amateur Champion to be crowned on Pebble Beach Golf Links. She sank a 15-foot putt on the 15th hole for birdie and a 40-footer for birdie on 16 to defeat Oregon's 18-year-old Amanda Neely 3&2 in the final.

THE STATE WOMEN'S STROKE-PLAY CHAMPIONSHIP

A third tournament called the California Women's State Championship was born at Torrey Pines in 1996. Unlike the other two California Women's Amateurs, this tournament is a 54-hole stroke-play event. The championship is run by a committee comprised of two representatives each from the Pacific Women's Golf Association, the Women's Golf Association of Northern California, the Women's Southern California Golf Association, and the San Diego County Women's Golf Association. To date, this championship has been contested three times at the Poppy Hills Golf Course at Pebble Beach, in 1997, 1999, and 2006. Among the champions of this newest California Women's Amateur is Natalie Gulbis who won this event in 2000 after winning the California (match play) Women's Amateur at Quail Lodge in 1997.

Only time will tell how the multiple California women's championships will shake out, but one thing that seems clear is that California will continue to create many future champions in the sport.

After finishing runner-up in 1951 and 1953, Pomona dentist Dr. Frank M. "Bud" Taylor (left) won the California Amateur back-to-back in 1954 and 1955. (PBC-J.P. Graham)

"Bud" Taylor (left) was a semifinalist for the first time in the State Amateur when Ken Venturi was still a first-grader; but when the 33-year-old dentist met the 20-year-old San Jose State sophomore in 1951, the youngster won 7&6. (PBC-J.P. Graham)

THE MEN'S CALIFORNIA AMATEUR CHAMPIONSHIP

The women weren't the only ones defining future champions; the men's State Amateur continued to be the top annual event for California's golfers. Some, like Ernie Pieper and Dr. Frank "Bud" Taylor, competed their entire lives as amateurs and frequently showed up as contenders in the State Amateur. Others competed in the State Amateur as youth before jumping into the professional ranks. Taylor was the victim of these future pros on more than one occasion and still managed to become a multiple winner in the event.

Taylor also entered the championship in his youth, first breaking into the semifinals in 1937. In the postwar era, Dr. Taylor again reached championship pace in 1951. That year, he defeated two-time champion Bruce McCormick in the semifinals only to face 20-year-old Ken Venturi in the finals. Venturi won the match 7&6. Taylor again reached the final match in 1953. That time he lost 5&4 to 23-year-old Gene Littler. Littler also won the 1953 U.S. Amateur and was a member of that year's Walker

1956 Champion Ken Venturi denied "Bud" Taylor a three-peat by beating him a second time in 1956. (PBC-J.P. Graham)

Young future golf professionals continued to compete and hone their skills in the California Amateur; like 21-year-old Johnny Miller, who won it in 1968. (PBC- W.C. Brooks)1956. (PBC-J.P. Graham)

Lennie Clements (left) congratulates Mark O'Meara upon winning the 1979 State Amateur, for what was his first of many wins on the famed links. (PBC-W.C. Brooks)

Cup team. In 1954, after finishing as the runner-up amateur in the U.S. Open, Littler turned pro and did not return to defend his title. Venturi was serving a two-year stint in the army and also missed the competition. Taylor rose to the top of the State's amateurs and won the championship back-to-back in 1954 and 1955. In 1956, Taylor again reached the finals, but Venturi was back and reclaimed the title with a 2&1 victory. Venturi had also won the medal that year with a 68-71—139, tying the record medal score set by Bud Brownell before the war.

Venturi turned pro shortly thereafter, and Taylor never again reached the semifinals in the State Amateur, turning his focus instead to national play. From 1956 to 1961, Taylor qualified for five U.S. Amateurs, finishing runner-up in 1957. He was also, with an active dental practice, a member of the Walker Cup team in 1957, '59, and '61.

Johnny Miller won the California Amateur in 1968 and Bobby Clampett won it in 1978 and 1980, perhaps indicating that Pebble Beach identified not only top golf champions but also great golf commentators. Venturi, Miller, and Clampett each made a comfortable living as both. John Cook ('75), Mark O'Meara ('79), Duffy Waldorf ('84), and Jason Gore ('97) were among the future tour pros to win the California Amateur. Several other future stars competed in the California Amateur without claiming the top prize, including Craig Stadler (1974 medalist), Scott Simpson (1976 medalist), and Corey Pavin (1982 medalist). Future tour pros Kevin Sutherland, Paul Stankowski, John Mallinger, and Dave Stockton Jr., also competed in the California Amateur.

Of course, the most famous California golfer of the modern era also competed in the California Amateur at Pebble Beach. Tiger Woods, who at 18 had hoped to compete in the 1994 U.S. Amateur at Pebble Beach, had to settle for a berth in the 1994 California Amateur when the U.S. Amateur's return to Pebble Beach was delayed until 1999. Ironically, it was a different Woods, Steve Woods, who won the medal honors and went on to win the championship. Tiger Woods lost 2&1 in the semifinals to Ed Cuff Jr., or it would have been a Woods v. Woods final. Cuff, who vanquished Tiger Woods and lost to Steve Woods in 1994, returned in 1998 to win the State Championship. Tiger Woods won the U.S. Amateur at Sawgrass in 1994 (and again in 1995 and 1996) and famously returned to Pebble Beach in 2000 to win both the AT&T Pebble Beach National Pro-Am and the U.S. Open.

In 2006, with only one break since 1920 (the 2000 California Amateur was moved to Bayonet due to the U.S. Open at Pebble Beach), the State Amateur ended its long run of 86 State Championships contested over Pebble Beach Golf Links. The California Golf Association decided that it would play the annual championship over a variety of the state's courses, rotating each year between the North and South. The 2007 championship moved just across the forest to Monterey Peninsula Country Club's two renovated courses; the 2008 Championship was at Los Angeles' Lakeside Country Club; 2009 at Lake Merced Golf Club in Daly City.

"Chick" Evans of Chicago, age 68, who won the U.S. Amateur in 1916, caged a birdie off the course, but he couldn't capture enough on course to survive the quarterfinals of the 1958 U.S. Senior Amateur. (PBC- J.P. Graham)

1942 California Amateur Champion John Dawson knew the courses at Pebble Beach better than most and was a heavy favorite to win the U.S. Senior Amateur. (PBC-J.P. Graham)

4TH U.S. SENIOR AMATEUR

Before World War II, the USGA conducted only four annual championships. The U.S. Amateur, the U.S. Open, and the U.S. Women's Amateur each date to 1895. The U.S. Amateur Public Links Championship began in 1922. After World War II, as interest in golf grew, the USGA added the U.S. Junior Championship (1948), the U.S. Girls' Junior (1949), the Women's Open (1953), and then the U.S. Senior Amateur (1955). The USGA brought the 4th Annual U.S. Senior Amateur Championship to Pebble Beach in 1958 for the organization's sixth visit—its fourth visit since the end of the war. Like the 1952 Girl's Junior, the 1958 U.S. Senior was contested over the Dunes Course at Monterey Peninsula Country Club, which was still owned by Morse's Del Monte Properties Company.

The Senior Amateur was open to amateur golfers over the age of 55, and the event attracted 370 entries, 152 of which, through regional qualifying, reached MPCC on Monday, September 29, for the 18-hole medal round. Among the local senior golfers playing were five-time California Amateur champion Jack Neville and General Robert McClure, who was responsible for the creation of the Bayonet course at nearby Fort Ord. Adrian McManus of Fresno, who won the California Senior Amateur the prior week, was also in the field. California's former Open, Amateur, and Crosby champion Johnny Dawson was the clear favorite to win—especially after he practiced on Pebble Beach and Cypress Point over the weekend and returned scores of 67 and 69. Dawson was playing in his first Senior Championship as he had only turned 55 the previous December. Another favorite in the field was the affable Charles "Chick" Evans Jr., of Chicago. The 68-year-old Evans

had been the first golfer to win the U.S. Open and U.S. Amateur in the same year, a feat he accomplished in 1916. Evans had played in both previous U.S. Amateurs at Pebble Beach. He came out early and warmed up by competing in the California Senior where he finished second to McManus.

The medalist, however, was defending U.S. Senior champion J. Clark Espie of Indianapolis with a 71. Thirty-one golfers shot 78 or better in the qualifying, leaving the eight players who shot 79 vying for the 32nd spot in the championship flight. It went to Vincent Fitzgerald of New York, who birdied the second playoff hole. Fitzgerald lost in the first round of matches to Ross McDade, who finished second in the qualifying. Edward M. Smith of Upper Montclair, New Jersey, gave Espie a pretty good tussle before Espie took a 2&1 victory. Evans and Dawson also won their first-round matches by the same margin. Maurice Smith of Kansas City and Ray Robeson had the most closely contested match of the day, with Smith not recording his victory until the 20th hole.

Smith's second round was not nearly as close as he crossed clubs with a red-hot John W. McGuire. In just 12 holes, the 1934 Indiana State Champion fired six threes to defeat Maurice Smith 7&6. The favorites Espie, Evans, and Dawson also dominated their matches, respectively defeating Charles Williams of San Jose, California; Walter E. Barnes of Rockford, Illinois; and Calvin T. McCarthy of Peabody, Massachusetts—each match ending after 14 holes. In the second round's longest match, 59-year-old Egon "Eggs" Quittner, a textile manufacturer from Jenkintown, Pennsylvania, needed 22 holes to defeat John W. Roberts of Columbus, Ohio.

Defending champion J. Clark Espie of Indianapolis won the medal and then defeated Chicago's Chick Evans to reach the semifinals in the fourth annual Senior Amateur Championship. (PBC-J.P. Graham)

Ross McDade of El Centro, California, the 1944 Louisiana Amateur Champion, reached the semifinals of the Senior Amateur by defeating John McGuire of Indianapolis. (PBC-J.P. Graham)

Quittner fell in round three by a score of 3&1 to 65-year-old Thomas C. Robbins, who had sold sporting goods in New York before retiring to Pinehurst, North Carolina. Robbins reached the quarterfinals by previously defeating Richard Guelich and Martin McCarthy. Joining Robbins in the semifinals were pre-tournament favorites Espie and Dawson, along with Ross McDade of El Centro, California, who was the 1944 Louisiana State Champion. Chick Evans did not make it past round three, falling to Espie by a score of 4&3.

Dawson and McDade both played strong golf with Dawson 1 under par at the turn and only leading 2-up. The match stretched to the 17th hole before Dawson could relax with a 2&1 victory. The Robbins-Espie match was even tighter; the match was all square through 15. On 16 Espie played his approach shot poorly, missed the green, and lost the hole. They halved the 17th, and then Espie uncharacteristically hit his tee shot into the forest and, after failing to recover, conceded the match to Robbins.

There was little question that Dawson would win in the final match—that is, for everyone but Robbins. Robbins knew he would have to play at the top of his game to beat Dawson, and he rose to the occasion. With spectacular iron play, Robbins actually hit the flagstick on both the 7th and 9th holes and played a remarkable recovery from a drainage ditch on hole 8 for a birdie. His semifinal win over defending champion Espie was an upset. His 2&1 defeat of Dawson for the championship was a shocker. Still, no one could question that he had earned his victory and the championship.

Runner-up John Dawson (left) of Los Angeles joins champion Thomas C. Robbins of Pinehurst with the U.S. Senior Amateur trophy. (PBC-J.P. Graham)

Three-time British Champion Joe Carr came over to the States for the Walker Cup and, like many of his teammates, he stayed on for the U.S. Amateur. (PBC-Graham/Brooks)

Michael Bonallack, another Walker Cupper, had already won the 1961 British Amateur. (PBC-Graham/Brooks)

Jack Nicklaus had won the 1959 U.S. Amateur and was gunning for his second with a win at Pebble Beach. (PBC-Graham/Brooks)

Gene Andrews taught some of the younger Walker Cup players, including Jack Nicklaus, how to play a course "by the book." (PBC-Graham/Brooks)

THE 1961 U.S. AMATEUR

For the 1961 U.S. Amateur, the field was dominated by college players. Unlike earlier National Amateurs at Pebble Beach, the career amateurs were less of a factor. The PGA Tour was providing a living for the best golfers, so the young college stars had begun turning professional after graduation. The illustrious Charles "Chick" Evans Jr. returned to Pebble Beach, qualifying as a competitor at the age of 71. This appearance made Evans the only golfer to play in the three U.S. Men's Amateurs at Pebble Beach Golf Links to that date. It also made him the oldest golfer in the field. Evans went out in the first match 5&4. As in 1947, the 1961 championship began with no medal play. The field of 200 golfers went straight to matches.

Nine of the Great Britain-Ireland team and all 10 Americans from the recent 1961 Walker Cup Tournament were competing at Pebble Beach. Any one of them was capable of winning. Deane Beman, the 22-year-old defending U.S. Amateur Champion from Maryland, and the 1959 Champion, 21 year-old Ohio State senior, Jack Nicklaus, were among the American team. The GB-I team included British Amateur champions Joe Carr (1953, '58, and '60) and Michael Bonallack (1961).

A couple of local favorites were San Jose's Ernie Pieper Jr., and San Francisco's E. Harvie Ward. Ward had won the U.S. Amateur in 1955 and 1956 and the British Amateur in 1952. Both had also competed in the 1947 U.S. Amateur at Pebble Beach; Ward reached the quarterfinals.

Most of the golfers arrived the week prior to get in some practice rounds. Gene Andrews, a 48-year-old Walker Cup star from Whittier, California, had developed a habit local golf reporter Bob Bullock called playing "by the book." Also dubbed "the Gene Andrews method," it was picked

up by many of the younger players, as well. The method required using a small notebook to chart your club length to the layout of each hole in the competition, marking bunkers, trees, and other hazards. Players would check their books on every shot to make sure they were selecting the proper clubs. Young Jack Nicklaus used this method and reported stepping off each shot in the days prior to the tournament. "This is the first course I haven't been able to judge the distances," he stated.

The big news from the second day's play came when Billy Joe Patton, an alternate on the Walker Cup team out of North Carolina, ousted 1960 U.S. Amatuer Champion Deane Beman in a very tight match. They reached 18 with Patton 1-up. Tremendous drives followed by missed second shots put both golfers in the right rough. Patton's luck held as he landed his third shot about 6 feet from the pin. Beman's third shot landed in a greenside bunker. He blasted out to about 7 feet and then walked to the green where he conceded the hole and the match.

With Beman out, Harvie Ward's prospects were looking better. Ward trounced his second round opponent Harlan Lane of Pine Forest, Texas, by a score of 7&5.

Four cuppers from the GB-I team survived Day 2: Joe Carr, Ronnie Shade, Michael Bonallack, and Gordon Huddy. The American team advanced six (seven, if you count Patton). Charlie Coe and Charlie Smith each had short afternoons defeating their challengers 5&4. Jack Nicklaus' 4&3 victory over Oregon's Donald Kreiger was nearly as swift. Bob Gardner and Gene Andrews each won at 3&2, while Bud Taylor's match went to the 17th, where he ended the bid of Connecticut's Richard Siderowf, 2&1.

With the field trimmed to 64 players for Day 3, 32 matches were played in the morning with the survivors playing 16 matches in the afternoon.

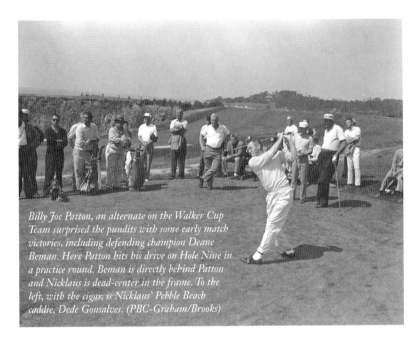

Billy Joe Patton, an alternate on the Walker Cup Team surprised the pundits with some early match victories, including defending champion Deane Beman. Here Patton hits his drive on Hole Nine in a practice round. Beman is directly behind Patton and Nicklaus is dead-center in the frame. To the left, with the cigar, is Nicklaus' Pebble Beach caddie, Dede Gonsalves. (PBC-Graham/Brooks)

Still in his early 20s, Ronnie D.B.M. Shade of the British Walker Cup team was yet to reach his peak as an amateur golfer (and later a pro), but he still made a strong showing at Pebble Beach. (PBC-Graham/Brooks)

Charlie Coe always looked relaxed and enjoyed amateur golf, never turning pro. He won two U.S. Amateurs (1949 and 1958), played on six Walker Cup teams, and he finished as low amateur at the Masters six times. (PBC-Graham/Brooks)

The 11 matches featuring the Walker Cup stars pulled the greatest crowds and featured some amazing upsets. Two of the GB-I team lost close matches in the morning—Bonallack to Ohio's Roger McManus in 18 and Huddy to James English of Colorado in 20.

Three American Cuppers were ousted in the morning. Gene Andrews was stunned by Jerry Jackson of Kokomo, Indiana, 5&4. Bob Gardner, a two-time California Champion and runner-up in the 1960 U.S. Amateur, found himself in the uncomfortable position of being down-4 after eight holes to University of Houston senior, Homero Blancas. Gardner battled back to within one after 16 but hit onto the rocks on 17 and lost the match 2&1. Even more bizarre was the defeat of Charlie Coe by unheralded Gene Francis of Westbury, New York. Coe was 2-up heading to the 16th tee. Francis remarkably won the 16th and 17th, squaring the match. On the 18th, Coe crushed his drive. It sailed through the air and then stopped abruptly when it lodged 30 feet above the fairway in the branches of one of the two infamous pines. Invoking an unplayable lie penalty, he hit again and from the fairway hooked into the surf. He conceded the match, sending Francis to the fourth round with a 1-up victory.

Charlie Smith narrowly escaped defeat at the hands of crowd favorite Ernie Pieper. Pieper was 1-up on the 18th tee but put his drive in the ocean. The 1-stroke penalty cost him the hole and squared the match. Smith secured his victory on the 20th hole. The last morning blow to local fans came at the hands of H. Dudley Wysong, who defeated Harvie Ward, the popular 35-year-old auto dealer from San Francisco. Ward was playing near flawless golf, having neither lost a hole nor made a bogey in the first two rounds. In his third round, he was still bogeyless through eight yet down-1 to the young Texan. A bogey on 9 put Ward down-2. Ward's three-putt on 10, followed by a bogey on 12, put him down-4. Halves on the next three holes were not enough, and Wysong posted a 4&3 win.

Golf writers were starting to narrow the field of favorites, taking special note of Jack Nicklaus, who finished off William Edwards of Garden City, New York, 5&4.

In the afternoon matches, more of the Walker Cup stars went down to defeat. Only three survived: Ireland's Joe Carr, North Carolina's Charlie Smith, and Ohio's Jack Nicklaus. Carr and Nicklaus each won their afternoon matches 2&1. Smith's match went to sudden-death against Iowa's John Spray. On the first extra hole, Spray pushed his tee shot right, nicked a branch, and watched it bounce out of bounds, costing him the match.

In the first of eight matches on Day 4, Wysong continued his strong play with a 4&3 defeat of Edwin Hopkins, a 36-year old Texas oilman playing in his sixth U.S. Amateur. In the second match, two Oklahoma golfers teed off, with geologist Richard Norville getting the better of Gene Fowler with a 2-up win.

Joe Carr was dead even with Charles Courtney through five holes and won the next four holes. Carr lost the 10th but won 11 and 12 to go 5-up with only six holes left to play. Courtney then lit up the crowd by winning hole 13 with a par and holes 14, 15, and 16 with three straight birdies to pull within one. But it was not enough; Carr won the 17th to close out the match at 2&1.

Nicklaus had a tough round against the considerably older John Humm of New York. After five holes, Humm was 2-up. Nicklaus won the 9th to cut the lead to 1-up and proceeded to put on a long-drive exhibition that eventually brought him a 3&1 victory. Charlie Smith also put away Manhattan attorney Marvin Olshan 3&1, sending all three remaining Cuppers into the final eight.

Gene Francis won an upset victory over Charlie Coe when Coe's
tee shot on 18 lodged in a fairway tree and he had to take an
unplayable lie. (PBC-Graham/Brooks)

Wysong went into the afternoon well rested and made short work of
Richard Norville 6&5. The afternoon upset came when Marion "Sonny"
Methvin, a 21-year-old junior from Louisiana State University playing
in his first National Amateur, knocked out Charlie Smith 5&4. Sonny
was 1-up after 9 and then jumped ahead with solid pars on 10, 11, and
12, while Smith continually missed the greens. The 1960 Arkansas State
Champion was probably more surprised than anyone. The prospect of
taking on Jack Nicklaus in the semifinals was a real cause for concern, "I'll
have to play real good to beat him," Methvin opined.

Nicklaus earned a berth in the semifinals by defeating Indiana's Sam
Carmichael, 4&3. Joe Carr succeeded in the tightest of the quarterfinal
matches. Carr and 23-year-old Gene Francis of New York reached the
18th tee all square. Both players hit good drives, but Francis hooked his
second shot into the ocean—an unrecoverable error. Carr's 1-up victory
sent him to the semifinals to face H. Dudley Wysong.

With four golfers left, the matches were extended to 36 holes. The
experts were looking ahead to an international final between Nicklaus and
Carr, the last of the two Walker Cup representatives. Carr was hoping
to become the first foreign competitor to win the U.S. Amateur since C.
Ross "Sandy" Sommerville of Canada defeated Johnny Goodman in the
1932 finals at Baltimore Country Club.

Nicklaus and Methvin teed off first. Methvin knew he was out-
matched, and the toll on his nerves was obvious. On the first hole,
Nicklaus took the lead with a par. Methvin failed to reach a green
in regulation until the par-3 5th. By the end of the morning round,
Nicklaus had completed the first 18 in 71 strokes and was leading by
7-up. Methvin was much more composed in the afternoon, but the
damage was already done. Methvin made par on the next 10 holes, but
with two birdies over the same distance, Nicklaus closed out the match
by winning 9&8.

H. Dudley Wysong of Texas surprised nearly everyone but Byron Nelson, who had mentored the young golfer. Wysong captured everyone's attention when he defeated E. Harvie Ward in the third round. (PBC-Graham/Brooks)

Joe Carr watches as Charles Courtney blasts it onto the 5th green. At this point, the match was all square. (PBC-Graham/Brooks)

Among the more severe side-hill lies, Jack Nicklaus plays from the cliff with his faithful caddie Dede Gonsalves standing nearby. (PBC-Graham/Brooks)

A highlight of Wysong's fifth-round match against Norville was his remarkable play on the 8th hole. His tee shot went left, hit the hardpan, and scooted down the hill into the 6th fairway. From there he hit a 4 wood back to 8, within 25 feet of the pin, winning the hole. (PBC-Graham/Brooks)

"Sonny" Methvin of Louisiana had won the 1960 Arkansas State Amateur, but he knew he would have a tough semifinal match against Jack Nicklaus. (PBC-Graham/Brooks)

Nicklaus and the caddies watch from the fairway while Methvin hits out of the large bunker on 6. (PBC-Graham/Brooks)

Wysong was 2-up through 34 holes in his semifinal match with Joe Carr. Finding the bunker on 17 cost him the hole. (PBC-Graham/Brooks)

In the fog, with a must win 18th hole, Joe Carr hit long and was forced to seek a miracle shot off the rocks beneath the 18th green. (Chuck Brenkus)

Nicklaus hits his third shot out of the greenside bunker on the par-5 second hole to set up a birdie for the lead in the final match. (PBC-Graham/Brooks)

Nicklaus chips onto the 8th in the afternoon but loses the hole with a bogey to drop back to 6-up with 10 to play. He closed out the match 8&6 on the 12th. (PBC-Graham/Brooks)

In the other match, Joe Carr's unsteady play in the morning round was very uncharacteristic of the golf he had been playing up until that time. Shooting 80 to Wysong's 73 allowed Wysong an advantage of 5-up as they broke for lunch. Carr came back strong in the afternoon and steadily whittled away at Wysong's lead. They reached the 17th tee with Wysong 2-up with two holes to play. Carr needed to win both holes to force a playoff. Carr put his tee shot safely on the green; Wysong's found the large greenside bunker. He blasted out onto the green but still needed two putts, allowing Carr to win the hole with a par.

They reached the 18th tee, the 36th hole of the match. Both players hit good drives and followed with strong second shots. Carr needed to land his next shot close enough for a birdie and hope Wysong could do no better than par. He carefully selected the club he wanted, settled into his swing, and watched as his ball lofted up and then over the green and onto the rocks below. Wysong put his shot safely on the green.

Carr climbed down to the rocks. He had a shot if he could pluck it clean off the hard surface. The ball sharply sailed up over the rocks, but instead of finding the green it found a bunker. Carr blasted out to the green but was already laying five. He conceded the hole and match to Wysong who took the 2-up win into the finals.

H. Dudley Wysong had defied the odds, climbing over a two-time U.S Amateur Champion and two Walker Cup stars, including a three-time British Amateur Champion, to reach the finals of the 1961 U.S. Amateur. Nicklaus was the clear favorite, but Wysong was not put off by being

the underdog one more time. Nicklaus took the lead with a birdie on 2 and added to his lead with birdies on 4 and 7. Wysong went out in the morning round playing errorless golf and was down-3. Nicklaus just missed a 60-foot birdie putt on 9, or it would have been worse. Wysong quickly understood that Nicklaus was not going to make mistakes. To have a chance, Wysong was going to have to make something happen.

After halving the 10th hole, Wysong scored the first bogey of the match allowing Nicklaus go 4-up on the 11th. Nicklaus gave one back with his own bogey on 13 when his bunker shot flew over the green. Both golfers reached the large frontal bunker on the 14th hole. Wysong's third shot bounced over the green, while Nicklaus' landed softly 10 feet from the cup. Wysong conceded the birdie when his chip landed short of the green. On 15, Nicklaus again found a bunker, and his sand wedge left him a 12-foot putt, which he missed, allowing Wysong to pull back within three. Wysong went down-4 on 17 when Nicklaus converted on a sand-save and Wysong failed to do the same. They finished the morning round by playing the 18th in regulation. It is interesting to note this was only the second time in the entire competition that Nicklaus had played the 18th. The only other time was the day before in the initial 18 against Methvin. None of Nicklaus' 18-hole matches had gone the distance.

Despite two bogeys, Nicklaus' 33-36—69 in match play was exceptional; add the pressure of it being the final round of the U.S. Amateur and the performance defied belief. Wysong had played strong but not strong enough to win against the exhibition of Nicklaus.

(left) Jack Nicklaus holds his trophies for winning the 1961 U.S. Amateur at Pebble Beach. (PBC-Graham/Brooks)

(above) S.F.B. Morse and USGA president John G. Clock congratulate the 1961 winner Jack Nicklaus and runner-up H. Dudley Wysong. (PBC-Graham/Brooks)

In the afternoon Nicklaus won the first four holes with birdies on 1, 2, and 4. They reached the 5th tee with Nicklaus 8-up. Wysong got back one with a birdie on 7, and they traded bogey losses on 8 and 9. Nicklaus posted another bogey on 10 but then birdied the 11th. Wysong was dormie, down-7 with seven holes to play.

On the par-3 12th, both players again found the bunker. Wysong blasted out, leaving a 20-foot putt, and Nicklaus caressed his to within 6 feet. Wysong knew he had to sink the putt. A half on the hole would still give the match to Nicklaus. He gave it a good ride—it tracked on line but stopped just short of falling. Wysong turned to Nicklaus and conceded his par putt and the match. Nicklaus posted an impressive 8&6 victory.

Impressive is a word that underscores the overall performance of Jack W. Nicklaus of Ohio. In seven matches he played a total of 136 holes—26 less than scheduled. Nicklaus played these holes in 20-under-par with 34 birdies and one eagle against just 16 bogeys. "Playing by the book," Nicklaus' reliance on his annotated notes for each hole, certainly worked for the champion, but he also had a good luck charm with him. His caddie for the championship was Al "Dede" Gonzalves, the same caddie who carried Harrison Johnston's clubs to victory at Pebble Beach in 1929.

7TH U.S. SENIOR WOMEN'S AMATEUR

The U.S Senior Women's Amateur was first played in 1962 and, like the Girls' Junior and Men's Senior, visited Pebble Beach and competed at the Monterey Peninsula Country Club in its first few years of existence. Unlike the other Amateur championships, the Senior Women's was 54 holes of stroke play rather than match play. In its first six years, two dominant players each had two wins and each had been a runner-up: Maureen Orcutt (winner in 1962 and 1966) and Loma Smith (winner in 1964 and 1965). Marge Mason was the defending champion coming into Pebble Beach, having won in Atlantic City in 1967; Smith was her runner-up. Loma Smith happened to be a member of Monterey Peninsula Country Club and a heavy favorite to win a third time. Smith, age 55, had been born Loma Moulton in Pasadena and had been a top tennis and badminton player—four times winning the national championship in badminton. She started playing golf after marrying Hulet Smith in 1941. The pair moved to Pebble Beach in 1962.

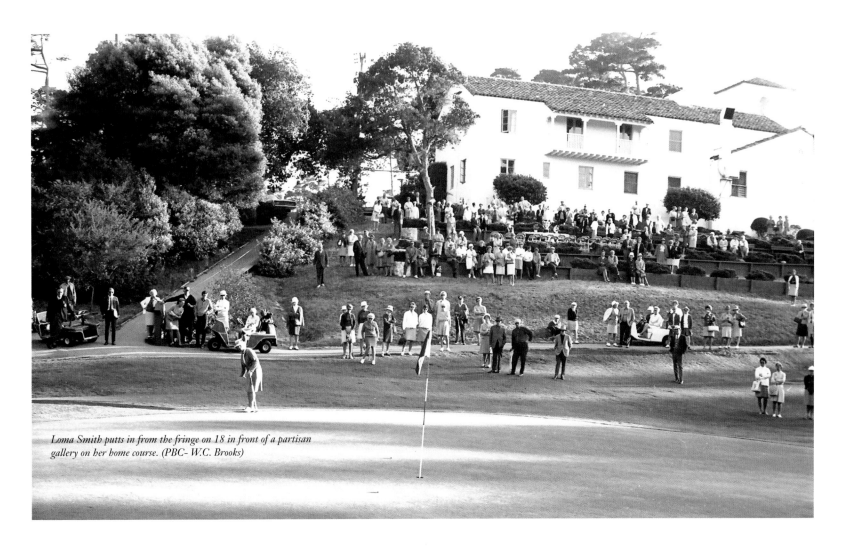

Loma Smith putts in from the fringe on 18 in front of a partisan gallery on her home course. (PBC- W.C. Brooks)

Marge Mason entered to defend her title, but with an opening 87 she was well back in the competition of 120 women. Maureen Orcutt was also on-hand to compete with Smith to become the tournament's first three-time winner. Orcutt opened with an 84, tying for seventh place. Smith's 82 put her in a three-way tie for second place, while tournament newcomer Carolyn Cudone was alone in first with an 80. Cudone was less than a month into her 50th year and newly eligible to compete in the Senior class, but she was quite familiar with championship golf. She had previously played in seven U.S. Women's Amateurs, three times reaching the quarterfinals and losing on the 19th hole to Polly Riley in the 1953 semifinals. The New Jersey native was also a five-time winner of the Women's Metropolitan Golf Association Championship (1955, '61, '63, '64, and '65) and a five-time New Jersey State Champion (1955, '56, '59, '60, and '63).

Both Cudone and Smith shot 79s in the second round and began to move away from the rest of the field; Cudone buried the field with a 77 in the final round for a 236 total. Smith closed with an 85 and still finished as runner-up, 10 strokes back. Defending champion Marge Mason closed with a pair of 80s at 247 to finish third, a stroke behind Smith.

Two-time Senior Champion Loma Smith (left) finished as runner-up in the 1968 U.S. Senior Women's Amateur to winner Carolyn Cudone, who claimed her first of five straight Senior Amateur championships at MPCC. (W.C. Brooks)

While neither Smith nor Orcutt ever officially got their third win, the Women's Senior also has Class winners and Smith won Class B (age 55-59), and Orcutt won Class C (age 60 and over). Furthermore, there was an official three-time future winner in the field. Cudone went on to win not only three but five straight Seniors titles between 1968 and 1972. Cudone stayed competitive and finished as the runner-up in 1974 and 1975.

15TH U.S. SENIOR WOMEN'S AMATEUR

The Women's Senior returned to Pebble Beach in 1976, and Cudone was again among the competitors, as was Loma Smith. Shooting a par-75 to take the first-round lead was San Rafel, California's Carol (Mrs. Lyle) Bowman, the 1952 Trans-Mississippi Champion and a veteran of three Women's Amateurs in the early 1950s. She balanced three bogeys against three birdies on the front nine for her 38-37—75. In second with a 78 was the newly senior Cecile (or "Ceil") Maclaurin of Savanah, Georgia, playing in her first Senior Women's Amateur just weeks shy of her 51st birthday. Maclaurin was one of Georgia's top women golfers, winning the Georgia State Championship 11 times—Match Play Championship (1952, '64, '65, and '70), Stroke Play Championship (1965, '68, '69, '72, '73, '74, and '75). Maclaurin's round was marred by a triple-bogey on the 7th hole at MPCC.

In the second round, Maclaurin shot the par score, and Bowman fell back into second place with an 80, 2 strokes back. Two strokes behind her in third place was Nancy (Mrs. I. Wayne) Rutter (80-77—157) of Williamsville, New York. Rutter had twice before finished as runner-up in this event (1972, '73), had been a medalist in the 1961 New York State Championship, and had won the New York State Women's Senior Amateur in 1972. The rest of the field of 120 golfers were significantly further back and led by Carolyn Cudone in fourth place at 81-81—162.

Maclaurin shot a third round 77 to win the championship by 7 strokes as Bowman finished with an 82 and Rutter an 81. Cudone won Class B (age 55-59) by 2 strokes over Helen Sigel Wilson, the runner-up in the 1948 U.S. Women's Amateur held at Pebble Beach. In Class C (over 60), MPCC's Loma Smith came in first (14th overall) at 83-91-81—255. The week before the USGA tournament, Smith captured the Club Championship for the eighth time.

In 1997, the U.S. Senior Women's Amateur was altered to become a match-play event like the USGA's other amateur championships.

(right) Cecile Maclaurin won the 1976 Women's Senior. (USGA)

The Walker Cup was presented by former USGA President George Herbert Walker to encourage gentlemanly international competition following World War I. (PBC-Archives)

THE 1981 WALKER CUP MATCHES

International team championships began in 1919 (the same year Pebble Beach opened for play) when a U.S. team went to Canada and won. Two years later, to encourage amateur competition between the United States and Britain, the USGA sent a team to Hoylake for the British Amateur and had an informal event, which the U.S. also won. The next year, the Brits accepted an invitation to a more formal team event played on the National Golf Links at Southampton, New York. The trophy was supplied by George Herbert Walker, an avid amateur golfer from St. Louis. Coincidentally, his daughter, Dorothy, married U.S. Senator Prescott Bush on August 6, 1921, in Kennebunkport, Maine. Bush later became president of the USGA. Their second son, George Herbert Walker Bush, would become the 41st president of the United States and an avid amateur golfer himself—but that's another story.

The first Walker Cup Match was played on August 28–29, 1922, and was won by a U.S. team that included Bobby Jones, Francis Ouimet, and Chick Evans. It was held annually for three years and bi annually thereafter, alternating between courses in the United States and Great Britain. The USGA selects the U.S. team, and the Royal and Ancient Golf Club of St. Andrews selects the team that is open to golfers from Great Britain (England, Scotland, Wales, and Northern Ireland) and Ireland.

The star of the U.S. Team in 1981 was 23-year-old Hal Sutton, the 1980 U.S. Amateur champion. To win the Amateur crown, he defeated teammates Jodie Mudd (age 21) in the quarterfinals, Jim Holtgrieve (age 33) in

(left) After a strong start, the team of Hal Sutton (shown here) and Jay Sigel found trouble and lost their opening match—the only USA loss in the morning. (courtesy Cypress Point Club) (above) GBI Captain Rodney Foster (right) greets US Captain James Gabrielsen. (courtesy Cypress Point Club)

the semifinals, and Bob Lewis Jr., (age 37) in the final match. With the exception of Mudd, the other three were teammates for the 1979 Walker Cup as was the other star of the 1981 team, 37-year-old Jay Sigel, the 1979 British Amateur champion. Lewis defeated Sigel in the 1980 U.S. amateur quarterfinal and teammate Dick von Tacky (age 24), the Northeast Amateur champion, in the semifinals. Joey Rassett (age 23) had finished second to von Tacky in the Northeast Amateur and was low amateur in the 1981 U.S. Open. Frank Fuhrer III (age 22), Ron Commans (age 22), and Corey Pavin (age 21) rounded out the U.S. Team, captained by James Gabrielsen, a member of the 1971 team.

At age 39, Ian Colin Hutcheon was the "old man" of the visiting team—a veteran of the last three Walker Cup teams and a three-time champion of the Scottish Open Stroke Play Championship. Geoffrey Frank Godwin (age 30) also played on the 1979 team, as did Peter McEvoy (age 28), the British Amateur Champion in 1977 and 1978, and Peter George Dibble (age 27), the English Amateur Champion in 1976 and 1980. The younger team members included Duncan Evans (age 22), the 1980 British Amateur champion; Roger Michael Chapman (age 22), the 1979 English Amateur champion; Colin Dalgleish (age 20), the 1980 Belgian Junior champion; Philip Walton (age 19), the Spanish Amateur champion; Paul Graham Way (age 18), the 1981 English Stroke Play champion; and Ronan Patrick Rafferty (age 17),

the Irish Amateur champion. The captain was Rodney Foster, a veteran of five Walker Cup teams.

The United States had not lost since 1971, and it appeared that the visitors had their hopes pinned to the youth. The format was four 18-hole Scotch (alternate-shot) foursomes in the morning and eight 18-hole singles matches in the afternoon for each of two days. A win was worth a point, and a tie earned one-half point.

In the opening match, Foster put up two of his youngsters, Walton and Rafferty, against the star U.S. pairing of Sutton and Sigel. The Americans were 3-up in the first three holes, and the Captain's strategy seemed faulty. But then the kids got hot and took nine of the next 11 holes, finishing off the Americans 4&2 when Rafferty chipped in for a birdie on the par-3 16th hole after Walton had done the same on the 15th. That win was their only good news of the morning as the Americans won the other three matches.

Sutton took his revenge on Rafferty in the afternoon but not without a fight. Sutton needed six birdies through 17 holes to defeat the teenager 3&1. American youth barely won in another match when Jodie Mudd, who had five birdies on the first nine holes, needed to sink a 12-foot putt for par on 18 to win 1-up over Godwin of England. Walton of Ireland took a 3-up lead over Commans on the 9th hole of the third match, showing a deft touch around the greens. But things tightened up, and Commans pulled to within one by the 18th hole. A remarkable save from behind some trees in the fairway left Commans with a 15-foot putt for birdie. He missed by inches for a conceded par. Walton needed to sink a 3-foot, pressure-filled putt for par to win the match. He did. Walton and Pavin, who defeated Ian Hutcheon 4&3 in the afternoon, were the only golfers to record two wins on Day 1. Still the Americans dominated, winning five of the singles matches to take an 8-4 lead in the match.

(left) Ron Commans celebrates as his chip on the final hole drops, winning the hole and securing a half in his final match. (courtesy Cypress Point Club) (above) The US team hoists the Walker Cup in celebration of a 15-9 team victory (l-r) Jim Holtgrieve, Jodie Mudd*, Joe Rassett, Hal Sutton*, Bob Lewis, Ron Commans (kneeling), Frank Fuhrer*, Corey Pavin, Dick Von Tackey, Jay Sigel and James Gabrielsen. (courtesy Cypress Point Club) * behind others

DAY 2

Captain Gabrielsen left three of his four teams intact, but Foster switched his around, keeping only Rafferty and Walton together. Foster's strategy worked with the visitors taking three of the four morning matches and bringing the overall score to a very competitive U.S. 9, GBI 7. Only the new U.S. pairing of Rassett and Mudd was successful, defeating Hutcheon and Godwin 5&4.

It all came down to the singles matches. Foster put his strongest players in the early rounds, hoping to get some momentum going for the team. But what he didn't know was that the honorary captain of the U.S. team, Jack Westland, had a discussion with Jay Sigel on the putting green. Westland, a former U.S. Representative from Washington, had won the 1952 U.S. Open and played on the Walker Cup teams of 1932, 1935, and 1952. Westland had retired to Pebble Beach after leaving Congress. He saw Sigel was frustrated by his morning loss. "I've watched you," Westland said. "You've got all the shots. Just hit them." It was the inspiration Sigel needed. He shared it with the team. While the early matches battled it out, Sigel went out, hit his shots, scored six birdies, and ended his match against Paul Way 6&5. Jodie Mudd, in the match following Sigel, played just as inspired

and with five birdies and an eagle defeated Colin Dalgleish 7&5. The momentum had shifted for the Americans. They led 11-7 and needed only one more win to retain the cup. Joey Rassett, with five birdies in his match against Peter Deeble, looked like he would provide that win, but his 4&3 victory was just icing as the early rounds started to end. Frank Fuhrer defeated Philip Walton 4&2, while Jim Holtgrieve finished off Ronan Rafferty 2&1. The only GBI win of the afternoon was the first match, which went 18 holes before Chapman recorded a 1-up victory over Hal Sutton.

The final two matches—Pavin vs. Evans and Commans vs. Godwin— were halved, but not without a little gutting-it-out magic by Commans. Godwin was 2-up with two to play. Commans won the 17th with a bogey. On the par-4 18th, Godwin was on in regulation, while Commans' shot had landed short in heavy rough with a horrible lie. His only shot was to try and pop it out with a sand wedge and hope for the best. The ball landed on the green and rolled through half of the green before finding the bottom of the cup for a birdie to win the hole and halve the match.

On paper it was just one more win for the U.S., who now led 25-2-1 in 28 contests, but for those involved it was as memorable as they come.

THE 1999 U.S. AMATEUR

The United States Amateur had not come to Pebble Beach since 1961, when it was won by Jack Nicklaus. Dreams of future stardom danced in the eyes of the record 7,920 golfers who entered regional qualifying for the U.S. Amateur at Pebble Beach. It had been scheduled to return in 1994 but was delayed due to ownership changes at Pebble Beach. Probably no one person was more impacted by that change than Tiger Woods with his Jack Nicklaus checklist. Nicklaus had won the U.S. Amateur and the U.S. Open at Pebble Beach—the only golfer to win both on the same course. Woods entered his first U.S. Amateur in 1994, and instead of Pebble Beach, he won it at the TPC Sawgrass; he won it again in 1995 and 1996 and then turned professional. Woods would not have the opportunity to play the U.S. Amateur at Pebble Beach, but 312 other amateurs—young and old—would. The large initial field was made possible by the decision to allow medal rounds to be split over two courses—156 golfers on Pebble Beach Golf Links and 156 on Spyglass Hill Golf Course on Monday, with the fields shifting on Tuesday. Only the low 64 would continue to match play on Wednesday.

Among the leaders after the first round was pre-tournament favorite Matt Kuchar with a 73 at Spyglass Hill, just 3 strokes off the lead held by Justin Bolli of Roswell, Georgia. Kuchar had won the 1997 U.S. Amateur—the first one in four years that didn't have Tiger Woods. That win earned him an invitation to the 1998 Masters where he finished 21st. Kutchar also reached the quarterfinals in the 1998 U.S. Amateur before losing to Sergio Garcia. To everyone's surprise, in 1999 Kuchar shot an 81 at Pebble Beach on Day 2 and missed the cut. Also missing the cut was Tom McKnight, the 1998 U.S. Amateur runner-up who defeated Garcia before falling to Hank Kuehne. Kuehne turned pro and was not defending his title. Other surprise cuts came with Hunter Mahan,

the 1999 U.S. Junior Champion, (74-79—153) and Landry Mahan, a 1998 U.S. Amateur quarterfinalist (75-80—155). Relatively unknown at the time and gathering little news for missing the cut was a 17-year-old visitor for Medellin, Columbia, Camilo Villegas (78-86—164); and a future U.S. Open Champion, Lucas Glover (77-79—165), then a Sophmore at Clemson.

Gene Elliott of West Des Moines, Iowa, won the medal rounds with a solid 71-72—143. Fifty-seven players shot 151 or better. First-round leader Justin Bolli ballooned to an 81 on Pebble Beach but still made the cut. The higher scores on Pebble Beach Golf Links attest to the challenge of the USGA par-71 setup. Seven spots remained for the 17 players who shot 152. Ten players lost in a playoff before the matches could begin. Medalist Elliott went out in the first round to Jason Martin, one of the seven players who survived the playoff. Martin won 2-up. Three of the playoff survivors won upset victories. Canada's David Hearn beat Matthew Jones in 19 holes; Jones had finished second in qualifying. John Pate of Santa Barbara defeated Australia's Adam Scott 2&1. Scott finished tied for third in qualifying and has gone on to become one of the top-ranked golfers in the world, claiming his first professional title in January 2001—the Alfred Dunhill Championship.

The other two golfers who tied for third in qualifying won their first-round matches against the playoff survivors and met in the quarterfinals. They were Andrew Sanders of Merritt Island, Florida, and Ben Curtis of Kent, Ohio. Curtis, who had won the 1999 Ohio Amateur, was one of the strongest golfers in the field and reached the semifinals by defeating Sanders 7&6.

James Oh of Lakewood, California, who tied for sixth in qualifying, knocked out the other playoff survivor and continued to the quarterfinals. Oh faced 17-year-old Sung Yoon Kim of South Korea in the quarterfinals

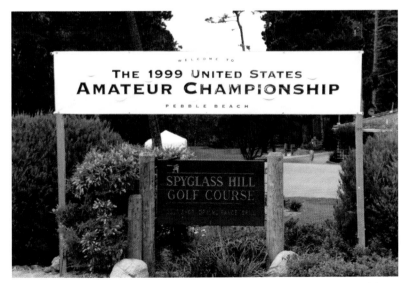

Spyglass Hill Golf Course shared the honors with Pebble Beach Golf Links by hosting medal rounds in a split field that had the 312 qualifiers playing 18 holes on each course to determine the cut for the 62 golfers that would continue to match play. (PBC-Archives)

Bryce Molder was the top-ranked college golfer in 1999 but pulled a tough bracket, needing 21 holes to secure his second match and then losing in 23 holes to James Oh of Lakewood, California, in round three. (PBC-C. Bush)

David Gossett's talent was focused by professional Tour caddie Andy Martinez to keep him winning— reaching the finals with a 2&1 victory over Ben Curtis, the Ohio Amateur Champion, who would go on to win the 2003 British Open. (PBC-Archives)

and had a tough battle before Kim won the match 2-up. Oh recently returned to Pebble Beach as a professional and finished tied for 39th in the 2009 AT&T Pebble Beach National Pro-Am.

In the other quarterfinal matches, David Gossett (age 20) of Tennessee, a sophomore at the University of Texas, defeated Virginia college senior James Driscoll of Brookline, Massachusetts, 4&3, and Hunter Haas (age 22), the 1999 U.S. Public Links Champion, defeated Charlie Woerner, a senior at the University of Southern California. The oldest semifinalist was 22—three college golfers and a high school student from South Korea would be playing for the national championship title.

The semifinal matches were played on Saturday under calm overcast skies. The USGA had measured the green speed at 11.5 (very fast), and with the setup, the slope rating was 155—as tough as it gets. First off the tee were David Gossett and Ben Curtis. Gossett jumped to an early lead winning the first two holes, but Curtis won the next two to square the match, and they halved the 5th. Gossett won the 6th and Curtis the 7th to again square the match. On 8, Curtis drove right, hitting a marshal with his ball landing in the deep rough. He had to lay up short of the chasm. Both golfers then found the front right bunker—Gossett lying two, Curtis three. Curtis blasted out to within 12 feet and was putting uphill for bogey. Gossett had about a 25-foot curling putt for par. Gossett lagged within inches and Curtis conceded the bogey. Curtis' putt just missed, and Gossett went 1-up. Curtis found the rough off the tee at 9 and struggled to even reach the green in four. Gossett went 2-up.

They halved holes 10, 11, and 12, and Gossett went 3-up by sinking a tough 12-footer on 13. Gossett seemed to be steadied all the way by his caddie, Andy Martinez. Martinez was actually professional golfer Tom Lehman's caddy. Lehman introduced the two and they hit it off. Martinez was happy to caddy for Gossett at Pebble Beach. They not only had a good time together, but it gave Martinez a good chance to study the USGA setup first hand, knowing that would help while caddying for Lehman in the 2000 AT&T and U.S. Open.

Curtis' approach on 14 hit the green and bounced over into the chipping area behind the green. He scrambled for a par to halve the hole but was running out of time—down-3 with four holes to play. Curtis hit his approach shot on 15 to within a couple of feet of the pin, while Gossett took three to reach the green. Curtis putted for birdie to win the hole, but it lipped out. Gossett conceded the Curtis par and then made his own. Curtis had to win every remaining hole to keep the match alive.

Both found the fairway on 16, but Gossett's approach shot went left, just off the green, while Curtis hit it stiff. Gossett opted to putt from the rough, and the ball went well past the flag. When he missed the comebacker, he conceded the hole to Curtis. On 17, the pin was on the right of the hourglass green. Curtis again hit it stiff, leaving a short putt for birdie. Gossett also found the green but was about 15 feet away. He and Martinez studied the line, and when Gossett drained the putt, it ended the match with a 2&1 victory.

In the other match, Hunter Haas was the clear favorite. Through an interpreter, Sung Yoon Kim, the South Korean Amateur champion, explained he had hoped to reach the quarterfinals and was amazed to find himself in the semifinals. He actually had a plane ticket back to South Korea on Sunday. The pair were even through 3, and Haas took 4 with a birdie. Kim took it back with a birdie on 5, and Haas was again 1-up with a birdie on 6. They halved 7 with pars, and on 8 they each found the right front bunker. Haas blasted out to within a couple of feet. Kim barely got it out and was still off the green. He chipped on softly but was still away. When he missed his putt for bogey, he conceded the hole to Haas, who went 2-up.

Haas found the rough off the tee on 9, his second shot was still short. He chipped on but missed his putt for par. Kim made his par, and then followed it up with a birdie on 10 to square the match. They both bogeyed 11. Haas blocked his tee shot and hit the right front bunker on 12. Kim hit his softly to the front and watched his ball trickle onto the green. Haas punched out to about 6 feet and conceded Kim's par after Kim lagged his 35-foot second stroke to within 2 feet. Haas lined up his putt but missed. Kim went 1-up. Haas hit his drive on 13 left of the long fairway bunker and lost another hole. Kim hit a beautiful shot into the 14th green. Haas hit the firm green and bounced into deep rough. He chipped on, barely, and made a clutch putt for par. It was for naught as Kim sunk his putt for birdie to go 3-up.

Kim hit a huge drive on 15, leaving a pitching wedge into the green, and the ball spun just off the green. Haas' approach went just left of the green. He chipped on but stopped short of the pin. Kim putted from off the green and missed his birdie by inches. Haas conceded the par, perhaps expecting the same. When he putted out and missed, the match went to Kim 4-up with three to play. Sung Yoon Kim was going to need to change his flight plans.

Sung Yoon Kim and David Gossett met on the 1st tee under sunny skies and ideal conditions for a 36-hole final match. One low-lying cloud bank shrouded Arrowhead Point in fog, while the rest of the course was bathed in sunshine. Kim was not playing nearly as well as he had the day before against Haas, while Gossett's steady play got him off to an early lead—going 6-up through the first nine holes, despite an eight-minute weather delay on hole 8 waiting for the fog to clear. Kim got one back with a long birdie on the 11th hole. On 17, Kim was long left in the deep rough and likely had brief visions of Watson's chip-in from 1982. He went down-6 with a bogey. On 18, Kim crushed his drive and went for the green in two. He had the distance and landed in the bunker between the green and the seawall. He chipped on and narrowly missed his long birdie putt. It was enough to win the hole as Gossett took four to reach the green, and could not convert. The morning round ended with Gossett in a commanding 5-up lead.

In the afternoon, Gossett acted as if he were anxious to end the match quickly. He won the 1st, 2nd, and 4th holes with birdie-par-birdie to go 8-up. Bunker trouble cost Gossett the 5th hole. After halving the 6th in fog, Kim found the left bunker and took 2 strokes to reach the 7th green before conceding the hole. Gossett landed his tee shot 3 feet from the pin. A birdie on 8 for Gossett gave him a 9-up lead, and halves on holes 9 and 10 ended the match with a score of 9-up with eight holes to play.

David Gossett, officially of Germantown, Tennessee, was headed to the University of Texas in 1999 and proudly displayed the "horns" symbol while parading his trophy. (PBC-Archives)

Championship Director RJ Harper surveyed the competition from his golf car and gives his smile of approval. (PBC-C. Bush)

(left) In 1972, Harold Firstman, then the golf professional at Laguna Seca, launched the invitational pro-am now known as the Callaway Golf Pebble Beach Invitational. (courtesy Harold Firstman) (right) Bobby Clampett, who grew up on the Monterey Peninsula, won the Invitational in 1980 while still an amateur. A few months later he won his second California Amateur Championship; Nicklaus (1972), Clampett (1980) and Tiger Woods (2000) are the only golfers to record two victories on Pebble Beach Golf Links in the same year. (courtesy Harold Firstman)

THE CALLAWAY GOLF PEBBLE BEACH INVITATIONAL (1972–)

The Pebble Beach Invitational is truly one of the most unique tournaments in golf. As a post-season golf event, it is not sanctioned by any of the professional tours, yet it annually attracts golfers from each of the tours and it is the one event where members of the PGA, LPGA, Champions, and several of the mini-tours compete head to head.

However, it is not strictly a professional event; it is also a team pro-am. Four-person amateur teams record the two best balls on each hole to determine the team score. But each day, the team plays with a different pro, and the pro's score can count as one of the team scores. Each day, the pros and teams also play on a different course, with those pros and teams making the cut playing a final round over Pebble Beach Golf Links.

In general, the format has remained constant since the event first began in December 1972, but prior to 1993, the championship saw several variations in the courses used and in the name provided by the title sponsor. Since 1993, the Pebble Beach Invitational has consistently played a three-course rotation each November over Pebble Beach Golf Links, Spyglass Hill Golf Course, and Del Monte Golf Course, with the fourth and final round over Pebble Beach Golf Links. Callaway Golf has been the title sponsor since 1997.

The tournament was the creation of Harold Firstman, then the golf professional at Laguna Seca Golf Ranch, a Robert Trent Jones (Sr. and Jr.)–designed golf course between Monterey and Salinas that was opened in 1970. Firstman was good friends with Bill Henry, the course professional who took over at Del Monte when Nick Lombardo left for his other courses. The new Monterey Hyatt House that had opened on Del Monte Golf Course signed on as an initial sponsor, and the tournament was born as the "Laguna Seca–Del Monte Hyatt Pro-Am."

The first tournament was won by Rafe Botts (70-67-71-71—279) by 2 strokes over Jim Wiechers and 3 over John Jacobs. Botts was 23 years old when he joined the PGA Tour in 1961 and was the second black golfer to do so; Charlie Sifford was the first. Winless on the Tour, Botts was still winning off the Tour and playing well. A month before playing at Del Monte, he finished second in the $12,500 Gardena Valley Open. After winning at Del Monte in December 1972, he won the Southern California Professional Match Play Championship in July 1973.

The short-lived Confidence golf equipment company was the sponsor in years two and three, and Lynx golf equipment sponsored the tournament for the fourth year when it was played in January and went to a three-course rotation for the first time—using Laguna Seca, Corral de Tierra, and Rancho Cañada—all inland courses off the peninsula.

For the fifth year, Spalding became the sponsor. The tournament moved back to December and Bayonet, the top course at nearby Fort Ord, replaced Corral de Tierra. This was also the first year that LPGA golfers were included in the field. The event continued as the Spalding for the next several years, and the courses continued to shift. Spyglass Hill Golf Course was used for the first time in the seventh year, December 1978, and Pebble Beach was first used the next year, but not for the rotation, only for the final round for those making the cut.

For the 8th Annual Invitational Pro-Am, Firstman invited 1979 Amateur of the Year Bobby Clampett to play in one of the professional spots. Clampett, a student at Brigham Young University, accepted and played in a professional spot as an amateur. After shooting sub-par rounds at Corral de Tierra and Del Monte Golf Course, Clampett jumped into the lead after 54 holes when he shot a course record 65 at Spyglass Hill Golf Course, birdying the last four holes. As he teed off in the final round at Pebble Beach, excited to be leading in his first professional tournament, he hooked his first shot out-of-bounds and quickly lost his lead. Composing himself, he played well for the rest of the round, finishing with a 71—272, and beating professional Mike Reid by a single stroke for the championship. Clampett was very content to accept the trophy and let Reid take the $22,500 first-place money. Among the LPGA stars playing that year, the top lady was the very popular Jan Stephenson, who finished at 297.

For the 10th Championship, Pebble Beach Golf Links joined the rotation along with Del Monte Golf Course, Corral de Tierra, and the new Carmel Valley course at Quail Lodge. They played a four-course rotation before making the cut for a fifth round at Pebble Beach. Jay Haas won the marathon 90-hole event with a 22-under-par 337, and only Bobby Clampett could make it a contest. Haas started the final round at Pebble Beach with a 2-stroke lead and worked it to 6 strokes after nine holes. A hard-driving Clampett pulled it back to near even, but Haas birdied holes 14, 15, and 17 to close out with a 69 and a 3-stroke victory. No one else was even close.

That was the only year the tournament played 90 holes. Corral de Tierra was dropped, keeping Pebble Beach, Del Monte, and Quail Lodge in

(left) Australian Jan Stephenson, winner of three majors in the early 1980s, and equally known for her sex-appeal, played in several Invitationals, seen here in 1986 with Nathaniel Crosby, another regular during his professional career. (courtesy Harold Firstman)

In 1990 Juli Inkster became the first woman to win the multi-tour competition known as the Callaway Golf Pebble Beach Invitational. (PBC-Archives)

the rotation for the next four years—a run that saw British star Peter Oosterhuis win twice (1982 and 1984) and Oostie's Ryder Cup opponent Johnny Miller win in 1983. The two competitive golfers went on to become competitive television analysts, Oosterhuis for CBS and Miller for NBC.

For the next three years (January 1987–89), Del Monte was replaced with the new Pete Dye–designed Carmel Valley Ranch, which was built on the old Ed Holt Ranch property previously owned by Pebble Beach Company. In January 1988, Jan Stephenson made the first serious showing for the LPGA. She was in the running the entire tournament, and missed a 6-foot putt on the final hole, finishing 1 stroke out of a playoff for the championship. Lennie Clements also missed a putt, his at 10 feet, on the final hole of regulation that would have given him the win. Instead he finished at 69—213, tying with Dan Pohl and allowing Ken Green and Tim Norris to make it a four-way tie when they made their clutch birdie putts on the final hole. The playoff began and ended on the 420-yard 15th hole at Carmel Valley Ranch when Clements snaked in a 35-footer for birdie.

The January 1989 championship replaced Pebble Beach with the Poppy Hills Golf Course, marking the first time since 1979 that Pebble Beach Golf Links was not in the rotation. Also missing in 1989 was the LPGA due to a scheduling conflict. The next winter, Firstman had trouble working anything out with the courses in the Monterey area, so he moved the tournament to Arizona utilizing three courses there. It was not a popular decision, and for December 1990, the event returned to the Monterey Peninsula. Firstman arranged a rotation foreshadowing the 1991 change in the AT&T rotation—Pebble Beach, Spyglass Hill, and Poppy Hills.

In the 1990 tournament, Howard Twitty held a 2-stroke lead over LPGA star Juli Inkster who, nine years earlier, had won the California Women's

Amateur at Pebble Beach. Twitty fell back, while Inkster fired a final round 71 to win the tournament with a 4-under-par 284, 1 stroke ahead of Mark Brooks. The $60,000 first-place money was the fourth largest payday of Inkster's seven-year career. It was the last year of the Spalding.

A few months before the 1990 championship, Pebble Beach was bought by Japanese businessman Minuro Isutani. Isutani actually first bought the Ben Hogan Company and used it to buy Pebble Beach Company. Hogan CEO David Heuber insisted that Spalding, a competitor of Hogan's, was not going to have another tournament on Pebble Beach as long as Hogan owned the company, so for 1991 (pushed to January 1992) the tournament became the Ben Hogan Pebble Beach Invitational. With 1992 U.S. Open excitement building, ABC decided to televise the tournament. Another Hogan connection was discovered when Firstman revealed that as a boy, he was cast as the young Ben Hogan in the movie *Follow the Sun*, which was partially filmed at Pebble Beach in 1953 and starred Glenn Ford as the adult Ben Hogan.

Galleries can get up close to the action at the Callaway Golf Pebble Beach Invitational. Nick Watney closes out his victory in 2005 from the front bunker on the 18th green while the gallery and fellow competitor Hunter Haas watch. (PBC-C. Bush)

Loren Roberts won the one and only Hogan, as two months later Isutani's financial empire crumbled and Hogan sold Pebble Beach to Taiheiyo Golf Clubs of Japan. Spalding, who felt unfairly jilted, declined to come back as a sponsor. Pebble Beach Company stepped in to help run the tournament without a sponsor, and when the January 1993 tournament was rain-shortened to 54 holes, the company decided to shift the event to November for future years. Poppy Hills was replaced by Del Monte and the November 1993 playing of the 22nd Pebble Beach Invitational set the standard for all future events.

Todd Fisher, age 22, took a 5-under-par 211 1-stroke lead into the final round of the 1993 Invitational. Bruce Fleisher, a 45-year-old club professional from Florida, was at 4 under, and Lauri Merten, U.S. Women's Open champion, was in the hunt at even par. In the final round, it was all up to the two leaders. Fleisher fell back 2 strokes when he bogeyed the 15th. Not giving up, he evened it up with a birdie on 16, while Fisher struggled to a bogey. They each parred the 17th and Fisher, who found the bunker off the 18th tee, struggled to save par and force a playoff from the 16th hole. Fleisher won when Fisher's putt for par lipped out.

In 1997, Callaway Golf signed on as the title sponsor, and with the future of the event in good hands, Firstman sold the tournament to Pebble Beach Company and began to phase out of active participation. In 1999, Annika Sorenstam made a great run, closing with a 69 for a second-place finish. Rocco Mediate bested her by a single stroke for the win. Other past champions include Tom Lehman, Mark Brooks, John Daly, and Nick Watney, but in 37 years there has been only one back-to-back winner, Tommy Armour III, who won in 2007 and 2008.

The Callaway Golf Pebble Beach Invitational continues to be one of the more popular weeks at Pebble Beach, with a waiting list of teams hoping to get into the tournament each year.

Many other amateur events are played each year at Pebble Beach. One of the newer events, begun in 2008, that is perhaps destined to become one of the great events is the Clay Walker Classic to benefit BAMS—Bands Against Multiple Sclerosis. The country music star, who has MS that for now is successfully being treated, hosts the event, which includes golf and music for the attendees and raises money to help fund needed research. ■

EXHIBITION GOLF

In the early days of the sport, golf exhibitions were designed to give players an opportunity to see professional-quality golf and develop interest in the game. One of the first exhibitions at Del Monte was the 1901 Open won by Willie Smith, the 1899 U.S. Open Champion who was visiting during the winter from Chicago. Walter Hagen made his first exhibition stop at Del Monte and Pebble Beach on his 1922 barnstorming world tour with Australian pro Joe Kirkwood. Hagen made another exhibition stop in 1938 when A.L. Watts filled in for Kirkwood and lost to the Puget brothers over 18 holes at Del Monte.

Four-time British Women's Amateur champion Joyce Wethered turned professional to make a world tour in 1935 that also included stops at Pebble Beach and Del Monte.

She arrived at Del Monte Lodge for a scheduled Sunday match on August 18, the day before the 1935 State Open. Paired with Willie Goggin, the Northern California Open champion, Wethered challenged Henry and Cam Puget in an 18-hole team match.

This was her first visit to Del Monte, but she had heard about it from many golfers in the East. A thousand spectators gathered for the match and watched as the slender Wethered held her own against the men while playing from the men's tees. The Puget brothers got off to a shaky start, losing two of the first four holes in the best ball match. On her own ball, Wethered went out in 39 strokes, and while the brothers made back one on the 9th, they headed home trailing by 1. On the back side, the course played tougher for the newcomer. She closed with a 43, giving her a total of 82. Her partner managed 77 for the round, which left enough room for the Pugets to close out with a 2&1 victory for the match with Henry besting his brother 75 to 76. They played out the 18th, which ranked as one of Wethered's favorite holes, and left her longing to come back for another match.

Officials invited her to play in the 1935 California Open, but her schedule did not allow it. She left Del Monte for another exhibition match but was back in Monterey six days later to face some younger competition. At Del Monte's No. 1 course, she paired with amateur Don Edwards, the Stanford star who finished second in the 1934 State Amateur, to challenge San Jose's Ernie Pieper Jr., and 15-year-old Clara Callender. Pieper carried the day with a 67 on the old course.

In the years after World War II, exhibitions became made-for-television events. In August 1959, Bing Crosby's brother, Bob, filmed some matches at Pebble Beach to sell a concept for a television series called *World Championship Golf*, pitting professional golfers in match-play competitions on different courses with larger paydays at each stage of the event. While they were not the first matches broadcast, the first matches filmed featured E.J. "Dutch" Harrison defeating Jack Fleck and Ken Venturi

Walter Hagen returned to Del Monte for a 1938 exhibition and partnered with A.L. Watts of the Calcutta Country Club. (PBC-J.P. Graham)

Joyce Wethered drives from the 11th tee in her August 1935 match at Pebble Beach. Of her swing Bobby Jones opined, "Miss Wethered has the finest swing of any golfer, male or female, I have ever seen." (PBC-J.P. Graham)

Gathering for an exhibition match at Pebble Beach, the local Puget brothers accepted a challenge from British Women's Amateur champion Joyce Wethered and Willie Goggin, refereed by Peter Hay (left to right): Hay, Wethered, Henry and Cam Puget, and Goggin. (PBC-J.P. Graham)

Youthful amateurs Ernie Pieper and Clara Callender study the putting stroke of Joyce Wethered on the practice green at Del Monte Golf Course. (PBC-J.P. Graham)

Filming World Championship Golf *action on the 14th green at Pebble Beach. With camera set-ups, each round lasted nearly eight hours. (PBC-J.P. Graham)*

Gene Sarazen visits with Nicklaus and Snead before the match, while announcer George Rogers listens in. Nicklaus won the event by a single stroke with a birdie on 18. (PBC-W.C. Brooks)

World Championship Golf, *a series of made-for-television match play events hosted by Bob Crosby, began at Pebble Beach—in real time. The first match filmed in August 1959, was between Ken Venturi and Shelly Mayfield at Pebble Beach Golf Links—it was actually the fifth match aired on November 22, 1959. Venturi won 5&4. (PBC-J.P. Graham)*

As winners of their first-round matches, Dutch Harrison (right) and Venturi greet each other for their match at Monterey Peninsula Country Club, which aired on November 29, 1959. Harrison used his wiles to defeat Venturi 3&2. (PBC-J.P. Graham)

(top) Challenge Golf *at Pebble Beach (left to right): Byron Nelson, Gary Player, Arnold Palmer, and Ken Venturi in a 1963 made for television match-play event. Pebble Beach professional Cam Puget stands near Venturi. (PBC-W.C. Brooks)*

(bottom) As the sun sets, golf professionals (left to right): John Daly, Fuzzy Zoeller, Tom Kite, and Davis Love III visit with ABC's Mark Rolfing and Chrysler executives after completing a grueling tournament where over two weekends they played 18 holes jetting between 18 different golf courses and finishing with the 17th hole played on hole 4 at Spyglass Hill and the 18th at Pebble Beach hole 18. Love was the big winner. (PBC-Archives)

defeating Shelly Mayfield —both at Pebble Beach Golf Links. Harrison and Venturi then matched off at MPCC, with Harrison besting the young pro and teaching him a valuable lesson. On the par-3 10th Venturi looked in Dutch's bag and saw Dutch hit a 6 iron—he thought that was odd, but decided he'd follow suit. Venturi blew it over the gallery. Dutch said, "I saw you looking in my bag," he said. "Don't ever do that. I'll play with your mind and hit it soft." Venturi used that, and for years the story on tour was, "Don't look in Venturi's bag. He'll get into your head." The *World Championship Golf* matches ran weekly from October 1959 through June 1960 with Cary Middlecoff defeating Mike Souchak in the final match.

Gene Sarazen hosted *Shell's Wonderful World of Golf* in the 1960s, which featured one-on-one matches between the pros on great golf venues around the world. The sole U.S. venue in 1962 was Pine Valley, and in 1963 it was Pebble Beach when wily veteran Sam Snead took on a young Jack Nicklaus in a late February match that went to the final hole—the young gun won with a birdie.

Arnold Palmer also launched a television series in 1963 called *Challenge Golf*. He partnered with South African professional Gary Player to take on challenges from other pairs of professionals. Byron Nelson and Ken Venturi were the challengers in 1963 and handily defeated their hosts.

In more recent years, events have included *Chrysler's Great American 18* in 1993 and a revitalized *Shell's Wonderful World of Golf*, where Jack Nicklaus and Tom Watson faced off at Pebble Beach in 1995. ■

CHAPTER *Five*

PROFESSIONAL GOLF IN THE MODERN ERA AT PEBBLE BEACH

S.F.B. Morse built a tremendous resort and saw it through 50 turbulent years. He died on May 10, 1969—the end of an era. (PBC-W.C. Brooks)

Defining the beginning of an era, especially one in which we are living, can be challenging. Still, the 1970s seem to be a logical beginning to the modern era, especially at Pebble Beach. Among the major demarcation points of 1969 were Woodstock, the Moon Landing, and at Pebble Beach, the death of Samuel Finley Brown Morse. At Pebble Beach, we can most easily identify the 50-year pre-Morse Pacific Improvement Era (1868–1918), the 50-year Morse Era (1919–1969), and the Modern Era (since 1970). The growth of golf's initial popularity bridged the period into the Morse Era, where golf professionals were seen as instructors and exhibitionists and the stars of golf were the great amateurs like Francis Ouimet, Bobby Jones, and Marion Hollins. The growing popularity of professional golf bridged the period into the Modern Era, when new stars like Arnold Palmer and Jack Nicklaus became household names.

The change was reflected in the growth of tournament prize money. In the first decade of the Morse Era, the Los Angeles Open made headlines in 1926 by offering a $10,000 purse, with $2,000 going to the winner. Few purses exceeded $5,000 until 1947 when the PGA established $10,000 as the minimum. At the end of the Morse Era, the purse of the Crosby Pro-Am had grown to $150,000, with the winner receiving $25,000. The growth of purses in the Modern Era has been dramatic; despite decades of playing at Pebble Beach by Jack Nicklaus and Mark O'Meara, each with multiple wins and top 10 finishes, Tiger Woods, after less than four years as a professional in 2000, leaped to the top of the lifetime earnings list at Pebble Beach as wins in the AT&T Pebble Beach National Pro-Am ($720,000) and U.S. Open ($800,000) pushed his career Pebble Beach winnings to nearly $1.7 million. Even that number has since been passed by multiple golfers, including Davis Love III, Phil Mickelson, Vijay Singh, and even Dustin Johnson is quickly approaching Tiger Woods' total with $1.2 million in just two appearances in the annual Pro-Am—tied for seventh in 2008 and a victory in 2009 that alone was worth $1,080,000, plus an $18,000 kicker for finishing in a tie for first in the team competition. The total purse in 2009 was $6.1 million.

Most notably at Pebble Beach in the Modern Era is that in addition to the annual AT&T Pebble Beach National Pro-Am, each decade has been accented by the playing of the U.S. Open—1972, 1982, 1992, and 2000, and it is returning in 2010 for a fifth time—more times than it has visited any other course since 1970. Pebble Beach Golf Links was the first public-access course to host a U.S. Open and until 1999 was the only public-access course to do so. Since 1999, the U.S. Open has been held on public-access courses more often than private clubs: Pinehurst (1999 and 2005), Pebble Beach (2000 and 2010), Bethpage (2002 and 2009), and Torrey Pines (2008)—a seven-to-five advantage for public access courses.

Jack Nicklaus visits with the media after his victory at the 1967 Crosby—his first of three Pro-Am victories. (PBC-W.C. Brooks)

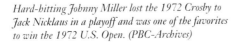

Hard-hitting Johnny Miller lost the 1972 Crosby to Jack Nicklaus in a playoff and was one of the favorites to win the 1972 U.S. Open. (PBC-Archives)

Jack Nicklaus defeated Johnny Miller on the first playoff hole to win the 1972 Crosby. (PBC-W.C. Brooks)

THE 1970S

As the 1970s began, the green fee at Pebble Beach was $22, Jack Nicklaus was in his prime, and the Palmer-Nicklaus duel was waning but still alive. Palmer began playing in the Crosby in 1958 and had finished as high as second to Don Massengale in the 1966 Crosby (Nicklaus was T-24). Nicklaus had won the U.S. Amateur at Pebble Beach in 1961 and began playing as a professional in the Crosby in 1962, winning it for the first time in 1967 (Palmer was third). In 1970, Nicklaus finished second to Bert Yancey, and in 1971 Palmer finished second to Tom Shaw, and another name began appearing on many leaderboards, Johnny Miller, who had won the 1968 California Amateur at Pebble Beach. In 1971, Miller finished (T-8) 6 strokes behind Palmer and 6 strokes ahead of Nicklaus (T-34).

In 1972, Pebble Beach Golf Links was prepping for its first U.S. Open when the Crosby came to town, and many of the pros were looking forward to seeing what that meant. Jack Nicklaus took the early lead in the Crosby with a 66 at Cypress Point, 3 strokes ahead of Lee Trevino, who had only twice made the cut at Pebble Beach before then. Palmer did not play in the Crosby that year. Nicklaus and Trevino each shot 74s at Spyglass Hill. British sensation Tony Jacklin, who first played in the 1968 Crosby before winning the 1969 British Open and 1970 U.S. Open, moved into a tie with Nicklaus for first with rounds of 70-70 at Cypress Point and Spyglass Hill. With a record low 68 at Spyglass Hill, Johnny Miller moved into a tie with Trevino 3 strokes back.

As the leaders moved to a third round at Pebble Beach, conditions were ideal—warm and windless. Miller continued to play strong, taking a bogey on hole 6. He lost two more on the way in to finish with a 73. Jacklin was also inching up despite several 3-putt greens and had earned a share of the lead by the 10th hole. He then double-bogeyed the 11th to fall back. He was tied in the tournament with Trevino as they reached the 18th tee, but then put his tee shot on the rocks, leading to another double bogey, a 77, and a tie for sixth place. Even Herb Hooper briefly shared the final round lead before he buried his approach shot into the large frontal bunker on 14 leading to his double bogey and loss of momentum. He also ended with a 77 for the round and in a tie for 14th place, 6 strokes back.

That left the conclusion to the final pairing. Nicklaus had caught Miller, and they were tied on the 16th tee. Both hit fine drives, but with a slight downhill lie, Miller flat-out shanked his 7 iron into the crowd. "I haven't shanked a ball even in practice since I was 12," commented the 24-year-old Miller. Buried behind a tree, his only shot was to pitch to a bunker. His great shot from the bunker nearly went in, but the bogey-5 gave Nicklaus a 1-stroke lead going to the 17th.

Not to be left out of the "game of giveaway," Nicklaus three-putted the 17th, and the leaders were again tied 2 strokes ahead of Trevino. They both finished 18 with pars and went to the 15th for a playoff. Nicklaus sank a 25-foot birdie putt to record his fifth win in his last six starts. He was looking forward to playing even better when he returned in June for the U.S. Open. Most of the Crosby leaders would be back to challenge him again—and for the U.S. Open, Arnold Palmer would also be on hand.

THE 1972 U.S. OPEN

Together, Frank Tatum and P.J. Boatwright of the USGA, with the assistance of original course designer Jack Neville, reinterpreted the course for the 1972 U.S. Open, bringing into balance the original shot values with improvements in equipment. The changes were modest. After all, the USGA knew Pebble Beach was a great course. The primary changes were in course conditioning and bunkering.

The rough was seeded with fescue grass during the preceding winter and allowed to grow in deep and thick. In those days, the rough received no irrigation other than what nature provided through rain and fog. By letting the grass grow with no mowing throughout the spring, it developed into a good thick stand with some tufts reaching knee high. Golfers playing in April and May were actually losing their clubs if they casually laid them down before taking a shot. Just before the tournament, the crew mowed the rough to a more uniform height of 5 to 6 inches.

The fairways were, however, narrowed dramatically, so much so that during the practice rounds, Arnold Palmer raised a protest about the 8th hole. At the last minute the USGA agreed to add four yards to the fairway width making it more fair and allowing a 40-yard width in the landing area. "The 8th was unrealistic before," Nicklaus said. "The way it was, the tee shot went from left to right, which put the ball in the rough. The

Tony Jacklin had three top 10 finishes at Pebble Beach in the 1970s; losing to Watson by a single stroke in 1977. (PBC-W.C. Brooks)

1-stroke lead over Nicklaus and Jacklin with his 67 to their 71s. Given the optimal conditions, they were all disappointed their sub-par rounds weren't lower. Miller thought he missed at least four makeable birdies. Rod Funseth shot a course record 33-31—64, using eight birdies to best the old course record of 65. Over at Spyglass Hill, Dan Sikes and Ken Towns each shot 66 to replace the course record shot the day before by Miller and Herb Hooper. Sadly for Towns, he still missed the cut by 5 strokes due to an opening round 85. Trevino was tightening his gap until he double-bogeyed the 17th hole and remained 3 strokes off the lead with a 70 and tied at 213 with Herb Hooper. A stroke back were the hot shooters that moved up— Rod Funseth (64), Dan Sikes (66), and Australian Bruce Crampton (69).

With eight golfers within 4 strokes anything was possible, but as great weather continued no one would have guessed that best score among the leaders would be a 73. In the final round, Nicklaus and Miller were paired in the final grouping, but Trevino, opening with three birdies to take a share of the lead, was setting the pace. He then led the way in what was dubbed a "game of giveaway" by shanking a 5 wood and taking a double-

Preparing Pebble Beach for the 1972 U.S. Open are (left to right): USGA vice president Lynn A. Smith, course designer Jack Neville, PBC's head of golf Roger Larson, USGA Board member Sandy Tatum, USGA Executive Director P.J. Boatwright, and NCGA Executive Director Bob Hanna. (W.C. Brooks)

fairway is still narrow, but where the ball caught the rough before, it's now in the fairway. It restores the finest second shot in golf."

Coming into the tournament, the heavy favorite was Jack Nicklaus. Earlier in the year he played in 12 tournaments and finished in the top 10 eight times, including wins at the Crosby, Doral, and the Masters. After his win in Augusta, many prognosticators were even projecting Nicklaus for the Grand Slam. Host professional Art Bell, himself a veteran of 10 U.S. Opens, picked Nicklaus for the win stating:

"He's played Pebble Beach so well in the past. He's the type of player who hits the ball high and is very strong in getting out of the rough. The thing that makes Pebble Beach tough is that the links are not protected by trees. Winds make oceanside courses hard to play. Figuring at least one or two days of westerly winds, which are not real strong winds, I'd say 290 should be in the top three."

Other contenders, as Bell put it included any of the top 20 money-winners, including George Archer, Bruce Crampton, Doug Sanders, and defending Open champion Lee Trevino, who was stricken with viral pneumonia. He spent the week before the Open in the hospital, while many others were on site practicing. But nothing was going to keep him away. Trevino arrived on the scene just before competition began with a case full of medications. The 42-year-old Arnold Palmer was a long-shot favorite with a faithful army of fans even though it had been a few years since he dominated golf.

Among the youngsters in pursuit of their first major were Johnny Miller, who had narrowly lost the 1972 Crosby; Tom Watson, fresh out of

Stanford; and the heavily touted 22-year-old rookie Lanny Wadkins, who had won the 1970 U.S. Amateur. A few top-rated amateurs also dreamed of glory. Jim Simons of Pennsylvania was back to defend his 1971 low amateur crown, which he accomplished with a third round 65 to tie for the lowest round ever by an amateur in U.S. Open competition. Other hopeful amateurs included a powerful pair of teammates from the University of Texas, Ben Crenshaw and Tom Kite.

With overcast skies and little wind, the first day's play started with several golfers going out in sub-par numbers for the opening holes. One of the best among these was Texan Homero Blancas, who fired six birdies on holes 2, 3, 4, 5, 7, and 8. After a more difficult back nine, however, his 33-41—74 opening round left him three shots back of a six-way tie at 71 for the lead between Jack Nicklaus, Orville Moody, Tom Shaw, Kermit Zarley, Chi Chi Rodriguez, and Mason Randolph. Under similar conditions, Nicklaus and Zarley fired 73s on Day 2 to maintain a share of the lead. Nicklaus might have had the lead alone, but after shooting 2 under through 10, he uncharacteristically bogeyed holes 14, 15, and 16, giving him 1-over for the day and even par for the tournament. The big news of the day was young Lanny Wadkins' 33-35—68 which, after an opening round 76, moved him into a tie at the top. Bruce Crampton and Homero Blancas also moved into the tie with 70s, and Cesar Sanudo made the sixth with his steady 72-72—144.

Trailing the leaders by 1 stroke alone in seventh place was Arnold Palmer. Energized by his army, Palmer, who had prepared for this competition more than he had in many years, fired a 35-33—68, tying Wadkins for the low round of the tournament. Featuring six birdies, Palmer's round could have been even better. He missed nine putts inside of 20 feet, including a 2-footer on 8 that accounted for one of his two bogeys. After the round, Palmer told reporters, "I missed makeable putts at 5 (15 feet), 6 (12 feet), and 7 (6 feet), then a little 2-footer at 8. I was madder than I have ever been on a golf course. I thought I had something going. But anyway, that 68 is the best competitive round of the year for me." And with it, Arnie's Army was charged up to see its hero back in the race, hitting the ball well, and with a real chance at the tournament.

Three amateurs made the cut. Tom Kite (75-73—148) led Jim Simons by 2 strokes. Daniel O'Neill, a senior at Penn State, was the only other amateur to qualify, doing so with a 154 right at the cutline. A shot that made the highlight reel was Jerry McGee's hole-in-one on the 160-yard 5th hole. This ace marked the first in a U.S. Open since 1956 and helped McGee into the finals.

Nicklaus finally emerged alone at the top after a cloudy and blustery third day at Pebble Beach. Sitting at even par, 71-73-72—216, Nicklaus had a 1-stroke lead over Lee Trevino, Bruce Crampton, and Kermit Zarley. "It's nice to be in a position to win," Nicklaus said. "But wait until tomorrow and we'll see if it's an advantage playing last." Among the amateurs, Tom Kite held on to his lead, despite falling back in the contest. Both he and Jim Simons could muster only 79s in the increasingly difficult conditions.

With more cloudy weather anticipated, the USGA decided against watering the greens on Saturday night. What they had not anticipated was the strong westerly wind that blew in on Sunday. The seas were so rough that the sailboats that had frolicked off the shore through Saturday's round remained safely moored in the confines of Stillwater Cove. It was a tough day for most of the golfers, too. After his round, Nicklaus reflected, "I can't recall a day like this when we were almost not playing golf. Golfing skills were almost eliminated. Half the greens were dead. They were dried out by the wind, and every green had a different speed. I don't think the USGA was looking for this much wind the last day and rolled the greens the night before. If you made a putt it was luck, not skill. All you could do was avoid 3-putting. It was just like a seaside course in Britain, and I had been expecting something like this all week." [20/21]

The conditions created the high drama for which the ABC film crew had hoped—great names young and old and close enough that anything could happen. Even Trevino seemed ready for anything as he joked with reporters from the putting green showing his jocularity that had been subdued by his illness most of the week. As the contenders teed off, it was as if they were stepping into a lion's den. No one went out charging but rather hoped to keep from being eaten alive on national TV. By the time Nicklaus sank his birdie putt on the 2nd hole he had a 3-stroke lead in the tournament. Trevino, who had matched par on the 1st, was showing signs of wear by the 2nd hole. His earlier humor had been masking the fact that he was still sick and lacked the strength he would need to compete under these conditions. He hit his tee shot on 2 into the left rough and failed to clear the rough on his second. He sailed his third beyond the green before finally getting down in 6. At the same time, Crampton was making 6 on the 3rd hole. From here, all Nicklaus needed was to hold on for the win, but could he?

Reaching the 10th, Nicklaus tested the wind, planned his shot into the sloping fairway, and teed up his ball. As he completed his backswing and was coming into the ball, a gust of wind from the west knocked him off-balance. His drive sailed way to the right, landing on the beach below the bluffs of the coastline. Opting to accept the 1-stroke penalty for a lateral hazard, Nicklaus dropped a ball above the bluff and selected a 2 iron to go for the green. Given the wind it was not enough, and his ball landed short of the green, tailing off into the tall grass on the steep bank of the bluff, again within the lateral hazard. When he reached the spot, he could see his ball. He had caught a break, and it was sitting up nicely. He was able to get it onto the green with a wedge and 2-putt for a double-bogey 6. But his lead had dwindled.

Palmer, despite a bogey himself on 10, had made par on 11 and 12 and was just 2 strokes back at 4-over for the tournament. Palmer had been rock solid in his play except for putting. Although he told nobody else until after the tournament, Palmer had snapped the shaft on his putter while attempting some minor adjustments on the eve of the final round. He ended up playing the final round with a similar model putter he borrowed from Australian David Graham.

Palmer and Nicklaus respectively finished 13 and 11 with pars setting up a key moment of high drama especially poignant for those watching on

Teens sit in a tree near the 13th green to get a better view of the action. (PBC-W.C. Brooks)

Chi Chi Rodriguez watches as Lee Trevino tees off on the first hole at the 1972 U.S. Open. Trevino's face mask is an attempt to keep him healthy while he plays through a bad lung infection. (PBC-W.C. Brooks)

Arnold Palmer tees off at the 1972 U.S. Open. (PBC-W.C. Brooks)

television. On the long, uphill, par-5 14th hole, Palmer hit two great shots leading to a lob wedge that landed 8 feet from the pin for a makeable birdie. At the same time, Nicklaus hit a low 3 iron into the narrow green of the 205-yard par-3 12th. It hit the green near the flag but proceeded to bounce into the thick mat of grass on the slope behind the green. From there he attempted to chop it out, managing only to get it to the edge of the rough. His next chip slid 8 feet past the hole.

In perhaps the most dramatic split-screen image in the sport's history, the two greatest names in active golf, Palmer and Nicklaus, were each looking at 8-foot putts that could change the outcome of the tournament. If Palmer made his and Nicklaus missed, it would be a 3-stroke swing that would give Palmer the lead. At the very least, if they both made it there would be a tie. The cameras rolled as their nearly simultaneous putts inched toward the targets. Palmer's just missed as Nicklaus' dropped into the cup and out of sight. Nicklaus held the lead by 1 stroke as Palmer tapped in for par.

From there Palmer soon dropped back to third. When Nicklaus reached the tee of the par-3 17th, he had a 3-shot lead over Bruce Crampton. With the wind howling in his face, Nicklaus hit a low-flying 1 iron directly at the flagstick 218 yards away. It landed just short of the cup, bounced once, hit the flagstick, and came to rest 6 inches from the hole. After the tap-in birdie and a safely played closing bogey at 18, Jack was again the Open champion with a total score of 290—exactly what course professional Art Bell had predicted.

The victory was Jack's 13th major, and it tied him with the great Bobby Jones, a once unthinkable feat. In the press tent, the questions flew. To illustrate how tense the week had been, Nicklaus tugged at his waistband and said, "You know, the first part of the week I could hardly get into my slacks. Now look how roomy they are after one week of competition. Last night, I woke up from nervous tension and began thinking how I would play the finishing holes if I had a 3- or 4-stroke lead. I kept thinking: How would I play the 17th hole if the wind was blowing?"

However, there was another story attracting reporters' attention. A group of protestors (one report called them "scruffy youngsters") had chained themselves to the huge pine tree on 18 that grows in the landing area of the tee shot. After padlocking themselves in place, they unfurled signs protesting the Vietnam War, and stayed most of the afternoon. As the final pair passed by them, everyone noticed Lee Trevino say something that made Nicklaus laugh. The comment? "Put a match to that tree and the key will appear mighty fast."

There are other great stories, but what mattered most to Pebble Beach was that everyone deemed the first U.S. Open to be played on the Monterey Peninsula a success. It was so successful, in fact, that it piqued the interest of another group. The PGA of America soon expressed interest in holding the PGA Championship at Pebble Beach and would do so in 1977.

On a windy final day, an intense Jack Nicklaus stayed focused and earned his way into a playoff for the 1973 Crosby championship. (PBC-W.C. Brooks)

THE CROSBY CONTINUES

The Crosby returned to Pebble Beach in January, and while Nicklaus did not get his Grand Slam (he finished second to Trevino in the British Open and T-13, and 6 shots back of Gary Player in the PGA Championship), he won again at Pebble Beach, creating a legendary "sandwich"—surrounding the U.S. Open win with two Crosby's for three professional victories at Pebble Beach in a year's time. Both his victories were narrow and resolved with a playoff. Going into the final round of the 1973 Crosby, Orville Moody (71-66-69—206) had a 4-stroke lead over Lanny Wadkins and Don Iverson. Ray Floyd, Billy Casper, and Nicklaus were tied for fourth at 211.

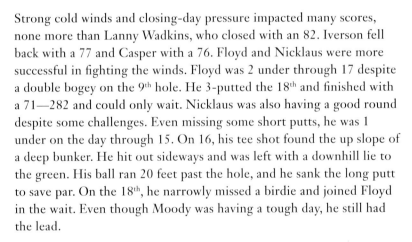

Playing with his amateur partner Clint Eastwood, Ray Floyd battled the winds to a final round 71, despite a 3-putt bogey on 18. (PBC-W.C. Brooks)

Third-round leader Orville Moody (nicknamed "Sarge"), fell back in the final round. Here he grimaces as he misses a short putt for par on 18 that would have given him the victory. Instead, he joined Nicklaus and Floyd in a three-way playoff. (PBC-W.C. Brooks)

Strong cold winds and closing-day pressure impacted many scores, none more than Lanny Wadkins, who closed with an 82. Iverson fell back with a 77 and Casper with a 76. Floyd and Nicklaus were more successful in fighting the winds. Floyd was 2 under through 17 despite a double bogey on the 9th hole. He 3-putted the 18th and finished with a 71—282 and could only wait. Nicklaus was also having a good round despite some challenges. Even missing some short putts, he was 1 under on the day through 15. On 16, his tee shot found the up slope of a deep bunker. He hit out sideways and was left with a downhill lie to the green. His ball ran 20 feet past the hole, and he sank the long putt to save par. On the 18th, he narrowly missed a birdie and joined Floyd in the wait. Even though Moody was having a tough day, he still had the lead.

Moody's trouble started early, when his tee shot on hole 4 went right and rolled down the bank into the hazard. Amazingly, he found the ball and hit a blind wedge to the green to save his par. He was not as lucky on hole 7, when the wind blew his tee shot into a bunker, and while he blasted out successfully, he 3-putted for a double bogey. When he 3-putted hole 15, he was 3-over on the day and reached the 18th with a 1-shot lead over Nicklaus and Floyd. He hit a great drive, a fine second shot, and an approach that stopped about 30 feet from the pin. A lag putt left a 2-footer for the win, but he missed as the ball squirted to the right.

The threesome headed to the 15th tee for a playoff. Nicklaus and Floyd hit 1 irons, and Moody outdistanced them with a 3 wood. The approach was the payoff; Floyd's went long into the rough, Nicklaus' landed softly 12 feet from the pin, and Moody was on the green with a tough but makeable 20-footer. Floyd chipped on and still had a long way for par. Moody's putt stopped well short, and Nicklaus sank his birdie for the win. It was Nicklaus' fifth win at Pebble Beach—he became the first golfer to win three Crosby's and was also the only golfer to have won the U.S. Amateur and U.S. Open on the same course.

Johnny Miller won the rain-shortened 1974 Crosby, which was only the second time the tournament had been shortened by weather since coming to Pebble Beach. Rookie golfer Gary McCord, now a CBS golf commentator, got off to a horrible start in his first-ever tournament on the regular tour. Through 15 holes at Cypress Point on Thursday he was 17 over par, but as the rains picked up and only 20 golfers completed play, tournament officials called off the entire day and started anew on Friday. Grateful for the fresh start, McCord fired a 7-under-par 65 on Cypress Point on Friday to take the first-round lead. Despite rain and even hail on Saturday, McCord managed a 73 on Spyglass Hill to share the lead with Miller, who made it around Spyglass Hill in 70. McCord lost his lead on Sunday with an 80. Starting on the 10th tee, his troubles started when he reached the 17th and knocked his ball beyond the green into the ocean with a 4 iron. He barely saved a double-bogey, and then bogeyed the next two holes. As the day progressed, he found himself praying for another rainout, but it was not to be. He found the ocean again on hole 4. On 8, his drive went over the cliff but caught up in the brush. He knocked it up where he could hit it, but by the time he dropped the putt, he had another double bogey. They played through the rain, and some golfers did okay. Miller opened up a 4-stroke lead with a 70, and Tom Kite moved into a tie for third with a 68. McCord's prayers were answered a day late—continued storms resulted in no play on Monday an end to the tournament after 54 holes.

Gene "The Machine" Littler methodically played through Pebble Beach, dominating the leaderboard from beginning to end…almost. (PBC-W.C. Brooks)

THE 59TH PGA CHAMPIONSHIP

Winners in the next three years leading into the 1977 PGA Championship were Gene Littler, Ben Crenshaw, and Tom Watson. Any of them were likely winners in the PGA, but Tom Watson, a two-time British Open champion who loved Pebble Beach, was the likely favorite.

With the commitment of the PGA, the tournament came to Pebble Beach despite the worst drought in the course's history. The little water available was used to perfect the greens. The rough was hard and consisted mainly of drought-tolerant weeds. The fairways were not a lot better. The rye-seeded fairways were brown, and in many areas the dry ground had

formed cracks in the soil. To adjust for the small fissures, tournament officials adopted a local rule that allowed relief should one's ball come to rest in such an area. The limited rough, coupled with the extra roll from the firm ground, led to a much different tournament than was seen at the 1972 Open.

Twenty-eight of the 141 golfers completed the opening round in par or better. Gene Littler, opening with two birdies and finishing his first round with a score of 67, virtually led the field from the start on Day 1. Tom Watson, Jerry McGee, and Mark Hayes were each a stroke behind Littler and tied for second, while Nicklaus, George Cadle, and Lanny Wadkins were crouched 2 strokes back at 69.

Lee Trevino gives encouragement to Arnold Palmer on the 18th. Trevino's 71 and Palmer's 73 were better than average but still well back of Gene Littler, who opened the championship with a 67. (PBC-W.C. Brooks)

Overcast skies and little to no wind was again the pattern for Day 2. Accordingly, 28 golfers again shot par or better, but only ten golfers managed the feat on both days.

1	Gene Littler	67-69—136
2	Jerry McGee	68-70—138
T-3	Jack Nicklaus	69-71—140
T-3	Lanny Wadkins	69-71—140
T-5	Joe Inman, Jr.	72-69—141
T-5	Al Geiberger	71-70—141
T-5	Charles Coody	70-71—141
T-9	Fuzzy Zoeller	70-72—142
T-15	Lon Hinkle	72-72—144
T-15	Bob Murphy	72-72—144

Watson had fallen back with a 73, and though still among the 28 golfers standing at par or better for the tournament, he was becoming a long shot at 5 strokes back. The story was Gene Littler, now the first- and second-round leader. He was 2 strokes ahead of his nearest competitor and had gotten there with superb, bogey-free golf. A San Diego golfer, Littler had been playing Pebble Beach for years. Going back as far as the 1947

California Amateur Championship, Littler had known the course in its more ragged days, which may have lent some advantage. He narrowly missed winning the State Amateur in 1949 (losing on the 3rd hole of sudden-death) and did win it in 1953 (the same year he won the U.S. Amateur in Oklahoma City). He also won the Crosby in 1975. Low scores for the second round (68) belonged to Dr. Gil Morgan and Miller Barber. The low round that had everyone talking, however, was that of 65-year-old Sam Snead. After an opening round of 80, his 71 on Friday inched him into a berth for the final two days, tied for 64th with seven others at 151.

Seventy-one golfers remained in the competition with 15 strokes separating first and last place. For the first time all week, the sun broke through and the gallery grew to about 15,000. Jerry Pate, starting the day tied for 12th, made the first early move by completing the front nine in 31—four pars and five birdies. Although he finished with 38 on the backside, his 69 was enough to move him into a tie for fourth place. Nicklaus also jumped out with a strong start, scoring an eagle on the 502-yard 2nd hole and a birdie on number 6. Littler, however, was even hotter, birdying four of the first seven holes. Standing on the 8th tee, Littler was 12-under-par for the tournament with a 5-stroke lead over Nicklaus, his closest competition.

In Gene Littler's (right) first playoff for a championship at Pebble Beach 28 years earlier, he lost on the third extra hole to "Mac" Hunter (left) for the 1949 California Amateur. (PBC-J.P. Graham)

Lanny Wadkins was ecstatic over his sudden-death victory on the 3rd hole at Pebble Beach. This marked his first victory in a major. (PBC-W.C. Brooks)

After 43 holes without a bogey, the odds finally caught up with Littler as he bogeyed the 8th. While he made two more bogeys offset by just one birdie on the way in, his third round 70 kept him 4 strokes ahead of Nicklaus, who also shot 70. Charles Coody slipped into solo control of third place with his 70, just 1 stroke behind Nicklaus. Five players were tied for fourth at 212: Jerry Pate, Tom Watson, Gil Morgan, George Cadle, and Lanny Wadkins. And what about Sam Snead? He followed his Friday 71 with a repeat of the same on Saturday. Still out of contention, his second sub-par round was enough to jump him from last place to 44th.

Play on the final day followed the pattern of starting play on the 1st and 10th tees. Littler's consistent play left little doubt that he would win the $45,000 first place check. The contest would be for second. For the first time that week, the wind was noticeable, which added a little more challenge. Still, par was the standard among the leaders. Through nine holes, Littler was 1 under, stretching his lead to 5 strokes. Gene "the Machine" Littler was living up to his reputation, and his friends couldn't have been happier that he was about to win his second Major. (He had won the 1961 U.S. Open at Oakland Hills.)

Then, just when it seemed the winner was a foregone conclusion, Littler's approach into 10 caught in the wind, falling short and into a bunker. Blasting out and two putts later, he recorded a bogey. He calmed himself with a par on 11, then 3-putted 12 for another bogey. On 13, a miss-hit approach and a flubbed wedge led to his third bogey of the round. He found the fairway bunker with his tee shot on 14 and bogeyed again—four bogeys in five holes. His over-powering lead was shaved to just 1 stroke, but it wasn't over. His approach shot on

15 found a bunker, and with a fifth bogey, he was in a tie with Jack Nicklaus. Concurrently, Nicklaus was making par on 16 for the first time all week. Nicklaus looked at the real possibility of taking the lead on two of his favorite holes. While he was teeing it up on 17 (where he had hit the pin in the 1972 U.S. Open), Lanny Wadkins was on the 18th green sinking a birdie putt to finish at 70 and slide into a three-way tie with Nicklaus and Littler. The formerly unexciting tournament was instantly transformed into a nail-biter.

From the tee at 17, Nicklaus launched at the green. This time, instead of bouncing off the flagstick, it bounced off the crown of the green and into the thick rough of the green complex. The narrow and firm green would not hold the pitch from the deep rough. The ball slid 25 feet past the cup for a 2-putt bogey. When Nicklaus could not drop his long birdie attempt on the 18th, Wadkins breathed a sigh of relief and waited to see what Littler would do.

Littler dodged a bullet on 17 when his tee shot also found the gnarly rough. He chipped on and sank a long, difficult putt for par. He needed a birdie on 18 to win, but it was not to be. Littler's par set off the first sudden-death finish in major history—the PGA had adopted the immediate tiebreaker for its championship just that year.

Gene Littler (right) congratulates Lanny Wadkins (center), knowing he really beat himself on the final day of play. (PBC-W.C. Brooks)

Grabbing a quick swig from a friend's beer, a confident 27-year-old Wadkins met a disconcerted Littler—two decades older—on the 1st tee. Littler could not believe he blew a 5-stroke lead but had no one to blame but himself. He would have to shake it off and return to the solid golf he had played all week. When the playoff began, Littler was on in 2 and looking good. The anxious Wadkins had found the deep grass off the green with his second shot. An incredibly deft touch got the ball to stop on the green, but Wadkins was left with a tricky 12-foot putt for a tying par. He made it.

At the par-5 2nd, both players reached the oblong green in 2 and were down with birdies. At the 3rd hole, following a too-short approach by Littler, a pumped-up Wadkins watched his ball fly the green and drop down on the hill behind. Going first, Littler hit his shot fat and his ball stopped 20 feet from the pin. Was it déjà vu? Had Littler been thinking of his last sudden-death playoff on this very hole? Mac Hunter had defeated

Littler on this spot in 1949, a few months before Wadkins was born. The parallels were stunning.

Wadkins examined the line, popped his ball softly to the edge of the green and watched it trickle toward the pin. It stopped 4 feet short on a precarious downhill line. Littler, putting for a much needed par, made a good lag putt for an easy bogey. Wadkins gave his ball a gentle stroke, and when it dropped, he exploded into a victory dance. This marked his first win in a major.

In truth, it was Wadkins' first victory of any kind in four years. He had joined the Tour in 1972 with much of the fanfare that had accompanied Nicklaus a decade earlier. He was to be golf's new superstar. Allergies and a gall bladder operation slowed him down over the first few years, but this dramatic win in the PGA Championship made him the man of the hour and earned him the cover on *Sports Illustrated.*

Nathaniel Crosby was just 16 when his father Bing died, and he stepped up as a player and host of the famed tournament. He later won the 1981 U.S. Amateur and tried a stint on the pro circuit. (PBC-W.C. Brooks)

THE CROSBY CONTINUES

Tom Watson finished tied for sixth in the PGA Championship, just 4 strokes back of the leaders, but he was still the defending champion of the Crosby. Missing from the Crosby was Bing, who had passed away on October 14, 1977, just after finishing a round of golf on La Moralaeja Golf Course near Madrid in Spain; he was 74. His youngest son, Nathaniel, then just 16, took over host duties with the help of his mother Kathryn. Also missing from Thursday's first round was the golf. Heavy rains on Wednesday had made the course unplayable. What a change from the drought that had challenged the PGA Championship just a few months earlier.

When play started on Friday, Watson led the first round with a 66 at Cypress Point. He fell to fourth place after the second round, a stroke behind three golfers tied at 139: Ray Floyd, Tommy McGinnis, and Hale Irwin. After three rounds, Watson and Floyd were tied at 211, just 1 stroke ahead of four golfers: Mike Morley, Tom Weiskopf, David Graham, and Dave Stockton. Six more—Hale Irwin, Ben Crenshaw, Andy North, Don Bies, Tommy McGinnis, and Gibby Gilbert—were at 213. A dozen players were within 2 strokes of the lead.

Watson took control early on the still soggy golf course. Playing lift-clean-and-place, Watson went out in record pace taking just 30 strokes on the first nine holes. He struggled some coming in with a 39 and left room for the competition but was still 3 under par on the day. Floyd was 3-over and fell back. Irwin made a run playing 5 under par through 16. A visit to the greenside bunker on 17 led to his only bogey of the round and a lipped-out putt on 18 caused him one stroke too many to make a playoff. One golfer was able to force a playoff—Ben Crenshaw, whose 32-35—67 was able to close the gap.

The playoff started on 16, where both made par. On 17, Watson hit to the right side of the hour-glass green, and Crenshaw found the front bunker. Watson lagged a beautiful putt over the ridge but still had a 3-footer left. Crenshaw blasted out of the sand and had 10 feet left. Crenshaw failed to convert, and Watson made his putt to become only the third golfer to win back-to-back in the Crosby.

Playoffs seemed to become more common. Lon Hinkle won in 1979 in a three-way playoff over three holes, and the tournament's largest playoff took place in 1981—one perhaps caused by bad information. Heavy rains delayed the start of the first round until Saturday, by which time it had been decided to make it a 54-hole tournament. John Cook, Amateur Champion of California in 1975 and the U.S. in 1978, fired a 66 at Cypress Point to take the first-round lead. Three others shot 67 at Cypress Point, and Bobby Clampett, in his first Crosby after twice winning the California Amateur, earned a first-round 67 on Pebble Beach. Watson shot a 69 on Pebble Beach to tie Brad Brant for the second-round lead, but when the co-leaders each slipped down to 74 in the third and final round, there was room for others to climb up. The challenge was that the golfers were spread around the three courses and, without electronic score boards, no one was really sure where anyone stood. Barney Thompson had moved into the lead with a 67 on Cypress Point for a 7-under-par 209. Cook, who had been bogey-free through the first two rounds, had one bogey but offset it with a birdie to shoot even par for his final round at Spyglass Hill and tie for the lead. Hale Irwin, also at Spyglass Hill, made four birdies on the last nine holes to finish with a 70 and also tie at 209. Ben Crenshaw was feeling good at 8 under for the tournament with just three holes to play at Spyglass Hill, but a 3-putt on the long 7th green dropped him back, and he also found himself caught in the growing web of the playoff. Over at Cypress Point, one player still had a chance. Bobby Clampett was 2 under through 17 holes on the day and 8 under for the tournament.

Knowing he was close to the lead but with no leaderboard in sight, Clampett looked desperately for an official who could tell him where he stood. He recognized a couple of NCGA officials and asked what they knew. He was told he was in a three-way tie with Watson and Nicklaus. Clampett hit a sand wedge into the slick 9th green to within 10 feet of the hole. He knew he needed birdie for a possible win, but his downhill putt lipped out and went 6 feet beyond the hole. He missed the comebacker and closed with a bogey. Had he known he had the lead, Clampett would have played for the par rather than birdie, and there would have been no playoff. Instead, he went from thinking he was out of it to finding out he was instead in a PGA Tour record five-way playoff that did not include either Watson or Nicklaus, who respectively finished 1 and 2 shots back.

The five-some gathered on the 1st tee of Pebble Beach Golf Links. Cook and Irwin found the fairway. Crenshaw pushed his tee shot into the trees to the right, and Clampett found the left side rough, partially blocked by a tree. Thompson skied his tee shot, hit his second shot left, and pitched on with his third, but a par was no longer likely. Irwin and Cook were on in regulation. Crenshaw made a remarkable recovery from the trees and knocked his third shot close for a likely par. Clampett managed to hook an iron shot around the tree and onto the green, but the ball went 12 feet beyond the pin, leaving a tough downhill putt for his birdie try. Cook sank his birdie, and Thompson and Crenshaw picked up. Irwin also made birdie. Clampett stroked his putt, and the partisan crown audibly sighed as the local star's putt slid past the hole.

Only Irwin and Cook continued. Cook found the rough off the tee and had to lay up short of the barranca on the 2nd hole; a pitch to the green and two putts gave him par. Irwin played the 2nd hole beautifully and had a 6-footer for birdie, but when he missed, they moved on to the 3rd hole. Both found the fairway, but as night closed in, Irwin's 9 iron shot hit the green and bounced over the back. Cook's approach stopped just 4 feet from the pin. Irwin chipped on to within 7 feet; his putt slid by, and he tapped in for bogey. Cook had two putts for the win, and when his first one lipped out, he was grateful for the extra margin.

Tom Watson won the Crosby Pro-Am back to back in 1977 and 1978. (PBC-W.C. Brooks)

John Cook receives kisses for his 1981 playoff victory, joining the growing ranks of former State Amateur Champions to win at Pebble Beach as professionals. (PBC-W.C. Brooks)

Tom Watson chips onto the 17th green and sinks the birdie shot. (Getty Images)

THE 1982 U.S. OPEN

Mother Nature made no delay in taking part in the 82nd U.S. Open. A strong westerly wind caught up with a number of players on the opening round. Danny Edwards, one of only two dozen players to compete in both of the previous Majors at Pebble Beach, sped to the top of the leaderboard by going 3 under with a birdie-eagle on the first two holes. Edwards ended up shooting a remarkable 31 on the front nine but struggled on the back and finished the day in a five-way tie for third at 71, 1 stroke behind co-leaders Bruce Devlin and 1981 British Open champion Bill Rogers. The early favorites were scattered further back. Tom Watson bogeyed the first three holes but rallied to close at 72. Nicklaus was back a little further at 74.

For 87 of the 154 competitors, Friday was the unlucky cut day. Among those missing the cut were Chi Chi Rodriguez, Lee Trevino, John Cook, Arnold Palmer, Seve Ballasteros, and Fred Couples. Ray Floyd made the cut by 1 shot. One of the few players who stayed hot was first round co-leader Bruce Devlin. After a second round 69, Devlin was now at 5 under and in the lead all alone by 2 strokes over the field. In second place was Larry Rinker, who fired a 67 and sent many reporters scrambling to find out who he was. A more familiar 26-year-old Scott Simpson moved into third place with a 69. Local favorite Bobby Clampett stayed close with a shaky 73 and was in a group at even par, 5 strokes off the lead. This group included Tom Kite, Tom Watson, and Jack Nicklaus. The only amateurs to continue were Corey Pavin and 1981 U.S. Amateur champion Nathaniel Crosby.

As so often happens in an Open, round three resulted in some major shifts in the leaderboard. Devlin, who hadn't won a tournament in 10 years, and the young Rinker each exploded to a 75 on a day when, in the words of Tom Watson, the course was "defenseless." When the day's play ended, the new co-leaders—by 2 strokes—were Watson and Rogers with 68 and 69 respectively. Defending champion David Graham joined Devlin, George Burns, and Scott Simpson in a four-way tie for third. Nicklaus and Calvin Peete were 1 stroke back. Clampett was at even par.

On Sunday, the golfers in the best position to win were in the final six pairings—12 golfers lumped within 4 strokes. Nicklaus and Peete teed off about a half-hour before the leaders. Down by 3, Jack got aggressive, perhaps too aggressive. His bogey on the 1st hole left him 1 more stroke to make up. But after a par on the 2nd, he birdied the next five holes.

Meanwhile, Watson birdied the 2nd and bogeyed the 3rd, thereby putting himself, Rogers, Devlin, and Nicklaus in a four-way tie at 4 under par when Nicklaus birdied the 6th. From that point on, players jumped off and on the leaderboard. In a final surge, Bobby Clampett was laying 246 yards from the 18th green after a tremendous drive. He was at 1 under for the day and the tournament. On 18, the pin was tucked front right. He and his caddie, long-time friend Mike Chapman, had stood in the 18th fairway many times playing out scenarios that would justify going for the green in 2 strokes. There had been no risk-reward justification until now. Three strokes off the lead in the U.S. Open, he confidently hit a driver 250 yards. All he could think of was getting down in 3 and applying pressure to the veterans yet to finish. He knew he shouldn't, but he knew he had to. He did it. The shot was on the money right up the gap but just short. He hit a simple chip and sank the birdie-putt and became the leader in the clubhouse at 2 under. A few minutes later, Dan Pohl joined him in a tie.

On the long par-5 14th, Watson faced a 35-footer for birdie that would move him out of a tie for first with Nicklaus. Watson and his caddy, Bruce Edwards, discussed the line and the speed of the curving putt. To the astonishment of perhaps everyone but Watson, the putt found the bottom of the cup. He later reported, "It was the putt that won the tournament for me. The pressure was gone. I had control of the situation, the game was on. I led Jack by one, with Bill Rogers 3 behind. It was a two-man battle, with Jack going for a record fifth Open and me for my first. I knew what I was trying to do and I was doing it, and I was enjoying myself for the first time in the round. It's the greatest feeling you can have in golf."[22]

Still, the tournament wasn't over, and Watson knew it was too early to celebrate. His missed par putt at 16 and Nicklaus' missed birdie putt at 18 meant they were tied for the lead once again.

For the final round, the USGA used the back tee on 17 to stretch out the entire 209 yards, leaving little forgiveness if one is long or left. Watson attempted a gentle hook with a 2 iron, but the ball hit the left collar and bounded into the thick, kikuyu rough, 8 feet back of the narrow green. Watson surveyed the situation. The ball was actually sitting up in the leggy grass. He could get a sand wedge under the ball, but could he stop it with just 12 feet of green? When his caddie encouraged him to "Just get it close," Watson fired back, "I'm not going for close—I'm going to sink it." He then played the delicate shot with the touch of a surgeon. The ball landed softly just off the fringe, took a gentle hop, and then started to track. Watson seemed to shift his body as if to steer the ball, and when it fell for the birdie, he began a celebratory dance of unbridled exuberance. He quickly calmed himself in order to play the final hole.

Nicklaus watched the event unfold on a monitor in the scorer's tent. It was possible that Watson had found a way to nip Nicklaus in a close match. Watson now stood on the verge of his first U.S. Open win. All he needed was a par on 18.

Following two conservative shots up the fairway, Watson's 9 iron approach stopped 20 feet from the flagstick. As he reached the green, the 20,000 fans gave him an even more resounding cry of appreciation than they had moments earlier when they were cheering for a Nicklaus victory. Watson needed a 2-putt par for the win and just wanted to get it close. He read the line and tapped it a little harder than intended. His ball, however, knew its duty and dove for the bottom of the cup and a second birdie. Nicklaus, always equally gracious in defeat as well as victory, greeted Watson coming off the green. "Why you SOB," Nicklaus said smiling, "you're something else. I'm really proud of you."

Tom Watson and his caddie Bruce Edwards celebrate the sweet victory of the 1982 U.S. Open. (PBC-W.C. Brooks)

Almost lost in the drama of the victory was the performance of 20-year-old Nathaniel Crosby, who finished as low amateur. With two years to go at the University of Miami, Crosby confessed joining the PGA Tour was among his goals. His golf game over the next couple of years would determine the outcome.

In the aftermath, Pebble Beach once again proved it could define champions and championship moments. There was no question it would again host an Open. The only question was when.

Tom Kite set a new course record 62 on Pebble Beach Golf Links en route to winning the 1983 Crosby. (Ted Durien Collection)

In 1986, the annual Pro-Am got a new sponsor and a new name. (PBC-Archives)

THE CROSBY CONTINUES AND CHANGES

Tom Kite set a new course record 62 in winning the 1983 Crosby. Hale Irwin bounced one off the rocks on 18 in the final round of 1984, saved par, and won the tournament in a playoff. Mark O'Meara won his first Crosby in 1985, and perhaps ironically, it was the last Crosby. Purses had grown to the point where no tournament could compete without a title sponsor. The 1985 Crosby carried a $440,000 purse, $640,000 was needed for 1986. AT&T came forward and offered to share the title as the AT&T Crosby National Pro-Am. Kathryn Crosby did not like the idea of linking the Crosby name with a corporate sponsor.

Assured by Pebble Beach owner Marvin Davis that he would not let anything happen to the tournament she did not approve, she felt betrayed when Davis agreed to the AT&T sponsorship. She pulled the Crosby name from the Pebble Beach event and started a new Crosby celebrity amateur event in North Carolina. Sons Harry and Nathaniel continued to serve on the board of the Pebble Beach tournament, keeping the Crosby connection alive, but the tournament was renamed the AT&T Pebble Beach National Pro-Am.

The first AT&T Pebble Beach National Pro-Am in 1986 was a rain-shortened affair won by Fuzzy Zoeller. Many called the rain Crosby's revenge for pulling his name from the tournament. Johnny Miller won a second time in 1987, and newcomer Steve Jones won a playoff in 1988 for his first PGA Tour win.

THE NABISCO CHAMPIONSHIPS OF GOLF

In 1986, the PGA Tour created what would become the Tour Championship—a professional event where only the top 30 money leaders are invited to compete in an event with a large purse. Some have called it the Fifth Major. Nabisco was the title sponsor for the first three years—two at Oak Hills Country Club in San Antonio and the third at Pebble Beach Golf Links. The purse in 1988 was $2 million, with $360,000 going to the winner; more than double the $700,000 purse of the 1988 AT&T Pebble Beach National Pro-Am with the winner's share at $126,000. In addition, the Nabisco had $1 million in bonus money that would be paid to the top money winners of the season, based on totals after the event—some big pay days were assured. Nabisco was also putting up $2 million for charity that would be allotted to the charities based on the winnings of the five-man teams selected by each tournament.

Going in, the leading money winner was Chip Beck at $776,018. He, or any of the golfers in the top 13, could become the first golfer to win $1 million on the Tour in one year. Australian Greg Norman had achieved combined winnings of $1.25 million in 1986, and Welshman Ian

Nabisco
Championships

Pebble Beach November 7-13, 1988

The short-lived Nabisco Championships made one stop at Pebble Beach in 1988. The tournament is now known as the Tour Championship, with only the top 30 money leaders invited to play.

The action on hole 3 during the 1988 Nabisco Championships. (PBC-Archives)

Woosnam totaled $1.8 million in 1987, but no one had ever reached that winnings mark on the U.S. Tour—Curtis Strange, with $925,941 in 1987, was the closest anyone had ever come.

With the weather promising sunny skies and temperatures in the high-50s, Curtis Strange, the 1988 U.S. Open champion, made it clear that he wanted to be the million-dollar man. He went out and birdied the first two holes and, in a bogey-free round, added four more birdies and an eagle on 11 to post an 8-under-par 64 and a 3-shot lead over Ken Green. Green's round was punctuated by an eagle on hole 2. Tom Kite had set the course record with a 62 at Pebble Beach in winning the 1983 Crosby. Kite was in the Nabisco field but well back with a first round 72. At the back of the pack was Mark Weibe with a 4-over-par 76. Greg Norman was only a stroke better. Norman began the day with a double bogey on 1 and ended with a double bogey on 18 for a first round 75.

Weibe may have been quietly humming Bing Crosby's favorite golf tune, "Tomorrow's My Lucky Day," but he likely didn't know how lucky. On Day 2, Weibe shot his way back into the tournament with his own 64. Strange held on to the lead with a 71, but Weibe had jumped from the bottom rung into a tie for seventh, just 5 strokes back. Green held on to a tie for second, 2 strokes back, with a 70 that included another eagle on hole 2, this one a spectacular shot from the green-side bunker. Moving into a tie for second were Bruce Lietzke with a 68 and Tom Kite with a solid 65. Norman followed up his 75 with a 76 and was alone at the bottom.

Another day, another 64. On Day 3 it was Payne Stewart's turn. It lifted him into a tie for fourth place, just 2 strokes behind Strange. Strange briefly gave up the lead when a string of mid-round bogeys followed his early eagle on hole 2, but he regained it with birdies on holes 15 and 16. It had narrowed to just a single stroke. Ken Green remained in second place with a 69 and was joined there by his former caddie, Mark Calcavecchia, who moved up with an impressive 65. Green, who led the Tour with 18 eagles on the year leading into the Nabisco, made it 21 with his third straight eagle in three days on the 2nd hole.

Curtis Strange's win at the 1988 Nabisco Championships made him the first golfer to win more than $1,000,000 in a single year. (PBC-P. Lester)

After three beautiful days, a storm crashed in on mid-day Sunday, forcing a one hour and 27 minute hiatus in the middle of the final round. One pairing was not bothered by the storm. Greg Norman (75-76-74—225) and Mark O'Meara (70-73-77—220) were first out, and out of the big money, but each had a $32,000 guarantee for completing the event. They went out in an effort to set a course record—they had no visions of shooting 61, they wanted to see how fast a PGA Tour round could be played. They completed their round in one hour and 28 minutes, each shooting 79, which for the alacrity was respectable and got them in before the storm hit.

As the storm blew away any hopes of sub-par scoring, the early 79s were not even the day's high score. Chip Beck also shot a 79, and Joey Sindelar made 80. Play resumed under near ideal conditions as the winds totally subsided. When the delay was called, Strange was on the 11th green, still with a 1-shot lead over Ken Green and 2 over Tom Kite. Each was 2 over on the day at that point, and the others had fallen back further. Kite birdied the 12th to join a tie for second, which soon also included Payne Stewart and Mark Calcavecchia. With a birdie on 13, Strange padded his lead to 2 strokes, but as twilight arrived, Strange found the right greenside bunker on 17 and bogeyed. At the same time, Kite made birdie on 18 to tie the leader. Strange could do no better than par on the final hole, and the pair were set for a playoff. Green, Stewart, and Calcavecchia were each a stroke back.

It was too late in the day and darkness prohibited going immediately to a playoff, so Tom Kite and Curtis Strange would resume in the morning. Kite was motivated. He had not gone a season without a win in the last six years—the longest active streak in the game—but was winless in 1988. He had made the top money list with a number of top 10 finishes, including three second place finishes. While Kite was experienced at finishing second, Strange was experienced at winning playoffs. Two of Strange's three victories in 1988 had come through playoffs, including an 18-hole playoff with Nick Faldo in the U.S. Open and a sudden-death playoff with Greg Norman in the Houston Open that lasted three holes.

The playoff for the Nabisco began on the 16th hole, which each player parred. On the 17th Strange hit first and the ball tracked like a heat-seeking missile to the back-left pin, stopping just 18 inches from the cup. Kite's shot flew the green and landed in a back bunker. Skilled with his wedges, Kite got it out and within 3 feet for a par, but he still lost to Strange's birdie. The $360,000 first place money was coupled with a $175,000 bonus, bringing his year's earnings to $1,147,644, and putting him third (behind Nicklaus and Watson) on the lifetime earnings list at $4,263,133. Kite won $216,000 with a $40,000 bonus in fifth on the year's money list, rising to fourth on the career list at $4,205,413.

BACK TO THE AT&T PEBBLE BEACH NATIONAL PRO-AM

Mark O'Meara set the speed record at the Nabisco, but getting back to the fun of the Pro-Am, he won back-to-back victories in 1989 and 1990 to join Nicklaus as the only three-time winners of the event. Paul Azinger won in 1991, the year Poppy Hills replaced Cypress Point in the rotation. O'Meara set another milestone, winning a record fourth Pro-Am in 1992. It required a playoff with Jeff Sluman. With four victories at Pebble Beach since the 1982 U.S. Open, O'Meara was the clear favorite going into the 1992 U.S. Open.

THE 1992 U.S. OPEN

The five months between the Open and the Pro-Am flew by. The third U.S. Open to be held on the Monterey Peninsula featured many European players, some of whom had never played Pebble Beach before. One newcomer, Ian Woosnam, set off a local stir when he expressed his surprise at all of the acclaim garnered by the Pebble Beach course. Of the short but scenic 7th, the diminutive (5'4") Welchman decried, "It looks like a little practice hole." And in summarizing his criticism of the course, "There are just too many blind shots." Standing alongside him for the latter comment, Nick Faldo (6'3") countered, "At your height, I'm sure that's true."

Calm and gray skies covered the course as the threesomes began play on Thursday. The lack of wind accounted for some of the lowest scoring ever seen in U.S. Open play. Andy Dillard, a young pro out of Oklahoma, set a U.S. Open record by birdying each of the first six holes to take the early lead. He gave up a couple on the backside and finished with a 68—good enough to be tied for third in a group of 29 golfers that beat par in the opening round. Tied with Dillard at 68 were Steve Pate and Tour rookie Phil Mickelson, the latter of whom chose this Open to make his professional debut.

Curtis Strange showed a prowess that had been lacking over the past few years since he won back-to-back Opens in 1988 and 1989. His early 67 made him the leader in the clubhouse for most of the afternoon. But as dusk closed in on the first day's play, Dr. Gil Morgan came up to 18 also at 5 under. Curling in a 15-foot birdie putt, Morgan went to 6 under to take the lead. British favorite Nick Faldo, after shooting a 2-under-par 70, prophetically suggested what lay ahead for those with lower scores. "This is the U.S. Open. Guys will take a run, but they'll come back to you progressively as the week goes on."

First round leader Gil Morgan would have no part of Faldo's theory. He had an early round on Friday and posted a second sub-par round to distance himself from the field with a 66-69—135. A chip-in birdie

Wee Welshman Ian Woosnam, playing Pebble Beach for the first time at the 1992 Open, remarked there were too many blind shots. (PBC-P. Lester)

Unknown Andy Dillard (aka "Bib") rocked the opening rounds of the U.S. Open with a "Joe Average"–style while he birdied the first six holes he played in the 1992 U.S. Open and later chipped one in for eagle on 14. (PBC-P. Lester)

Phil Mickelson made his professional debut at the 1992 U.S. Open but missed the cut with a 68-81—149. (ALSPORT)

at 14 helped Dillard take an uncontested second place at 68-70—138. The low score for Friday went to Wayne Grady, whose 74-66—140 was good enough to move into a tie for third with 1986 Open Champion Ray Floyd. With more verve than prophecy, Floyd echoed Faldo's earlier sentiments. "There's only one player at 9 under. That tells you what the golf course is doing to the rest of the field. All I can say is you can lose a championship in any one or two rounds, but I don't think you can win in any one or two rounds. If Gil continues at this level of play, all records are going to be broken. It's not likely."

Among those missing the cut were early leaders Steve Pate, Phil Mickelson, and all three amateurs in the field. David Duval (76-76—152) was the low amateur, besting Mitch Voges and Matt Gogel by 3 and 9 strokes, respectively. Curtis Strange exploded to a 78, but did make the cut. Mark O'Meara, the 1992 Pro-Am winner, did not.

For a third straight day the players were allowed to score with minimal interference from nature. Morgan's birdie at the seventh was his third birdie of the round and allowed the Oklahoman to set a record—it was the first time any player had ever reached 12 under in a U.S. Open. Now holding a 7-stroke lead on the field, Morgan was playing flawless golf

and was beginning to seem unreachable—but this is golf, and in the U.S. Open anything can happen.

Over the next three holes—with a double bogey, a bogey, and another double bogey—Morgan lost 5 shots from his lead. "The Cliffs of Doom," as course architect Tom Doak christened the stretch of 8, 9, and 10, had lived up to their name. Dr. Gil Morgan could only hope the inland trek would provide the cure. It did not. With bogeys on 11 and 12 and another double at 14, Morgan had lost his lead and was tied at 3 under par with Tom Kite, Mark Brooks, Ian Woosnam, and Gary Hallberg. The latter fell to 2 under with a bogey on 17, but Kite, Brooks, and Woosnam finished the third day at 3 under.

Morgan's wild ride continued with a birdie on 16, a bogey on 17, and then a 25-foot putt for birdie on 18 to finish at 4 under. He was still in the lead but never so glad to have a round behind him. The drama of Morgan's fall overshadowed Andy Dillard's fall, which was even worse. With a 79, Dillard dropped from second place to a tie for 23rd. And then there was Wayne Grady. Tied for third when play began, Grady had the day's worst round at 81 and fell to a tie for 51st.

Dr. Gil Morgan took the first round lead at 6 under par, and in round three he became the first player to reach 12 under par in a U.S. Open…it didn't last. (PBC-P. Lester)

David Duval did the best of any amateur in the field, but his 76-76—152 missed the cut by 6 strokes. (PBC-P. Lester)

Weather forecasters predicted a final day of overcast skies. The USGA directed only light irrigation to assure fast greens and a challenging final round. Scores among the first groups of golfers to finish ranged from 70 for Tray Tyner to 80 for Peter Jacobsen. A 71 for Nick Price made him the early leader in the clubhouse with a four-round total of 3 over par.

Shortly after Price finished, however, the wind began to blow away the clouds and whatever was left of the low scoring. As the ABC-TV broadcast began around 1:00PM, the sun shone brightly and Pebble Beach never looked better…except to those still on the course. The wicked wind of the west can tear apart a golfer's scorecard on a good day. Under U.S. Open conditions, the wind can tear apart a golfer's heart. Commentating

from the TV booth on Sunday was Jack Nicklaus. He predicted that the leaders, who were just starting out, would be hard pressed to shoot anything close to par.

Before Morgan finished his 5th hole, Scotland's Colin Montgomerie finished with a 70-71-77-70—288, even par to take over as leader in the clubhouse. As he was ushered in to the tower on 18, Nicklaus greeted him saying, "Congratulations, Colin. How does it feel to win your first Open?" At the time, Morgan and Kite were tied at 3 under, both recording a double bogey on the 4th hole. The difference was that Kite offset his double with birdies at 1 and 6, and Morgan had only one birdie on the 5th. Just prior to Montgomerie's arrival in the tower, Kite had missed the 7th

David Feherty, now a CBS Golf announcer, played in the 1992 U.S. Open paired with Corey Pavin and Andrew McGee. Feherty missed the cut, so perhaps he was honing his interview skill here with Nick Price and Hale Irwin who did make the cut. (PBC-P.Lester)

The crowd cheers as Tom Kite sinks a long birdie putt on 12 to hold his lead. (PBC-P. Lester)

Colin Mongomerie finished the 18th just as the winds began to whip and was the leader in the clubhouse. With little chance of the leaders scoring well in the strong winds off the ocean, he was in a very good position. (ALSPORT)

green with a punched 6 iron. With winds in excess of 30 mph, Nicklaus' belief was reasonable but ill timed. Before Montgomerie could properly respond, Kite's chip bounced twice and then rolled smoothly across the green, slipping into the cup for an exhilarating birdie. At nearly the same time, Morgan double-bogeyed the 6th to fall into a tie for second with Woosnam at 1 under. In mere minutes, Kite went from being tied for first to having a 3-stroke lead. Kite later reported that he thought about doing a Watson-like dance at that moment but controlled his emotions knowing plenty of trouble lay ahead.

The strong wind quickly dried out the greens, creating a consistency more like concrete than turf. Only those who could adapt their game to the conditions had a chance. Most failed. Scott Simpson ballooned to an 88. Payne Stewart shot 83, as did the usually competitive Davis Love III. Coming in with an 81, Ray Floyd disgustedly called the course setup a "joke." In response, the USGA's David Eger acknowledged that had they anticipated the winds, they would have provided more water to the greens and adjusted a few pin placements.

Out on the golf course, Kite was trying to stay focused. This was difficult, because his playing partner, Mark Brooks, was collapsing in the wind with the rest of the field. Playing as carefully as he could, Kite made a par on the 8th, a "good" bogey on 9, then two more pars at 10 and 11. At the par-3 12th, Kite bounced his tee shot onto the right side of the green some 30 feet from the cup. Miraculously, he made the birdie putt and was now 4 under with a 4-shot lead on Montgomerie. "Stick to the game plan," he told himself. "Positive thoughts; one shot at a time." Kite later admitted he struggled with negative thoughts a few times in the round, but no one saw it in his play.

After a par at 13 and a superb birdie at 14, Kite was now at 5 under. To his surprise, though, his lead was still only 4 strokes. Jeff Sluman, the 1988 PGA champion who began the day at even par, managed to get to 1 under through exceptional play of his own. Sluman, not Montgomerie, was the leader in the clubhouse.

With a 4-stroke margin and only four holes to go, Kite seemed to relax just slightly. A scrambling par at 15 was followed by a bogey at 16 and his precarious lead was down to 3. At the 17th tee, Kite faced the fierce head-on gale that was making the famous par-3 play even longer than its fully stretched 209 yards. Even with a full 3 wood, Kite's tee-shot came up short and landed in the large bunker at the front left of the green. Unfortunately, a good shot with his sand wedge was followed by a missed putt and another bogey.

Kite stood at the 18th tee with a 2-stroke margin and more pressure than most could stand. Kite knew all too well that he was known on the circuit as the best golfer to never win a major. He was golf's all-time leading money winner, but the 42-year old Kite had never managed better than second in a major. Now just 545 yards away from putting that footnote to rest, he had to close his mind to everything but playing a tough par-5 with

a brutal crosswind. As he had all week, he pulled out his driver and ripped it across the bay and safely onto the fairway. Minutes later, his successful putt for a 5 finished off a sensational even-par round achieved on one of the toughest days in major tournament history.

Tom Kite, in yet another dramatic victory, joined Tom Watson and Jack Nicklaus as the three golfers identified by Pebble Beach Golf Links as the best. Could there be a better test than Pebble Beach under championship conditions? The USGA began wondering if ten years was too long to wait for another Open at Pebble Beach, and discussions for the next visit began before the USGA officials left town.

Tom Kite hoists the trophy—his first major in a successful 20-year career. (PBC-P. Lester)

Actor Jack Lemmon and his longtime professional partner Peter Jacobsen in 1995. "Jake" made the cut and won the tournament. As a team, they barely missed the cut. (Monterey Peninsula Foundation)

THE AT&T PEBBLE BEACH NATIONAL PRO-AM CONTINUES

While the Pro-Am continued in the 1990s, it was anything but predictable. Unknown Australian Brett Ogle won in 1993, and in a flashback to an earlier era, Johnny Miller and Tom Watson battled it out in the 1994 event with Miller winning his third victory in the event and becoming the only golfer to win at Pebble Beach in four different decades—1968 California Amateur, 1974 Crosby, 1987 AT&T, and 1994 AT&T. In 1995, Peter Jacobsen, perennial professional partner of actor Jack Lemmon, rose to the top. A double bogey on 18 at Poppy Hills in round two that Lemmon couldn't better may have been the two strokes that kept Lemmon from making the cut. In 1996, the tournament was rained out.

Tiger Woods made his first appearance in the AT&T Pebble Beach National Pro-Am in 1997. He turned pro just a few months earlier and had already won three events. Woods piqued public interest, but two other relative newcomers grabbed the headlines with 65s at Poppy Hills Golf Course—Jesper Parnevik and David Duval. Woods shot 72, while his mentor, Mark O'Meara, posted a 67. Jim Furyk made 65 at Poppy Hills in the second round to take the lead, while at Spyglass Hill Parnevik and Duval shot 70 and 71, respectively. Woods shot 72, and O'Meara posted another 67. Things heated up at Pebble Beach in the third round. O'Meara posted a third 67, which had him tied with Furyk, who shot 69.

The story of the day, though, was David Duval's record-tying 62, which gave him a 3-shot lead. Almost lost in the story was Tiger Woods, who shot a blazing 63 on Pebble Beach to move within 4 strokes of O'Meara and Furyk.

Woods had come to win, and he followed up his 63 with a 64 in the final round, the lowest 36 holes in the history of the tournament, but would 19-under-par be enough? Duval was at even par on the day as he reached the 16th and saw Tiger's final birdie posted. O'Meara had made up 3 strokes and was tied with Duval, 1 stroke behind Woods. O'Meara got serious and birdied the next two holes, edging into the lead. Duval was still trailing Woods by 1 as they reached 18. While O'Meara was studying his par putt for the win, Duval made his birdie on the final hole to tie Woods. Now it was O'Meara's turn—would he sink the putt for the win, or would there be another playoff? He sunk it for his fourth 67 of the week and a tournament record 20-under-par to accent his fifth tournament victory.

Phil Mickelson won for the first time at Pebble Beach in 1998, but it took more than six months to secure the victory as an *El Niño* storm rolled in and ransacked the course. Two rounds were completed in January, but there was no way weather would allow completion of the tournament in the short term. Rather than record a second rain-out in three years, it was decided to cancel only the Pro-Am and bring the pros back at a later date. The final round was played on August 17, and followed by a ruling that no tournament completion would ever be delayed more than a few days in the future.

Rain shortened the 1999 Pro-Am as well, and when it was called, Payne Stewart was the 54-hole leader and declared the winner. It was Stewart's first victory at Pebble Beach, and when he also won the 1999 U.S. Open at Pinehurst that June, it meant he would be returning to Pebble Beach in 2000 as the defending champion in two tournaments. It was a devastating blow when Stewart died in a plane crash on October 25, 1999. His memory was ever present in the events of 2000.

At the 2000 AT&T Pebble Beach National Pro-Am, players and gallery wore plaid ribbons in memory of Stewart. The opening round stayed on schedule, but rain caused a suspension of play with a plan to finish round one on Friday and play through Monday to complete 72 holes. Vijay Singh, David Duval, and Notah Begay led the first round with 66s at Poppy Hills. Duval fell back in round two and later withdrew, but Singh and Begay remained the leaders with 67 and 68 respectively at Pebble Beach.

Tour-rookie Matt Gogel was just 4 strokes back after two rounds, a margin he made up in round three with a 67 at Pebble Beach, while Singh and Begay shot 72s at Spyglass Hill. Mark Brooks shared the lead with Gogel after recording a 66 at Poppy Hills; both were 12 under par. Tiger Woods, who had won five straight tournaments coming into Pebble Beach, looked like his streak was over as he stood 5 shots back. As he went out on Monday, he just couldn't get things going. After 11 holes, Woods trailed by 7 strokes. Woods had gotten to 10 under par, but Gogel had birdied five of the first seven holes to get to 17 under par. Woods continued to press. On 12 he hit a 5 iron to 5 feet and made the birdie putt and barely missed another birdie on 14. Watching the leaderboard, Woods saw Gogel start to struggle with bogeys on 11 and 12. Sensing an opportunity, Woods increased his intensity as only he can do. He crushed his drive on 15 and then finessed a 97-yard wedge that landed softly on the green and rolled into the cup for an eagle. In four holes, Woods had picked up 3 strokes while Gogel lost 2; the margin was now only 2 strokes.

Woods' energy grew as he nestled his approach into 16 for a tap-in birdie. Gogel's lead was 1. Gogel continued to falter with a bogey on 15; they were tied. Woods finished with a birdie on 18 for a 64—273, 15-under-par. Three over par on the back, Gogel found himself trailing Woods by a stroke. He struggled with emotions and made par on 16 and 17, but still needed a birdie on 18 just to force a playoff. He set it up like a more seasoned pro, leaving an 8-foot putt for the birdie. But there is no pressure like a high-stakes putt. The putt slid by, and then in frustration he missed the putt coming back. A bogey on 18 dropped Gogel back into a tie for second with Vijay Singh. Woods was proving his ever-growing legendary prowess on the course. He became the first player to win six straight tournaments since Ben Hogan did it in 1948, and his come-from-behind victory will not soon be forgotten.

Jack Nicklaus takes a moment to reflect on a remarkable career before playing what he expects will be his last hole in a U.S. Open. (PBC-P. Lester)

THE 2000 U.S. OPEN

The USGA selected Pebble Beach as the site for the playing of the 100th U.S. Open—a major venue for a major event. Pre-event activities at the 2000 U.S. Open included an unveiling of "Momentum," a colossal sculpture by artist Richard MacDonald to commemorate the event. Upon the base are engraved the names of all the past winners of the U.S. Open. A more solemn moment took place on the Wednesday morning before play started on Thursday. A memorial service for Payne Stewart was held on the 18th hole led by his close friend and fellow professional, Paul Azinger.

Appropriate to a 100th U.S. Open there are so many stories. Jack Nicklaus and Tom Watson, who won in 1972 and 1982, were given special exemptions to play, and while neither made the cut, it was an especially moving tribute to Nicklaus, who took a moment on the 18th tee in round two to reflect on all his great memories before playing the 18th for a final time in competition. He went for it in two and made it—arriving on the green to a well deserved standing ovation. As he was finishing his round, Tiger Woods was teeing off on the first hole, breathing new life into the ages-old game.

Local product Bobby Clampett, a regular visitor with the CBS crew broadcasting the AT&T, showed he could still play by opening the 1992 U.S. Open with a 3-under-par 68. (PBC-P. Lester)

Spain's Miquel Angel Jimenez shot an opening round 66 finishing just 1 stroke behind Tiger Woods. It was as close as anyone would get for the rest of the tournament. (PBC-P. Lester)

Thomas Bjorn was tied for second with Jimenez at the end of round two—both at 2-under-par, but 6 strokes back of the leader. (PBC-P. Lester)

Local golf fans were also inspired by the performance of Bobby Clampett. The gritty junior golfer that grew up on the peninsula and was also nicknamed "Tiger" in his youth had entered the professional ranks in 1980 with so much promise. He only won one professional event and eventually landed a job with CBS as a golf analyst. He qualified for the 2000 U.S. Open, and showed it was no fluke as he opened with a noteworthy 68. His second round 77 was enough to make the cut and revive dreams of a career as a professional golfer—perhaps on the Champions Tour? Clampett will turn 50 on April 22, 2010.

Playing as a par-71 course with the 2nd hole as a par-4, the course gave up a remarkable number of birdies in the first round. Twenty-eight golfers shot par or better, the low man, to no one's surprise, was Tiger Woods with a bogey-free 33-32—65. Just behind him was Miguel Angel Jimenez of Spain. With seven birdies and two bogeys, he returned a card of 31-35—66. John Huston also opened with seven birdies, but with three bogeys, he was 1 stroke back of Jimenez. Only about half of the field finished the first round on Thursday. At 3:57 in the afternoon, David Meeks, the USGA's Director of Rules and Competitions, suspended play due to a thick fog that had blanketed the coast and impaired players' vision of the course. He asked golfers to stay on the course in the hopes it would clear, but at 6:28 PM he called it off for the day, asking golfers to return at 6:30 AM to complete their rounds.

Golfers arrived early the next morning to find the coast still shrouded in fog. The resumption was delayed until 8:15 AM, jeopardizing completion of the second round. The first round was completed and the second round continued until 8:15 PM when the USGA called the suspension of play due to darkness. A third of the field was still on the course, including tournament leader Tiger Woods, who had picked up five more birdies with two bogeys to get to 9 under par with six holes to finish on Saturday morning. He had extended his lead to 3 strokes over Jimenez, who was 1 under through seven.

Morning came early, and seemed to affect golfers and their scores. Tiger, who looks at par-5s as birdie opportunities, bogeyed the long 14th hole. He birdied 15, but on the 18th he pulled his tee shot into the ocean and then toughed out four shots for a net bogey with the penalty to end the second round at 65-69—134, 8 under par. Jimenez, however, was affected even more making five bogeys on his final 11 holes before birdying the 18th for a 66-74—140 to fall 6 strokes back of Woods and into a tie for second with Thomas Bjorn. When the second round was tallied, Tiger Woods again had the day's low round, equaled only by Dave Eichelberger.

After 36 holes, the Open field is cut to "the low 60 scorers and any tying for 60th place and any player within ten strokes of the leader." Eleven golfers were tied for 53rd place at 149. Amazingly, only 18 golfers were within 10 strokes of the leader, so that point was moot. Therefore, while Eichelberger's second round 69 helped him make the cut, his first round 78 left him 13 strokes off the lead in a tie for 36th with the likes of Ernie Els, Colin Montgomerie, and Nick Price—making the cut, but well out of contention for the win unless the unthinkable happened. There were still some recalling the large lead that Gil Morgan built up in 1992 before the wheels came off.

(above) From an awkward stance, Tiger Woods looks for a way to get his club on the ball to extract it from the tall grass on the 3rd hole. He took a triple bogey and then just smiled as if to say, "Stuff happens." (PBC-P. Lester)

(right) Tiger Woods nails a birdie on hole 14 and, despite his triple bogey on the 3rd, finished with a par round and held a 10-stroke lead. (PBC-P. Lester)

The third round began at 10:40 AM after all the second round scores were in and pairings were set. There was no sign of fog and conditions were ideal, but scoring remained difficult. After just two holes Tiger Woods increased his lead to 8 strokes with a 1st hole bogey by Jimenez and a 2nd hole birdie by Woods. Bjorn had quickly fallen out of contention. And then it happened. There was a chink in the armor. Woods' approach to the third green fell short and right of the green, not in the bunker, but in the thick grass surrounding the sand, forcing a very awkward stance. He sized up the shot and took a hack—the ball barely moved. He lined up again and moved the ball over the bunker, but still in deep rough short of the green—now laying 4. He chipped it to the green without much study and still had a 10-foot putt. He left it short and recorded an un-Tiger-like triple-bogey 7. Visions of Gil Morgan again emerged. Woods simply

shook his head and smiled. He still had a 5-stroke lead and now a new goal—no more mistakes.

Woods parred 4 and 5 but found trouble again on 6. His tee shot landed in the deep rough at the base of the hill. He had muscled it out of there the day before and did so again, but this time his ball sailed left and found the thick grass around a bunker—shades of hole 3. This time he popped it out clean, landing it softly on the green tracking for the hole, and sliding just by the flag. He sank the putt, turning possible disaster into a birdie.

Tiger Woods capped off his momentous victory with a bogey-free final round, playing smart golf and adding three birdies to set several U.S. Open records—not the least of which was winning by 15 strokes over his nearest competitors. (PBC-P. Lester)

He followed it up with a birdie on 7, bogeyed the 8th, and birdied the 9th. After a roller-coaster nine holes he was even-par on the day, but had stretched his lead to 9 strokes as Jimenez made bogeys on 5 and 8.

Woods was in trouble again on 10. His approach shot went over and halfway down the hill above Carmel Beach. Deep in the long grass of the embankment he found and chose to play his ball from the hazard. It came out too clean and rolled through the green. He chipped it close to save bogey. He got the stroke back with a birdie on 14 and finished with an even-par round despite the excitement. Meanwhile, Jimenez bogeyed 16 and 17, coming in to finish with a 76, trailing Woods by 11 strokes. Ernie Els, however, recorded five birdies and two bogeys en route to a 68, the only sub-par round of the day. The score moved him into second place, 10 strokes behind Woods. The race was now for second place, and the leaderboard was dominated by the foreign players. Els of South Africa in second place; Spain's Jimenez and Ireland's Padrig Harrington tied for third; and tied for fifth, Spain's Jose Maria Olazabal and Phil Mickelson.

Tiger's goal for round four was to play a bogey-free round. He knew he could not be caught unless he collapsed, and he was not about to do that. The day was almost anticlimactic. It was more like a coronation awaiting the final putt to drop and see just how many records Woods could break on his way to victory. It was clearly the most remarkable performance in the history of the game and took place on golf's most remarkable venue during the remarkably significant 100th playing of the National Championship. The stars certainly aligned to make a memorable championship.

When the round was over, Woods had accomplished his goal of a bogey-free round and added four birdies to his performance, finishing at 272 and 12 under par. Els and Jimenez tied for second at 287 and 3 over par. Woods won by 15 strokes, shattering records that went back 100 years. Willie Smith had held the record of winning by 11 strokes in 1899, but he only beat seven other golfers. This new record is destined to stand for all time.

But perhaps lost in the excitement of Tiger Woods' performance is the performance of Pebble Beach Golf Links. With the exception of Woods, the relatively short (playing to 6,846 yards in 2000) Pebble Beach Golf Links challenged the best golfers in the world, and while a few beat par in a round or two, only Tiger Woods beat par over four days. Such is the nature of a classic course like Pebble Beach that was built by golfers for golfers. It can be made playable for the duffer or challenging for the best of the best depending on how it is set up.

Tiger Woods continues to dominate golf in the Modern Era, and while his fifth-place finish at the Masters in 2000 ended thought of his winning the Grand Slam in 2000, he used his U.S. Open victory to launch his own "Tiger Slam" and won the 2000 British Open, the 2000 PGA Championship, and the 2001 Masters to become the only golfer to hold all four major titles at the same time. What lies ahead is anyone's guess.

Tiger Woods' victory at Pebble Beach was a storybook epic befitting the 100th playing of the U.S. Open. It also launched his "Tiger Slam" as he won the next three majors to become the only player to hold the four modern Major titles concurrently. (PBC-P. Lester)

THE AT&T PEBBLE BEACH NATIONAL PRO-AM CONTINUES

One has to believe Tiger Woods had Jack Nicklaus in his mind when he returned to Pebble Beach for the 2001 AT&T Pebble Beach National Pro-Am. Nicklaus had won the Pro-Am on either side of his 1972 U.S. Open victory, and Tiger was looking at an open-face sandwich, having won the first two legs of the feat. Tiger opened with a 66—a score his friend and playing partner, Jerry Chang, couldn't better. But David Berganio could; he shot a course record 64 at Spyglass Hill to take the first round lead. After a second round 73, Woods fell out of contention, and this time there were no spectacular finishes by Woods. Phil Mickelson (70-66-66—202) shared the third round lead with Olin Browne, with Vijay Singh 2 strokes back. But on the final day, Davis Love III fired a 63 to leap to a 1-stroke victory over Singh.

Matt Gogel, who collapsed in 2000, held firm in 2002 and benefitted from the collapse of third round leader Pat Perez. Gogel shot a final round 69, while Perez hit out-of-bounds on 18 for a triple-bogey 8, ending his round with a 76 and losing to Gogel by 3 strokes.

Love became a two-time winner in 2003, and Vijay Singh recorded his first win in 2004. Phil Mickelson became a two-time winner in 2005, aided by his first round 62 for a course record at Spyglass Hill. In 2006, Pebble Beach crowned Arron Oberholser with his first PGA Tour victory—he was the first golfer to win his first Tour victory at Pebble Beach since Brett Ogle did it in 1993. Whereas Ogle was from far-away Australia, Oberholser was from nearby San Jose.

In 2007 Phil Mickelson became the fourth golfer to record three Pro-Am victories at Pebble Beach, and he did it impressively, tying O'Meara's record 20 under par performance. He also tied the tournament record of winning by a 5-stroke margin of victory.

Vijay Singh nearly won his second Pro-Am victory in 2008, but with three straight bogeys coming in on the final round, he was lucky to force a playoff with Steve Lowery with a birdie on the 18th. Lowery, who had not won in his last 198 starts, birdied the 18th for the best payday of his life. From the journeyman to the future, Dustin Johnson, in only his second appearance at Pebble Beach, won a rain-shortened 54-hole tournament in 2009. Johnson, age 24, had won his first Tour event the previous October at Turningstone and the 2009 AT&T Pebble Beach National Pro-Am was his second. In 2008 at Pebble Beach, he finished in a tie for seventh place.

Reading the green together in 2004 are Jay Haas of the Champions Tour and his junior partner Sydney Burlison of nearby Salinas. Burlison, while only 14 at the time, was already a veteran of the U.S. Women's Open having been its youngest qualifier in 2003. (Reproduced by Permission of the Walmart First Tee Open at Pebble Beach)

Craig Stadler and Aaron Woodard of The First Tee of Denver won the inaugural Walmart First Tee Open at Pebble Beach in 2004. (Reproduced by Permission of the Walmart First Tee Open at Pebble Beach)

THE WALMART FIRST TEE OPEN

The First Tee program is an initiative of the World Golf Foundation begun in 1997 to introduce more young people to the game of golf and the values that it offers. In addition to teaching the fundamentals of the sport, The First Tee stresses the Nine Core Values—Honesty, Integrity, Sportsmanship, Respect, Confidence, Responsibility, Perseverance, Courtesy, and Judgment—values that are important in golf and life. The First Tee has a growing number of chapters across the U.S. and a few other countries. The First Tee of Monterey County was launched in 2004 with the strong support of the Monterey Peninsula Foundation.

The board of the Monterey Peninsula Foundation, which runs the annual AT&T Pebble Beach National Pro-Am and includes Pebble Beach owners Peter Ueberroth, Clint Eastwood, and Paul Leach wanted to do more to support the organization. The board worked with The First Tee, the Champions Tour, and title sponsor Walmart to create The Walmart First Tee Open at Pebble Beach, first played on Labor Day weekend 2004. The nationally televised tournament pairs 78 senior professionals with 78 junior players (ages 13-18) in a pro-am format similar to the AT&T Pebble Beach National Pro-Am—two additional amateurs round out each foursome and play as a second team. The juniors may be boys or girls, and the amateurs may be men or women.

In 2004, the tournament was played in a split field with 18 holes at Fort Ord's Bayonet course and 18 holes at Pebble Beach Golf Links. The professionals and low teams then played a final round on Pebble Beach for the championship. Craig Stadler won the inaugural event—both sides, closing with a 66 to beat Jay Haas by 3 strokes for the individual honors

and pairing with Aaron Woodard of Denver to win the pro-junior team event. It was Stadler's first victory at Pebble Beach, who had several top 10 finishes in the Crosby/AT&T Pro-Am as early as 1977. He and the other pros expressed how much they liked the format and playing with the juniors.

Sydney Burlison, who at age 12 was runner-up in the California Women's Amateur and managed a top 10 finish in four of the first five First Tee Open events; she paired with Fuzzy Zoeller in 2008 to win team honors in her final year of eligibility. (Reproduced by Permission of the Walmart First Tee Open at Pebble Beach)

2008 Champion Jeff Sluman accepts the individual trophy. In 2009, he became the event's first back-to-back champion. (Reproduced by Permission of the Walmart First Tee Open at Pebble Beach)

Paula Creamer, still a junior golfer in 2004, appears quite at home on Pebble Beach, flanked by the more seasoned professionals—Peter Jacobsen and Gary Player. (Reproduced by Permission of the Walmart First Tee Open at Pebble Beach)

Since 2005, Del Monte Golf Course has shared the hosting honors with Pebble Beach, and the number of The First Tee chapters represented through regional qualifying has continued to grow. Of the first five professional winners, only Hale Irwin (2005) had a previous victory at Pebble Beach (1984 AT&T). For team victories, Craig Stadler (2004) and Fuzzy Zoeller (2008) each scored team victories in the AT&T (1999 and 1986 respectively).

The juniors, however, are a big part of the event, and while many have no visions of becoming professional golfers, others do and have. Among the junior golfers in the 2004 Walmart First Tee Open was Paula Creamer, now an LPGA star. It is likely we will see other First Tee juniors among the top professional and amateur golfers of the future.

Pebble Beach has been, and will continue to be, a strong force in developing and defining great golf and great champions. To reiterate the prophecy of Earle Brown after the 1926 Monterey Peninsula Open, "We have had our first stellar championship with the majority of Kings competing. We shall have them all in the future." With a history of golf that began more than a century ago at Del Monte Golf Course, Pebble Beach has hosted all of the greats of the game, and not just the "Kings." The queens, princes, and princesses of golfing royalty have all found their way to the courses of Pebble Beach, and the best have been crowned as champions.

This tradition will doubtlessly continue, but beyond the championships and the beauty and quality of the courses and golf experience—whether a casual round or a national championship—Pebble Beach stands alone in offering the only course that has perennially been ranked among the top 10 courses in the world that is open to the general public, three courses in the top 100 since the rankings began, and as diverse a mix of great golf courses as is available on the planet. Pebble Beach and the Monterey Peninsula truly is "The Golf Capital of the World."

Come, enjoy, and build your own tradition at Pebble Beach. ■

APPENDIX 1: THE CHAMPIONSHIPS

DEL MONTE CUP – MEN'S CHAMPIONSHIP (1898-1908)
The Men's Championship in 1898 was for a silver cup, but 1899 was the first year it was actually referenced as the Del Monte Cup

			FINALISTS			SEMI FINALISTS					
Year	Mo	Winner		Runner-up	Score	Lost to Winner	Score	Lost to Runner-up	Score	Medalist	Score
1898	Aug	J. Downey Harvey	d.	C.R. Scudder	2 & 1	Captain Payson	Dn-2	F.F. Ryer	Dn-4	J.V. Coleman	58-57—115
1899	Aug	Charles E. Maud	d.	E.B. Tufts	5 & 2	R.M. Fitzgerald		Walter Cosby		Conde Jones	85
1900	Aug	Ernest R. Folger	d.	J.W. Byrne	10 & 8					E.J. McCutcheon	83
1901	Aug	Charles E. Maud	d.	H.M. Sears	4 & 3	N.F. Wilshire	7 & 5	Charles Hubbard	6 & 4	Fred S. Stratton	78
1902	Aug	J. Athearn Folger	d.	R.L. McCleay	4 & 3					C.B. Knapp	76
1903	Aug	Charles E. Orr	d.	Dr. C.H. Walter	2-up					Dr. J.R. Clark	
1904	Aug	Chapin F. Tubbs	d.	Douglas Grant	11 & 10						
1905	Sep	Charles E. Maud	d.	Charles Zueblin	7 & 6					Charles E. Maud	74-75—149
1906	Aug	C. Templeton Crocker	d.	H. Warner Sherwood	3 & 2					Charles E. Maud	69-77—146
1907	Sep	Robin Y. Hayne	d.	R.G. Hanford	6 & 4	Chapin F. Tubbs	21st	W.B. Walton	Dn-1	Robin Y. Hayne	78-73—151
1908	Sep	Thomas P. Mumford	d.	W.F. Garby	5 & 3					Charles E. Maud	72-81—153

DEL MONTE MEN'S CHAMPIONSHIP (1909-1912)

			FINALISTS			SEMI FINALISTS					
Year	Mo	Winner		Runner-up	Score	Lost to Winner	Score	Lost to Runner-up	Score	Medalist	Score
1909	Sep	Frank C. Newton	d.	F.D. Frazer	5 & 3	Douglas Grant	4 & 3	Chapin Tubbs	3 & 2	Robin Y. Hayne	74-69—143
1910	Aug	Campbell D. Whyte	d.	Austin White	3 & 2	Douglas Grant	4 & 3	Vincent Whitney	2 & 1	Douglas Grant	71-71—142
1911	Sep	Ervin S. Armstrong	d.	Dr. D.P. Fredericks	10 & 9	J.F. "Jack" Neville	2 & 1	Judge Frederickson	Dn-1	Frank C. Newton+	72-72—144
1912	Sep	J.F. "Jack" Neville	d.	Ervin S. Armstrong	2-up	Chapin Tubbs	37th	Vincent Whitney	2-up	J.F. "Jack" Neville	149

+ Newton won in an 18-hole playoff (35-36—71) with Dr. D.P. Fredericks (39-33—72) and Robin Hayne (40-34—74), who also scored 144 in the qualifying rounds.

CALIFORNIA STATE AMATEUR CHAMPIONSHIP (1912-2007)
The Del Monte Men's Championship was last played in 1912, the following weekend, the first State Amateur was played. Jack Neville won them both. From then on, the annual championship for men at Del Monte was only the State Amateur. Through 1919, the tournament was played only at Del Monte Golf Course, beginning in 1921 (except for a few years when there was no medal play), the medal play was on multiple courses (originally Del Monte and Pebble Beach) and the championship flight of match play was held on Pebble Beach Golf Links. The first exception was in 2000 (Bayonet), then in 2007, the CGA decided to rotate the championship. The 2007 Championship was played at MPCC.

MULTIPLE WINNERS

5 – John Francis "Jack" Neville	1912, 1913, 1919, 1922, 1929
3 – John J. McHugh	1923, 1927, 1928
2 – Dr. Paul Hunter	1920, 1921
2 – Roger Kelly	1937, 1938
2 – Ernest O. Pieper, Jr.	1941, 1944
2 – Bruce McCormick	1945, 1946
2 – Robert Gardner	1947, 1950
2 – Eli Bariteau, Jr.	1948, 1958
2 – Ken Venturi	1951, 1956
2 – Dr. Frank "Bud" Taylor	1954, 1955
2- Mike Brannan	1973, 1976
2 – Bobby Clampett	1978, 1980
2 – Casey Boyns	1989, 1993
2 – Verne Callison	1959, 1965

MULTIPLE MEDALISTS (*co-medalist)

3 – Douglas Grant	1917, 1918, 1919
3 – Roger Kelly	1936, 1938, 1939
3 – John W. Dawson	1945, 1949*, 1955*
2 – Robin Y. Hayne	1912, 1916
2 – E. "Scotty" Armstrong	1913, 1922
2 – Heinrich Schmidt	1914, 1915
2 – Gene Littler	1949*, 1952
2 – Ken Venturi	1953, 1956
2 – Dr. William O'Neal	1954, 1957
2 – Dan Morgan	1958, 1959*
2 – Dr. Arthur Butler	1960, 1965
2 – Sandy Galbraith	1971, 1991
2 – Mark Johnson	1990*, 1995
2 – Steve Woods	1994, 2006

MEDALIST/WINNER THE SAME YEAR

Douglas Grant	1918
Dr. Paul Hunter	1921
Roger Kelly	1938
Ken Venturi	1956
Bob Eastwood	1966*
Mike Brannan	1973
Bobby Clampett	1980
Duffy Waldorf	1984
Sam Randolph	1985
Casey Boyns	1993
Steve Woods	1994

			FINALISTS			SEMI FINALISTS					
Year	Ann	Winner		Runner-up	Score	Lost to Winner	Score	Lost to Runner-up	Score	Medalist	Score
1912	1st	J.F. "Jack" Neville	d.	Dr. D.P. Fredericks	2 & 1	Campbell D. Whyte	7 & 6	Robin Y. Hayne	1-up	Robin Y. Hayne	78-74—152
1913	2nd	J.F. "Jack" Neville	d.	E. "Scotty" Armstrong	5 & 3	Clinton La Montagne	10 & 9	Vincent Whitney	10 & 9	E. S. Armstrong	74-76—150
1914	3rd	Harry K.B. Davis	d.	Heinrich Schmidt	5 & 4	J.F. "Jack" Neville	2-up	Al A. French	2 & 1	Heinrich Schmidt	70-72—142
1915	4th	E. "Scotty" Armstrong	d.	Heinrich Schmidt	6 & 5	Dr. Eaves	6 & 4	Al A. French	7 & 6	Heinrich Schmidt	72-72—144
1916	5th	Larry Cowing	d.	Robin Y. Hayne	5 & 4	E.K. Johnstone	5 & 4	E. "Scotty" Armstrong	4 & 3	Robin Y. Hayne	75-74—149
1917	6th	Dr. Charles H. Walter	d.	Douglas Grant	1-up	Dr. A. Don Hines	9 & 8	J.F. "Jack" Neville	6 & 4	Douglas Grant	74-70—144
1918	7th	Douglas Grant	d.	J.K. Wadley	8 & 7	Arthur Vincent	6 & 5	Charles E. Maud	37th	Douglas Grant	74-74—148
1919	8th	J.F. "Jack" Neville	d.	Dr. Charles H. Walter	5 & 4	Gus Schwartz	9 & 8	Frank Tatum	7 & 6	Douglas Grant	74-74—148
1920	9th	Dr. Paul M. Hunter	d.	E. "Scotty" Armstrong	6 & 4	Dr. A. Don Hines	8 & 7	Fred R. Upton	1-up	Robert Hunter	76-73—149
1921	10th	Dr. Paul M. Hunter	d.	Fitzgerald Marx	6 & 5	Frank A. Kales	8 & 7	E. "Scotty" Armstrong	1-up	Dr. Paul M. Hunter	78-75—153
1922	11th	J.F. "Jack" Neville	d.	Robert Hunter	11 & 9	Fred J. Wright, Jr.	1-up	Norman Macbeth	3 & 1	E. S. Armstrong	71-74—145
1923	12th	John J. McHugh	d.	Fred J. Wright, Jr.	9 & 8	J.F. "Jack" Neville	6 & 5	George Ritchie	5 & 4	Willie Hunter	72-72—144
1924	13th	Capt A. Bullock-Webster	d.	Rudolph Wilhelm	7 & 5	E. "Scotty" Armstrong	6 & 5	Frank Godchaux	4 & 3	Frank Godchaux	78-72—144
1925	14th	George VonElm	d.	Frank Dolp	2 & 1	C.D. "Chuck" Hunter, Jr.	11 & 10	Harold Thompson	6 & 4	H. Chandler Egan	73-71—144
1926	15th	H. Chandler Egan	d.	John J. McHugh	3 & 1	Dr. Paul M. Hunter	1-up	C.D. "Chuck" Hunter, Jr.	2-up	Oswald Carlton / Donald Moe	73-70—143 / 75-68—143
1927	16th	John J. McHugh	d.	C.D. "Chuck" Hunter, Jr.	8 & 7	Heinrich Schmidt	1-up	Frank Dolp	3 & 1	George VonElm	68-72—140
1928	17th	John J. McHugh	d.	H. Chandler Egan	6 & 5	Russell Thompson	6 & 5	Harold Thompson	6 & 4	Jack Gaines	75-75—150
1929	18th	J.F. "Jack" Neville	d.	Frank C. Stevens, Jr.	3 & 1	John J. McHugh	3 & 1	Fay Coleman	1-up	Fay Coleman / John J. McHugh	77-76—153 / 80-73—153

Year	No.	Champion		Runner-up		Semifinalist		Semifinalist		Medalist	Score
1930	19th	Francis H.I. Brown	d.	Fay Coleman	10 & 9	John J. McHugh	2 & 1	Harry Eichelberger	4 & 3	W. Lawson Little, Jr.	73-75—148
1931	20th	David Martin	d.	Ernie O. Pieper, Jr.	10 & 8	John Robbins	7 & 6	Guy E. Hanson	4 & 3	No Qualifying	
1932	21st	Neil White	d.	Harold Thompson	3 & 2	David Martin	1-up	Ernie O. Pieper, Jr.	3 & 1	No Qualifying	
1933	22nd	Charles Seaver	d.	Dr. Cliff Baker	3 & 1	Harold Thompson	6 & 5	Jack Finger	3 & 2	No Qualifying	
1934	23rd	Stuart Hawley, Jr.	d.	Don Edwards	1-up	Frank Hixon	3 & 2	Ernie O. Pieper, Jr.	2-up	John Robbins / Jack Nounnan	71-71—142 / 71-71—142
1935	24th	Jack Gaines	d.	Stuart Hawley, Jr.	2 & 1	Ernie O. Pieper, Jr.	6 & 5	Harry Wesbrook	4 & 3	Ernie O. Pieper, Jr.	75-71—146
1936	25th	Mat Palacio, Jr.	d.	Jim M. Rea	1-up	Jack Nounnan	2 & 1	Tom Teffler	7 & 6	Roger Kelly	72-71—143
1937	26th	Roger Kelly	d.	Mat Palacio, Jr.	12&10	Frank "Bud" Taylor	20th	Jack Nounnan	1-up	Ernest Combs*	73-70—143
1938	27th	Roger Kelly	d.	Bob McGlashen	8 & 7	Jack Westervelt	8 & 6	Ralph Hoffman	4 & 3	Roger Kelly	74-70—144
1939	28th	Jack Gage	d.	Walter Gilliam, Jr.	3 & 2	Jack Finger	4 & 3	Ernie O. Pieper, Jr.	3 & 3	Roger Kelly	71-72—143
1940	29th	Ed Monaghan	d.	Jack Gage	7 & 5	George Coleman	5 & 4	Frank "Bud" Taylor	3 & 2	Rennie Kelly	73-72—145
1941	30th	Ernie O. Pieper, Jr.	d.	Robert Gardner	4 & 2	Tom Dwyer	3 & 2	John Hanley	6 & 5	Ralph Lomelli	72-74—146
1942	31st	John W. Dawson	d.	Robert Gardner	8 & 7	Smiley Quick	3 & 1	Frank Hixon	5 & 3	"Bud" Brownell, Jr.	73-66—139
1943	32nd	Elmer Cites	d.	Bob Rosburg	8 & 6	Phillip Stearns	4 & 2	Ralph Hall	3 & 1	Henry Suico	70
1944	33rd	Ernie O. Pieper, Jr.	d.	Bob Rosburg	5 & 4	John W. Dawson	8 & 7	H.M. "Mac" Hunter	10 & 9	Bob Rosburg	72
1945	34th	Bruce McCormick	d.	Jack Nounnan	4 & 3	Barge Pease	5 & 4	George Schoux	4 & 2	John W. Dawson	69-75—144
1946	35th	Bruce McCormick	d.	Ernie O. Pieper, Jr.	2 & 1	Mike Ferentz	1-up	Tal Smith	8 & 7	Eli Bariteau, Jr.	71
1947	36th	Robert Gardner	d.	Smiley Quick	2 & 1	Verne Callison	8 & 6	Paul Millett	3 & 2	Morgan Fottrell	71
1948	37th	Eli Bariteau, Jr.	d.	Bob Rosburg	37th	Bobby Harris	3 & 2	Clarke Hardwicke	9 & 8	Russell "Buddy"York*	72
1949	38th	Henry M. "Mac" Hunter	d.	Gene Littler	39th	Verne Callison	6 & 5	John W. Dawson	2 & 1	Gene Littler / John W. Dawson / Tal Smith	69 / 69 / 69
1950	39th	Robert Gardner	d.	Willie Barber	7 & 5	Bud McKinney	9 & 8	Gene Littler	37th	Fred Jordan	72
1951	40th	Ken Venturi	d.	Dr. Frank "Bud" Taylor	7 & 6	Gene Littler	5 & 4	Bruce McCormick	3 & 1	Bud Holscher	74-68—142
1952	41st	Bob Silvestri	d.	Bruce McCormick	1-up	Jerry Douglas	9 & 8	Bud Holscher	38th	Gene Littler	71-71—142
1953	42nd	Gene Littler	d.	Dr. Frank "Bud" Taylor	5 & 4	Jock Richardson	9 & 8	Chuck Soper	11 & 9	Ken Venturi	68-71—139
1954	43rd	Dr. Frank "Bud" Taylor	d.	Walter Gilliam, Jr.	3 & 2	George Galios	4 & 2	Frank Hoover	7 & 6	Dr. William O'Neal	69-73—142
1955	44th	Dr. Frank "Bud" Taylor	d.	Jack Lovegren	3 & 1	Bob Silvestri	3 & 2	Aldo Galletti	37th	Tom Draper / John W. Dawson	74-67—141 / 72-69—141
1956	45th	Ken Venturi	d.	Dr. Frank "Bud" Taylor	2 & 1	Ted Gleichmann	5 & 3	Ernie O. Pieper, Jr.	2-up	Ken Venturi / Bob Silvestri	72-70—142 / 72-70—142
1957	46th	Tal Smith	d.	Dick Giddings	7 & 6	Gene Andrews	3 & 1	Bob McAllister	1-up	Dr. William O'Neal	68-72—140
1958	47th	Eli Bariteau, Jr.	d.	Dan Morgan	1-up	Steve Stimac	4 & 3	George Galios	4 & 3	Dan Morgan	73-69—142
1959	48th	Verne Callison	d.	Dick Runkle	6 & 4	George Galios	1-up	Frank Zack	21st	Dan Morgan / Bob Roos	73-72—145 / 69-76—145
1960	49th	Larry Bouchey	d.	George Galios	7 & 5	Jack Bariteau	7 & 5	John Lotz	6 & 4	Dr. Arthur F. Butler	72-73—145
1961	50th	John Richardson	d.	John Lotz	2 & 1	Ed Castagnetto	9 & 8	Dr. Arthur F. Butler	4 & 3	No Qualifying	
1962	51st	Dick Lotz	d.	Ron Cerrudo	5 & 3	Bud Shank	8 & 6	John Lotz	2-up	John Lotz	71-70—141
1963	52nd	Dr. Paul Travis	d.	Dick Runkle	3 & 2	James Rheim	1-up	David Bohannon	6 & 4	Peter Choate	75-66—141
1964	53rd	Steve Opperman	d.	Guy Bill	37th	Dr. Don Keith	4 & 3	Ross Randall	2 & 1	Ron Cerrudo	76-69—145
1965	54th	Verne Callison	d.	Dr. Arthur F. Butler	5 & 4	Jim Johnson	8 & 7	Vic Loustalot	3 & 1	Dr. Arthur F. Butler	72-71—143
1966	55th	Bob Eastwood	d.	Vic Loustalot	3 & 2	Dallan Ragland	2-up	Eli Bariteau, Jr.	8 & 7	Bob Eastwood*	75-74—149
1967	56th	Bob E. Smith	d.	James Rheim	7 & 5	Harry Taylor	2-up	Guy Bill	6 & 5	Arne Dokka	71-72—143
1968	57th	Johnny Miller	d.	Les Peterson	12&10	Forrest Fezler	9 & 7	Ernie O. Pieper, Jr.	3 & 2	Les Peterson	72-72—144
1969	58th	Forrest Fezler	d.	Steve Stimac	8 & 6	Dick Runkle	9 & 8	John Brodie	2 & 1	Ted Lyford	73-72—145
1970	59th	Bob Risch	d.	Vic Loustalot	39th	Jerry Hedding	5 & 4	Dick Runkle	7 & 6	Tom Smith	75-72—147
1971	60th	Doug Nelson	d.	Sandy Galbraith	8 & 7	Aly Trompas	7 & 6	Bruce Robertson	6 & 4	Sandy Galbraith	72-73—145
1972	61st	H. M. "Mac" Hunter, Jr.	d.	Bob Roos	2-up	Ray Leach	2 & 1	Harry Fischer	3 & 1	Mark Pfeil	73-73—146
1973	62nd	Mike Brannan	d.	Dick Runkle	37th	John Abendroth	4 & 2	Bill Malley	8 & 6	Mike Brannan	70-71—141
1974	63rd	Curtis Worley	d.	Mike Brannan	1-up	Dick Runkle	2 & 1	Lee Mikles	5 & 4	Craig Stadler	73-73-78—224
1975	64th	John Cook	d.	Bob Bloomberg	2 & 1	John Richardson	1-up	Doug Talley	6 & 4	Clem Richardson*	74-77-77—228
1976	65th	Mike Brannan	d.	Ron Commans	3 & 2	John Richardson	6 & 5	Lee Davis	19th	Scott Simpson	72-70-76—218
1977	66th	Lee Mikles	d.	Ted Lyford	2 & 1	Ron Commans	6 & 4	Brett Mullin	2-up	Tom Culligan III*	74-74-74—222
1978	67th	Bobby Clampett	d.	Ray Pellegrini	5 & 4	Mark Tinder	3 & 2	Chris Gutilla	3 & 2	Don Levin	70-71-78—219
1979	68th	Mark O'Meara	d.	Lennie Clements	8 & 7	Bryan Pini	2 & 1	Tim Norris	5 & 4	Lennie Clements	72-74-68—214
1980	69th	Bobby Clampett	d.	Jim Kane	6 & 4	Don Bliss	2 & 1	Mark O'Meara	3 & 2	Bobby Clampett	69-70-71—210
1981	70th	Joe Tamburino	d.	Brian Lindley	4 & 2	Don Bliss	1-up	Eddie Luethke	2 & 1	Mike Barnblatt*	72-73-72—217
1982	71st	Gary Vanier	d.	Bob Bloomberg	3 & 2	Craig Steinberg	19th	Ray Pellegrini	2 & 1	Corey Pavin	70-74-71—215
1983	72nd	Kris Moe	d.	Tracy Nakazaki	8 & 6	Bruce Zulalca	6 & 5	Jeff Wilson	5 & 4	Gregg Twiggs*	68-77-72—217
1984	73rd	Duffy Waldorf	d.	Mark Phillips	2 & 1	Gary Vanier	5 & 4	Doug Thompson	2 & 1	Duffy Waldorf	70-76-68—214
1985	74th	Sam Randolph	d.	Brad Greer	5 & 4	Dennis Paulson	3 & 2	Jim Myers	2 & 1	Sam Randolph	69-70-73—212
1986	75th	Terrence Miskell	d.	Mike Blewett	5 & 4	Eric Woods	2-up	Carl Wagner	20th	Dana Banke	70-70-74—214
1987	76th	Mike Springer	d.	Bob May	4 & 3	Perry Parker	2 & 1	Kevin Sutherland	4 & 3	Bob Lasken*	70-72-77—219
1988	77th	Don Parsons	d.	Randy Haag	5 & 4	Steven McMichael	1-up	Bob Marten	4 & 3	Aaron Meeks	75-72-68—215
1989	78th	Casey Boyns	d.	Dave Stockton, Jr.	4 & 3	Jack Spradlin	1-up	Tom Kennaday	4 & 2	Jerry Michaels*	69-72—141
1990	79th	Charlie Wi	d.	Gary Vanier	3 & 2	Paul Stankowski	19th	Terrence Miskell	1-up	Mark Johnson*	73-69—142
1991	80th	Harry Rudolph III	d.	Sandy Galbraith	3 & 2	Gary Vanier	3 & 2	Eddie Davis	6 & 5	Sandy Galbraith	70-75—145
1992	81st	Todd Dempsey	d.	David Berganio, Jr.	5 & 4	Mark Johnson	1-up	Charlie Wi	1-up	Harry Rudolph III	74-69—143
1993	82nd	Casey Boyns	d.	Joey Ferrari	3 & 1	Gary Vanier	3 & 2	Kevin Riley	20th	Casey Boyns*	73-70—143
1994	83rd	Steve Woods	d.	Ed Cuff, Jr.	5 & 3	Steve Burdick	2-up	Eldrick "Tiger" Woods	2 & 1	Steve Woods	69-73—142

Year	#	Winner	d.	Runner-up	Score	Lost to Winner	Score	Lost to Runner-up	Score	Medalist	Score
1995	84th	Jeff Sanday	d.	John Pate	1-up	Bob Niger	6 & 4	Craig Steinberg	4 & 3	Mark Johnson	72-72—144
1996	85th	Mark Johnson	d.	Brian Crocker	8 & 7	David Burroughs	2 & 1	Randy Haag	3 & 1	Jeff Gilchrist	69-73—142
1997	86th	Jason Gore	d.	Scott Watson	6 & 5	Ed Cuff, Jr.	1-up	Tim Hogarth	4 & 3	Tim Hogarth	71-67—138
1998	87th	Ed Cuff, Jr.	d.	Bobby Rodger	5 & 4	Rodd Rose	3 & 2	Daniel Arroyo	2 & 1	Craig Steinberg	73-68—141
1999	88th	Tim Hogarth	d.	Gary Vanier	38th	Dong Yi	5 & 3	John Mallinger	3 & 2	Ed Cuff, Jr. / Steve Conway	72-70—142 / 73-69—142
2000	89th	Nick Jones	d.	Troy McKinley	2-up	Jim Skinner	2 & 1	John Enright	26th	Todd Miller / James Stewart	73-70—143 / 71-72—143
2001	90th	Darryl Donovan	d.	Travis Johnson	4 & 3	Scott McGihon	2 & 1	James Hay	4 & 3	Jeff Wilson	69-72—141
2002	91st	Eddie Heinen	d.	Jonathan Echols	1-up	Mark "Buzz" Peel	1-up	Scott Terry	20th	Don DuBois	75-71—146
2003	92nd	Patrick Nagle	d.	Spencer Levin	4 & 3	Eddie Heinen	1-up	Scott Almquist	4 & 3	Roy Moon	71-70—141
2004	93rd	Spencer Levin	d.	Mark "Buzz" Peel	4 & 3	Casey Boyns	20th	Mark Warman	5 & 4	Mark Sear	75-67-68—210
2005	94th	Don DuBois	d.	Joseph Bramlett	2 & 1	Eric Riehle	20th	Rick Reinsberg	6 & 5	Jordan Cox	71-69-72—212
2006	95th	Jordan Nasser	d.	Jeff Gilchrist	3 & 2	David Bartman	2-up	Joseph Bramlett	3 & 2	Steve Woods	71-70-66—207
2007	96th	Josh Anderson	d.	Joe Greiner	4 & 3	Shiwan Kim	20th	John McClure	19th	Blake Trimble	67-74—141

DEL MONTE CUP – WOMEN'S CHAMPIONSHIP (1898-1908)

Early championships were played for donated cups: 1899 – George Crocker Cup; 1900 – Henry T. Scott Cup. In 1901 and 1902 it stood as the Pacific Coast Golf Association (PCGA) Women's Amateur Championship.

Year	Mo	Winner	Score	Net Handicap	Score	
1898	Aug	Mrs. C.R. Scudder	75	Mrs. J.D. Harvey	67	80 (13) 67
1899	Aug	Miss Mary Scott	111			
1900	Aug	Mrs. R. Gilman Brown	99			

FINALISTS — SEMIFINALISTS

Year	Mo	Winner		Runner-up	Score	Lost to Winner	Score	Lost to Runner-up	Score	Medalist	Score
1901	Aug	Miss Caro Crockett	d.	Miss Alice Hager	1-up	Florence Ives	6 & 5	Bertha Dolbeer	2 & 1	Mrs. R. G. Brown	95
1902	Aug	Mrs. R. Gilman Brown	d.	Edith Chesebrough	6 & 3						
1903	Aug	Edith Chesebrough	d.	Bertha Dolbeer	5 & 4						
1904	Aug	Mrs. H.(Charlotte) Munn	d.	Mrs. R. Gilman Brown	Playoff						
1905	Sep	Mrs. W.S. Martin	d.	Mrs. R. Gilman Brown	2-up						
1906	Aug	Mrs. H.H. Sherwood	d.	Mrs. W.S. Martin	def.						
1907	Sep	Mrs. J. Leroy Nickel	d.	Miss West	3 & 2	Mrs. W.S. Martin		Mrs. W.F. George		Mrs. W.S. Martin	91
1908	Sep	Edith Chesebrough	d.	Mrs. G.W. Lane	3 & 2	Mrs. J.V. Eliot	7 & 6	Mrs. W.F. George	5 & 4		

DEL MONTE WOMEN'S CHAMPIONSHIPS (1909-1943)

The Del Monte Championship was played concurrently with the Men's Championship, which became the California Amateur Championship. While there was also a Women's State Amateur, the Del Monte Women's Championship continued to be a prestigious and popular tournament until World War II, regularly attracting the top women golfers of the state, and occasionally from other areas. It was played on Del Monte Golf Course every year except 1943 at Cypress Point.

MULTIPLE WINNERS
6 – Edith Chesebrough VanAntwerp 1911, 1912, 1918, 1919, 1921, 1923
5 – Clara Callender 1932, 1934, 1935, 1940, 1942
3 – Helen Lawson Shepherd 1927, 1936, 1937
3 – Kathleen Wright 1917, 1925, 1926
2 – Alice Warner Law 1913, 1914
2 – Leona Pressler 1929, 1930

MULTIPLE MEDALISTS (* CO-MEDALIST)
4 – Kathleen Wright 1917, 1924*, 1925, 1927
4 – Clara Callender 1932*, 1934, 1936, 1942
3 – Edith Chesebrough VanAntwerp 1913*, 1918, 1920
2 – Alice Warner Law 1912, 1913*
2 – Doreen Kavanagh 1921, 1922
2 – Helen Sheedy 1924*, 1928
2 – Sylvia Potter 1931, 1932*
2 – Helen Lawson Shepherd 1932*, 1935
2 – Iva Liston 1932*, 1933*
2 – Catherine Shuster Lunn 1939, 1941

MEDALIST/WINNER THE SAME YEAR
3 – Clara Callender 1932, 1934, 1942
2 – Alice Warner Law 1913, 1919
1 – Kathleen Wright 1917
1 – Edith Chesebrough VanAntwerp 1918
1 – Mildred "Babe" Zaharias 1943

FINALISTS — SEMIFINALISTS

Year	Mo	Winner		Runner-up	Score	Lost to Winner	Score	Lost to Runner-up	Score	Medalist	Score
1909	Sep	Alice Hager	d.	Mrs. T.W. Bishop	6 & 4	Mrs. H.(Charlotte) Munn	4 & 3	Miss H.M. Pillans	7 & 5	Katherine Mellus	92
1910	Aug	Margaret Morris	d.	Mrs. G.R. Field	1-up	Miss M. Ebner	4 & 2	Ethel Havemeyer	4 & 3	Mrs. G.R. Field	88
1911	Sep	Edith Chesebrough	d.	Mrs. J.V. Eliot	4 & 2	Alice Warner	7 & 6	Mrs. Edgar Hodge	1-up	Jennie Crocker	85
1912	Sep	Edith Chesebrough	d.	Mrs. A.R.(Alice) Pommer	4 & 3	Mrs. Augustus Taylor	5 & 4	Alice Hager	3 & 2	Alice Warner	95
1913	Sep	Alice Warner	d.	Edith Chesebrough	4 & 3	Mrs. A.R.(Alice) Pommer	2 & 1	Alice Hager	3 & 2	Edith Chesebrough	94
1914	Sep	Alice Warner	d.	Katherine Mellus	4 & 3	Mrs. H.S. VanDyke	3 & 2	Mrs. W.S. Martin	2-up	Mrs. A.R. Pommer	90
1915	Sep	Mrs. A.R.(Alice) Pommer	d.	Mrs. Thomas S. Baker	4 & 3	Edith Chesebrough	2-up	Mrs. Henry S. VanDyke	5 & 4	Mrs. A. Swinnerton	89
1916	Sep	Miss Josephine Johnson	d.	Mrs. Malcolm Whitman	3 & 2	Mrs. Eli Wiel	6 & 4	Cornelia Armsby	4 & 3	Mrs. Emery T. Smith / Mrs. Robert A. Roos	88 / 88
1917	Sep	Kathleen Wright	d.	Mrs. Guy Cochrane	7 & 5	Mrs. Al Roscoe	2 & 1	Mrs. M.C. Milton	4 & 3	Kathleen Wright	91
1918	Sep	Edith Chesebrough	d.	Miss Josephine Moore	19th	Maud Kegley	8 & 7	Miss Rosenfeld	1-up	Edith Chesebrough	88
1919	Aug	E. Chesebrough 89-88—177		Mrs. Charles F. Ford 86-94—180		Mrs. Thomas F. Baker 95-86—181		Miss Alice Hanchett 92-93—185		36-hole medal play; no matches	
1920	Sep	Margaret Cameron	d.	Mrs. W.C. VanAntwerp	2-up	Kathleen Wright	def.	Mrs. Luther Kennett	2 & 1	Mrs. W VanAntwerp	82
1921	Sep	Mrs. W.C. VanAntwerp	d.	Margaret Cameron	4 & 2	Mrs. Thomas S. Baker	5 & 4	Mrs. Herbert Rothschild	7 & 6	Doreen Kavanagh	86
1922	Sep	Miss Mary K. Browne	d.	Doreen Kavanagh	3 & 1	Mrs. Robert A. Roos	2 & 1	Kathleen Wright	6 & 5	Doreen Kavanagh	86

1923	Sep	Mrs. W.C. VanAntwerp	d.	Miss Mary K. Browne	1-up	Mrs. Brent (Sylvia) Potter	2 & 1	Hester Uhl	6 & 4	Mrs. F.S. Hardin	89
1924	Sep	Mrs. Joe Mayo	d.	Mrs. F.S. Hardin	1-up	Kathleen Wright	1-up	Mrs. George Weber	19th	Kathleen Wright	89
										Mrs. H. Grossman	89
										Mrs. Frank Sheedy	89
1925	Sep	Kathleen Wright	d.	Mrs. F. (Helen) Sheedy	5 & 3	Mrs. L. (Helen) Lengfeld	3 & 2	Mrs. Milton Bernard	2 & 1	Kathleen Wright	78
1926	Sep	Kathleen Wright	d.	Mrs. Harry Grossman	5 & 4	Mrs. Gregg Lifur	3 & 2	Mrs. H.D. Hammond	2 & 1	Mrs. T.H. Pike	82
1927	Sep	Helen Lawson	d.	Mrs. Brent (Sylvia)Potter	1-up	Mrs. J.M. Yount	3 & 1	Kathleen Wright	Dn-1	Kathleen Wright	77
1928	Sep	Marjorie Kirkham	d.	Mrs. F. (Helen) Sheedy	4 & 3	Mrs. C.A. Webster	3 & 2	Barbara Lee	21st	Mrs. Frank Sheedy	86
Year	Mo	Winner		Runner-up	Score	Lost to Winner	Score	Lost to Runner-up	Score	Medalist	Score
1929	Jun	Mrs. H. (Leona) Pressler	d.	Mrs. Gregg Lifur	19th	Mrs. Brent (Sylvia) Potter	4 & 2	Esther Scott	5 & 3	Mrs. Gregg Lifur	79
1930	Sep	Mrs. H. (Leona) Pressler	d.	Mrs. Brent (Sylvia)Potter	6 & 5	Rea Gottlieb	4 & 3	Hermine Wocker	19th	Barbara Lee	80
1931	Sep	Mrs. Brent (Sylvia)Potter	d.	Esther Scott	6 & 5	Clara Callender	Dn-2	Mrs. Herbert Rothschild	20th	Mrs. Brent Potter	82
1932	Sep	Clara Callender	d.	Mrs. Brent (Sylvia) Potter	3 & 2	Mary Lou Powers	4 & 2	Helen Lawson	5 & 4	Clara Callender	84
										Helen Lawson	84
										Mrs. Brent Potter	84
										Iva Liston	84
1933	Sep	Jane Douglas	d.	Clara Callender	5 & 4	Betty Vetterlein	5 & 4	Mrs. C.K. Bellew	19th	Mrs. R.C. Noble	83
										Iva Liston	83
1934	Sep	Clara Callender	d.	Mrs. George Lewis	7 & 6	Elizabeth Abbott	6 & 5	Mrs. Charles Woerner	2 & 1	Clara Callender	76
1935	Sep	Clara Callender	d.	Mary Hayne	3 & 2	Barbara Ransom	5 & 4	Mrs. C.B. Mugridge	5 & 4	Mrs. W.E.Shepherd	75
1936	Aug	Mrs. W.E. Shepherd	d.	Ruth Tustin	6 & 4	Barbara Ransom	Dn-1	Margaret Bushard	1-up	Clara Callender	78
1937	Aug	Mrs. W.E. Shepherd	d.	Clara Callender	2 & 1	Mary Morse	Dn-1	Mrs. L.T. Tescher	6 & 5	Barbara Ransom	75
1938	Aug	Barbara B. Thompson	d.	Mrs. R.S. Morimoto	3 & 1	Elizabeth Hicks	3 & 2	Clara Callender	Dn-1	Elizabeth Hicks	75
1939	Aug	Barbara Ransom	d.	Mrs. W.E. Shepherd	7 & 6	Mrs. R.S. Morimoto	4 & 3	Frances Glover	6 & 4	Catherine Shuster	77
										Mrs. R.S. Morimoto	77
1940	Sep	Clara Callender	d.	Frances Glover	1-up	Mrs. Arthur McArthur	4 & 3	Mary Morse	5 & 4	Mrs. Allan Pattee	77
1941	Sep	Marion Hollins	d.	Mrs. Joseph Lunn	1-up	Patricia McPhee	4 & 3	Mrs. Roxie Setrakian	Dn-1	Mrs. Joseph Lunn	80
1942	Sep	Clara Callender	d.	Marion Hollins	9 & 8	Mrs. A.A. Bolton	4 & 2	Mrs. Simon J. Anink, Jr.	2 & 1	Clara Callender	71
1943	Sep	Mrs. Geo. Zaharias	d.	Mrs. Walter McCarthy	13-12	Peggy Rutledge	Dn-2	Mrs. Decker McAllister	2 & 1	Mrs. Geo. Zaharias	79

DEL MONTE WOMEN'S CHAMPIONSHIPS (1947-1953)

The Del Monte Championships were not played in 1944, 1945, 1946, and 1952. In its post-war years it was much more a diversion from the Men's State Amateur, poorly attended and lacking its former prestige. It was strictly stroke play and in 1950, eclectic – adding the low scores per hole of two rounds. Below are the top three finishers:

1947 – 54 holes
1 – Barbara Ransom 84-87-82—253
2 – Mrs. Paul Gardner 86-85-xx—xxx
3 – Barbara Dawson 83-89-xx—xxx

1948 – 54 Holes
1 – Mary Sargent 78-80-81—239
2 – Barbara Ransom 85-84-76—245
3 – Mrs. Cory (Mary) Briggs 83-84-81—248

1949 – 54 Holes
1 – Mrs. Cory (Mary) Briggs 85-77-85—247
2 – Mrs. Calvin Tiden 85-87-82—254
3 – Mrs. Harry Winters 82-90-84—256

1950 – 36 Holes - Eclectic
1 – Mrs. Calvin Tilden 70 (1) 69
2 – Mrs. William Millar 75 (3) 72
3 – Mrs. Jack Holmes 77 (0) 77

1951 – 36 Holes
1 – Mrs. Jack Holmes 82-78—160
2 – Mrs. Paul Gardner 82-89—168
3 – Barbara Ransom 87-82—169

1953 – 36 Holes
1 – Gloria Armstrong 73-82—155
T-2 – Mrs. H.O. Milds 85-82—167
T-2 – Mrs. Harry Winters 8 5-81—167

CALIFORNIA WOMEN'S AMATEUR – (1901-1920)

The Pacific Coast Golf Association instituted a women's championship in 1901 that was played at Del Monte Golf Course for its first two years. It moved to Los Angeles in 1903 to draw a larger field; it did not and was discontinued. The 1902 Champion, Mrs. R. Gilman Brown of San Francisco, led the charge to form the California Women Golfers Association in 1905, reinstituting a women's championship in 1906 that utilized the earlier perpetual trophy used for the PCGA championship. It rotated between courses in northern and southern California. It was canceled in 1918 due to World War I, and in 1919 the ladies opted to use the scheduled Del Monte Championship match play as the Women Golfers State Amateur and play a 36-hole stroke play championship as the Del Monte Championship, separate from the regularly scheduled qualifying medal round and match play event. Alice Warner Law, who had won the 1916 and 1917 state championships, won the 1919 championship and was awarded possession of the perpetual trophy for her three straight wins.

		FINALISTS				SEMIFINALISTS					
Year	Mo	Winner		Runner-up	Score	Lost to Winner	Score	Lost to Runner-up	Score	Medalist	Score
1901	Aug	Miss Caro Crockett	d.	Miss Alice Hager	1-up	Florence Ives	6 & 5	Bertha Dolbeer	2 & 1	Mrs. R.G. Brown	95
1902	Aug	Mrs. R. Gilman Brown	d.	Edith Chesebrough	6 & 3						
1919	Sep	Mrs. Hubert E. Law	d.	Mrs. Robert A. Roos	20th	Doreen Kavanagh	Dn-1	Edith Chesebrough	19th	Mrs. H. E. Law	87

CALIFORNIA WOMEN'S AMATEUR – (1920-2007)

In 1920 the Women's Golf Association of California was reorganized and the earlier championships were no longer deemed official, even though the championship continued to be match play and rotated between courses north and south. This version of the Women's California Amateur Championship made but one stop on the Monterey Peninsula. The 2008 Championship was cancelled and the event is to be reorganized for the future.

		FINALISTS				SEMIFINALISTS					
Year		Winner		Runner-up	Score	Lost to Winner	Score	Lost to Runner-up	Score	Medalist	Score
1952	MPCC	Miss Barbara Romack	d.	Mrs. Ruth McCullah	5 & 3	Mrs. Peter Patch		Mrs. Fred Apostoli	19th	Romack / Ferrie	79
1958	MPCC	Barbara Romack Porter	d.	Mrs. George Downing	11 & 9	Mrs. William H. Hartson	3 & 1	Mrs. James Ferrie	3 & 1	Mrs. Wm. H. Hartson	

THE WESTERN AMATEUR CHAMPIONSHIP (1916)

The Western Golf Association was founded in 1899, and its headquarters have always been in Chicago, Illinois—then considered the West. It came to California with its championships more quickly than the USGA, bringing the Western Amateur to Del Monte in 1916. Free rail transportation from Chicago to Del Monte was offered to competitors, making it easier to attract a strong field. The USGA ruled any golfer accepting the free transportation would be stripped of their amateur status. The dispute over this aspect of control, and the WGA Board's acquiescence to the authority of the USGA, ended the battle for control of golf in America in favor of the USGA. The WGA never returned to the Monterey Peninsula.

18TH WESTERN AMATEUR CHAMPIONSHIP DEL MONTE GOLF COURSE, JULY 17-22, 1916
Medalist: Heinrich Schmidt, 73-72—145

MEDAL SCORE	QUARTERFINALISTS (36 HOLES)	SEMIFINALISTS	FINALISTS	WINNER
73-72—145	Heinrich Schmidt, Claremont, CA	Heinrich Schmidt 5 & 4		
75-74—149	E. Hoover Bankard, Jr., Chicago, IL		Heinrich Schmidt 13 & 12	
79-78—157	Roger Lapham, San Francisco, CA	Roger Lapham 4 & 3		Heinrich Schmidt Claremont, CA7 & 6
80-74—154	Harold Lamb			
76-72—148	Douglas Grant, Burlingame, CA	Douglas Grant 6 & 5		
74-80—154	E. "Scotty" Armstrong, Los Angeles, CA		Douglas Grant 5 & 4	
70-76—146	Clarence Mangham, San Antonio, TX	Clarence Mangham 2 & 1		
78-81—159	Walker Salisbury, Salt Lake City, UT			

PEBBLE BEACH UN-OFFICIAL OPENING DAY TOURNAMENT (APRIL 1, 1918)

Jack Neville organized an opening tournament for Pebble Beach Golf Links in 1918, attracting several top golfers from Northern California and a few visitors. The course condition was so poor and the scores so high, that "the course is in an early state of development and it will be many months before all the fairways and greens are in condition for real tournament play." The top finishers are listed below.

1	Mike Brady, Boston	79-75—154	T-6	John Black, Claremont	87-85—172
2	Harold Sampson, Pebble Beach	88-79—167	T-6	Tom McQuarree, Rock Island	84-88—172
3	a-John Francis "Jack" Neville, Claremont	84-81—165	8	Harold Clark, Marin	86-88—174
4	a-Dr. D.P. Fredericks, Claremont	87-81—168	9	William Kamens	92-84—176
5	Tom Hughes, Burlingame	85-85—170	10	Robert Clark, Belvedere	86-91—177
			11	Peter Hay, Stockton	91-91—182

THE CALIFORNIA OPEN

Open Championships on the West Coast date to the turn of the century. The early championships in California, like those in the east, were dominated by the Scottish and British Immigrants that served as the first golf professionals. The first official California Open was played at Del Monte Golf Course in 1919 and continued annually with the exception of 1928 and 1929. The winners of the earlier Opens at Del Monte were often credited as the California Open Champion.

Aug-1901	Del Monte	Robert Johnstone	1907	Del Monte		Sep-1913	Del Monte	Abe Espinosa
Aug-1902	Del Monte	F.J. Riley	1908	Del Monte		Sep-1914	Del Monte	
Aug-1903	Del Monte	Robert Johnstone	Aug-1909	Del Monte	George Smith	Sep-1915	Del Monte	Charlie Thom
Aug-1904	Del Monte	a-Charles E. Maud	Aug-1910	Del Monte	MacDonald Smith	Sep-1916	Del Monte	
Sep-1905	Del Monte	F.J. Riley	Aug-1911	Del Monte	Abe Espinosa	Sep-1917	Del Monte	a-Douglas Grant
Sep-1906	Del Monte	George Smith	Sep-1912	Del Monte	George Smith	Sep-1918	Del Monte	

1st California Open, Del Monte Golf Course		
August 31 – September 2, 1919		
1	John Black (Oakland)	70-71-71-71—284
2	a-Douglas Grant (Del Monte	71-72-73-71—287
3	Abe Espinosa (San Jose)	76-71-72-70—289
4	George Turnbull (Del Monte)	74-69-72-76—291
T-5	Harold Sampson (Pebble Beach)	71-72-73-77—293
T-5	Bob Lager (San Francisco)	74-74-72-73—293
T-7	Elmer Holland (Culver City)	74-80-74-71—299
T-7	Bill Hanley (Pasadena)	72-72-77-78—299
T-7	Mortie Dutra (Del Monte)	79-68-76-76—299
T-10	Al Espinosa (San Francisco)	76-71-78-75—300
T-10	Tom Hughes	80-74-74-72—300

15th California Open, Pebble Beach Golf Links		
August 20-22, 1935		
1	Cam Puget (Pebble Beach)	70-72-75-69—286
2	Willie Hunter (Culver City)	72-71-72-75—290
3	Mike DeMassey (Modesto)	73-73-76-72—294
T-4	Ted Longworth (Portland)	71-71-75-78—295
T-4	Fred Morrison (Pasadena)	70-77-72-76—295
6	a-Ernie Pieper (San Jose)	76-72-73-72—297
T-7	Charles Sheppard (Pleasanton)	75-72-75-76—298
T-7	Jack Finger (Burlingame)	75-76-77-70—298
T-9	Fay Coleman (Los Angeles)	72-78-70-79—299
T-9	Les Madison (Hollywood)	75-78-68-78—299
11	Dewey Longworth	74-78-73-75—300

16th California Open, Pebble Beach Golf Links		
August 18-20, 1936		
1	Fred Morrison (Pasadena)	72-73-75-72—292
T-2	Mark Fry (Oakland)	74-73-75-73—295
T-2	Benny Coltrin (San Francisco)	74-75-73-73—295
T-2	a-Roger Kelly (Los Angeles)	71-72-77-75—295
T-5	Joe Hunter (Santa Barbara)	73-75-76-75—299
T-5	Art Bell (Pasadena)	76-78-72-73—299
7	a-Don Edwards (San Jose)	74-75-82-70—301
8	Olin Dutra (Los Angeles)	77-72-73-80—302
9	Harold Sampson (Burlingame)	75-75-78-75—303
10	Les Madison (Hollywood)	77-80-73-74—304

28th California Open, Pebble Beach Golf Links		
April 30 – May 2, 1948		
1	Smiley Quick (Los Angeles)	71-75-71-74—291
2	Art Bell (San Francisco)	73-76-75-71—295
T-3	Ellsworth Vines (Pasadena)	74-72-77-75—298
T-3	a-Ernie Pieper (San Jose)	70-75-75-78—298
5	Ted Rhodes (Los Angeles)	77-75-72-75—299
6	Bill Nary (Monterey Park)	71-78-76-76—301
7	Paul Runyon (Pasadena)	74-73-78-79—304
T-8	a-Jack Bariteau (San Jose)	77-76-77-75—305
T-8	Ted Dorius San Diego)	76-74-80-75—305
10	Harry Bassler (Culver City)	76-76-77-78—307

PEBBLE BEACH GOLD VASE CHAMPIONSHIPS (1919-1932)

Pebble Beach Golf Links officially opened on Washington's Birthday 1919, and while the opening tournament was not officially for the Gold Vase, it led to a tradition of the Gold Vase which was awarded to the low gross medalist in the qualifying round for the match play of the annual Washington's Birthday tournament. In 1921 and 1922 The Gold Vase was played in March and while the associated match play is recorded below, the Washington's Birthday Tournament was still held in February. In 1923 M.A. McLaughlin, the two-time (1915, 1919) Colorado State Amateur Champion won the Gold Vase a third time. A new vase and 36-hole qualifying was instituted for 1924.

	Gold Vase Championship		Washington's Birthday Tournament			SEMIFINALISTS			
Year	Winner	Score	Winner	Runner-up	Score	Lost to Winner	Score	Lost to Runner-up	Score
1919	Douglas Grant	80 (0) 80							
1920	M.A. McLaughlin	85 (2) 83	D. Kerr (Portland)	J.A. Rithet (Victoria, BC)	1-up	Sam Russell	Def.	A.E. de Armond (Claremont)	5 & 4
1921	M.A. McLaughlin	80 (4) 76	A.E. de Armond (Claremont)	Fred LaBlond, Jr. (Berkeley)	1-up	M.A. McLaughlin (Denver)	1-up	Dr. William Moffatt	19th
1922	Robert Hunter	82 (5) 77	Clinton E. La Montagne (Mry)	M.A. McLaughlin (Denver)	3 & 2	George H. Mullin	6 & 5	Jack F. Morrill	5 & 4
1923	M.A. McLaughlin	79 (5) 74	Stuart Haldorn (San Francisco)	Dr. H.G. Meek (Sequoya CC)	6 & 5	Byington Ford (PB)	3 & 2	Daulton Mann	3 & 2
1924	A. Bullock Webster	73-79—152	E.O. Cornish (Vancouver, BC)	Glenn Littlefield (Casper, WY)	3 & 2	Stuart Haldorn (SF)	5 & 4	E.W. Hamber (Vancouver)	4 & 3
1925	Malcolm McBurney	79-80—159	Chuck D. Hunter, Jr. (Tacoma)	R.A. Stranahan (Ohio)	23rd	W.E. Egan	4 & 3	Malcolm McBurney	5 & 4
1926	J.B. Ryerson	77 (4) 73	John De Paolo	B. Goward	3 & 2	L.S. Ackerman	5 & 4	C.R. Harold	5 & 4
1927	Dick Lang	82-79—161							
1928	Jack Neville	76-76—152							
1929	A.G. Sato	80 (3) 77	Lloyd Thomas	H.C. Howe	4 & 3	A.G. Sato (San Francisco)	1-up	Earle Riley, Jr.	3 & 2
1930	H. Chandler Egan	79	W. Lawson Little, Jr.	John B. Ryerson (Cprstn, NY)	4 & 3	A.G. Sato (San Francisco)	3 & 2	Herman G. Bullock (MPCC)	19th
1931	Milton Latham	77-78—155							
1932	Wilbur Johnson	85 (0) 85	Stanley Heron (Carmel)	W.W. Holt (Pebble Beach)	2 & 1	J.A. Moore (Berkeley)	5 & 3	Wilbur Johnson (Los Angls)	2 & 1

The 1928 and 1931 winners of the Washington's Birthday Tournament remain undocumented, but we know the finalists.

1928 – Finalist John B. Ryerson (Cooperstown, NY) def. H.B. "Dutch" Leonard 2&1 in the semifinals
Finalist G.W. Foelschow (San Diego, CA) def. J.W. Roberts 1-up in the semifinals

1931 – Finalist A.G. Sato (San Francisco, CA) def. John S. Chapman 2-up in the semifinals
Finalist Stanley Heron (Carmel, CA) def. S.D. Ledig (Salinas, CA) 6&4 in the semifinals

CALIFORNIA JUNIOR CHAMPIONSHIPS (1920-1937)

Played at Del Monte Golf Course each year, originally for boys and girls who had not reached the age of 16. In 1925 they raised the age limit and 17-year-olds could compete, There was a separate division for Boys under 16. There is no record of it continuing after 1937. The NCGA and SCGA Junior Championships seemed to fill the need for statewide junior competitions. Peter Hay replaced it with his own championship in 1938 for local youth.

		FINALISTS			SEMIFINALISTS					
Year	Mo	Winner		Runner-up	Score	Lost to Winner	Score	Lost to Runner-up	Score	Medalist	Score
1919	Nov	Ashton Stanley (13)	d.	Don Carlos Hines	5 & 4					Don Carlos Hines	91
1920	Jul	E.B."Togo"Osbourne (15)	d.	Ashton Stanley (14)	6 & 5	Don Davin	6 & 5	Phillip Block	9 & 8	E.B. Osbourne	87
1921	Jul	Bobby Ross (15)	d.	Ashton Stanley (15)	21st					Bobby Ross	83
1922	Jul	Jimmy Wade (15)	d.	Don Davin	2-up	Robert D. Syer, Jr.	4 & 3	George K. McDaniels	6 & 4	Jimmy Wade	82
1923	Jul	George K. McDaniels	d.	Robert D. Syer, Jr.		Herbert Fleishhacker, Jr.		J.D. French		Don Davin	80
1924	Jul	Charles Helganz (15)	d.	David Martin	3 & 1	Leslie Hensley	6 & 4	Allen Moser	2 & 1	Allen Moser	81
1925	Jul	Norman MacBeth, Jr.	d.	Leslie Hensley	4 & 2	Justin W. Esberg	5 & 4	Elmer Duffus	7 & 5	Leslie Hensley	80
1926	Jul	Leslie Hensley	d.	Julian Cahn	1-up	Russell Pierce	Dn-2	David Martin	Dn-2	N. MacBeth, Jr.	76
1927	Jul	Leslie Hensley	d.	Clark Potter		Rudolph Bain	Dn-1	Don Nittinger	5 & 4	Dan H. Sangster	74
1928	Jul	Ernest F. Coombs (15)	d.	Harry Eichelberger	4 & 2	Norman MacBeth, Jr.	2 & 1	Bob Ballin	6 & 5	Harry Eichelberger	74
										Warren Johnson	74
1929	Jul	Ernie Pieper (17)	d.	Ernest F. Coombs (16)	1-up	Bert Honey (16)	Dn-1	Don Edwards (14)	4 & 3	Hugh Sill+	70
1930	Jul	Curtis Williams (17)	d.	Danny Sangster (17)	2-up	Don Edwards	4 & 3	Louis Cass, Jr.	6 & 5	Danny Sangster	71
1931	Jul	Dalton Henderson	d.	Don Edwards		Rex Bailes	1-up	Don Nittinger	5 & 4	Don Nittinger	72
1932	Jul	Bob Fahy (17)	d.	Mat Palacio, Jr.		Dalton Henderson	19th	William Halla	5 & 4		
1933	Jul	Mat Palacio, Jr.	d.	Walter Myers	2-up	Henry VanDyke	3 & 2	Jack Wallace	3 & 1	Mat Palacio, Jr.	69
1934	Jul	Robert Roos, Jr.	d.	Walter Myers	2-up	Charles Finger	4 & 3	Henry VanDyke	2 & 1	Jack Wallace	74
										Eddie Burns, Jr.	74
1935	Jul	Walter Myers	d.	Randolph Weinmann		Warner Keeley	8 & 7	Bud Fox	Dn-2	Randolph Weinman	71
1936	Jul	Charles Finger (17)	d.	Ray "Bud" Brownell	2 & 1	Warner Keeley	2 & 1	Don Kennedy	1-up	Bud Brownell	71
1937	Jul	Jerry Gundert (17)	d.	Bill McLaughlin	3 & 2	Sherman Selix	5 & 4	Ray "Bud" Brownell	1-up	Bud Brownell	76

+ *won medal honors in a playoff with Bob Marsky, Jr. who also shot 70 in the qualifying round*

THE $5,000 MONTEREY PENINSULA OPEN (DECEMBER 1926)

Seeking a way to bring national attention to Pebble Beach Golf Links as a championship caliber course, Morse arranged for the first significant professional tournament to be played at Pebble Beach, in the month preceding the Los Angeles Open. It attracted over 130 of the top professional and amateur champions of the era. Gene Sarazen was involved in the early publicity but did not return a card and Walter Hagen, pulled out at the last minute to accept an invitation to an exhibition match in the San Francisco area that offered a guarantee appearance fee greater than this tournament's first place prize of $1,200.

1	Harry Cooper, Los Angeles, CA	75-70-73-76—293	T-8	a-George von Elm, Los Angeles	76-71-77-75—299	T-14	Joe Turnesa, New York, NY	77-75-75-73—300
2	Larry Nahholtz, Cleveland, OH	76-73-69-77—295	T-8	Willie Hunter, Los Angeles, CA	76-71-77-75—299	T-16	Hutt Martin, Los Angeles	73-78-74-76—301
T-3	Bill Melhorn, Chicago, IL	72-70-79-75—296	T-8	Tommy Armour, New York, NY	75-73-74-77—299	T-16	Bobby Cruickshank, NY	74-75-74-78—301
T-3	Johnny Farrell, New York	77-71-69-79—296	T-8	Dick Linares, Long Beach, CA	77-72-72-78—299	T-16	Mike Brady, New York, NY	96-74-73-78—301
T-5	Abe Espinosa, Chicago, IL	78-73-73-73—297	T-8	Olin Dutra, Fresno, CA	78-70-74-77—299	T-16	Duncan Sutherland, Edmtn	76-72-76-77—301
T-5	Al Watrous, Grand Rapids, MI	75-72-72-78—297	T-8	Leo Diegel, Washington, DC	78-75-73-73—299	T-20	Bert Wilde, Bellingham, NY	75-79-76-72—302
7	Johnny Golden, Patterson, NJ	75-70-77-78--298	T-14	Geo. Joe Martin, Long Beach	74-71-75-80—300	T-20	Cyril Walker, Englewood, NJ	75-73-80-74—302

PEBBLE BEACH CHAMPIONSHIP FOR WOMEN (1923-1951)

Marion Hollins, the 1921 U.S. Women's Amateur Championship came to Pebble Beach in 1922 and established this championship in 1923. Through the start of World War II Hollins both attracted the finest players to compete in this event as well as she dominated the tournament herself. It was played on Pebble Beach Golf Links all but two years: 1928 at MPCC and 1933 at Cypress Point. The format was altered from match play in 1943 and 1951 due to poor turn-out.

Multiple Winners
7 – Marion Hollins 1923, 1924, 1925, 1926, 1928, 1933, 1942
3 – Dorothy Traung 1934, 1936, 1939
3 – Clara Callender 1937, 1938, 1941
2 – Patty Berg 1946, 1947
2 – Grace DeMoss 1949, 1950

Multiple Medalists (* co-medalist)
6 – Marion Hollins 1923, 1925, 1927*, 1930, 1932, 1933
3 – Dorothy Traung 1935, 1936, 1940
3 – Clara Callender 1937, 1938, 1941
2 – Patty Berg 1946, 1947
2 – Mrs. Decker McAlister 1942, 1943

Medalist/Winner the same year
3 – Marion Hollins 1923, 1925, 1933
3 – Clara Callender 1937, 1938, 1941
2 – Patty Berg 1946, 1947
1 – Mrs. Melvin Jones 1927*
1 – Dorothy Traung 1936
1 – Grace DeMoss 1950

FINALISTS / SEMI FINALISTS

Year	Mo	Winner		Runner-up	Score	Lost to Winner	Score	Lost to Runner-up	Score	Medalist	Score
1923	Feb	Marion Hollins	d.	Doreen Kavanagh	6 & 5	Mrs. Fred C. Letts, Jr.	Dn-2	Miss D.L. Higbie	9 & 7	Marion Hollins	88
1924	Feb	Marion Hollins	d.	Mary K. Browne	5 & 4	Mrs. H.G. Hutchings	2 & 1	Mrs. Brent Potter	2 & 1	Edith Cummings	86
1925	Feb	Marion Hollins	d.	Louise Fordyce	5 & 4	Margaret Cameron	6 & 4	Mary K. Browne	3 & 2	Marion Hollins	83
1926	Feb	Marion Hollins	d.	Mrs. W.C. VanAntwerp	6 & 5	Mrs. Frank Sheedy	4 & 3	Mrs. W.W. Campbell[1]	2-up	Mrs. H.G. Hutchings	87
1927	Feb	Mrs. Melvin Jones	d.	Marion Hollins	4 & 3	Alice Hanchett	3 & 2	Mrs. Lee Mida	7 & 5	Marion Hollins	96
										Mrs. Melvin Jones	96
1928	Feb	Marion Hollins	d.	Miriam Burns Horn	20th	Mrs. Ingalls Alker	5 & 4	Mrs. Joe Mayo	8 & 7	Miriam Burns Horn	74
1929	Feb	Mrs. Jim Yount	d.	Mrs. Fred C. Letts, Jr.	6 & 4	Mrs. E.M. Hodges	Dn-2	Mrs. A.W. Clapp	4 & 3	Mrs. Guy E. Riegel	95
1930	Mar	Mrs. Gregg Lifur	d.	Marion Hollins	25th	Mrs. Vera Hutchings	3 & 1	Helen Lawson	19th	Marion Hollins	93
1931	Mar	Helen Lawson	d.	Barbara Lee	37th	Mrs. James Davies		Mrs. Hermine Wocker		Hermine Wocker	86
1932	Mar	Mrs. Roy Green	d.	Marion Hollins	5 & 3	Mrs. Edward Stevens	5 & 4	Mrs. A.H. Means	5 & 3	Marion Hollins	91[2]
1933	Mar	Marion Hollins	d.	Dorothy Traung	1-up	Mrs. J.W. Proctor	2 & 1	Miss Jane Douglas	Dn-1	Marion Hollins	83
1934	Mar	Dorothy Traung	d.	Mrs. Helen Lengfeld	9 & 8	Marion McDougall	3 & 1	Helen Lawson	Dn-1	Helen Lawson	84
1935	Mar	Elizabeth Abbott	d.	Dorothy Traung	1-up	Mary Morse	3 & 1	Mrs. F.F. Sayward-Wilson	3 & 1	Dorothy Traung	85
1936	Mar	Dorothy Traung	d.	Alice Hanchett	8 & 6	Barbara B. Thompson	5 & 4	Clara Callender	2 & 1	Dorothy Traung	84
1937	Mar	Clara Callender	d.	Marion Hollins	4 & 2	Barbara B. Thompson	3 & 2	Peggy Graham	2 & 1	Clara Callender	83
1938	Mar	Clara Callender	d.	Mrs. Arthur MacArthur	11-10	Mary Morse	5 & 4	Mrs. Helen Lengfeld	2 & 1	Clara Callender	82
1939	Mar	Dorothy Traung	d.	Elizabeth Hicks	8 & 7	Clara Callender	5 & 3	Mrs. R.S. Morimoto	5 & 4	Elizabeth Hicks	92
1940	Mar	Peggy Graham	d.	Marion Hollins	7 & 6	Mrs. R.S. Morimoto	5 & 4	Barbara Ransom	2 & 1	Dorothy Traung	80
1941	Mar	Clara Callender	d.	Marion Hollins	5 & 4	Barbara Ransom	4 & 2	Dorothy Traung	5 & 4	Clara Callender	80
1942	Mar	Marion Hollins	d.	Mrs. Frederick Sheldon	9 & 8	Mrs. Rod LaRocque	3 & 2	Mrs. Decker McAllister	Dn-1	Mrs. D. McAllister	90
1943	Apr	Ellen Kieser		-9	Mrs. R.G. Rawlins	-8	Special Format - Match Play against par due to poor turn-out				Mrs. D. McAllister	87
1944 -1945		No Tournament due to World War II									
1946	May	Patty Berg	d.	Mary Sargent	9 & 8	Barbara Thompson	5 & 4	Mrs. D. G. Copping	4 & 2	Patty Berg	78
1947	May	Patty Berg	d.	Beverly Hanson	8 & 6	Mary Sargent	2 & 1	Helen Dettweiller	2 & 1	Patty Berg	79
1948	Mar	Mary Sargent	d.	Dorothy Traung	1-up	Dorothy Kielty	4 & 3	Ellen Kieser	4 & 3	Dorothy Kielty	84
										Beverly Hanson	84
1949	Apr	Grace DeMoss	d.	Roxie Setrakian	6 & 4	Barbara Dawson	7 & 5	Mrs. Calvin Tilden	4 & 3	Dorothy Traung	80
1950	Mar	Grace DeMoss	d.	Ann Pedroncelli	9 & 7	Mrs. William Rainey	5 & 4	Barbara Dawson	4 & 3	Grace DeMoss	81
1951	Mar	Barbara Romack		82-94-80—256 (no matches)		Mrs. Peter Patch 84-93-94—271		Angie Vote 85-94-95—274			

[1] *The former Doreen Kavanagh married W.W. Campbell.*
[2] *Hollins and Green tied at 91 in qualifying, Hollins won an 18-hole playoff 82 to 96 for the medal honor.*

PACIFIC COAST INTER-COLLEGIATE CHAMPIONSHIP (1924-1938)

The first Pacific Coast Inter-Collegiate was held in 1923 at Waverly Country Club in Portland, Oregon and won by Jack Westland, The 1924 event was held at Seattle Country Club and on by Bryan Winter. The event at Del Monte originated in 1924 as the California Inter-Collegiate, in 1925 it became the Pacific Coast Inter-Collegiate. In its early years it was played on Del Monte Golf Course, but in 1926 the event was moved to Pebble Beach Golf Links where it remained until 1938 when it moved to other locales (Frank Newell won the Intercollegiate at Lakeside in April 1940; Bud Brownell won it in April 1941 at Stanford).

Year	Winner	Runner-up	Score	Lost to Winner	Score	Lost to Runner-up	Score	Medalist	Score
1924	Lauren Upson (UC-B)	Stanton Haight (UC-B)	7 & 6	Jack Westland (UW)	Dn-2	Lloyd Thomas (UC-B)	Dn-2	Jack Westland (UW)	74
1925	Lauren Upson (UC-B)	Lloyd Thomas (UC-B)	6 & 4	Eddie Meyberg (Stnfrd)	9 & 8	Jack Nounnan (UC-B)	8 & 6	Lauren Upson (UC-B)	75
1926	Harold Thompson (UCSB)	Ward Edmonds (Stnfrd)	9 & 7	Dick Lang (Stnfrd)	1-up	Horace Hendry (Stnfrd)	1-up	Scotty Tait (UC-B)	77
1927	Edwin Meyberg (Stnfrd)	Harold Thompson (UCSB)	2-up	Ward Edmonds (Stnfrd)	1-up	R.D. Syer (Stnfrd)	3 & 2	H. Fleishhacker, Jr.	79
1928	Gibson Dunlap (UCLA)	Allen Moser (USC)	5 & 4	Larry Staley (Stanford)	2 & 1	Edwin Meyberg (Stnfrd)	23rd	Gibson Dunlap (UCLA)	73
1929	Allen Moser (USC)	Richard Stevenson (Stfd)	1-up	Warner Edmonds (Stfd)	5 & 4	Bob Brownstein (Stfd)	3 & 2	Gibson Dunlap (UCLA)	80
1930	Richard Stevenson (Stfd)	Russell Thompson (USC)	1-up	Allen Moser (USC)	21st	Warner Edmonds (Stfd)	5 & 4	Warner Edmonds (Stf)	73
1931	Harry Eichelberger (Stfd)	Stuart Hawley (Stnfrd)	3 & 1	Harry Lawson (USC)	19th	Winston Fuller (USC)	4 & 2	Warner Edmonds (Stf)	71
1932	Winston Fuller (USC)	Bud Lawson (USC)	5 & 4	Herman Hellman (Stfd)	3 & 1	Pliny Holt (Stanford)	4 & 2	Gail Stockton (USC)	75
1933	W. Lawson Little, Jr. (Stf)	Neil White (USC)	6 & 5	Harry Eichelberger (Stf)	1-up	"Bud" Cantwell (USC)	6 & 5	Louis Bastanchury	76
1934	W. Lawson Little, Jr. (Stf)	Roy Ryden (UCLA)	2 & 1	August Drier (St. Mary)	2 & 1	Charles DeBrettville	2 & 1	August Drier (St. Mry)	76
1935	Don Nittinger (USC)	Bill Van (USC)	6 & 5	Dalton Henderson (Stf)	4 & 3	Tom Dwyer (Stanford)	2 & 1	Tom Dwyer (Stanford)	77
1936	Bob Thompson (Stanford)	Mat Palacio, Jr. (USF)	37th	Willis Iseminger (USC)	2 & 1	Bill Hogan (USF)	1-up	Don Edwards (Stfd)	85
1937	Roger Kelly (Loyola)	Jack Wallace (Stanford)	5 & 3	Carl Johnson (UW)	2 & 1	Bob McGlashan (USF)	20th	Jack Wallace (Stfd)	76
1938	Willard McCay (UC-B)	Bob Herrmann (USC)	3 & 1	Jack Robinson (USC)	5 & 4	Bill Boyd (Stanford)	19th	Alan Hyman (Stfd)	83

THE WEATHERVANE TRANSCONTINENTAL WOMEN'S OPEN GOLF CHAMPIONSHIP

The LPGA was founded in 1950, and the unique Weathervane tournament was one of its first championships continuing for four years. It was played over four courses across the county each year, with each 36-hole tournament carrying its own prizes and a $5,000 bonus going to the lowest combined score. Pebble Beach was used in each of the first two year, and coincidentally, the winner at Pebble Beach also won the combined score bonus/

1st Weathervane Championship – Leg 1, Pebble Beach Golf Links			
April 29-30, 1950		Pebble Beach	over-all
1	Mrs. Mildred (Babe) Zaharias (Prairie View, IL)	79-79—158	167-145-159—629
2	a- Grace DeMoss (Corvallis, OR)	80-79—159	
3	Patty Berg (Chicago, IL)	81-79—160	172-153-162—647
4	Louise Suggs (Atlanta, GA)	83-78—161	160-156-155—632
5	a-Mrs. James Ferrie (Long Beach, CA)	80-82—162	
T-6	a-Beverly Hanson (Indio, CA)	79-85—164	
T-6	Betty Jameson (San Antonio, CA)	79-85—164	170-162-169—665
T-8	a- Barbara Dawson (Piedmont, CA)	80-88—168	
T-8	a- Betty MacKinnon (Mt. Pleasant, TX)	83-85—168	
10	Mrs. Bettye Mims Danhoff (Dallas, TX)	81-88—169	175-164-170—668

2nd Weatervane Championship - Leg 2, Pebble Beach Golf Links			
May 5-6, 1951		Pebble Beach	over-all
1	Patty Berg (Chicago, IL)	76-76—152	153-147-149—601*
2	Mrs. Mildred (Babe) Zaharias (Tampa, FL)	76-80—156	149-145-151—601
3	Louise Suggs (Atlanta, GA)	77-82—159	158-147-150—614
4	a- Beverly Hanson (Indio, CA)	79-82—161	
5	Betty MacKinnon (Mt. Pleasant, TX)	80-82—162	
T-6	Betsy Rawls (Austin, TX)	79-83—162	159-151-153—625
T-6	Helen Dettweiler (Indio, CA)	83-80—163	
T-6	Betty Jameson (San Antonio, CA)	79-84—163	155-157-158—633
T-6	Alice Bauer (Midland, TX)	79-84—163	156-158-156—638
10	Shirley Spork (Bowling Green, OH)	85-80—165	

* Berg and Zaharias had a 36-hole playoff at Scarsdale CC in Great Neck NY on June 16-17, 1951; Berg: 71-75—146; Zaharias: 71-76—147.

THE TRANS-MISSISSIPPI CHAMPIONSHIP

Often simply called the Trans-Miss, there are actually two distinct organizations for the men's and women's amateur golf championships; one that operates the The Men's organization was established in 1901, in large part to address the need for competitions west of the Mississippi—a region ignored in the early years by both the USGA and the Western Golf Association based in Chicago. The long-lived regional championship shares many of the names that have won the U.S. Amateur, including winners at Pebble Beach: Skee Riegel and Jack Nicklaus. Among the top amateurs that competed at Spyglass Hill that year, two later came back to win the U.S. Open at Pebble Beach—Tom Kite who finished second in the medal qualifying (72-76—148) before going out in the third round to future pro Barry Jaekel; Stanford golfer Tom Watson qualified with an 82-77-159 (right at the cut line) and went out in the second round to Greg Pitzer.

The Women's Trans-Mississippi Golf Association was established in 1927 as an expansion of the Tri-State Golf Association (OK, MO & KS). Among the future professionals that won the Trans-Miss as well as championships at Pebble Beach were Betty Jameson, Patty Berg and Babe Didrickson Zaharias.

Women's Trans-Mississippi MPCC Dunes Course, October 9-14, 1956									
Year	Winner	Runner-up	Score	Lost to Winner	Score	Lost to Runner-up	Score	Medalist	Score
1956	Margaret " Wiffie" Smith	Mrs. James Ferrie	8 & 6	Miss Barbara Romack	4 & 3	Miss Polly Riley	2 & 1	Marg. " Wiffie" Smith	38-36—74

Men's Trans-Mississippi Spyglass Hill Golf Course, July 12-18, 1971									
Year	Winner	Runner-up	Score	Lost to Winner	Score	Lost to Runner-up	Score	Medalist	Score
1971	Allen Miller	Alan Tapie	3 & 1	Artie McNickle	20th	Barry Jaekel	Dn-1	Bruce Robertson	77-70—147

CALIFORNIA WOMEN'S AMATEUR – (1967-   )

Helen Lengfeld convinced S.F.B. Morse to open up Pebble Beach Golf Links each December for a new California Women's Amateur Championships which would not require being a member of any golf association, and while most were, in 1984 the championship was won by Sue Tonkin of Australia. Many of the competitors went on to become stars of the LPGA and a couple (Bretton and Voss-Kruger) have played as amateurs in the AT&T Pebble Beach National Pro-Am. The tournament continued at Pebble Beach through 1986, and then moved to Carmel Valley where it still continues under the direction of the California Women's Amateur Championships (www.cwacgolf.org)

Year		Winner		Runner-up	Score	Lost to Winner	Score	Lost to Runner-up	Score	Medalist	Score
						FINALISTS		SEMIFINALISTS			
1967	PBGL	Shelley Hamlin	d.	Harriet Glanville	5 & 4	Susan Meze	4 & 3	Noni Schneider	3 & 2	Harriet Glanville	78
1968	PBGL	Shelley Hamlin	d.	Carol Skala	3 & 1	Shelia Moss Hopkins	2 & 1	Barbara Handley	4 & 2	Shelley Hamlin	78
1969	PBGL	Shelley Hamlin	d.	Noni Schneider	2 & 2	Mary Elizabeth Shea	2-up	Joan Damon	8 & 6	Mrs. Walt Bowering	78
1970	PBGL	Shelley Hamlin	d.	Barbara Handley	3 & 2	Laura Baugh	1-up	Roberta Albers	21st	Joan Damon	77
1971	PBGL	Barbara Handley	d.	Laura Baugh	3 & 2	Mary Elizabeth Shea	4 & 3	Kathy Martin	5 & 4	Laura Baugh	78
1972	PBGL	Barbara Handley	d.	Linda Maurer	3 & 1	Debbie Meisterlin	8 & 6	Laura Baugh	1-up	Linda Maurer	79
1973	PBGL	Amy Alcott	d.	Debbie Skinner	2 & 1	Linda Maurer	5 & 4	Cassandra Freeman	1-up	Carolyn Hill	79
1974	PBGL	Mary Elizabeth Shea	d.	Amy Alcott	1-up	Alice Miller	3 & 2	Lauren Howe	2-up	Amy Alcott	70
1975	PBGL	Patricia Cornett	d.	Holly Hartley	4 & 3	Shelley Gates	4 & 3	Patty Snyder	1-up	Patricia Cornett	71
1976	PBGL	Marianne Bretton	d.	Susan Stanley	6 & 4	Barbara Handley	20th	Julie Young	1-up	Lulong Hartley	75
1977	PBGL	Patty Sheehan	d.	Irene Zuniga	6 & 5	Cathy Hanlon	1-up	Dayna Benson	19th	Alice Miller	38-35—73
1978	PBGL	Patty Sheehan	d.	Sharon Barrett	21st	Sue Bennett	3 & 2	Ellen Bowering	5 & 3	Sally Voss	73
1979	PBGL	Sally Voss	d.	Linda Maurer	1-up	Patricia Cornett	1-up	Mary Enright	2 & 1	Patty Sheehan / Sally Voss	76 / 76
1980	PBGL	Mary Enright	d.	Sally Voss	3 & 2	Edi Hathaway	1-up	Kathy Kostas	22nd	Juli Simpson Inkster	41-34—75
1981	PBGL	Juli Simpson Inkster	d.	Juli Ordonez	4 & 2	Carol Hogar	4 & 3	Sally Voss	2 & 1	Juli Simpson Inkster	38-36—74
1982	PBGL	Debbie Weldon	d.	Patricia Cornett	1-up	Juli Ordonez	6 & 5	Mary Enright	3 & 2	Loretta Aldrete / Cindy Scholefield	74 / 74
1983	PBGL	Patricia Cornett	d.	Kareen Gibson	2 & 1	Ann Walsh	2-up	Susan Tonkin (Australia)	3 & 1	Nancy Harrison	75
1984	PBGL	Susan Tonkin (Australia)	d.	Kim Cathrein	3 & 2	Patricia Cornett	3 & 2	Deborah McHaffie	1-up	Libby Wilson	76
1985	PBGL	Anne Quast Sander	d.	Patricia Cornett	3 & 2	Shelly Rule	4 & 3	Kris Neiman	3 & 2	Cindy Scholefield	70
1986	PBGL	Cindy Scholefield	d.	Amanda Nealy	3 & 2	Cindy Mah-Lyford	3 & 2	Patricia Cornett	4 & 3	Sally Voss	73

THE MORSE CUP MATCHES

The 1st Morse Cup Match, Seattle GC			July 9-10, 1949		
Scotch Foursomes			**score**	**PNGA**	**CGA**
Dawson-McCormick	lost to	Givan-Westland	6 & 4	1	-
McKinney-Evans	lost to	Mawhinney-Doud*	1-up	1	-
Pieper-Bariteau	tied	Campbell-Clark	even	_	_
Lowery-Bean	defeated	Owens*-Weston	3 & 2	-	1
Singles Matches					
Johnny Dawson	tied	Harry Givan	even	_	_
Bruce McCormick	lost to	Jack Westland	4 & 2	1	-
Eli Bariteau, Jr.	lost to	Bill Mawhinney	1-up	1	-
Ernest O. Pieper, Jr.	lost to	Ray Weston, Jr.	3 & 2	1	-
Ralph Evans	defeated	James Ronald Clark	2 & 1	-	1
Bud McKinney	lost to	Glenn Sheriff	1-up	1	-
Dr. Jackson Bean	lost to	Lou Stafford	1-up	1	-
Edward Lowery	lost to	Albert Campbell	1-up	1	-
*Dave Doud / Guy Owens				9	3

The 2nd Morse Cup Match, Cypress Point			Sep. 30 – Oct. 1, 1950		
Scotch Foursomes			**score**	**PNGA**	**CGA**
Dawson-McCormick	defeated	Givan-Westland	4 & 2	-	1
Smith-Venturi	defeated	Mawhinney-Weston	3 & 1	-	1
Rosburg-Bariteau*	lost to	Mengert-Littler	3 & 2	1	-
Taylor-Ferrie	lost to	Yost-Clark	6 & 5	1	-
Singles Matches					
Bob Cardinal	lost to	Bill Mawhinney	2 & 1	1	-
Bruce McCormick	defeated	Jack Westland	4 & 3	-	1
Jim Ferrie	lost to	Al Mengert	2 & 1	1	-
Johnny Dawson	defeated	Ray Weston, Jr.	4 & 3	-	1
Tal Smith	defeated	Harry Givan	4 & 3	-	1
Ken Venturi	defeated	James Ronald Clark	2 & 1	-	1
Dr. Frank Taylor	defeated	Gene Littler	3 & 2	-	1
Jay Sigel	defeated	Dick Yost	2 & 1	-	1
*Eli Bariteau, Jr.				4	8

The 3rd Morse Cup Match, Spokane G&CC			July 21-22, 1951		
Scotch Foursomes			**score**	**PNGA**	**CGA**
Dawson-McCormick	defeated	Givan-Westland	6 & 5	-	1
Smith-Cardinal	defeated	Mawhinney-Parent	3 & 2	-	1
Venturi-Ferrie	defeated	Yost-Atkinson	4 & 3	-	1
Gardner-Taylor	lost to	Mengert-Weston	3 & 1	1	-
Singles Matches					
Tal Smith	defeated	Bob Atkinson	1-up	-	1
Ken Venturi	lost to	Bill Mawhinney	2 & 1	1	-
Bob Gardner	lost to	Al Mengert	4 & 2	1	-
Bruce McCormick	lost to	Jack Westland	1-up	1	-
Jim Ferrie	tied	Dick Yost	even	_	_
Bob Cardinal	tied	Erv Parent	even	_	_
Dr. Frank Taylor	defeated	Ray Weston, Jr.	5 & 4	-	1
Johnny Dawson	defeated	Harry Givan	3 & 2	-	1
				5	7

The 4th Morse Cup Match, Cypress Point			September 20-21, 1952		
Scotch Foursomes			**score**	**PNGA**	**CGA**
Seaver-Ferrie	lost to	Mawhinney-McElroy	3 & 1	1	-
Smith-Venturi	defeated	Draper-Mengert	2 & 1	-	1
Taylor-Pieper	defeated	Yost-Cudd	3 & 1	-	1
Dawson-McCormick	defeated	Westland-Parent	2-up	-	1
Singles Matches					
Ernest O. Pieper, Jr.	defeated	Bruce Cudd	2 & 1	-	1
Jim Ferrie	tied	Dick Yost	even	_	_
Dr. Frank Taylor	tied	Walter McElroy	even	_	_
Charles Seaver	lost to	Erv Parent	4 & 3	1	-
Tal Smith	lost to	Ed Draper	2 & 1	1	-
Johnny Dawson	lost to	Bill Mawhinney	2 & 1	1	-
Ken Venturi	lost to	Al Mengert	1-up	1	-
Bruce McCormick	lost to	Jack Westland	2-up	1	-
				7	5

The 5th Morse Cup Match, Columbia-Edgewood Club			July 18-19, 1953		
Scotch Foursomes			**score**	**PNGA**	**CGA**
Smith-Ferrie	defeated	McElroy*-Fleming	3 & 2	-	1
Seaver-Taylor	defeated	Parent*-Draper	2-up	-	1
Bariteau-Littler	defeated	Atkinson-McReynolds	1-up	-	1
Jacobs-Silvestri	tied	Cudd-Weston	even	_	_
Singles Matches					
Gene Littler	defeated	Dick Yost	2-up	-	1
D.J. "Bob" Silvestri	defeated	Bruce Cudd	2 & 1	-	1
Jim Ferrie	defeated	Ray Weston, Jr.	2 & 1	-	1
Charlie Seaver	defeated	Bob Atkinson	3 & 2	-	1
Tom Jacobs	lost to	Bob Fleming	1-up	1	-
Dr. Frank Taylor	lost to	Bob McReynolds	5 & 4	1	-
Eli Bariteau, Jr.	lost to	Dick Price	3 & 2	1	-
Tal Smith	tied	Ed Draper	even	_	_
* Walter McElroy / Erv Parent				4	8

The 6th Morse Cup Match, Cypress Point			September 18-19, 1954		
Scotch Foursomes			**score**	**PNGA**	**CGA**
Seaver-Pennell	defeated	Yost-Getchell	1-up	-	1
Dawson*-McCormick	defeated	Parent-Weston	1-up	-	1
Taylor-Richards	defeated	Cudd-Draper	5 & 4	-	1
Ward-Silvestri	defeated	Fleming-Crawford	2 & 1	-	1
Singles Matches					
Charlie Seaver	defeated	Ray Weston, Jr.	6 & 5	-	1
Cy Pennell	defeated	Phil Getchell	6 & 5	-	1
Bruce McCormick	tied	Dick Yost	even	_	_
Jim Ferrie	tied	Erv Parent	even	_	_
Ted Richards	lost to	Lyle Crawford	3 & 2	1	-
Dr. Frank Taylor	lost to	Ed Draper	1-up	1	-
D.J. "Bob" Silvestri	defeated	Bob Fleming	4 & 2	-	1
E. Harvie Ward, Jr.	defeated	Bruce Cudd	5 & 3	-	1
* Johnny Dawson				3	9

The 7th Morse Cup Match, Inglewood CC			July 9-10, 1955		
Scotch Foursomes			**score**	**PNGA**	**CGA**
Roos-Giddings	defeated	Parent-Yost		-	1
Seaver-Smith	defeated	Crawford-Cudd		-	1
Pennell-McBeath	defeated	Funseth-Givan		-	1
Pieper-Bariteau	lost to	Getchell-Beechler		1	-
Singles Matches					
David McBeath	lost to	Rod Funseth	2 & 1	1	-
Jack Bariteau	lost to	Phil Getchell	4 & 2	1	-
Richard Giddings	lost to	Harry Givan	1-up	1	-
Cy Pennell	tied	George Beechler	even	_	_
Robert Roos	lost to	Lyle Crawford	3 & 2	1	-
Ernest O. Pieper, Jr.	defeated	Erv Parent	1-up	-	1
Charlie Seaver	lost to	Dick Yost	2 & 1	1	-
Tal Smith	tied	Bruce Cudd	even	_	_
				7	5

The 9th Morse Cup Match, Pebble Beach Golf Links		August 7-8, 1968		
Northern California Golf Team	312	292	604	
Jack Bariteau, Dick Giddings, Forrest Fezler, Johnny Miller, Harry Taylor, Yost-Getchell (non-playing captain) Robert A. Roos				
Southern California Golf Team	308	303	611	
David Barber, Bob Bouchier, Greg Pitzer, Dick Runkle, Jim Rheim, Joe Simpson, (non-playing captain) Gordon Booth				
Other Teams: Pacific Northwest (613); Arizona (639); Utah (642); Montana (657)				
PCGA Champion: Ed Morris (San Jose, CA)	73-71-83-72—299			

The 37th Morse Cup Match, Poppy Hills Golf Course		July 30-31, 1996		
Northern California Golf Team	146	139	285	
Casey Boyns, Randy Haig, Jeff Gilchrist				
Other Teams: So. California, Pacific Northwest, Colorado, Idaho, Utah, No. Nevada, So. Nevada, Oregon, Washington, Wyoming, Alberta, British Columbia, Taiwan				
PCGA Champion: Scott Johnson (Kennewick, WA)	70-70-71-76—287			

THE UNITED STATES AMATEUR CHAMPIONSHIP

The United States Amateur Championship was first played in 1895 at Newport, Rhode Island. It was not played in 1917 or 1918 because of World War I, and missed 1942-1945 because of World War II. Prior to professional golf's popularity, the U.S. Amateur had greater prestige than the U.S. Open, and in fact amateur golfers did well in the Open as well. The early championships traveled throughout the northeastern states, often making it as far west as the Chicago area. It reached out in 1921 to the St. Louis Country Club just across the Mississippi River. It was not until 1929, that the U.S.G.A. would host a championship west of the Continental Divide, and that was the 33rd playing of the U.S. Amateur. It has returned to the west coast ten times since then, three more time to Pebble Beach—in 1947, 1961 and 1999. Each of the latter champions at Pebble Beach became golf professionals – Jack Nicklaus later becoming the only pro to win the U.S. Amateur (1961) and U.S. Open (1972) on the same course.

Year	Winner	Runner-up	Score	Lost to Winner	Score	Lost to Runner-up	Score	Medalist	Score
1929	Harrison R. Johnston	Dr. Oscar F. Willing	4 & 3	Francis Ouimet	Dn-1	H. Chandler Egan	6 & 5	Robert T. Jones Eugene Homans	70-75—145 72-73—145
1947	Robert H. "Skee" Riegel	John W. Dawson	2 & 1	Felice J. Torza	2 & 1	John H. Selby	5 & 4	No medal rounds	
1961	Jack W. Nicklaus	H. Dudley Wysong	8 & 6	Marion C. Methvin, Jr	9 & 8	Joseph B. Carr	Dn-2	No medal rounds	
1999	David Gossett	Sung Yoon Kim	9 & 8	Ben Curtis	2 & 1	Hunter Haas	4 & 3	Gene Elliot	71-72—143

THE UNITED STATES WOMEN'S AMATEUR CHAMPIONSHIP

The United States Women's Amateur Championship was first played in 1895 at Hempstead, NY. Like the Men's Amateur, it was not played in 1917 or 1918 because of World War I, and missed 1942-1945 because of World War II. It reached out in 1924 to the St. Louis Country Club, its first venture across the Mississippi River. It was first played on the West Coast at Los Angeles Country Club in 1930. Its second visit west was in 1940 at Pebble Beach for the 40th Championship. It returned in 1948 after the war for the 44th Championship.

Year	Winner	Runner-up	Score	Lost to Winner	Score	Lost to Runner-up	Score	Medalist	Score
1940	Miss Betty Jameson	Miss Jane S. Cothran	6 & 5	Miss Clara Callender	4 & 3	Mrs. James Ferrie	Dn-2	Miss Dorothy Traung	36-42—78
1948	Miss Grace S. Lenczyk	Miss Helen Sigel	4 & 3	Mrs. Jack Holmes	4 & 2	Miss Beverly Hanson	6 & 5	Bettye Mims White	77

THE UNITED STATES GIRLS' JUNIOR AMATEUR CHAMPIONSHIP

Prior to World War II, the USGA conducted only four championships. As golf gained popularity after the war, the USGA saw the need to add championships for various groups. The fifth USGA championship was the Junior Amateur (1948) for boys age 17 and under; the sixth was the Girls' Junior (1949) or girls 17 and under. The third annual Girls' Junior was played at Pebble Beach and had four future Hall-of-famers in the semifinals.

3rd U.S. Junior Girls' Amateur Championship MPCC Dunes Course, August 18-21, 1952									
Medalist: Anne Quast, Everett, WA, 37-39—76 *(won medal in a playoff with Mickey Wright, 39-37—76)*									
Year	Winner	Runner-up	Score	Lost to Winner	Score	Lost to Runner-up	Score	Medalist	Score
1952	Margaret K. " Mickey" Wright	Miss Barbara McIntire	1-up	Judy Bell	2 & 1	Miss Anne Quast	7 & 6	Miss Anne Quast	37-39—76

THE UNITED STATES SENIOR AMATEUR CHAMPIONSHIP

The U.S. Senior Amateur was first played in 1955 and the fourth annual Senior Amateur was played at Pebble Beach. It is open to amateur golfers over the age of 55 and attracted veterans of many championships including Chick Evans, John Dawson and defending Senior Champion J. Clark Espie. Remarkably, the championship was won by a golfer that did not take up the game until age 31.

4th U.S. Senior Amateur MPCC Dunes Course, September 29 – October 4, 1958									
Year	Winner	Runner-up	Score	Lost to Winner	Score	Lost to Runner-up	Score	Medalist	Score
1958	Thomas C. Robbins	John W. Dawson	2 & 1	J. Clark Espie	Dn-2	Ross McDade	2 & 1	J. Clark Espie	35-36—71

THE UNITED STATES WOMEN'S SENIOR AMATEUR

The first U.S. Women's Senior Amateur was played in 1962. It is open to women over the age of 50 and attracts many experienced players and the top players are often former members of the Curtis Cup teams, including their captains. The first winner was Maureen Orcutt, a veteran of four Curtis Cup teams in the 1930s, and the runner-up was Glenna Collett-Vare, the six-time U.S. Women's Amateur Champion ('22,'25,'28,'29, '30, and '35), and a member of the first (and three later) Curtis Cup team as well as a four-time captain of the team. The Women's Senior is a 54-hole stroke-play competition and has twice been played over the Dunes Course of the Monterey Peninsula Country Club at Pebble Beach.

7th Annual U.S. Women's Senior Amateur, MPCC Dunes Course		
October 2-4, 1968		
1	Mrs. Philip (Carolyn) Cudone, Myrtle Beach, SC	80-79-77—236
2	Mrs. Hulet (Loma) Smith, Pebble Beach, CA	82-79-85—246
3	Mrs. Marge Mason, West Englewood, NJ	87-80-80—247

15th Annual U.S. Women's Senior Amateur, MPCC Dunes Course		
September 29 – October 1, 1976		
1	Cecile Maclaurin, Savanah, GA	78-75-77—230
2	Mrs. Lyle (Carol) Bowman, San Rafel, CA	75-80-82—237
3	Mrs. Wayne Rutter, Williamsville, NY	80-77-83—240
4	Mrs. Philip (Carolyn) Cudone, Myrtle Beach, SC	81-81-82—244
5	Mrs. Albert Bower, Pelham, NY	85-80-81—246
T-6	Mrs. Helen Sigel Wilson, Gladwyne, PA	84-80-84—248
T-6	Mrs. Peter Patch, Lafayette, CA	82-84-82—248

THE WALKER CUP

Named for a cup donated in 1921 by George Herbert Walker, the USGA President of 1920 for an international team championship between the best amateurs representing the two ruling bodies of golf—The USGA and the R&A. The event was played annually from 1922-24, and biennially thereafter with the exception of 1940-46 due to World War II. The competition is played alternately on courses of the U.S. and U.K. 1981 marked its first playing in California and its second on the West Coast. It was played in Seattle in 1961, just prior to the 1961 U.S. Amateur at Pebble Beach.

THE 28TH WALKER CUP MATCH, CYPRESS POINT

Friday, August 28, 1981					
Scotch Foursomes			Score	GB/Irel	USA
Sutton-Sigel	lost to	Walton-Rafferty	4 & 2	1	-
Holtgrieve-Fuhrer	defeated	Chapman-McEvoy	1-up	-	1
Lewis-von Tackey	defeated	Deeble-Hutcheon	2 & 1	-	1
Commans-Pavin	defeated	Evans-Way	5 & 4	-	1
Singles Matches					
Hal Sutton	defeated	Ronan Rafferty	3 & 1	-	1
Joey Rassett	defeated	Colin Dalgleish	1-up	-	1
Ron Commans	lost to	Philip Walton	1-up	1	-
Bob Lewis	lost to	Roger Chapman	2 & 1	1	-
Jodie Mudd	defeated	Geoffrey Godwin	1-up	-	1
Corey Pavin	defeated	Ian Hutcheon	4 & 3	-	1
Dick von Tacky	lost to	Paul Way	3 & 1	1	-
Jay Sigel	defeated	Peter McEvoy	3 & 2	-	1
				4	8

Saturday, August 29, 1981					
Scotch Foursomes			Score	GB/Irel	USA
Sutton-Sigel	lost to	Chapman-Way	1-up	1	
Holtgrieve-Fuhrer	lost to	Walton-Rafferty	6 & 4	1	
Lewis-von Tackey	lost to	Evans-Dagleish	3 & 2	1	
Rassett-Mudd	defeated	Hutcheon-Godwin	5 & 4		1
Singles Matches					
Hal Sutton	lost to	Roger Chapman	1-up	1	
Jim Holtgrieve	defeated	Ronan Rafferty	2 & 1		1
Frank Fuhrer III	defeated	Philip Walton	4 & 2		1
Jay Sigel	defeated	Paul Way	6 & 5		1
Jodie Mudd	defeated	Colin Dalgleish	7 & 5		1
Ron Commans	tied	Geoffrey Godwin	even	–	–
Joey Rassett	defeated	Peter Deeble	4 & 3		1
Corey Pavin	tied	Duncan Evans	even	–	–
				5	7
				9	15

THE CALLAWAY GOLF PEBBLE BEACH INVITATIONAL (1972 -   )

Golf Professional Harold Firstman, then with Laguna Seca Golf Ranch, created the tournament known since 1997 as the Callaway Golf Pebble Beach Invitational. While the event has evolved and had a number of sponsors over the years, the general concept has remained the same—pairing a team of amateurs with a different professional golfer each day; the professionals compete with the other professionals with their individual scores and the team uses the best ball score for each hole and can use their pro's score for the team score. Making the tournament truly unique is that pros from the PGA, LPGA, Champions, and mini tours, as well as club professionals, compete head to head. The event also uses multiple courses; these two have changed over the years, but since 1979, the pros and the teams that make the cut have played the final round on Pebble Beach Golf Links. Since 1993, the rotation has been fixed with one-third rotating across Del Monte, Spyglass Hill and Pebble Beach day prior to the cut.

	Date	Courses	Professional	Score	Team	
Laguna Seca-Del Monte Hyatt Pro-Am						
1st	Dec-1972	DMGC & LSGR	Rafe Botts	279		
Confidence Pro-Am						
2nd	Dec-1973	CTGC & LSGR	Rod Funseth	272		
3rd	Jan-1975	DMGC & LSGR	Forrest Fezler	276		
Lynx-Golf Pro-Am						
4th	Jan-1976	CTGC, RC (East) & LSGR	David Glenz	277		
Spalding Invitational Pro-Am						
5th	Dec-1976	RC (East), FO (Bayonet) & LSGR	Mark Pfeil	211		
6th	Dec-1977	CTGC, RC (East) & LSGR	Rod Funseth	271		
7th	Dec-1978	SHGC, RC (East) & LSGR	Al Geiberger	276		
8th	Jan-1980	CTGC, DMGC, SHGC – cut to PBGL	Bobby Clampett	272		
9th	Dec-1980	CTGC, DMGC, SHGC – cut to PBGL	John Mahaffey	279		
10th	Dec-1981	CTGC, DMGC, CVQL & PBGL	Jay Haas	337		
11th	Dec-1982	DMGC, CVQL & PBGL	Peter Oosterhuis	274		
12th	Dec-1983	DMGC, CVQL & PBGL	Johnny Miller	270		
13th	Dec-1984	DMGC, CVQL & PBGL	Peter Oosterhuis	277		
14th	Jan-1986	DMGC, CVQL & PBGL	Tim Norris	277		
15th	Jan-1987	CVR, PBGL & CVQL	Ken Green	274		
16th	Jan-1988	CVR, PBGL & CVQL	Lennie Clements	271		
17th	Jan-1989	CVR, PHGC & CVQL	Bob Gilder	276		
18th	Dec-1989	DHGC, RGC & Boulders	Mark Calcavecchia	276		
19th	Dec-1990	PBGL, SHGC & PHGC	Juli Inkster	284		
Ben Hogan-Pebble Beach Invitational						
20th	Jan-1992	PBGL, SHGC & PHGC	Loren Roberts	281		
Pebble Beach Invitational						
21st	Jan-1993	PBGL, SHGC & PHGC	Mark Brooks	208		
22nd	Nov-1993	PBGL, SHGC & DMGC	Bruce Fleisher	283		
23rd	Nov-1994	PBGL, SHGC & DMGC	Robert Gamez	277		
24th	Nov-1995	PBGL, SHGC & DMGC	Ronnie Black	277		
Merrill Lynch- Pebble Beach Invitational						
25th	Nov-1996	PBGL, SHGC & DMGC	Kirk Triplett	274		
Callaway Golf-Pebble Beach Invitational						
26th	Nov-1997	PBGL, SHGC & DMGC	Loren Roberts	276		
27th	Nov-1998	PBGL, SHGC & DMGC	Tom Lehman	273		
28th	Nov-1999	PBGL, SHGC & DMGC	Rocco Mediate	282		
29th	Nov-2000	PBGL, SHGC & DMGC	Kevin Sutherland	275		
30th	Nov-2001	PBGL, SHGC & DMGC	Olin Browne*1	271	Don McMath Peter Schwartz Paul Coffey Mike Alkier	474
31st	Nov-2002	PBGL, SHGC & DMGC	Mark Brooks	272	Stuart Holland, Mark Kowalczyk, Ron Kruzenski, Bill Robinson	508
32nd	Nov-2003	PBGL, SHGC & DMGC	John Daly	279	Michael Cooper, Cory Thabit, Kris Thabit, George Thabit	511
33rd	Nov-2004	PBGL, SHGC & DMGC	Jeff Brehaut	279	Chris Mahowald Dave Andrews Gordon Smith Stewart Kim	518
34th	Nov-2005	PBGL, SHGC & DMGC	Nick Watney	270	John Justice, John Justice III, Hunter Edwards, Butch Cone	505
35th	Nov-2006	PBGL, SHGC & DMGC	Jason Bohn	274	Don McMath, Edward Price, Richard Meyer, Danny Schaus	504
36th	Nov-2007	PBGL, SHGC & DMGC	Tommy Armour III	272	Mark Marshall, Frank Keener, Wally Kemp, Bob Holmes	499
37th	Nov-2008	PBGL, SHGC & DMGC	Tommy Armour III*2	278	Peter Werth, Jason Higton, Eaton Chen, Rick Becker	513

*1 Won third playoff hole to break tie with Todd Barrenger, who forced the tie with a final round 63 to Browne's 71.
*2 Won first playoff hole to break tie with Brock Mackenzie & Scott Simpson.

Golf Course Abbreviations
• Boulders – The Boulders Resort, Scottsdale, AZ
• CTGC – Corral de Tierra Golf Club, Salinas
• CVQL – Carmel Valley Golf Club at Quail Lodge, Carmel Valley
• CVR – Carmel Valley Ranch, Carmel Valley
• DHGC – Desert Highlands Golf Club, Scottsdale, AZ
• DMGC – Del Monte Golf Course, Monterey
• FO (Bayonet) – Fort Ord's Bayonet Golf Course, Seaside
• LSGR – Laguna Seca Golf Ranch, Monterey
• PBGL – Pebble Beach Golf Links, Pebble Beach
• PHGC – Poppy Hills Golf Course, Pebble Beach
• RC (East) – Rancho Cañada Golf Club (East Course), Carmel Valley
• RGC – Renegade Golf Course, The Desert Mountain Club, Scottsdale, AZ
• SHGC – Spyglass Hill Golf Course, Pebble Beach

THE U.S. OPEN

The U.S. Open has been played annually since 1895 with the exception of two years during World War I and four years during World War II. It has always been a stroke-play championship open to professionals and amateurs, although no amateur has won it since 1933. Like the other early championships, it was slow to come west. It came as far west as Colorado in 1938 and made its first trip to California in 1948 at the Riviera Country Club in Los Angeles. It was played at the Olympic Club in San Francisco in 1955 and 1966, and finally came to Pebble Beach in 1972, and will be returning to Pebble Beach for a fifth time in 2010. Only two golfers have made the cut in all four U.S. Opens at Pebble Beach: Tom Kite, who won the event in 1992 and three-time U.S. Open Champion Hale Irwin, whose highest finish in an Open at Pebble Beach was T-36 in 1972.

72nd U.S. Open Championship, Pebble Beach Golf Links June 15-18, 1972		
1	Jack Nicklaus	71-73-72-74—290
2	Bruce Crampton	74-70-73-76—293
3	Arnold Palmer	77-68-73-76—294
T-4	Lee Trevino	74-72-71-78—295
T-4	Homero Blancas	74-70-76-75—295
6	Kermit Zarley	71-73-73-79—296
7	Johnny Miller	74-73-71-79—297
8	Tom Weiskopf	73-74-73-78—298
T-9	Cesar Sanudo	72-72-78-77—299
T-9	Chi Chi Rodriguez	71-75-78-75—299

82nd U.S. Open Championship, Pebble Beach Golf Links June 17-20, 1982		
1	Tom Watson	72-72-68-70—282
2	Jack Nicklaus	74-70-71-69—284
T-3	Bobby Clampett	71-73-72-70—286
T-3	Dan Pohl	72-74-70-70—286
T-3	Bill Rogers	70-73-69-74—286
T-6	Gary Koch	78-73-69-67—287
T-6	Jay Haas	75-74-70-68—287
T-6	Lanny Wadkins	73-76-67-71—287
T-6	David Graham	73-72-69-73—287
T-10	Calvin Peete	71-72-72-73—288
T-10	Bruce Devlin	70-69-75-74—288

92nd U.S. Open Championship, Pebble Beach Golf Links June 18-21, 1992		
1	Tom Kite	71-72-70-72—285
2	Jeff Sluman	73-74-69-71—287
3	Colin Montgomery	70-71-77-70—288
T-4	Nick Price	71-72-77-71—291
T-4	Nick Faldo	70-76-68-77—291
T-6	Jay Don Blake	70-74-75-73—292
T-6	Bob Gilder	73-70-75-74—292
T-6	Billy Andrade	72-74-72-74—292
T-6	Mike Hulbert	74-73-70-75—292
T-6	Tom Lehman	69-74-72-77—292
T-6	Joey Sindelar	74-72-68-78—292
T-6	Ian Woosnam	72-72-69-79—292

100th U.S. Open Championship, Pebble Beach Golf Links June 15-18, 2000		
1	Eldrick "Tiger" Woods	65-59-71-67—272
T-2	Miguel Angel Jimenez	66-74-76-71—287
T-2	Ernie Els	74-73-68-72—287
4	John Huston	67-75-76-70—288
T-5	Lee Westwood	71-71-76-71—289
T-5	Padraig Harrington	73-71-72-73—289
7	Nick Faldo	69-74-76-71—290
T-8	Vijay Singh	70-73-80-68—291
T-8	Stewart Cink	77-72-72-70—291
T-8	David Duval	75-71-74-71—291
T-8	Loren Roberts	68-78-73-72—291

THE PGA CHAMPIONSHIP

The PGA of America, an association of club professionals created the PGA Championship in 1916 before there was a formal tour for playing professionals. "Long" Jim Barnes, a naturalized citizen who learned the game in England and was one of the early professionals to compete at Del Monte, won the first PGA Championship and after a two-year break for World War I, won the second PGA Championship in 1919. The 12th PGA Championship in 1929, was the first contested in California, as Hillcrest Country Club in Los Angeles. It missed only one year during World War II (1943) and returned to the West Coast at Portland, Oregon in 1946. Its third playing in the West was at Pebble Beach in 1979. It was a match play event until 1958 when it shifted to a 72-hole stroke-play event, and together with the U.S. Open, British Open and Masters is one of the four Majors of the modern Grand Slam. It was the first major to adopt a sudden-death playoff to resolve a tie, and the first such playoff was at Pebble Beach.

59th PGA Championship, Pebble Beach Golf Links, June 18-21, 1992			Playoff began on hole #1		
1	Lanny Wadkins	69-71-72-70—282*	Par – Birdie – Par	4-4-4—12
2	Gene Littler	67-69-70-76—282	Par – Birdie – Bogey	4-4-5—13
3	Jack Nicklaus	69-71-70-73—283		
4	Charles Coody	70-71-70-73—284		
5	Jerry Pate	73-70-69-73—285		
T-6	Lou Graham	71-73-71-71—286		
T-6	Jerry McGee	68-70-77-71—286		
T-6	Al Geiberger	71-70-73-72—286		
T-6	Don January	75-69-70-72—286		
T-6	Tom Watson	68-73-71-74—286		

THE NABISCO GOLF CHAMPIONSHIPS OF GOLF / THE TOUR CHAMPIONSHIP

In 1987, the PGA TOUR created what would become the TOUR Championship – a professional event where only the Top 30 money leaders are invited to compete in an event with a large purse; some have called it "the Fifth Major." Nabisco was the title sponsor for the first four years—the first at Oak Hills CC in San Antonio and the second at Pebble Beach Golf Links. The purse in 1988 was $2 million with $360,000 going to the winner; more than double the purse of the 1988 AT&T Pebble Beach National Pro-Am which was $700,000 with the winners share being $126,000.

The 3rd Nabisco Championships of Golf		Pebble Beach Golf Links, November 10-13, 1988			
1	Curtis Strange	64-71-70-74—279*	T-14	Lanny Wadkins	72-70-67-77—286
2	Tom Kite	72-65-70-72—279	T-17	Paul Azinger	73-70-69-75—287
T-3	Payne Stewart	73-70-64-73—280	T-17	Sandy Lyle	72-71-68-76—287
T-3	Mark Calcavecchia	70-71-65-74—280	T-17	Steve Pate	70-72-69-76—287
T-3	Ken Green	67-70-69-74—280	T-17	David Frost	69-71-70-77—287
6	Peter Jacobsen	71-70-67-73—281	T-21	Ben Crenshaw	72-71-69-76—288
7	Fred Couples	75-67-67-73—282	T-21	Joey Sindelar	68-73-67-80—288
T-8	Mile Reid	72-72-68-73—285	23	Dan Pohl	72-69-71-78—290
T-8	Gary Koch	71-72-68-74—285	T-24	Mark Weibe	76-64-74-78—292
T-8	Scott Verplank	69-70-72-74—285	T-24	Chip Beck	71-69-73-79—292
T-8	Bob Tway	69-70-71-75—285	T-26	Jeff Sluman	72-75-71-75—293
T-8	Jodie Mudd	70-71-68-76—285	T-26	Larry Nelson	75-69-73-76—293
T-8	Bruce Lietzke	69-68-70-78—285	28	Scott Hoch	70-76-70-78—294
T-14	Mark McCumber	73-70-70-73—286	29	Mark O'Meara	70-73-77-79—299
T-14	Jay Haas	69-71-70-76—286	30	Greg Norman	75-76-74-79—304

THE WALMART FIRST TEE OPEN AT PEBBLE BEACH

The First Tee is a national organization devoted to "impact[ing] the lives of young people by providing learning facilities and educational programs that promote character development and life-enhancing values through the game of golf. A 1997 initiative of the World Golf Foundation, The First Tee reaches over 500,000 youth around the United States and a growing chapters around the world. In 2004, The Champions Tour partnered with Walmart to start The First Tee Open at Pebble Beach where a junior golfer is paired with a professional to play in a televised tournament at Pebble Beach. The first year, the tournament split the field with half playing Pebble Beach Golf Links on Day One and half playing the nearby Bayonet Golf Course in Seaside, switching on Day Two and then those that made the cut played Day Three at Pebble Beach Golf Links. Since 2005, the tournament has used Del Monte Golf Course and Pebble Beach Golf Links.

1st Annual Walmart First Tee Open at Pebble Beach, September 3-5, 2004

1	Craig Stadler	72-63-66—201	1	Craig Stadler / Aaron Woodard (Denver, CO)	69-62-63—194
2	Jay Haas	70-66-68—204	T-2	Jay Haas / Sydney Burlison (Salinas, CA)	69-63-66—198
T-3	Hale Irwin	73-66-70—209	T-2	Hubert Green / Colin Peck	69-64-65—198
T-3	Tom Kite	73-66-70—209	T-2	Dana Quigley / Paula Creamer	67-66-65—198
T-5	David Eger	67-73-70—210	T-5	D.A. Weibring / Alan Fowler	65-70-64—199
T-5	D.A. Weibring	68-71-71—210	T-5	Hale Irwin / Teddy Collins	68-65-67—199
T-7	Bruce Lietzke	70-74-67—211	T-7	Dale Douglass / June Lee	60-64-67—201
T-7	Ed Dougherty	71-69-71—211	T-7	Gibby Gilbert / Chris Kilmer	70-65-66—201
T-9	Lonnie Nielsen	73-70-69—212	T-7	David Eger / Julianna Uhrik	64-70-67—201
T-9	Peter Jacobsen	70-73-69—212	T-10	6-way tie: January/Garcia; Dougherty/Bergman	203
T-9	Doug Tewell	73-69-70—212		Lye/McCready; Bean/Little; Hatalsky/French; Davis/Hack	

2nd Annual Walmart First Tee Open at Pebble Beach, September 2-4, 2005

1	Hale Irwin	66-69-68—203	T-1	Jim Thorpe / Amit Odaiyar (Sacramento, CA)	64-68-65—197
T-2	Morris Hatalsky	69-68-67—204	T-1	Lonnie Nielsen / Colby Smith	63-64-70—197
T-2	Craig Stadler	69-68-67—204	T-3	Curtis Strange / Thomas Klingman	64-68-66—198
T-2	Gil Morgan	70-65-69—204	T-3	Dale Douglass / Chris Killmer	67-63-68—198
T-5	Jim Thorpe	69-70-66—205	T-3	Keith Fergus / Joshua Leppo	65-65-68—198
T-5	Don Pooley	70-67-68—205	T-6	Hale Irwin / Jacques Gatera	65-68-66—199
T-5	Bruce Fleisher	72-67-66—205	T-6	Mark Johnson / Cameron Rappleye (Elk Grove, CA)	65-69-65—199
8	Mark McNulty	68-73-65—206	T-6	Jay Haas / Katrina Delen-Briones	68-63-68—199
T-9	Jay Haas	69-70-69—208	T-9	Vicente Fernandez / Jonathan Keane	66-68-66—200
T-9	Lonnie Nielsen	70-67-71—208	T-9	Craig Stadler / Aaron Woodard (Denver, CO)	67-66-67—200

3rd Annual Walmart First Tee Open at Pebble Beach, September 1-3, 2006

1	Scott Simpson	67-69-68—204	1	Dana Quigley / Scott Langley (Little Rock, AR)	67-65-63—195
T-2	David Edwards	67-70-68—205	T-2	Scott Simpson / Robert Carter	63-66-67—196
T-2	Jay Haas	66-69-70—205	T-2	David Edwards / Hillary Packard	64-67-65—196
4	Massy Kuramoto	69-72-65—206	T-4	Tom Kite / Mina Harrigae (Monterey, CA)	65-63-70—198
T-5	Tom Kite	69-65-73—207	T-4	Gary McCord / Andrew Cortez	64-65-69—198
T-5	Eduardo Romero	69-67-71—207	T-4	Mike McCullough / Brian Langley	67-65-66—198
T-7	Mike McCullough	68-68-72—208	T-4	Rick Rhoden / Gregor Main	64-68-66—198
T-7	Loren Roberts	67-71-70—208	T-4	Larry Nelson / Robert Hoadley	65-67-66—198
T-7	Des Smyth	68-70-70—208	T-9	Fuzzy Zoeller / Sydney Burlison (Salinas, CA)	66-65-68—199
T-7	D.A. Weibring	64-71-73—208	T-9	Jim Thorpe / Amit Odaiyar (Sacramento, CA)	66-65-68—199

4th Annual Walmart First Tee Open at Pebble Beach, August 31 – September 2, 2007

1	Gil Morgan	70-65-67—202	1	Morris Hatalsky / Harold Varner (Gastonia, NC)	62-65-66—193
2	Hale Irwin	70-65-69—204	2	James Mason / Cameron Rappleye (Elk Grove, CA)	67-66-64—197
3	Tom Watson	67-70-69—206	T-3	Jay Sigel / Sydney Burlison (Salinas, CA)	67-67-64—198
T-4	Scott Simpson	72-69-67—208	T-3	Eduardo Romero / Andres Pumariega (Miami, FL)	63-68-67—198
T-4	Des Smyth	71-74-73—208	T-3	Bruce Vaughn /J.D. Archibald (Simi Valley, CA)	59-70-69—198
T-4	Don Pooley	70-71-67—208	T-3	D.A. Weibring / Brandon Vicory (Aurora, IL)	70-63-65—198
T-7	Jay Haas	73-65-71—209	T-3	Joe Ozaki / Sam Mysock (Tulsa, OK)	66-62-70—198
T-7	D.A. Weibring	72-67-70—209	T-8	Chip Beck / Tucker Harper (Pebble Beach, CA)	67-63-69—199
T-7	Joe Ozaki	72-65-72—209	T-8	Gil Morgan / Lee Prince (Tulsa, OK)	69-64-66—199
T-10	4-way tie: Jacobsen, Baiocchi, Langer, Hatalsky	210	T-8	Des Smyth / John Dustin Allen (Savannah, GA)	68-61-70—199

5th Annual Walmart First Tee Open at Pebble Beach, August 29-31, 2008

1	Jeff Sluman	69-66-67—202	1	Fuzzy Zoeller / Sydney Burlison	62-62-67—191
T-2	Fuzzy Zoeller	66-72-69—207	2	Nick Price / John Catlin	64-68-67—199
T-2	Craig Stadler	70-66-71—207	T-3	Gene Jones / Andrew Garcia	67-67-66—200
T-4	Chip Beck	66-74-68—208	T-3	Jeff Sluman / Michael Guardiola	67-66-67—200
T-4	Mark McNulty	68-71-69—208	T-5	Tom Kite / Elena Warren	67-67-67—201
T-4	Fred Funk	67-70-71—208	T-5	Tom McKnight / Xander McDonald-Smith	70-63-68—201
T-4	Phil Blackmar	67-68-73—208	T-7	Phil Blackmar / Brett Silvernail	66-67-70—203
T-8	Scott Simpson	69-72-68—209	T-7	David Eger / Ariana Patterson	67-68-68—203
T-8	David Eger	70-68-71—209	T-7	Fred Funk / Gabriel Bell	67-68-68—203
T-8	Steve Thomas	67-70-72—209	T-7	Lonnie Nielsen / JT Harper	70-65-68—203
			T-7	Steve Thomas / Paul Chirdon	66-66-71—203
			T-7	Bruce Vaughn / Hannah Martin	67-67-69—203

6th Annual Walmart First Tee Open at Pebble Beach, September 4-6, 2009

1	Jeff Sluman	65-73-68—206	1	David Eger / Will Bishop	63-69-67—199
2	Gene Jones	68-70-70—208	2	Jeff Sluman / Erica Schneider	65-68-67—200
T-3	Tom Lehman	71-65-73—209	3	Ben Crenshaw / Nicklaus Janss	67-65-69—201
T-3	Mark O'Meara	67-67-75—209	4	Scott Simpson / Justin Thomas	66-68-68—202
T-5	David Eger	68-73-69—210	T-5	Andy North / Carly Goldstein	66-69-68—203
T-5	Olin Browne	66-73-71—210	T-5	Loren Roberts / Clifton Jordan	64-66-73—203
T-5	Loren Roberts	66-66-78—210	T-7	Lonnie Nielsen / Brett Denap	69-66-69—204
T-8	Fred Funk	69-71-71—211	T-7	Chip Beck / Samuel Odi	68-66-70—204
T-8	Tom Watson	70-69-72—211	T-7	Mark McNulty / Louis Reismann III	67-68-69—204
T-8	Tom Jenkins	72-66-73—211	T-7	Tom Lehman / Isaiah Huerta	69-64-71—204
T-8	Mark McNulty	68-70-73—211			

THE AT&T PEBBLE BEACH NATIONAL PRO-AM (1947 -)

Bing Crosby had operated a tournament at Rancho Santa Fe, California from 1936-42. It was canceled following the onset of World War II. After the war, Crosby resumed the tournament in January of 1947 utilizing a three course rotation on the courses at Pebble Beach. From 1947-1985 the tournament was officially known as "The Bing Crosby National Pro-Am, " and more casually as "The Crosby," in honor of the founder and host. Since 1986, AT&T has been the title sponsor and the tournament has been called by its current name. It is one of the longest running PGA Tour events, was one of the first televised tournaments, and is truly unique in that amateurs that "make the cut" with their pro-am team play through the final day. Below are the top finishers year by year. On the left are the professionals' individual finishing scores and positions. On the right are the top team scores including the professional's scores and the team's net better ball score.

From 1947-1951 all players played the same course each day over a 54-hole tournament. Round 1: Cypress Point, Round 2: MPCC Dunes; Round 3: Pebble Beach Golf Links. There was no cut.

1947 Bing Crosby National Pro-Am, January 11-13, 1947

Pos	Professional	CP	MP	PB	Total		Pos	Professional	CP	MP	PB		Total	Amateur	CP	MP	PB	Total	Help to Pro
T-1	George Fazio	68	70	75	213		T-1	Sam Snead	76	70	70		216	Roger Kelly	64	66	66	196	-20
T-1	Ed Furgol	72	69	72	213		T-2	Al Zimmerman	74	75	73		222	Bud Ward	65	67	67	199	-23
T-3	Lloyd Mangrum	72	68	76	216		T-2	Newt Bassler	71	74	71		216	F.A. "Buck Hennekin	65	66	68	199	-17
T-3	Sam Snead	76	70	70	216		4	Ed Furgol	72	69	72		213	Bill Higgins	66	67	67	200	-13
T-3	Newt Bassler	71	74	71	216		5	Jim Milward	74	73	73		220	Don Edwards	66	67	70	203	-17
T-6	Ed Oliver	70	70	77	217		T-6	Dick Metz	67	73	79		219	Fred Dold	64	67	73	204	-15
T-6	Elsworth Vines	71	70	76	217		T-6	Harold McSpaden	73	72	80		225	Ed Lowery	70	66	68	204	-21
8	Dick Metz	67	73	79	219		T-6	George Payton	73	72	79		224	Jack Anderson	67	69	68	204	-20
T-9	Johnny Bulla	72	73	75	220		T-6	Johnny Bulla	72	73	75		220	Del Webb	67	69	68	204	-16
T-9		74	69	77	220		T-10	2-way tie						2-way tie				205	

1948 Bing Crosby National Pro-Am, January 9-11, 1948

Pos	Professional	CP	MP	PB	Total		Pos	Professional	CP	MP	PB		Total	Amateur	CP	MP	PB	Total	Help to Pro
1	Lloyd Mangrum	70	67	68	205		1	Ben Hogan	72	69	70		211	Johnny Dawson	70	63	64	197	-14
2	Stan Leonard	71	67	72	210		T-2	Chandler Harper	74	68	80		222	Warner Keeley	67	64	68	199	-23
3	Ben Hogan	72	69	70	211		T-2	Bobby Locke	73	69	70		212	Frank Stranahan	67	67	65	199	-13
4	Bobby Locke	73	69	70	212		T-2	Lloyd Mangrum	70	67	68		205	Bob Simmers	68	66	65	199	-6
T-5	Johnny Palmer	75	66	75	216		5	Stan Leonard	71	67	72		210	T. Suffern Tailer	65	63	72	200	-10
T-5	Jackie Burke	75	70	71	216		T-6	Herman Keiser	No card				na	Bob Gardner	70	64	68	202	na
T-7	Cary Middlecoff	77	71	69	217		T-6	Skip Alexander	73	72	78		223	Morgan Fottrell	68	66	68	202	-21
T-7	Jimmy Demaret	73	70	74	217		8	Jimmy Demaret	73	70	74		217	Dan Searle	70	66	67	203	-14
9	Martin Rose	71	69	78	218		T-9	4-way tie					0					0	0
T-10	five-way tie				219														

1949 Bing Crosby National Pro-Am, January 14-16, 1949

Pos	Professional	CP	MP	PB	Total		Pos	Professional	CP	MP	PB		Total	Amateur	CP	MP	PB	Total	Help to Pro
1	Ben Hogan	70	68	70	208		1	Bill Nary	66	73	74		213	Lefty O'Doul	61	66	69	196	-17
2	Jim Ferrier	69	70	71	210		2	Jon Barnum	69	75	73		217	Harrison Goodwin	61	66	71	198	-19
3	Jimmy Demaret	69	70	72	211		3	Ben Hogan	70	68	70		208	Johnny Dawson	65	65	69	199	-9
4	Bill Nary	66	73	74	213		T-4	Emery Zimmerman	71	70	73		214	Doug Lewis	64	68	68	200	-14
T-5	Emery Zimmerman	71	70	73	214		T-4	Jimmy Demaret	69	70	72		211	Warren Ingersoll	67	66	67	200	-11
T-5	Joe Brown	68	73	73	214		6	Cary Middlecoff	76	65	75		216	Frank Stranahan	67	62	72	201	-15
7	Chick Harbert	69	73	73	215		T-7	Jim Ferrier	69	70	71		210	Forrest Tucker	66	67	69	202	-8
T-8	Art Bell	73	72	71	216		T-7	Art Bell	73	72	71		216	Tom Dwyer	67	67	68	202	-14
T-8	Lew Worsham	72	69	75	216		T-9	5-way tie					0					0	0
T-8	Cary Middlecoff	76	65	75	216														

1950 Bing Crosby National Pro-Am, January 13-15, 1950

Pos	Professional	CP	MP	PB	Total		Pos	Professional	CP	MP	PB		Total	Amateur	CP	MP	PB	Total	Help to Pro
T-1	Jackie Burke	75	67	72	214		T-1	Ralph Bloomquist	73	71	75		219	Bud Moe	69	64	68	201	-18
T-1	Dave Douglas	71	73	70	214		T-1	Marty Furgol	72	69	80		221	Don Edwards	68	64	69	201	-20
T-1	Sam Snead	69	72	73	214		3	Dave Douglas	71	73	70		214	Johnny Weissmuller	66	69	67	202	-12
T-1	Smiley Quick	72	69	73	214		T-4	Jackson Bradley	73	72	75		220	Leo Durocher	70	67	68	205	-15
T-5	E.J. "Dutch" Harrison	74	70	73	217		T-4	Bud Ward	77	71	73		221	Ralph Kiner	68	66	71	205	-16
T-5	Fred Haas, Jr.	74	79	74	227		T-4	Fred Hawkins	72	73	74		219	Ed Lowery	66	69	70	205	-14
T-7	Fred Hawkins	72	73	74	219		T-4	Fred Haas, Jr.	74	79	74		227	Howard Parker	68	67	70	205	-22
T-7	Ralph Bloomquist	73	71	75	219		T-8	Ed Vines	81	79	nc		na	C. Pard Erdman	69	67	70	206	na
T-9	Ray Gafford	73	74	73	220		T-8	Bob Watson	77	75	77		229	Tom Ray, Jr.	69	67	70	206	-23
T-9	Jackson Bradley	73	72	75	220		T-8	Byron Nelson	75	74	78		227	Ed Flynn	68	67	71	206	-21
T-9	Cary Middlecoff	74	68	78	220														

1951 Bing Crosby National Pro-Am, January 12-14, 1951

Pos	Professional	CP	MP	PB	Total		Pos	Professional	CP	MP	PB		Total	Amateur	CP	MP	PB	Total	Help to Pro
1	Byron Nelson	71	67	71	209		1	E.J. "Dutch" Harrison	72	69	75		216	Phil Harris	69	60	67	196	-20
2	Cary Middlecoff	76	67	69	212		2	Joe Kirkwood, Jr.	71	70	73		214	Ben Gage	67	64	67	198	-16
T-3	Ed Furgol	75	70	78	223		T-3	Ed Furgol	75	70	78		223	William C. Boyd	70	66	64	200	-23
T-3	George Fazio	71	71	71	213		T-3	Skee Riegel	73	72	74		219	Dr. John Johnston	67	67	66	200	-19
T-3	Julius Boros	72	72	69	213		T-5	Earl Stewart	71	71	77		219	Paul Gardner	67	65	70	202	-17
6	Joe Kirkwood, Jr.	71	70	73	214		T-5	Byron Nelson	71	67	71		209	Ed Lowery	68	65	69	202	-7
T-7	Smiley Quick	76	69	70	215		T-5	Cary Middlecoff	76	67	69		212	Ed Crowley	73	63	66	202	-10
T-7	Pete Cooper	70	73	72	215		T-5	Jackie Burke	75	73	72		220	George Coleman	70	65	67	202	-18
T-7	Jim Ferrier	70	73	72	215		9	Lew Worsham	72	74	74		220	Ralph Kiner	70	66	67	203	-17
10	E.J. "Dutch" Harrison	72	69	75	216		T-10	4-way tie										204	

Everyone played Round 1 at Cypress Point in a strong wind. Rain washed out the scheduled Round 2 at MPCC, and the rain-shortened 36-hole event concluded with the final round played at Pebble Beach Golf Links.

1952 Bing Crosby National Pro-Am, January 10-12, 1952

	Professional	CP	MP	PB	Total		Professional	CP	MP	PB	Total	Amateur	CP	MP	PB	Total	Help to Pro
1	Jimmy Demaret	74	-	71	145	T-1	Art Bell	75	-	72	147	William Hoelle	70	-	63	133	-14
2	Art Bell	75	-	72	147	T-1	Bob Toski	78	-	72	150	Dr. Bob Knudson	68	-	65	133	-17
3	Doug Ford	78	-	70	148	3	Jimmy Demaret	74	-	71	145	Bob Hope	70	-	64	134	-11
T-4	Jim Ferrier	78	-	71	149	4	Earl Stewart	80	-	71	151	Ken Venturi	70	-	66	136	-15
T-4	Al Brosch	75	-	74	149	T-5	Stanley Horne	80	-	79	159	Tom Dwyer	70	0	67	137	-22
T-6	Everett Goulart	77	-	73	150	T-5	Byron Nelson	77	-	76	153	Ed Lowery	70	-	67	137	-16
T-6	Bob Toski	78	-	72	150	T-6	Doug Ford	78	-	70	148	James French, Jr.	73	-	66	139	-9
T-6	John Barnum	76	-	74	150	T-6	Marty Furgol	81	-	77	158	Stan Moore	72	-	67	139	-19
T-9	Earl Stewart	80	-	71	151	T-6	John Barnum	76	-	74	150	Bob Goldwater	71	-	68	139	-11
T-9	Al Besselink	79	-	72	151	10	Jack Shields	79	-	79	158	Jimmy Saphier	71	-	69	140	-18
T-9	Lloyd Mangrum	79	-	72	151												

From 1953-1957 the field was expanded to 100 teams and a split field; half played the Round 1 at Cypress Point and Round 2 at MPCC Dunes. The other half played the opposite. Only those making the cut (including the low 45 teams) played Round 3 at Pebble Beach Golf Links.

1953 Bing Crosby National Pro-Am, January 9-11, 1953

	Professional	CP	MP	PB	Total		Professional	CP	MP	PB	Total	Amateur	CP	MP	PB	Total	Help to Pro
1	Lloyd Mangrum	67	66	71	204	T-1	Cary Middlecoff	69	67	74	210	Ed Crowley	63	65	62	190	-20
2	Julius Boros	69	67	72	208	T-1	Gene Webb	71	71	71	213	Col. I.F. Wintermute	61	63	66	190	-23
3	W. Lawson Little II	70	70	69	209	T-1	Paul Runyon			MC	na	Bob Vaillancourt	62	61	67	190	na
T-4	Johnny Bulla	70	68	72	210	T-4	Julius Boros	69	67	72	208	Jack Walsh	62	63	68	193	-15
T-4	Al Besselink	71	71	68	210	T-4	Willie Goggin	72	67	75	214	William Hoelle	59	65	69	193	-21
T-4	Cary Middlecoff	69	67	74	210	T-6	Max Evans			MC	na	Wheeler Farish	62	67	65	194	na
T-7	Jackie Burke	67	70	75	212	T-6	Lloyd Mangrum	67	66	71	204	Milt Wershow	66	64	64	194	-10
T-7	Doug Ford	68	73	71	212	T-8	E.J. "Dutch" Harrison	72	71	70	213	Phil Harris	66	65	64	195	-18
T-9	6-way tie				213	T-8	Doug Ford	68	73	71	212	Charles de Limur	64	64	67	195	-17
						T-8	Tommy Bolt	70	66	78	214	Julie Bescos	64	61	70	195	-19

1954 Bing Crosby National Pro-Am, January 15-17, 1954

	Professional	Rd1	Rd2	PB	Total		Professional	Rd1	Rd2	PB	Total	Amateur	Rd1	Rd2	PB	Total	Help to Pro
1	E.J. "Dutch" Harrison	71	68	71	210	T-1	Bud Ward	73	75	70	218	E. Harvie Ward, Jr.	64	67	62	193	-25
2	Jimmy Demaret	73	68	70	211	T-1	Walter Burkemo	74	71	71	216	Lefty O'Doul	66	62	65	193	-23
3	Tommy Bolt	71	70	71	212	T-1	Art Wall, Jr.	77	77	MC	154	Gene Littler	62	65	66	193	na
4	Doug Ford	71	71	71	213	T-1	Doug Ford	71	71	71	213	Monty Moncrief	66	62	65	193	-20
T-5	Earl Stewart	74	70	70	214	5	Peter Thomson	73	70	71	214	Gen. Robert McClure	64	65	66	195	-19
T-5	Peter Thomson	73	70	71	214	T-6	Bill Nary	75	73	72	220	Gerry Priddy	67	65	64	196	-24
T-7	Jimmy Clark	69	74	73	216	T-6	Shelley Mayfield	77	69	73	219	Jack Cendoya	70	61	65	196	-23
T-7	Bob Toski	72	71	73	216	T-8	Fred Hawkins	70	75	74	219	Bones Hamilton	62	71	64	197	-22
T-7	Walter Burkemo	74	71	71	216	T-8	Art Bell	74	74	75	223	William Hoelle	64	67	66	197	-26
T-10	4-way tie				217	T-8	Vic Ghezzi	77	72	74	223	Nick Hilton	65	64	68	197	-26

1955 Bing Crosby National Pro-Am, January 14-16, 1955

	Professional	Rd1	Rd2	PB	Total		Professional	Rd1	Rd2	PB	Total	Amateur	Rd1	Rd2	PB	Total	Help to Pro
1	Cary Middlecoff	69	69	71	209	1	Byron Nelson	70	75	nc	na	Ed Lowery	64	68	63	195	na
T-2	Paul Maguire	68	75	70	213	2	Cary Middlecoff	69	69	71	209	Ed Crowley	66	64	66	196	-13
T-2	Julius Boros	70	71	72	213	T-3	Stan Leonard	66	73	76	215	Jack Walters	65	65	67	197	-18
T-4	Vic Ghezzi	69	75	71	215	T-3	Fred Wampler	70	72	78	220	Julie Bescos	61	68	68	197	-23
T-4	Stan Leonard	66	73	76	215	T-3	Bob Rosburg	72	67	77	216	Hank Mann	62	61	74	197	-19
T-6	Gene Littler	70	70	76	216	T-6	Julius Boros	70	71	72	213	Howard Everitt	64	66	68	198	-15
T-6	Doug Ford	67	74	75	216	T-6	Doug Ford	67	74	75	216	Randolph Scott	62	67	69	198	-18
T-6	Bob Rosburg	72	67	77	216	T-8	Gardner Dickinson	74	72	72	218	Wheeler Farish	68	67	64	199	-19
T-9	Ed Furgol	72	70	75	217	T-8	Art Doering	76	70	75	221	Gen. Omar Bradley	65	66	68	199	-22
T-9	Jackie Burke	69	72	76	217	T-8	Al Mengert	72	82	MC	na	Rod Funseth	64	66	69	199	na
T-9	Jimmy Demaret	72	71	74	217												

1956 Bing Crosby National Pro-Am, January 13-15, 1956

	Professional	Rd1	Rd2	PB	Total		Professional	Rd1	Rd2	PB	Total	Amateur	Rd1	Rd2	PB	Total	Help to Pro
1	Cary Middlecoff	66	68	68	202	1	Ralph Blomquist	no card			na	George Galios	61	60	67	188	na
2	Mike Souchak	64	71	72	207	2	Donald Whitt	73	72	74	219	Dr. Ed Lambert	62	64	65	191	-28
T-3	Bill Ogden	68	69	74	211	3	John Barnum	70	72	WD	na	Dennis O'Keefe	62	61	69	192	na
T-3	Bob Rosburg	69	65	77	211	4	Bud Ward	72	72	73	217	E. Harvie Ward, Jr.	64	63	66	193	-24
T-5	Dow Finsterwald	69	69	74	212	T-5	Cary Middlecoff	66	68	68	202	Ed Crowley	64	64	66	194	-8
T-5	Doug Ford	70	67	75	212	T-5	Art Bell	71	71	79	221	Ken Venturi	64	63	67	194	-27
7	Bo Wininger	68	69	76	213	T-5	Don Addington	75	69	76	220	Frank Pace, Jr.	64	62	68	194	-26
8	Mike Fetchick	65	78	71	214	T-8	George Buzzini	76	73	MC	na	William Higgins	63	64	68	195	na
T-9	E.J. "Dutch" Harrison	71	69	75	215	T-8	Bob Rosburg	69	65	77	211	Hank Mann	65	61	69	195	-16
T-9	Gardner Dickinson	70	70	75	215	T-8	Glen Spivey	78	71	MC	na	Pete Geyer	66	60	69	195	na

1957 Bing Crosby National Pro-Am, January 11-13, 1957

	Professional	Rd1	Rd2	PB	Total			Professional	Rd1	Rd2	PB	Total	Amateur	Rd1	Rd2	PB	Total	Help to Pro
																		Team Score
1	Jay Hebert	74	69	70	213		1	Cary Middlecoff	76	67	72	215	Ed Crowley	62	59	66	187	-28
2	Cary Middlecoff	76	67	72	215		2	Jay Hebert	74	69	70	213	Roger Kelly	65	63	68	196	-17
3	Stan Leonard	68	74	74	216		3	Ed Oldfield	78	71	NC	na	Ernie Nevers	65	60	71	196	na
4	Walter Burkemo	72	71	76	219		T-4	Wesley Ellis	76	69	75	220	Boyd O'Donnell	70	60	68	198	-22
T-5	Wesley Ellis	76	69	75	220		T-4	Smiley Quick	69	78	76	223	Adolph Schmidt, Jr.	59	70	69	198	-25
T-5	Lloyd Mangrum	73	75	72	220		T-6	Gardner Dickinson	79	71	75	225	Wheeler Farish	68	63	68	199	-26
T-5	Paul O'Leary	73	71	76	220		T-6	George Buzzini	81	72	MC	na	William Higgins	68	63	68	199	na
T-5	Ken Venturi	73	71	76	220		T-6	John Zontek	88	70	MC	na	Nelson Cullenward	67	64	68	199	na
9	Ed Furgol	71	71	79	221		T-6	Al Besselink	73	74	75	222	Bob Goldwater	63	67	69	199	-23
T-10	6-way tie				222		T-10	5-way tie									200	

In 1958 the tournament was expanded to 72 holes with the final round televised for the first time. The first two rounds were again split with half playing Round 1 at Cypress Point and Round 2 at MPCC Dunes and the other half playing the opposite. Only those making the cut played the final two rounds on Pebble Beach Golf Links.

1958 Bing Crosby National Pro-Am, January 9-12, 1958

	Professional	Rd1	Rd2	Rd3	PB	Total			Professional	Rd1	Rd2	Rd3	PB	Total	Amateur	Rd1	Rd2	Rd3	PB	Total	Help to Pro
1	Billy Casper	71	66	69	71	277		1	Jay Hebert	69	72	71	73	285	Roger Kelly	65	65	64	66	260	-25
2	Dave Marr	69	70	70	72	281		2	Billy Casper	71	66	69	71	277	Bob Reynolds	67	61	68	65	261	-16
T-3	Ken Venturi	68	74	70	72	284		T-3	Paul Harney	76	71	74	69	290	Phil Harris	68	63	67	65	263	-27
T-3	Dow Finsterwald	73	67	69	75	284		T-3	Ken Venturi	68	74	70	72	284	Charles French	63	69	65	66	263	-21
T-3	Jackie Burke	72	68	71	73	284		T-5	Johnny Pott	68	76	74	78	296	John Miles	63	68	67	66	264	-32
6	Jay Hebert	69	72	71	73	285		T-5	Bob Harris	71	69	71	75	286	Ralph Kiner	69	64	64	67	264	-22
T-7	Bob Harris	71	69	71	75	286		T-5	Jack Fleck	68	76	71	78	293	Frank Souchak	65	66	66	67	264	-29
T-7	Tommy Bolt	67	71	74	74	286		T-5	Dow Finsterwald	73	67	69	75	284	Fred Briskin	69	62	62	71	264	-20
T-7	Cary Middlecoff	72	69	72	73	286		T-5	Byron Nelson	72	74	73	80	299	Ed Lowery	64	63	67	70	264	-35
T-10	Bob Rosburg	65	67	74	81	287		T-10	Ted Kroll	72	72	72	74	290	Bob Goldwater	66	65	67	67	265	-25
T-10	Chick Harbert	71	68	74	74	287		T-10	Tommy Jacobs	74	74	MC		na	Bob Lemon	63	65	68	69	265	na

1959 Bing Crosby National Pro-Am, January 15-18, 1959

	Professional	Rd1	Rd2	Rd3	PB	Total			Professional	Rd1	Rd2	Rd3	PB	Total	Amateur	Rd1	Rd2	Rd3	PB	Total	Help to Pro
1	Art Wall, Jr.	69	65	70	75	279		1	Art Wall, Jr.	69	65	70	75	279	Charles Coe	65	60	62	65	252	-27
T-2	Jimmy Demaret	74	64	70	73	281		2	Doug Ford	73	74	68	70	285	Art Anderson	66	64	64	63	257	-28
T-2	Gene Littler	73	67	70	71	281		3	Gene Littler	73	67	70	71	281	Jack Munger	66	65	66	62	259	-22
T-4	Bob Rosburg	71	70	70	72	283		T-4	Smiley Quick	77	72	72	75	296	Morgan Barofsky	66	62	66	66	260	-36
T-4	John McMullin	68	73	71	71	283		T-4	Art Bell	78	73	75	MC	na	Robert Roos, Jr.	64	63	65	68	260	na
T-6	Don January	70	72	70	73	285		T-4	Jimmy Demaret	74	64	70	73	281	Pete Elliott	66	60	65	69	260	-21
T-6	Doug Ford	73	74	68	70	285		7	Wesley Ellis, Jr.	70	71	71	80	292	Frank Tatum, Jr.	63	63	65	71	262	-30
T-8	Billy Maxwell	67	74	72	73	286		T-8	Ellsworth Vines	76	70	70	79	295	Willard Parker	65	66	63	69	263	-32
T-8	Lloyd Mangrum	73	71	70	72	286		T-8	Bob Rosburg	71	70	70	72	283	Nelson Cullenward	67	64	65	67	263	-20
T-8	Arnold Palmer	69	77	67	73	286		T-8	Gardner Dickinson	72	70	72	75	289	Fred Krammer, Jr.	67	64	65	67	263	-26
T-8	Jack Fleck	75	69	73	69	286															
T-10	Chick Harbert	71	68	74	74	287		T-10	Tommy Jacobs	74	74	MC		na	Bob Lemon	63	65	68	69	265	na

In 1960 the field was further expanded with one-third playing each of the three courses over the first three rounds, and those making the cut playing Round 4 on Pebble Beach Golf Links. For 1960-1966, the three course rotation remained Cypress Point, MPCC Dunes and Pebble Beach Golf Links.

1960 Bing Crosby National Pro-Am, January 21-24, 1960

	Professional	Rd1	Rd2	Rd3	PB	Total			Professional	Rd1	Rd2	Rd3	PB	Total	Amateur	Rd1	Rd2	Rd3	PB	Total	Help to Pro
1	Ken Venturi	70	71	68	77	286		1	Bud Ward	78	76	70	75	299	Bob Silvestri	70	63	63	66	262	-37
T-2	Julius Boros	73	71	72	73	289		T-2	Julius Boros	73	71	72	73	289	Don Schwab	67	64	64	70	265	-24
T-2	Tommy Jacobs	70	74	70	75	289		T-2	Ken Venturi	70	71	68	77	286	E. Harvie Ward, Jr.	65	66	65	69	265	-21
T-4	Ed Oliver	73	68	73	76	290		4	George Bayer	72	75	71	78	296	Morgan Barofsky	64	68	63	71	266	-30
T-4	Don January	72	71	69	78	290		5	Billy Maxwell	71	74	68	78	291	Dr. Bob Knudson	67	67	63	71	268	-23
T-6	Billy Maxwell	71	74	68	78	291		T-6	Doug Ford	73	76	70	73	292	Arne Boscacci	67	71	62	69	269	-23
T-6	Gene Littler	67	73	71	80	291		T-6	Ron Nicol	76	85	76	MC	na	Wheeler Farish, Jr.	68	67	65	69	269	na
8	Doug Ford	73	76	70	73	292		T-8	Mason Rudolph	77	73	66	82	298	Curtis Person	65	67	64	74	270	-28
T-9	Billy Casper	74	72	73	75	294		T-8	Bob Rosburg	84	74	70	MC	na	James Garner	72	65	64	69	270	na
T-9	Paul Harney	75	73	70	76	294		T-8	Lionel Hebert	84	76	73	MC	na	Pete Elliott	76	66	60	68	270	na
T-8	Jack Fleck	75	69	73	69	286															
T-10	Chick Harbert	71	68	74	74	287		T-10	Tommy Jacobs	74	74	MC		na	Bob Lemon	63	65	68	69	265	na

1961 Bing Crosby National Pro-Am, January 19-22, 1961

	Professional	Rd1	Rd2	Rd3	PB	Total			Professional	Rd1	Rd2	Rd3	PB	Total	Amateur	Rd1	Rd2	Rd3	PB	Total	Help to Pro
1	Bob Rosburg	69	67	74	72	282		1	Wesley Ellis, Jr.	71	72	69	77	289	Frank Tatum, Jr.	63	62	60	67	252	-37
T-2	Dave Ragan	68	71	70	74	283		2	Dow Finsterwald	69	70	72	75	286	Fred Krammer, Jr.	60	64	63	67	254	-32
T-2	Roberto deVicenzo	72	66	70	75	283		3	Tommy Jacobs	75	74	71	76	296	Wheeler Farish, Jr.	65	61	62	67	255	-41
T-4	Gardner Dickinson	70	71	72	71	284		4	Byron Nelson	76	70	77	MC	na	Ed Lowery	64	63	65	64	256	na
T-4	Arnold Palmer	70	68	71	75	284		T-5	Mason Rudolph	70	71	71	78	290	Curtis Person	64	61	65	69	259	-31
T-4	Ted Kroll	69	66	68	81	284		T-5	Ken Venturi	67	71	74	74	286	E. Harvie Ward, Jr.	63	67	63	66	259	-27
T-4	Bill Collins	67	68	74	75	284		T-5	Dave Ragan	68	71	70	74	283	William Hoelle	63	64	66	66	259	-24
8	Johnny Pott	73	72	69	71	285		T-5	Ted Kroll	69	66	68	81	284	Aubrey Duffy	65	63	65	66	259	-25
T-9	Jackie Burke	68	69	75	74	286		T-9	Tom Nieporte	74	66	78	78	296	Gordon MacRae	66	60	68	66	260	-36
T-9	Bo Wininger	70	72	70	74	286		T-9	Bob Harris	74	74	72	76	296	Eli Bariteau	67	66	63	64	260	-36
T-9	Ken Venturi	67	71	74	74	286		T-9	Jackie Burke	68	69	75	74	286	George Coleman	60	65	69	66	260	-26
T-9	Dow Finsterwald	69	70	72	75	286		T-9	Johnny Pott	73	72	69	71	285	James French	66	64	63	67	260	-25
T-9	Marty Furgol	70	72	67	77	286															

1962 Bing Crosby National Pro-Am, January 18-22, 1962

	Professional	Rd1	Rd2	Rd3	PB	Total			Professional	Rd1	Rd2	Rd3	PB	Total	Amateur	Rd1	Rd2	Rd3	PB	Total	Help to Pro
1	Doug Ford	70	73	69	74	286	*	1	Bob McCallister	73	78	69	79	299	Albie Pearson	59	64	62	70	255	-44
2	Joe Campbell	67	71	72	76	286		T-2	Stan Leonard	74	74	71	73	292	Dr. Bud Taylor	62	68	64	67	261	-31
3	Phil Rodgers	67	75	72	74	288		T-2	Dow Finsterwald	73	74	74	77	298	Fred Krammer, Jr.	65	65	65	66	261	-37
T-4	Dave Ragan	70	74	73	73	290		4	Doug Ford	70	73	69	74	286	H. Dudley Wysong	65	68	64	65	262	-24
T-4	Ken Venturi	72	69	73	76	290		5	Doug Sanders	73	69	74	77	293	Lloyd Pitzer	68	63	65	69	265	-28
T-6	Johnny Pott	69	75	73	74	291		T-6	Tommy Jacobs	71	75	70	75	291	Wheeler Farish, Jr.	61	67	68	70	266	-25
T-6	Mason Rudolph	68	77	74	75	294		T-6	Billy Maxwell	74	71	74	74	293	Dr. Bob Knudson	63	68	64	71	266	-27
T-6	Tommy Jacobs	71	75	70	75	291		T-6	Al Mengert	81	77	70	MC	na	Bob Goldwater	69	65	64	68	266	na
T-6	Don Massengale	72	76	73	71	292		T-9	George Bayer	72	73	74	78	297	Morgan Barofsky	64	66	68	70	268	-29
T-10	5-way tie					292		T-9	Miller Barber	84	77	73	MC	na	O'Hara Watts	69	67	65	67	268	na

* Ford won with a six-foot putt on the first hole

1963 Bing Crosby National Pro-Am, January 17-20, 1963

	Professional	Rd1	Rd2	Rd3	PB	Total			Professional	Rd1	Rd2	Rd3	PB	Total	Amateur	Rd1	Rd2	Rd3	PB	Total	Help to Pro
1	Billy Casper	73	65	73	74	285		1	Doug Sanders	74	74	69	71	288	Lloyd Pitzer	64	65	62	66	257	-31
T-2	Bob Rosburg	71	74	70	71	286		T-2	Bob Duden	70	73	67	77	287	Ted Gleichmann	66	63	63	68	260	-27
T-2	Dave Hill	68	69	76	73	286		T-2	Tommy Jacobs	74	73	71	74	292	Wheeler Farish, Jr.	69	62	65	64	260	-32
T-2	Art Wall, Jr.	71	71	72	72	286		T-4	George Bayer	68	73	71	76	288	Morgan Barofsky	65	67	64	65	261	-27
T-2	Gary Player	73	69	70	74	286		T-4	Jay Hebert	73	70	77	71	291	Roger Kelly	65	64	67	65	261	-30
T-2	Jack Nicklaus	71	69	76	70	286		6	Julius Boros	66	75	70	77	288	Don Schwab	64	68	63	67	262	-26
7	Bob Duden	70	73	67	77	287		T-7	Dave Hill	68	69	76	73	286	Phil Harris	63	64	68	68	263	-23
T-8	George Bayer	68	73	71	76	288		T-7	Mason Rudolph	74	71	68	76	289	Curtis Person	67	66	62	68	263	-26
T-8	Julius Boros	66	75	70	77	288		T-9	Bob Rosburg	71	74	70	71	286	John Brodie	65	68	65	66	264	-22
T-8	Doug Sanders	74	74	69	71	288		T-9	Jackie Burke	72	72	79	70	293	George Coleman	64	68	69	63	264	-29

1964 Bing Crosby National Pro-Am, January 16-19, 1964

	Professional	Rd1	Rd2	Rd3	PB	Total			Professional	Rd1	Rd2	Rd3	PB	Total	Amateur	Rd1	Rd2	Rd3	PB	Total	Help to Pro
1	Tony Lema	70	68	70	76	284		1	Mike Fetchick	70	74	75	77	296	Charles Seaver	58	65	66	69	258	-38
T-2	Gay Brewer	76	68	70	73	287		2	Tony Lema	70	68	70	76	284	Father John Durkin	63	60	66	70	259	-25
T-2	Bo Wininger	69	73	70	75	287		3	Rex Baxter	70	74	72	78	294	Dr. Bud Taylor	63	62	63	73	261	-33
T-4	Al Geiberger	80	67	68	73	288		T-4	Phil Rodgers	73	71	73	75	292	Jim Vickers	67	61	66	68	262	-30
T-4	Tommy Aaron	70	68	73	77	288		T-4	George Bayer	76	75	79	MC	na	Morgan Barofsky	68	65	60	69	262	na
T-6	George Knudson	72	76	68	73	289		T-4	Dave Ragan	73	72	77	MC	na	William Hoelle	65	63	68	66	262	na
T-6	Gardner Dickinson	71	73	70	75	289		T-7	Don January	74	71	72	75	292	H.R. "Potts" Berglund	69	62	66	67	264	-28
T-6	Bruce Devlin	69	67	74	79	289		T-7	Ken Venturi	76	80	73	MC	na	Roane Puett	62	64	66	72	264	na
T-6	Dave Marr	72	69	72	76	289		T-9	11-way tie											265	
T-10	4-way tie					290															

1965 Bing Crosby National Pro-Am, January 21-24, 1965

	Professional	Rd1	Rd2	Rd3	PB	Total			Professional	Rd1	Rd2	Rd3	PB	Total	Amateur	Rd1	Rd2	Rd3	PB	Total	Help to Pro
1	Bruce Crampton	75	67	73	69	284		T-1	George Bayer	72	77	69	75	293	Morgan Barofsky	65	67	61	67	260	-33
2	Tony Lema	71	65	79	72	287		T-1	George Archer	71	72	74	75	292	Nelson Cullenward	66	65	63	66	260	-32
T-3	Billy Casper	70	70	76	72	288		3	Gene Littler	71	74	75	79	299	Lou Oehmig	64	67	64	67	262	-37
T-3	Jack Nicklaus	72	68	77	71	288		T-4	Johnny Pott	71	72	77	76	296	Jimmy Day	66	62	67	68	263	-33
T-5	Harold Kneece	69	76	69	75	289		T-4	Charles Coody	74	71	77	74	296	Robert Cardinal	69	65	68	61	263	-33
T-5	Al Mengert	78	67	74	70	289		T-4	Lionel Hebert	75	72	77	80	304	Roger Kelly	66	63	68	66	263	-41
T-5	Rocky Thompson	74	70	68	78	290		T-4	Sam Carmichael	no card				na	Alvin Dark	66	67	67	63	263	na
T-5	Jacky Cupit	74	70	68	78	290		8	Dan Sikes	77	72	74	76	299	Johnny Thornton	72	61	64	67	264	-35
T-5	Ken Still	76	69	75	70	290		T-9	5-way tie											265	
T-10	3-way tie					291															

1966 Bing Crosby National Pro-Am, January 20-23, 1966

	Professional	Rd1	Rd2	Rd3	PB	Total			Professional	Rd1	Rd2	Rd3	PB	Total	Amateur	Rd1	Rd2	Rd3	PB	Total	Help to Pro
1	Don Massengale	70	67	76	70	283		1	Chuck Courtney	73	77	70	72	292	John Moler	64	66	63	62	255	-37
2	Arnold Palmer	70	70	73	71	284		2	Billy Martindale	72	71	69	73	285	Bob Roos, Jr.	63	62	61	69	255	-30
T-3	Billy Martindale	72	71	69	73	285		3	Arnold Palmer	70	70	73	71	284	Mark McCormack	63	64	69	60	256	-28
T-3	Al Geiberger	68	74	67	76	285		4	Randy Glover	73	72	72	70	287	Don Schwab	63	63	67	64	257	-30
T-5	Doug Sanders	75	70	71	71	287		5	Gay Brewer	74	74	76	75	299	Dale Morey	60	68	66	64	258	-41
T-5	Randy Glover	73	72	72	70	287		6	Mike Souchak	77	77	72	MC	na	Frank Souchak	67	67	62	63	259	na
T-7	R.H. Sikes	74	74	70	71	289		T-7	Jimmy Powell	76	75	76	MC	na	William Swederskas	67	64	65	64	260	na
T-7	Jack Rule	75	70	70	74	289		T-7	Dean Refram	73	83	73	MC	na	Richard Crane	63	64	69	64	260	na
T-7	Joe Campbell	71	75	73	70	289		T-7	Don Bies	75	72	79	MC	na	William Rudkin	66	60	66	68	260	na
T-10	Mason Rudolph	74	74	70	72	290		T-10	3-way tie												
T-10	Bob Goalby	74	74	67	75	290															

Spyglass Hill Golf Course opened in March 1966 and in January 1967 replaced MPCC Dunes in the rotation. The format remained unchanged and Cypress Point and Pebble Beach Golf Links remained as the other two courses with Round 4 at Pebble Beach Golf Links.

1967 Bing Crosby National Pro-Am, January 19-22, 1967

	Professional	Rd1	Rd2	Rd3	PB	Total			Professional	Rd1	Rd2	Rd3	PB	Total	Amateur	Rd1	Rd2	Rd3	PB	Total	Help to Pro
1	Jack Nicklaus	69	73	74	68	284		1	Mike Souchak	76	73	79	MC	228	Frank Souchak	65	61	66	67	259	na
2	Billy Casper	72	74	69	74	289		T-2	Chuck Courtney	71	75	76	73	295	John Moler	65	68	67	62	262	-33
3	Arnold Palmer	74	75	67	75	291		T-2	Ted Makalena	73	75	72	77	297	Paul J. Spengler, Jr.	65	62	66	69	262	-35
T-4	Bob Rosburg	72	75	72	74	293		T-2	Al Geiberger	73	71	75	75	294	Lew Leis	63	67	64	78	272	-22
T-4	Jackie Burke	70	75	74	74	293		T-5	Wesley Ellis, Jr.	73	75	71	75	294	Frank Tatum, Jr.	69	67	62	66	264	-30
T-4	Bill Parker	75	72	70	76	293		T-5	Jackie Burke	70	75	74	74	293	Virgil Sherrill	65	66	65	68	264	-29
T-7	Doug Sanders	73	78	72	71	294		T-7	Tom Nieporte	71	77	75	78	301	Richard Remsen	63	69	65	68	265	-36
T-7	Dave Hill	73	80	70	71	294		T-7	Bill Collins	74	76	75	74	299	James Fisher	67	66	67	65	265	-34
T-7	Gardner Dickinson	75	74	73	72	294		T-9	Ernie Vossler	73	76	77	77	303	William Higgins	68	67	63	68	266	-37
T-7	Frank Beard	72	75	75	72	294		T-9	Bob Rosburg	72	75	72	74	293	John Brodie	69	66	65	66	266	-27
T-7	Howie Johnson	73	76	72	73	294		T-9	Doug Sanders	73	78	72	71	294	Ed Crowley	63	71	64	68	266	-28
T-7	Wesley Ellis, Jr.	73	75	71	75	294															
T-7	Al Geiberger	73	71	75	75	294															
T-7	Bob McCallister	73	71	75	75	294															

1968 Bing Crosby National Pro-Am, January 11-14, 1968

	Professional	Rd1	Rd2	Rd3	PB	Total			Professional	Rd1	Rd2	Rd3	PB	Total	Amateur	Rd1	Rd2	Rd3	PB	Total	Help to Pro
1	Johnny Pott	70	71	71	73	285	*	1	Johnny Pott	70	71	71	73	285	Virgil Sherrill	59	66	67	61	253	-32
T-2	Billy Casper	73	69	73	70	285		2	Billy Casper	73	69	73	70	285	Bob Dickson	66	63	65	63	257	-28
T-2	Bruce Devlin	73	69	73	70	285		3	Ron Cerrudo	77	75	73	73	298	E. Harvie Ward, Jr.	66	61	63	68	258	-40
4	Deane Beman	74	71	72	70	287		T-4	Jack Nicklaus	71	75	70	73	289	Bob Hoag	64	65	68	62	259	-30
T-5	Raymond Floyd	79	68	71	70	288		T-4	Wesley Ellis, Jr.	75	72	74	71	292	Frank Tatum, Jr.	66	63	69	61	259	-33
T-5	George Knudson	73	71	74	70	288		T-4	Marty Fleckman	72	78	73	73	296	John Cain	64	67	60	68	259	-37
T-5	Bobby Nichols	76	68	72	72	288		7	Paul Bondeson	75	74	77	79	305	Tom Culligan	66	62	68	64	260	-45
8	Jack Nicklaus	71	75	70	73	289		T-8	Tom Nieporte	77	72	72	72	293	Richard Remsen	65	65	65	66	261	-32
9	Jack Rule	73	76	69	72	290		T-8	Chick Evans	80	73	81	MC	na	Bob Falkenburg	66	66	65	64	261	na
T-10	4-way tie					291		T-8	Frank Beard	76	72	74	75	297	Mickey Van Gerbig	63	65	67	66	261	-36

Pott won play-off with a chip-in for birdie on first play-off hole (No. 15)

1969 Bing Crosby National Pro-Am, January 23-27, 1969

	Professional	Rd1	Rd2	Rd3	PB	Total			Professional	Rd1	Rd2	Rd3	PB	Total	Amateur	Rd1	Rd2	Rd3	PB	Total	Help to Pro
1	George Archer	72	68	72	71	283		1	Bob Dickson	73	69	74	68	284	Jack Ging	65	63	65	64	257	-27
T-2	Bob Dickson	73	69	74	68	284		T-2	Billy Casper	70	76	74	70	290	Michael Bonnallack	61	65	67	65	258	-32
T-2	Dale Douglass	71	69	70	74	284		T-2	Gene Littler	73	74	70	72	289	John Moler	68	64	63	63	258	-31
T-2	Howie Johnson	71	69	71	73	284		T-2	Tom Nieporte	71	72	76	74	293	Richard Remsen	65	64	65	64	258	-35
5	John Lotz	71	75	67	72	285		T-2	Tom Shaw	72	77	78	MC	na	Richard Crane	62	61	68	67	258	na
6	Jack Nicklaus	71	73	73	70	287		T-6	Jack Nicklaus	71	73	73	70	287	Bob Hoag	64	65	69	61	259	-28
7	Lee Elder	71	75	73	69	288		T-6	Frank Beard	74	79	75	MC	na	Mickey Van Gerbig	62	68	64	65	259	na
T-8	Bruce Devlin	69	75	78	67	289		T-6	Al Geiberger	71	72	73	74	290	Lew Leis	62	65	65	67	259	-31
T-8	Bill Collins	71	73	76	69	289		T-9	Dale Douglass	71	69	70	74	284	Charles de Bretteville	64	64	68	64	260	-24
T-8	Ron Cerrudo	75	72	71	71	289		T-9	Lionel Hebert	74	71	75	73	293	Roger Kelly	69	63	62	66	260	-33
T-8	Don Massengale	72	75	70	72	289		T-9	Bob McCallister	71	73	75	73	292	Guy Madison	63	66	67	64	260	-32
T-8	Gene Littler	73	74	70	72	289															
T-8	Jimmy Powell	73	76	68	72	289															
T-8	Rod Funseth	72	71	73	73	289															

1970 Bing Crosby National Pro-Am, January 22-25, 1970

	Professional	Rd1	Rd2	Rd3	PB	Total			Professional	Rd1	Rd2	Rd3	PB	Total	Amateur	Rd1	Rd2	Rd3	PB	Total	Help to Pro
1	Bert Yancey	67	70	72	69	278		1	Bob Rosburg	71	72	73	73	289	John Brodie	61	63	64	64	252	-37
2	Jack Nicklaus	70	72	72	65	279		2	Mason Rudolph	70	75	68	75	288	Morgan Barofsky	64	64	62	63	253	-35
T-3	Howie Johnson	68	74	71	70	283		T-3	Bob Dickson	69	74	68	75	286	Jack Ging	63	65	63	64	255	-31
T-3	Bobby Nichols	71	73	69	70	283		T-3	Mac Hunter	75	76	70	MC	na	Jack Bariteau	64	68	62	61	255	na
T-5	George Archer	68	73	71	72	284		T-3	John Lotz	70	76	73	71	290	Jack Huiskamp	64	67	63	61	255	-35
T-5	Paul Harney	69	72	72	71	284		T-3	Rich Martinez	80	69	71	MC	na	U.T. Thompson	67	62	64	62	255	na
T-5	John Jacobs	74	72	69	69	284		T-7	Roberto Bernardini	70	70	76	76	292	Howard Keel	61	66	64	65	256	-36
T-5	Don Massengale	70	70	70	74	284		T-7	Johnny Miller	72	73	72	72	289	Charles de Bretteville	67	65	60	64	256	-33
T-9	Bob Goalby	67	72	71	75	285		T-7	Jack Nicklaus	70	72	72	65	279	Bob Hoag	66	65	63	62	256	-23
T-9	Rod Funseth	74	68	68	75	285		10	Ramon Sota	74	76	72	MC	na	Jose Gancedo	66	65	59	67	257	na
T-9	Bob Stone	72	74	68	71	285															
T-9	Tom Weiskopf	71	76	68	70	285															

1971 Bing Crosby National Pro-Am, January 14-17, 1971

	Professional	Rd1	Rd2	Rd3	PB	Total			Professional	Rd1	Rd2	Rd3	PB	Total	Amateur	Rd1	Rd2	Rd3	PB	Total	Help to Pro
1	Tom Shaw	68	71	69	70	278		1	Lou Graham	72	74	69	72	287	Father John Durkin	64	64	61	65	254	-33
2	Arnold Palmer	72	68	69	71	280		2	Jack Burke, Jr.	76	70	73	72	291	George Coleman	65	60	66	64	255	-36
3	Bob Murphy	71	69	73	69	282		3	Tony Clecak	78	81	79	MC	na	Grant Fitts	67	64	63	63	257	na
T-4	Jerry Heard	72	74	71	67	284		4	Jerry Heard	72	74	71	67	284	Downey Orrick	63	64	66	65	258	-26
T-4	Tom Weiskopf	71	73	68	72	284		T-5	Tom Shaw	68	71	69	70	278	Ed Crowley	64	64	67	65	260	-18
T-4	Howie Johnson	69	70	71	74	284		T-5	Larry Ziegler	74	DQ			na	Max Baer	64	67	65	64	260	na
7	Bobby Nichols	68	72	71	74	285		T-7	Gary Loustalot	83	75	78	MC	na	Alvin Dark	64	70	65	65	264	na
T-8	Johnny Miller	73	74	72	67	286		T-7	Doug Ford	79	74	75	MC	na	Ian McNab	67	65	65	65	261	na
T-8	Dave Eichelberger	72	71	71	72	286		T-7	Jimmy Wright	73	74	77	MC	na	Guy de la Valdene	63	68	63	65	261	na
T-8	Miller Barber	74	69	71	72	286		T-7	Larry Hinson	73	77	73	66	289	Andy Williams	67	65	67	62	261	-28

1972 Bing Crosby National Pro-Am, January 13-16, 1972

	Professional	Rd1	Rd2	Rd3	PB	Total			Professional	Rd1	Rd2	Rd3	PB	Total	Amateur	Rd1	Rd2	Rd3	PB	Total	Help to Pro
1	Jack Nicklaus	66	74	71	73	284	*	1	Lee Trevino	69	74	70	73	286	Don Schwab	66	67	59	64	256	-30
2	Johnny Miller	75	68	67	74	284		2	Bob Murphy	76	74	69	69	288	Tommy Vickers	68	67	60	65	260	-28
3	Lee Trevino	69	74	70	73	286		3	Dale Douglass	73	73	72	73	291	John Archer	65	66	66	64	261	-30
T-4	Fred Marti	72	73	71	71	287		T-4	Sam Snead	77	77	71	MC	na	Ed Tutwiler	65	69	64	67	265	na
T-4	Bruce Crampton	73	72	69	73	287		T-4	Dave Stockton	73	73	73	72	291	Bud Bradley	68	66	63	68	265	-26
T-6	Dan Sikes	76	72	66	74	288		T-4	George Archer	76	73	69	70	288	Robert Roos	67	69	66	63	265	-23
T-6	Bob Murphy	76	74	69	69	288		T-7	Don Bies	76	71	72	73	292	William Rudkin	67	66	67	65	265	-27
T-6	George Archer	76	73	69	70	288		T-7	Tom Weiskopf	70	73	75	71	289	John Swanson	66	67	67	65	265	-24
T-6	Tony Jacklin	70	70	71	77	288		9	Bobby Nichols	74	74	69	76	293	Glen Campbell	64	68	63	71	266	-27
T-10	4-way tie					289		T-10	Orville Moody	76	70	71	75	292	Dan Moss	66	66	66	69	267	-25
								T-10	Hale Irwin	72	76	72	72	292	Darius Keaton	69	68	65	65	267	-25

* Nicklaus won on first play-off hole(No. 15) with a 25-foot birdie putt

1973 Bing Crosby National Pro-Am, January 25-28, 1973

	Professional	Rd1	Rd2	Rd3	PB	Total			Professional	Rd1	Rd2	Rd3	PB	Total	Amateur	Rd1	Rd2	Rd3	PB	Total	Help to Pro
1	Jack Nicklaus	71	69	71	71	282	*	1	Lanny Wadkins	72	70	68	82	292	Billy Satterfield	64	58	62	71	255	-37
T-2	Raymond Floyd	71	70	70	71	282		2	Jim Simmons	72	76	72	78	298	Garth Reynolds	61	68	68	65	262	-36
T-2	Orville Moody	71	66	69	76	282		3	Billy Casper	66	67	78	76	287	Howard Kaskel	64	62	68	70	264	-23
4	Dave Marr	71	71	70	73	285		4	Dave Stockton	74	72	72	72	290	Bud Bradley	66	66	67	66	265	-25
T-5	Rod Funseth	72	74	71	69	286		5	Terry Wilcox	76	81	79	MC	na	Bill Celli	66	66	68	66	266	na
T-5	Lee Elder	76	68	69	73	286		6	Jack Lewis	76	75	72	MC	na	Mauricio Urdaneta	70	64	64	69	267	na
T-7	Billy Casper	66	67	78	76	287		7	B.R. "Mac" McClendon	71	75	75	73	294	David Kirkland	65	71	66	66	268	-26
T-7	Don Iverson	72	68	70	77	287		T-8	Orville Moody	71	66	69	76	282	W. H. Flowers	68	65	68	68	269	-13
T-9	Butch Baird	72	72	75	69	288		T-8	Tom Weiskopf	68	74	82	MC	na	John Mahoney	65	65	69	70	269	na
T-9	Lee Trevino	74	70	73	71	288		T-8	Al Geiberger	75	71	74	73	293	Lew Leis	67	68	68	66	269	-24
T-9	Howie Johnson	73	71	73	71	288		T-8	John Jacobs	74	71	72	75	292	Alvin Dark	68	67	65	69	269	-23
T-9	Gibbey Gilbert	74	67	73	74	288		T-8	Mason Rudolph	71	78	71	76	296	Morgan Barofsky	67	69	67	66	269	-27

* Nicklaus won on first play-off hole(No. 15) with a 12-foot birdie putt

1974 Bing Crosby National Pro-Am, January 3-7, 1974

	Professional	Rd1	Rd2	Rd3	PB	Total			Professional	Rd1	Rd2	Rd3	PB	Total	Amateur	Rd1	Rd2	Rd3	PB	Total	Help to Pro
1	Johnny Miller	68	70	70	-	208		1	Johnny Miller	68	70	70	-	208	Locke de Bretteville	64	67	65	-	196	-12
2	Grier Jones	71	69	72	-	212		2	B.R. "Mac" McClendon	72	78	71	-	221	David Kirkland	67	66	64	-	197	-24
T-3	Rod Funseth	72	70	72	-	214		T-3	Hubert Green	73	70	74	-	217	Louis Auer	67	64	67	-	198	-19
T-3	Tom Kite	71	75	68	-	214		T-3	Dwaine Knight	76	80	78	MC	na	James Murray III	62	69	67	-	198	na
T-3	Bruce Summerhays	74	71	69	-	214		T-3	Billy Casper	74	70	73	-	217	Howard Kaskel	67	65	66	-	198	-19
T-3	John Jacobs	74	68	72	-	214		T-3	Don Bies	74	76	73	-	223	William Rudkin	65	68	65	-	198	-25
T-7	Dave Eichelberger	69	74	72	-	215		7	Steve Melnyk	72	76	75	-	223	Ogden Phipps	67	67	65	-	199	-24
T-7	David Glenz	70	72	73	-	215		T-8	Hale Irwin	70	71	78	-	219	Darius Keaton	66	66	68	-	200	-19
T-9	6-way tie					216		T-8	Lanny Wadkins	67	73	77	-	217	Billy Satterfield	65	68	67	-	200	-17
								T-10	5-way tie											201	

1975 Bing Crosby National Pro-Am, January 23-26, 1975

	Professional	Rd1	Rd2	Rd3	PB	Total			Professional	Rd1	Rd2	Rd3	PB	Total	Amateur	Rd1	Rd2	Rd3	PB	Total	Help to Pro
1	Gene Littler	68	71	68	73	280		1	Bruce Devlin	73	71	69	76	289	Jacky Lee	67	63	63	67	260	-29
2	Hubert Green	66	75	74	69	284		T-2	Tom Watson	69	70	72	81	292	Robert Willits	64	64	68	67	263	-29
3	Tom Kite	70	76	69	70	285		T-2	Hubert Green	66	75	74	69	284	Louis Auer	61	68	67	67	263	-21
4	Lou Graham	72	70	70	75	287		4	Bruce Crampton	80	71	73	MC	224	Joe Denton	70	63	67	67	267	na
5	Forrest Fezler	71	73	72	72	288		5	Rod Curl	71	72	70	77	290	Tom Culligan	65	66	67	70	268	-22
T-6	Jack Nicklaus	71	74	72	72	289		T-6	Allen Miller	72	70	75	78	295	Dan Searle, Jr.	64	66	69	70	269	-26
T-6	Dave Hill	76	72	69	72	289		T-6	Gene Littler	68	71	68	73	280	John Moler	67	69	63	70	269	-11
T-6	Rik Massengale	72	71	74	72	289		T-6	Jim Simmons	71	75	75	76	297	Garth Reynolds	67	63	69	70	269	-28
T-6	Leonard Thompson	74	71	71	73	289		T-6	Lou Graham	72	70	70	75	287	Father John Durkin	68	65	69	67	269	-18
T-6	Johnny Miller	71	74	70	74	289		T-10	Joe Inman	76	71	75	73	295	Mauricio Urdaneta	66	66	67	71	270	-25
T-6	Bruce Devlin	73	71	69	76	289		T-10	B.R. "Mac" McClendon	73	77	71	72	293	George Burns III	67	67	65	71	270	-23

1976 Bing Crosby National Pro-Am, January 22-25, 1976

	Professional	Rd1	Rd2	Rd3	PB	Total			Professional	Rd1	Rd2	Rd3	PB	Total	Amateur	Rd1	Rd2	Rd3	PB	Total	Help to Pro
1	Ben Crenshaw	75	67	70	69	281		1	Hale Irwin	77	71	72	70	290	Darius Keaton	72	63	62	66	263	-27
2	Mike Morley	67	72	71	73	283		T-2	Hubert Green	72	70	74	73	289	Louis Auer	66	68	67	63	264	-25
T-3	George Burns	74	72	69	69	284		T-2	Johnny Miller	74	77	70	70	291	Dean Wendt	66	69	66	63	264	-27
T-3	Dave Hill	71	65	76	72	284		T-4	Dave Stockton	73	76	76	72	297	Rolly Fingers	66	66	66	68	266	-31
T-5	David Graham	69	69	73	75	286		T-4	Guy Walkingstick	76	72	74	76	298	Robert Rasmussen	65	64	69	68	266	-32
T-5	Tom Watson	73	72	70	71	286		T-6	Ben Crenshaw	75	67	70	69	281	Mickey Van Gerbig	71	61	67	68	267	-14
T-7	Bruce Crampton	72	76	72	67	287		T-6	George Burns	74	72	69	69	284	Virgil Sherrill	68	68	65	66	267	-17
T-7	Buddy Allin	74	68	71	74	287		T-6	Bruce Crampton	72	76	72	67	287	Roy Schenk	66	72	64	65	267	-20
T-9	Charles Coody	72	71	72	73	288		T-9	6-way tie											268	
T-9	Tom Weiskopf	76	70	70	72	288															

MPCC's Shore Course was substituted in 1977 for Spyglass Hill. The format remained unchanged and Cypress Point and Pebble Beach Golf Links remained as the other two courses with Round 4 at Pebble Beach Golf Links.

1977 Bing Crosby National Pro-Am, January 20-23, 1977

	Professional	Rd1	Rd2	Rd3	PB	Total			Professional	Rd1	Rd2	Rd3	PB	Total	Amateur	Rd1	Rd2	Rd3	PB	Total	Help to Pro
1	Tom Watson	66	69	67	71	273		1	Leonard Thompson	69	69	73	67	278	Jim Vickers	63	64	64	61	252	-26
2	Tony Jacklin	69	66	68	71	274		T-2	Craig Stadler	72	68	71	67	278	John Jennings	64	62	63	66	255	-23
3	Lee Elder	69	66	69	71	275		T-2	Hale Irwin	71	69	72	70	282	Darius Keaton	65	62	52	66	245	-37
4	Bill Rodgers	68	68	70	71	277		T-4	Dave Stockton	72	71	73	72	288	Rolly Fingers	62	66	64	64	256	-32
T-5	Leonard Thompson	69	69	73	67	278		T-4	Victor Regaldo	67	67	71	73	278	Mauricio Urdaneta	59	63	65	69	256	-22
T-5	Craig Stadler	72	68	71	67	278		T-4	Bob Shearer	72	73	69	74	288	Bob Gibson	63	63	64	66	256	-32
T-5	Hubert Green	65	76	68	69	278		7	Don Massengale	72	73	74	MC	na	Charles Johnson	64	66	63	64	257	na
T-5	Bruce Devlin	69	68	71	70	278		8	Jim Dent	71	74	71	71	287	Tommy John	62	65	65	66	258	-29
T-5	Victor Regaldo	67	67	71	73	278		T-9	Al Geiberger	72	71	71	70	284	Lew Leis	68	63	66	62	259	-25
10	Don Bies	68	72	67	72	279		T-9	Calvin Peete	73	71	74	MC	na	Wheeler Farish	66	62	65	66	259	na
								T-9	Art Wall, Jr.	70	71	73	68	282	Charles McLaughlin	62	66	66	65	259	-23

Spyglass Hill Golf Course returned to the rotation in 1978. The format remained unchanged and Cypress Point and Pebble Beach Golf Links remained as the other two courses with Round 4 at Pebble Beach Golf Links.

1978 Bing Crosby National Pro-Am, January 20-24, 1978

	Professional	Rd1	Rd2	Rd3	PB	Total			Professional	Rd1	Rd2	Rd3	PB	Total	Amateur	Rd1	Rd2	Rd3	PB	Total	Help to Pro
1	Tom Watson	66	74	71	69	280	*	1	Gibby Gilbert	70	71	72	73	286	Richard Gelb	65	63	67	65	260	-26
2	Ben Crenshaw	69	71	73	67	280		2	Tony Jacklin	74	70	73	68	285	Jim Mahoney	67	64	67	63	261	-24
3	Hale Irwin	69	70	74	68	281		T-3	Eddie Pearce	74	70	73	75	292	Fred Krammer, Jr.	67	67	67	62	263	-29
T-4	Hubert Green	69	71	74	69	283		T-3	Craig Stadler	72	71	72	73	288	John Jennings	65	64	65	69	263	-25
T-4	Mike Morley	71	73	68	71	283		T-3	Hale Irwin	69	70	74	68	281	Darius Keaton	65	66	64	68	263	-18
T-4	Don Bies	70	70	73	70	283		T-6	Dave Stockton	72	71	69	78	290	Rolly Fingers	65	65	65	70	265	-25
7	Andy North	74	70	69	71	284		T-6	David Graham	71	72	69	74	286	Kerry Packer	64	68	65	68	265	-21
T-8	Tony Jacklin	74	70	73	68	285		T-8	Lon Hinkle	69	72	75	70	286	Willie Mays	63	68	69	66	266	-20
T-8	Don Pooley	70	70	75	70	285		T-8	Hubert Green	69	71	74	69	283	Capt. Maurice Green	67	64	71	64	266	-17
T-8	Tom Weiskopf	70	71	71	73	285		T-10	5-way tie												

Watson won on second play-off hole with par

1979 Bing Crosby National Pro-Am, February 1-4, 1979

	Professional	Rd1	Rd2	Rd3	PB	Total			Professional	Rd1	Rd2	Rd3	PB	Total	Amateur	Rd1	Rd2	Rd3	PB	Total	Help to Pro
1	Lon Hinkle	70	68	69	77	284	*	1	Andy Bean	72	73	70	69	284	Bill Bunting	67	65	61	64	257	-27
T-2	Mark Hayes	73	73	66	72	284		T-2	Gary Koch	71	75	80	MC	na	Bob Michael	66	66	64	67	263	na
T-2	Andy Bean	72	73	70	69	284		T-2	Lee Trevino	75	78	75	MC	na	Don Schwab	65	66	65	67	263	na
T-4	Leonard Thompson	71	69	76	70	286		4	Lon Hinkle	70	68	69	77	284	John Bridges	68	64	65	67	264	-20
T-4	Brad Bryant	71	70	73	72	286		T-5	Tom Storey	73	73	74	77	297	Lebby Hudson	68	65	67	66	266	-31
T-6	Jim Nelford	72	74	70	71	287		T-5	J.C. Snead	74	72	69	73	288	John McCarthy	66	68	67	65	266	-22
T-6	Jay Haas	68	77	74	68	287		T-7	Vance Heafner	72	77	73	70	292	Brooks Barwick	64	72	67	64	267	-25
T-8	Curtis Strange	70	70	74	74	288		T-7	Jim Nelford	72	74	70	71	287	Bob Blomberg	69	68	66	64	267	-20
T-8	J.C. Snead	74	72	69	73	288		T-9	Steve Melnyk	76	74	73	73	296	Tom Culligan	69	71	64	64	268	-28
T-8	Gibby Gilbert	72	73	70	73	288		T-9	Eddie Pearce	73	79	83	MC	na	Bill Celli	66	71	66	65	268	na

Hinkle won on third play-off hole with birdie

1980 Bing Crosby National Pro-Am, January 31 - February 3, 1980

	Professional	Rd1	Rd2	Rd3	PB	Total			Professional	Rd1	Rd2	Rd3	PB	Total	Amateur	Rd1	Rd2	Rd3	PB	Total	Help to Pro
1	George Burns	71	69	71	69	280		T-1	George Cadle	76	71	75	MC	na	Wheeler Farish	62	65	66	65	258	na
2	Dan Pohl	72	70	72	67	281		T-1	John Mahaffey	68	74	72	68	282	Vern Peak	66	65	64	63	258	-24
T-3	John Mahaffey	68	74	72	68	282		3	Gibby Gilbert	73	69	76	69	287	Richard Gelb	68	62	68	61	259	-28
T-3	Keith Fergus	70	71	71	70	282		4	Pat McGowan	75	68	77	71	291	Barry Ruhl	66	64	66	65	261	-30
T-3	Bill Kratzert	70	74	68	70	282		T-5	Johnny Miller	72	68	75	72	287	Dean Wendt	66	63	66	67	262	-25
T-3	Larry Nelson	70	70	70	72	282		T-5	Curtis Strange	74	73	73	73	293	Paul J. Spengler, Jr.	68	65	63	66	262	-31
T-7	Tom Weiskopf	70	77	67	69	283		T-7	Gary Koch	73	75	73	MC	na	Bob Michael	67	66	66	64	263	na
T-7	Mike Reid	69	72	71	71	283		T-7	Gil Morgan	70	69	71	73	283	Card Walker	66	64	67	66	263	-20
T-7	David Edwards	67	69	72	75	283		T-9	Jerry McGee	71	73	74	73	291	Jim Vickers	65	66	66	67	264	-27
T-7	Gil Morgan	70	69	71	73	283		T-9	Dow Finsterwald	75	74	73	MC	na	James Murray III	67	66	67	64	264	na

1981 Bing Crosby National Pro-Am, January 29 - February 2, 1981

	Professional	Rd1	Rd2	Rd3	PB	Total			Professional	Rd1	Rd2	Rd3	PB	Total	Amateur	Rd1	Rd2	Rd3	PB	Total	Help to Pro
1	John Cook	66	71	72	-	209	*	1	George Cadle	72	71	72	-	215	Wheeler Farish	65	62	64	-	191	-24
T-2	Hale Irwin	70	69	70	-	209		2	Tom Kite	68	76	67	-	211	Tom Kite, Sr.	63	67	64	-	194	-17
T-2	Barney Thompson	71	71	67	-	209		T-3	Barney Thompson	71	71	67	-	209	Charles de Lemur	68	67	60	-	195	-14
T-2	Bobby Clampett	67	71	71	-	209		T-3	Bobby Clampett	67	71	71	-	209	Louis Auer	61	69	65	-	195	-14
T-2	Ben Crenshaw	67	70	72	-	209		T-5	Larry Nelson	70	69	72	-	211	J.C. Rathbone	65	66	65	-	196	-15
T-6	Brad Bryant	69	67	74	-	210		T-5	John Cook	66	71	72	-	209	James Garner	63	63	70	-	196	-13
T-6	Mike Reid	70	72	68	-	210		T-5	Andy Bean	70	69	71	-	210	Bill Bunting	64	66	66	-	196	-14
T-6	Jerry Pate	69	68	73	-	210		T-5	Bill Kratzert	71	72	74	-	217	Jim Vickers	61	66	69	-	196	-21
T-6	Tom Watson	67	69	74	-	210		9	Gibby Gilbert	74	79	74	-	227	Richard Gelb	68	67	62	-	197	-30
T-6	Andy Bean	70	69	71	-	210		10	Gary Koch	72	71	73	-	216	Peter Ueberroth	63	65	69	-	197	-19

Cook won on third play-off hole

1982 Bing Crosby National Pro-Am, February 4-7, 1982

	Professional	Rd1	Rd2	Rd3	PB	Total			Professional	Rd1	Rd2	Rd3	PB	Total	Team Score Amateur	Rd1	Rd2	Rd3	PB	Total	Help to Pro
1	Jim Simons	71	66	71	66	274		1	Jay Haas	73	68	73	73	287	Alfonso Fanjul	68	64	63	62	257	-30
2	Craig Stadler	71	71	64	70	276		2	Gibby Gilbert	72	70	71	72	285	Richard Gelb	65	60	68	65	258	-27
T-3	Johnny Miller	71	71	71	67	280		T-3	Jeff Mitchell	70	72	71	74	287	Jim Chew	66	63	63	67	259	-28
T-3	Mike Morley	72	76	65	67	280		T-3	Jim Simons	71	66	71	66	274	Richard Hoover	67	65	67	60	259	-15
T-3	Rex Caldwell	73	67	73	67	280		T-3	Craig Stadler	71	71	64	70	276	John Jennings	68	66	63	62	259	-17
T-3	Joe Inman	73	69	69	69	280		6	Jim Booros	71	72	71	77	291	Barry Ruhl	68	62	66	64	260	-31
T-3	Jack Nicklaus	69	70	71	70	280		T-7	Bob Gilder	71	70	72	69	282	Howard Clark	66	68	65	63	262	-20
T-8	Tommy Valentine	70	71	73	67	281		T-7	Mike Morley	72	76	65	67	280	Stan Rumbough	66	67	62	67	262	-18
T-8	Gene Littler	70	71	71	69	281		T-9	7-way tie											
T-8	George Burns	67	69	77	68	281															
T-8	Dave Stockton	71	70	70	70	281															

1983 Bing Crosby National Pro-Am, February 3-6, 1983

	Professional	Rd1	Rd2	Rd3	PB	Total			Professional	Rd1	Rd2	Rd3	PB	Total	Team Score Amateur	Rd1	Rd2	Rd3	PB	Total	Help to Pro
1	Tom Kite	69	72	62	73	276		1	Bob Gilder	72	69	66	72	279	Howard Clark	63	64	65	66	258	-21
T-2	Rex Caldwell	69	70	66	73	278		2	Victor Regaldo	73	70	73	72	288	Andres Kaneda	62	61	67	70	260	-28
T-2	Calvin Peete	68	70	70	70	278		3	Miller Barber	72	74	74	MC	na	Dr. Charles James	65	67	64	65	261	na
T-4	Bob Gilder	72	69	66	72	279		T-4	Mike Reid	71	75	70	72	288	Boss Brownlie	64	70	63	65	262	-26
T-4	Danny Edwards	70	69	69	71	279		T-4	Danny Edwards	70	69	69	71	279	Roger Penske	67	64	66	65	262	-17
6	Jack Nicklaus	71	71	66	72	280		T-4	Calvin Peete	68	70	70	70	278	Frank Tatum, Jr.	64	69	65	64	262	-16
T-7	Ken Green	66	68	71	76	281		T-7	Bill Rogers	73	67	75	75	290	Rick Rogers	68	63	63	69	263	-27
T-7	Tom Watson	67	73	72	69	281		T-7	Tim Simpson	74	71	73	MC	na	Dick Horne	66	65	65	67	263	na
T-9	David Graham	72	70	70	70	282		T-7	Tom Kite	69	72	62	73	276	James Robinson	67	69	60	67	263	-13
T-9	Gil Morgan	67	73	71	71	282		T-10	Roger Maltbie	74	65	72	75	286	Stan Rumbough	70	61	63	70	264	-22
T-9	Ben Crenshaw	69	72	68	72	281		T-10	John McComish	69	74	74	MC	na	Jacky Lee	65	65	68	66	264	na
T-9	Mike McCullough	69	72	70	71	282		T-21	Bob Nichols	69	74	73	82	298	Glen Campbell	61	70	67	70	268	-30

1984 Bing Crosby National Pro-Am, February 2-5, 1984

	Professional	Rd1	Rd2	Rd3	PB	Total			Professional	Rd1	Rd2	Rd3	PB	Total	Team Score Amateur	Rd1	Rd2	Rd3	PB	Total	Help to Pro
1	Hale Irwin	69	69	68	72	278	*	1	Mark O'Meara	68	74	68	70	280	J.P. Diesel	62	67	67	61	257	-23
2	Jim Nelford	67	73	70	68	278		2	Rex Caldwell	74	70	75	MC	na	Barry Ruhl	66	63	66	63	258	na
T-3	Mark O'Meara	68	74	68	70	280		T-3	Andy Bean	77	69	70	74	290	Bill Bunting	65	66	64	67	262	-28
T-3	Fred Couples	74	67	69	70	280		T-3	Jim Nelford	67	73	70	68	278	John Purcell	64	69	65	64	262	-16
5	Nick Faldo	70	72	71	68	281		T-3	Miller Barber	73	76	70	MC	na	Johnny Bench	69	66	64	63	262	na
T-6	Craig Stadler	72	66	74	70	282		T-6	Roger Maltbie	72	71	71	72	286	Stan Rumbough	69	65	64	65	263	-23
T-6	Hal Sutton	69	70	71	72	282		T-6	Bill Kratzert	71	74	73	73	291	Tim Sexson	66	68	65	64	263	-28
T-8	Lon Hinkle	72	71	72	68	283		T-6	Mike Donald	74	84	72	MC	na	Cris Collinsworth	61	66	69	67	263	na
T-8	John Fought	72	72	70	69	283		T-6	Danny Mays	81	77	79	MC	na	Don Strock	64	64	68	67	263	na
T-8	David Edwards	69	70	69	75	283		T-10	3-way tie											264	

Irwin won on second play-off hole (No. 16)

1985 Bing Crosby National Pro-Am, January 31 - February 3, 1985

	Professional	Rd1	Rd2	Rd3	PB	Total			Professional	Rd1	Rd2	Rd3	PB	Total	Team Score Amateur	Rd1	Rd2	Rd3	PB	Total	Help to Pro
1	Mark O'Meara	70	72	68	73	283		1	Hubert Green	72	72	75	73	292	Dean Spanos	65	63	61	66	255	-37
T-2	Kikuo Arai	73	69	71	71	284		T-2	Jack Nicklaus	76	72	73	67	288	Jack Nicklaus, Jr.	69	65	65	65	264	-24
T-2	Larry Rinker	73	72	70	69	284		T-2	Dave Eichelberger	77	76	81	MC	na	Pard Erdman	66	66	69	63	264	na
T-2	Curtis Strange	75	69	68	72	284		T-4	Gary McCord	75	70	72	77	294	Robert Vaux	65	67	63	70	265	-29
T-5	Rex Caldwell	75	72	72	66	285		T-4	Jay Delsing	80	76	75	MC	na	Jesse Yohanan	73	63	65	64	265	na
T-5	Payne Stewart	72	73	74	66	285		T-4	Jim Thorpe	76	69	71	76	292	Gary Grelick	65	64	66	70	265	-27
T-7	Tom Watson	75	71	71	69	286		7	Doug Tewell	72	70	72	73	287	Jerry Owens	69	63	67	67	266	-21
T-7	Greg Norman	74	68	73	71	286		8	Fred Couples	76	72	80	MC	na	Barry Ruhl	67	66	69	65	267	na
T-7	Berhard Langer	73	71	71	71	286		T-9	Willie Wood	69	77	74	71	291	John Zoller	67	72	65	64	268	-23
T-10	5-way tie					287		T-9	Hale Irwin	77	71	73	73	294	John Purcell	69	70	65	64	268	-26

AT&T became the title sponsor and the tournament's name was changed to the AT&T Pebble Beach National Pro-Am. The format remained unchanged and Spyglass Hill, Cypress Point and Pebble Beach Golf Links remained as the other three courses with Round 4 at Pebble Beach Golf Links (although in 1986 Round 4 was rained out).

1986 AT&T Pebble Beach National Pro-Am, January 30 - February 2, 1986

	Professional	Rd1	Rd2	Rd3	PB	Total			Professional	Rd1	Rd2	Rd3	PB	Total	Team Score Amateur	Rd1	Rd2	Rd3	PB	Total	Help to Pro
1	Fuzzy Zoeller	69	66	70	-	205		1	Fuzzy Zoeller	69	66	70	-	205	Mike Evans	66	62	65	-	193	-12
2	Payne Stewart	71	69	70	-	210		2	Lee Trevino	77	72	70	-	219	Don Schwab	70	68	59	-	197	-22
T-3	Mark Wiebe	70	69	72	-	211		T-3	Hubert Green	74	72	75	-	na	Dean Spanos	70	64	64	-	198	na
T-3	Tom Watson	71	67	73	-	211		T-3	Willie Wood	68	74	76	-	218	John Zoller	63	65	70	-	198	-20
T-3	Tony Sills	72	68	71	-	211		T-5	Mark Wiebe	70	69	72	-	211	Charles de Limur	68	66	65	-	199	-12
T-6	Dan Pohl	71	70	72	-	213		T-5	Bob Eastwood	70	70	73	-	213	Don Ohlmeyer	63	67	69	-	199	-14
T-6	Mark Pfeil	73	67	73	-	213		T-7	Ron Streck	76	76	71	-	na	Darrell Brown	68	72	60	-	200	na
T-6	Ken Brown	74	73	66	-	213		T-7	Craig Stadler	72	73	71	-	216	John Jennings, Jr.	66	69	65	-	200	-16
T-6	Bob Eastwood	70	70	73	-	213		T-7	Mike McCullough	77	72	72	-	na	Hord Hardin	70	65	65	-	200	na
T-10	3-way tie					214		T-10													

1987 AT&T Pebble Beach National Pro-Am, January 29 - February 1, 1987

Pos	Professional	Rd1	Rd2	Rd3	PB	Total		Pos	Professional	Rd1	Rd2	Rd3	PB	Total	Amateur	Rd1	Rd2	Rd3	PB	Total	Help to Pro
1	Johnny Miller	72	72	68	66	278		1	Fred Couples	70	70	72	69	281	George Brett	67	61	64	65	257	-24
2	Payne Stewart	69	69	69	72	279		2	Wayne Levi	73	77	78	MC	na	Jacky Lee	63	62	68	63	256	na
T-3	Berhard Langer	72	69	68	71	280		3	Kenny Perry	77	75	73	MC	na	Don Sutton	64	64	65	66	259	na
T-3	Lanny Wadkins	68	69	72	71	280		T-4	Tom Kite	74	70	74	69	287	Tom Kite, Sr.	64	63	67	66	260	-27
5	Fred Couples	70	70	72	69	281		T-4	Mark Wiebe	71	72	73	67	283	Charles de Limur	66	65	67	62	260	-23
T-6	Danny Edwards	70	69	72	71	282		T-6	Rex Caldwell	67	78	67	74	286	Dan Quayle	63	68	64	66	261	-25
T-6	Larry Mize	71	71	71	69	282		T-6	John Brodie	75	74	75	MC	na	Dan Marino	66	63	65	67	261	na
T-6	Dan Pohl	69	75	71	67	282		T-8	Brad Fabel	72	73	73	73	291	Jim Mahoney	66	64	68	64	262	-29
T-6	Bob Tway	72	71	72	67	282		T-8	Bill Glasson	72	73	73	72	290	Johnny Bench	64	65	68	65	262	-28
T-10	3-way tie					283		T-8	Ken Brown	73	70	71	69	283	Colm O'Connell	66	65	62	69	262	-21
								T-8	Johnny Miller	72	72	68	66	278	Telly Savalas	68	64	64	66	262	-16
								T-8	Rocco Mediate	75	75	83	MC	na	Darrell Brown	65	65	66	66	262	na
								T-8	Tommy Armour III	72	72	77	MC	na	Pete O'Brien	68	64	66	64	262	na

1988 AT&T Pebble Beach National Pro-Am, February 4-7, 1988

Pos	Professional	Rd1	Rd2	Rd3	PB	Total		Pos	Professional	Rd1	Rd2	Rd3	PB	Total	Amateur	Rd1	Rd2	Rd3	PB	Total	Help to Pro
1	Steve Jones	72	64	70	74	280	*	1	Dan Pohl	69	73	75	69	286	Dan Marino	64	63	64	64	255	-31
2	Bob Tway	72	73	67	68	280		T-2	Steve Jones	72	64	70	74	280	Dr. James Rheim	64	62	67	64	257	-23
3	Greg Norman	68	75	72	66	281		T-2	Johnny Miller	71	71	75	76	293	John Miller, Jr.	64	62	67	64	257	-36
T-4	Craig Stadler	68	70	71	73	282		4	Rick Pearson	73	70	75	71	289	Tom Crow	68	63	62	65	258	-31
T-4	Berhard Langer	72	67	70	73	282		T-5	Lennie Clements	70	75	72	72	289	Louis Auer	63	65	67	65	260	-29
T-4	Jim Carter	70	71	70	71	282		T-5	Andrew Magee	75	68	72	71	286	Jim Vickers	69	60	63	68	260	-26
T-4	Tom Sieckmann	69	68	75	70	282		T-5	Andy North	69	74	79	MC	na	George Gillett, Jr.	65	67	67	61	260	na
8	Mark Calcavecchia	67	69	75	72	283		T-8	Bob Eastwood	74	72	70	78	294	David Fisher	64	67	64	66	261	-33
T-9	Tom Watson	68	72	72	72	284		T-8	David Canipe	70	76	68	70	284	Tom Warde	67	68	61	65	261	-23
T-9	Mark O'Meara	69	73	71	71	284		T-10	Mike Hulbert	74	74	70	72	290	Rudy Gatlin	69	64	64	65	262	-28
T-9	David Canipe	70	76	68	70	284		T-10	Tommy Armour III	73	69	71	72	285	Pete O'Brien	67	63	65	67	262	-23
	Jones won on second play-off hole (No. 16) with a birdie							T-10	Tom Byrum	73	74	74	MC	na	David Kirkland	68	63	66	65	262	na

1989 AT&T Pebble Beach National Pro-Am, January 26-29, 1989

Pos	Professional	Rd1	Rd2	Rd3	PB	Total		Pos	Professional	Rd1	Rd2	Rd3	PB	Total	Amateur	Rd1	Rd2	Rd3	PB	Total	Help to Pro
1	Mark O'Meara	66	68	73	70	277		1	Steve Jones	71	69	71	70	281	Dr. James Rheim	64	64	63	64	255	-26
2	Tom Kite	67	70	72	69	278		2	Dan Pohl	73	75	72	MC	na	Dan Marino	64	65	64	63	256	na
T-3	Jim Carter	70	72	69	69	280		3	Mark Calcavecchia	71	72	75	72	290	Gary Carter	64	66	65	63	258	-32
T-3	Nick Price	66	74	67	73	280		4	Kenny Knox	75	75	72	MC	na	Jack Wagner	66	67	62	66	261	na
T-3	Sandy Lyle	68	72	72	68	280		5	Jack Kay, Jr.	74	73	74	MC	na	Joe Brown	66	64	68	64	262	na
T-6	Steve Jones	71	69	71	70	281		T-6	Lanny Wadkins	73	69	72	67	281	Finis Conner	66	68	65	64	263	-18
T-6	Lanny Wadkins	73	69	72	67	281		T-6	Andrew Magee	74	75	67	72	288	Jim Vickers	65	66	67	65	263	-25
T-6	Steve Pate	72	72	66	71	281		T-6	Lon Hinkle	73	74	78	MC	na	Dwight Clark	68	66	63	66	263	na
T-6	Hal Sutton	70	73	70	68	281		T-6	David Graham	78	77	78	MC	na	Harry Oranges	67	63	69	64	263	na
T-10	Dave Stockton	65	70	78	69	282		T-10	4-way tie											264	
T-10	Loren Roberts	67	72	76	67	282															

1990 AT&T Pebble Beach National Pro-Am, February 1-4, 1990

Pos	Professional	Rd1	Rd2	Rd3	PB	Total		Pos	Professional	Rd1	Rd2	Rd3	PB	Total	Amateur	Rd1	Rd2	Rd3	PB	Total	Help to Pro
1	Mark O'Meara	67	73	69	72	281		1	Hubert Green	74	76	72	MC	na	Dean Spanos	63	68	61	68	260	na
2	Kenny Perry	73	71	69	70	283		T-2	David Frost	74	71	73	67	285	Tom Crow	69	63	67	65	264	-21
T-3	Tom Kite	69	69	75	71	284		T-2	Bob Eastwood	69	72	77	70	288	David Fisher	67	65	69	63	264	-24
T-3	Payne Stewart	66	71	74	73	284		T-2	Mark Calcavecchia	69	71	74	72	286	Gary Carter	64	67	67	66	264	-22
5	David Frost	74	71	73	67	285		T-5	Roger Maltbie	71	71	75	73	290	Eddie DeBartolo, Jr.	66	64	69	69	268	-22
T-6	Richard Zokol	75	71	71	69	286		T-5	Payne Stewart	66	71	74	73	284	Orel Hershiser	65	66	68	69	268	-16
T-6	Mark Calcavecchia	69	71	74	72	286		T-5	Andrew Magee	74	69	76	72	291	Jim Vickers	64	64	71	69	268	-23
T-8	Rocco Mediate	69	68	73	77	287		T-5	Clark Burroughs	73	75	76	MC	na	Huey Lewis	69	69	62	68	268	na
T-8	Rick Fehr	70	72	73	72	287		T-5	Joel Edwards	70	79	75	MC	na	Robert Hoag	66	68	66	68	268	na
T-8	Brad Faxon	75	69	74	69	287		T-5	Jack Nicklaus, Jr.	81	76	87	MC	na	John Purcell	69	64	69	66	268	na
T-11	5-way tie					288		T-11	John Cook	70	68	78	77	293	James Garner	67	65	68	69	269	-24
								T-11	Jeff Wilson	70	75	77	MC	na	Stan Rumbough	67	67	67	68	269	na
								T-11	Barry Jaekel	75	74	73	MC	na	Gregg Davis	68	67	67	67	269	na
								T-11	Pat Fitzsimons	75	79	73	MC	na	Dave Rughetti	66	69	66	68	269	na

Cypress Point withdrew from the rotation after 1990 and Poppy Hills was its replacement. The format remained unchanged and Spyglass Hill and Pebble Beach Golf Links remained as the other two courses with Round 4 at Pebble Beach Golf Links. This format continued through 2009. For 2010 the redesigned MPCC Shore Course will replace Poppy Hills in the rotation.

1991 AT&T Pebble Beach National Pro-Am, January 31 - February 3, 1991

Pos	Professional	Rd1	Rd2	Rd3	PB	Total		Pos	Professional	Rd1	Rd2	Rd3	PB	Total	Amateur	Rd1	Rd2	Rd3	PB	Total	Help to Pro
1	Paul Azinger	67	67	73	67	274		1	John Cook	66	72	69	73	280	Jack Wagner	63	67	63	62	255	-25
T-2	Brian Claar	66	73	71	68	278		2	Bobby Wadkins	73	70	73	67	283	Vinnie Giles	64	64	66	62	256	-27
T-2	Corey Pavin	71	71	69	67	278		3	Larry Mize	71	66	73	70	280	Bill Bentley, Jr.	66	60	68	64	258	-22
T-4	Mike Smith	70	73	71	65	279		T-4	Payne Stewart	69	71	74	71	285	Orel Hershiser	65	67	64	64	260	-25
T-4	Rocco Mediate	69	67	69	74	279		T-4	Bob Borowicz	71	72	74	75	292	Brett Saberhagen	64	62	71	63	260	-32
T-4	Davis Love III	67	70	69	73	279		T-6	Chip Beck	70	70	69	74	283	Ray Knowles	66	60	66	69	261	-22
T-7	Jay Haas	68	70	74	68	280		T-6	Paul Azinger	67	67	73	67	274	Larry Colson	66	63	67	65	261	-13
T-7	John Cook	66	72	69	73	280		T-8	Brad Faxon	74	67	73	70	284	Peter Ueberroth	67	63	68	64	262	-22
T-7	Larry Mize	71	66	73	70	280		T-8	Corey Pavin	71	71	69	67	278	Jim Mahoney	63	69	65	65	262	-16
10	Mark Calcavecchia	71	72	71	67	281		T-8	David Canipe	77	73	78	MC	na	Tom Warde	68	61	65	68	262	na

1992 AT&T Pebble Beach National Pro-Am, January 30 - February 2, 1992

	Professional	Rd1	Rd2	Rd3	PB	Total			Professional	Rd1	Rd2	Rd3	PB	Total	Amateur	Rd1	Rd2	Rd3	PB	Total	Help to Pro
1	Mark O'Meara	69	68	68	70	275	*	1	Greg Norman	74	68	71	71	284	Kerry Packer	63	59	59	65	246	-38
2	Jeff Sluman	64	73	70	68	275		2	Fred Funk	71	75	67	72	285	Lawrence Taylor	62	66	62	62	252	-33
3	Paul Azinger	74	70	64	68	276		3	Brad Bryant	72	73	71	MC	na	Tom Candioti	64	66	61	62	253	na
T-4	Steve Elkington	70	70	69	68	277		4	Brian Claar	72	69	77	MC	na	Jason Batemen	60	65	68	62	255	na
T-4	Tom Lehman	70	71	67	69	277		T-5	Willie Wood	67	72	74	72	285	John Zoller	63	64	64	65	256	-29
T-4	Mark Wiebe	64	74	70	69	277		T-5	Payne Stewart	73	66	70	74	283	Orel Hershiser	65	62	63	66	256	-27
T-7	Larry Rinker	72	66	72	69	279		T-5	Mark Calcavecchia	71	71	74	MC	na	Gary Carter	64	65	65	62	256	na
T-7	Gil Morgan	71	69	69	70	279		8	Paul Azinger	74	70	64	68	276	Larry Colson	70	65	58	64	257	-19
T-9	Tom Watson	70	69	71	70	280		T-9	Gary Nicklaus	83	77	72	MC	na	John Purcell	64	67	61	66	258	na
T-9	Ben Crenshaw	71	71	71	67	280		T-9	Johnny Miller	76	69	71	MC	na	Bryant Gumbel	63	63	67	65	258	na
T-9	Chip Beck	67	71	73	69	280															

* O'Meara won on first play-off hole (No. 16) with a par

1993 AT&T Pebble Beach National Pro-Am, February 4-7, 1993

	Professional	Rd1	Rd2	Rd3	PB	Total			Professional	Rd1	Rd2	Rd3	PB	Total	Amateur	Rd1	Rd2	Rd3	PB	Total	Help to Pro
1	Brett Ogle	68	68	69	71	276		1	Payne Stewart	72	70	71	70	283	Jim Morris	63	65	63	66	257	-26
2	Billy Ray Brown	70	68	69	72	279		T-2	Perry Moss	71	72	70	77	290	Ken Bowden	62	65	64	67	258	-32
T-3	Greg Twiggs	69	72	70	69	280		T-2	Billy Andrade	70	74	68	71	283	Mark McGwire	65	66	63	64	258	-25
T-3	Joey Sindelar	69	72	70	69	280		T-2	David Edwards	71	79	70	MC	na	Mark Grace	65	66	63	64	258	na
T-3	Trevor Dodds	70	68	70	72	280		T-2	Willie Wood	76	75	71	MC	na	John Zoller	66	70	60	62	258	na
6	Lee Janzen	71	67	72	71	281		T-6	Olin Browne	71	74	71	74	290	Pandel Savic	65	66	63	65	259	-31
T-7	Grant Waite	71	70	72	69	282		T-6	Brett Ogle	68	68	69	71	276	Peter Pocklington	67	61	64	67	259	-17
T-7	Chip Beck	72	71	69	70	282		T-8	Larry Rinker	71	71	74	71	287	Richard Gelb	64	64	66	66	260	-27
T-9	8-way tie					283		T-8	John Inman	71	74	69	71	285	Stan Smith	62	63	67	68	260	-25
								T-8	Andrew Magee	70	74	77	MC	na	Jim Vickers	63	66	60	71	260	na

1994 AT&T Pebble Beach National Pro-Am, February 3-6, 1994

	Professional	Rd1	Rd2	Rd3	PB	Total			Professional	Rd1	Rd2	Rd3	PB	Total	Amateur	Rd1	Rd2	Rd3	PB	Total	Help to Pro
1	Johnny Miller	68	72	67	74	281		1	Dudley Hart	65	71	70	78	284	Robert Floyd	58	66	64	70	258	-26
T-2	Jeff Maggert	68	72	72	70	282		T-2	Jim Nelford	70	73	71	75	289	Rober McDonnell	59	68	66	68	261	-28
T-2	Corey Pavin	69	71	71	71	282		T-2	Tom Kite	68	70	72	79	289	Rudy Gatlin	61	64	67	69	261	-28
T-2	Kirk Triplett	69	74	67	72	282		4	Jack Nicklaus	74	73	73	MC	na	Steve Nicklaus	65	62	65	70	262	na
T-2	Tom Watson	69	67	72	74	282		5	Payne Stewart	68	73	73	77	291	Jim Morris	62	65	67	69	263	-28
6	Tom Lehman	69	68	73	73	283		T-6	Kirk Triplett	69	74	67	72	282	Michael Tucker	62	66	66	70	264	-18
T-7	Keith Clearwater	70	70	71	73	284		T-6	Robin Freeman	69	74	74	77	294	William Swing	63	60	70	71	264	-30
T-7	Ted Tryba	70	70	70	74	284		T-6	Mark Brooks	67	78	78	MC	na	Howard Lester	63	64	68	69	264	na
T-7	Blaine McCallister	68	71	72	73	284		T-9	David Duval	69	72	75	73	289	Hughes Norton	65	64	68	68	265	-24
T-7	Jay Delsing	66	75	70	73	284		T-9	Glen Day	73	69	75	79	296	Steve John	62	61	71	71	265	-31
T-7	Dudley Hart	65	71	70	78	284		T-9	Corey Pavin	69	71	71	71	282	Fletcher Pavin	63	66	69	67	265	-17

1995 AT&T Pebble Beach National Pro-Am, February 3-6, 1995

	Professional	Rd1	Rd2	Rd3	PB	Total			Professional	Rd1	Rd2	Rd3	PB	Total	Amateur	Rd1	Rd2	Rd3	PB	Total	Help to Pro
1	Peter Jacobsen	67	73	66	65	271		1	David Duval	72	67	67	67	273	Hughes Norton	69	60	61	64	254	-19
2	David Duval	72	67	67	67	273		2	Jack Nicklaus	71	70	67	70	278	Steve Nicklaus	67	63	61	64	255	-23
T-3	Kenny Perry	68	68	67	72	275		3	Jim Furyk	70	68	74	70	282	Jay Pierson	67	62	65	62	256	-26
T-3	Davis Love III	65	71	71	68	275		4	Davis Love III	65	71	71	68	275	Danny Sullivan	63	65	65	64	257	-18
5	Payne Stewart	71	67	69	70	277		T-5	Ben Crenshaw	73	72	69	66	280	Nathaniel Crosby	67	62	64	65	258	-22
T-6	Guy Boros	69	66	71	72	278		T-5	Nick Faldo	66	72	69	72	279	Huey Lewis	62	65	66	65	258	-21
T-6	Brad Faxon	70	64	72	72	278		T-7	Gil Morgan	73	69	68	75	285	Michael Franz	63	63	62	71	259	-26
T-6	Jack Nicklaus	71	70	67	70	278		T-7	Scott Simpson	72	75	70	MC	na	Bill Murray	63	66	63	67	259	na
T-9	Emlyn Aubrey	70	69	68	72	279		T-9	J.L. Lewis	76	76	67	MC	na	Davis Sezna	68	65	59	68	260	na
T-9	John Adams	72	66	71	70	279		T-9	Guy Boros	69	66	71	72	278	Stu Francis	64	63	65	68	260	-18
T-9	Mark O'Meara	73	68	70	68	279		T-11	Jeff Sluman	73	71	68	76	288	Mark Grace	65	62	64	70	261	-27
T-9	Nick Faldo	66	72	69	72	279		T-11	Billy Andrade	71	70	72	71	284	Joe Pesci	65	66	64	66	261	-23

1996 AT&T Pebble Beach National Pro-Am, February 1-4, 1996

	Professional	CP	MP	PB		Total			Professional	CP	MP	PB		Total	Amateur	CP	MP	PB		Total	Help to Pro
Rain-out																					

1997 AT&T Pebble Beach National Pro-Am, January 30 - February 2, 1997

	Professional	Rd1	Rd2	Rd3	PB	Total			Professional	Rd1	Rd2	Rd3	PB	Total	Amateur	Rd1	Rd2	Rd3	PB	Total	Help to Pro
1	Mark O'Meara	67	67	67	67	268		1	Paul Stankowski	67	67	74	69	277	Andy Garcia	62	58	67	58	245	-32
T-2	David Duval	65	71	62	71	269		T-2	Frank Lickliter	68	75	68	71	282	Joe Mayernik	60	65	58	65	248	-34
T-2	Tiger Woods	70	72	63	64	269		T-2	Glen Day	70	69	67	70	276	Paul Hazen	62	63	62	61	248	-28
4	Jim Furyk	67	65	69	72	273		T-2	Grant Waite	70	72	71	MC	na	Stan Humphries	65	62	63	58	248	na
T-5	Jesper Parnevik	65	70	67	72	274		T-5	Craig Stadler	70	69	66	69	274	Glen Frey	61	61	61	66	249	-25
T-5	Craig Stadler	70	69	66	69	274		T-5	Tiger Woods	70	72	63	64	269	Kevin Costner	64	66	60	59	249	-20
T-7	Billy Andrade	66	75	66	68	275		7	Tom Purtzer	74	69	69	74	286	John Purcell	65	62	62	61	250	-36
T-7	Paul Azinger	69	70	67	69	275		8	Brad Bryant	71	74	67	70	282	John Denver	66	60	61	64	251	-31
T-9	Mike Brisky	69	68	68	71	276		9	Brad Faxon	70	69	69	70	278	Thomas Ryan	62	64	60	66	252	-26
T-9	Glen Day	70	69	67	70	276		T-10	Mike Brisky	69	68	68	71	276	James Hoak	65	59	64	65	253	-23
								T-10	Roger Maltbie	73	71	75	MC	na	William Devane	66	63	61	63	253	na

1998 AT&T Pebble Beach National Pro-Am, January 29 - February 1, 1998 / August 17, 1998

Team Score — Help to Pro

	Professional	Rd1	Rd2	Rd3	PB	Total			Professional	Rd1	Rd2	Rd3	PB	Total	Amateur	Rd1	Rd2	Rd3	PB	Total	to Pro
1	Phil Mickelson	65	70	67	-	202			The Pro-Am was canceled with only two rounds completed											
2	Tom Pernice, Jr.	67	69	67	-	203														
T-3	Jim Furyk	69	67	68	-	204														
T-3	Paul Azinger	67	69	68	-	204														
T-3	J.P. Hayes	70	67	67	-	204														
T-6	Jay Haas	68	67	70	-	205														
T-6	Fuzzy Zoeller	70	70	65	-	205														
T-6	Steve Elkington	70	68	67	-	205														
T-9	Tom Watson	67	67	72	-	206														
T-9	Chris Smith	69	67	70	-	206														
T-9	Bob Gilder	68	70	68	-	206														

1999 AT&T Pebble Beach National Pro-Am, February 4-7, 1999

Team Score — Help to Pro

	Professional	Rd1	Rd2	Rd3	PB	Total		Professional	Rd1	Rd2	Rd3	PB	Total	Amateur	Rd1	Rd2	Rd3	PB	Total	to Pro
1	Payne Stewart	69	64	73	-	206	T-1*	Frank Lickliter	68	68	71	-	207	Robert MacDonnell	63	65	66	-	194	-13
2	Frank Lickliter	68	68	71	-	207	T-2	Craig Stadler	70	67	72	-	209	Glen Frey	65	60	69	-	194	-15
3	Craig Stadler	70	67	72	-	209	T-2	Neal Lancaster	73	70	68	-	211	Robert Scott	68	66	60	-	194	-17
T-4	Ronnie Black	71	69	70	-	210	T-4	Corey Pavin	69	76	73	-	218	Richard Ferris	64	64	67	-	195	-23
T-4	Fred Couples	72	65	73	-	210	T-4	Joe Ozaki	69	70	74	-	213	Jeff Halpin	65	62	68	-	195	-18
T-4	Justin Leonard	70	72	68	-	210	T-4	Payne Stewart	69	64	73	-	206	Jim Morris	63	64	68	-	195	-11
T-4	Jay Williamson	69	70	71	-	210	T-4	Jay Williamson	69	70	71	-	210	Kevin Macgillivary	62	67	66	-	195	-15
T-8	Neal Lancaster	73	70	68	-	211	T-8	Doug Martin	69	74	72	-	215	Sally Krueger	63	67	66	-	196	-19
T-8	Tommy Toles	71	70	70	-	211	T-8	David Ogrin	74	72	79	MC	na	Orel Hershiser	68	60	68	-	196	na
T-10	5-way tie						T-10	6-way tie											197	

* Lickliter-MacDonnell awarded 1st place on pro's score

2000 AT&T Pebble Beach National Pro-Am, February 3-6, 2000

Team Score — Help to Pro

	Professional	Rd1	Rd2	Rd3	PB	Total		Professional	Rd1	Rd2	Rd3	PB	Total	Amateur	Rd1	Rd2	Rd3	PB	Total	to Pro
1	Tiger Woods	68	73	68	64	273	1	Skip Kendall	72	74	66	73	285	David Gill	64	63	58	64	249	-36
T-2	Matt Goegel	69	68	67	71	275	2	Tiger Woods	68	73	68	64	273	Jerry Chang	63	62	65	63	253	-20
T-2	Vijay Singh	66	67	72	70	275	3	Matt Goegel	69	68	67	71	275	Alan Hoops	65	63	61	65	254	-21
T-4	Jerry Kelly	71	70	68	67	276	4	Tom Lehman	69	70	72	67	278	J.B. McIntosh	65	64	63	64	256	-22
T-4	Notah Begay III	66	68	72	70	276	5	Andrew Magee	69	75	67	67	278	John McCoy	65	66	64	63	258	-20
T-4	Jimmy Green	72	68	68	68	276	6	Jack Nicklaus	74	76	72	MC	na	Steve Nicklaus	64	67	66	63	260	na
T-7	Mark Brooks	71	67	66	74	278	T-7	Scott Dunlap	74	70	72	74	290	Gary Vanderweghe	67	64	61	69	261	-29
T-7	Tom Lehman	69	70	72	67	278	T-7	Kelly Gibson	72	72	73	MC	na	Ron Maggard	66	67	65	63	261	na
T-7	Andrew Magee	69	75	67	67	278	T-7	Willie Wood	73	71	72	75	291	Jim Davis	63	65	66	67	261	-30
T-7	Mike Weir	72	71	69	66	278	T-10	3-way tie											263	

2001 AT&T Pebble Beach National Pro-Am, February 1-4, 2001

Team Score — Help to Pro

	Professional	Rd1	Rd2	Rd3	PB	Total		Professional	Rd1	Rd2	Rd3	PB	Total	Amateur	Rd1	Rd2	Rd3	PB	Total	to Pro
1	Davis Love III	71	69	69	63	272	T-1	Tiger Woods	66	73	69	72	280	Jerry Chang	59	67	64	64	254	-26
2	Vijay Singh	66	68	70	69	273	T-1	Phil Mickelson	70	66	66	73	275	Kenny G	66	60	63	65	254	-21
T-3	Phil Mickelson	70	66	66	73	275	T-3	Joe Ogilvie	72	73	68	70	283	Terry O'Toole	64	65	60	66	255	-28
T-3	Olin Browne	68	69	65	73	275	T-3	Steve Flesch	71	72	66	73	282	Kevin Macgillivary	61	67	59	68	255	-27
5	Ronnie Balck	67	68	70	71	276	5	Olin Browne	68	69	65	73	275	Brady	63	65	60	69	257	-18
T-6	Glen Day	68	75	69	65	277	T-6	Jesper Parnevik	72	70	71	80	293	Scott McNealy	63	64	63	68	258	-35
T-6	Craig Barlow	67	71	67	72	277	T-6	Kevin Wentworth	72	71	71	71	285	Tom Dreesen	65	61	66	66	258	-27
T-8	Jerry Kelly	69	68	68	73	278	T-6	Cliff Kresge	71	72	74	MC	na	Alan Hoops	60	64	69	65	258	na
T-8	Mike Weir	70	70	65	73	278	T-9	Brad Elder	66	69	75	74	284	Jimmy Connors	62	61	69	67	259	-25
T-8	Franklin Langham	70	70	70	68	278	T-9	Chris Tidland	73	76	73	MC	na	Matt Lyons	67	68	60	64	259	na
T-8	Frank Nobilo	70	70	67	71	278														

2002 AT&T Pebble Beach National Pro-Am, January 31 - February 3, 2002

Team Score — Help to Pro

	Professional	Rd1	Rd2	Rd3	PB	Total		Professional	Rd1	Rd2	Rd3	PB	Total	Amateur	Rd1	Rd2	Rd3	PB	Total	to Pro
1	Matt Goegel	66	72	67	69	274	1	Brian Claar	74	72	73	MC	na	Randall Mays	65	63	61	66	255	na
2	Pat Perez	66	65	70	76	277	2	Craig Stadler	69	72	73	73	287	Glen Frey	60	66	66	64	256	-31
T-3	Lee Janzen	68	67	70	73	278	3	Andrew Magee	69	70	67	72	278	John McCoy	64	65	64	66	259	-19
T-3	Andrew Magee	69	70	67	72	278	4	Phil Tataurangi	67	72	70	71	280	Lon Haskew	64	63	66	67	260	-20
T-5	Jose Maria Olazabal	70	71	71	68	280	T-5	Paul Azinger	74	72	70	73	289	Peter Ueberroth	68	63	65	65	261	-28
T-5	Jerry Smith	67	69	72	72	280	T-5	Rory Sabbatini	69	72	72	70	283	David Calhoun	63	68	66	64	261	-22
T-5	Phil Tataurangi	67	72	70	71	280	T-7	Todd Fischer	71	73	71	68	283	Joe Jacob	65	67	64	66	262	-21
T-8	Matthew Goggin	69	72	68	72	281	T-7	Dudley Hart	69	71	72	74	286	Jimmy Connors	65	66	66	65	262	-24
T-8	Paul Goydos	72	70	67	72	281	T-7	Michael Heinen	77	74	73	MC	na	Ron Christman	67	63	66	66	262	na
T-8	Kent Jones	70	71	70	70	281	T-7	Craig Perks	70	71	72	77	290	Alan Hoops	61	67	66	68	262	-28
T-8	Vijay Singh	69	71	70	71	281	T-7	Tom Byrum	71	72	73	76	292	Kevin Hayes	67	64	64	67	262	-30

2003 AT&T Pebble Beach National Pro-Am, February 6-9, 2003

	Professional	Rd1	Rd2	Rd3	PB	Total		Professional	Rd1	Rd2	Rd3	PB	Total	Amateur	Rd1	Rd2	Rd3	PB	Total	Help to Pro
1	Davis Love III	72	67	67	68	274	T-1	Brad Faxon	70	70	70	70	280	Thomas Ryan	66	63	64	64	257	-23
2	Tom Lehman	68	70	70	67	275	T-1	Phil Tataurangi	68	73	70	69	280	Craig Heatley	64	66	63	64	257	-23
T-3	Mike Weir	67	74	67	68	276	3	Davis Love III	72	67	67	68	274	Jonathon Linen	65	62	66	65	258	-16
T-3	Tim Herron	69	69	72	66	276	4	Jesper Parnevik	72	74	76	MC		Tom Brady	64	64	68	63	259	na
T-5	Rocco Mediate	70	71	68	70	279	5	Rory Sabbatini	71	69	70	71	281	Andy Hunter	67	64	62	67	260	-21
T-5	Jim Furyk	71	66	73	69	279	T-6	Tom Lehman	68	70	70	67	275	J.B. McIntosh	64	68	65	64	261	-14
T-7	Brad Faxon	70	70	70	70	280	T-6	John Senden	72	79	68	MC	na	Thomas Siebel	62	72	62	65	261	na
T-7	Paul Stankowski	71	67	73	69	280	T-8	Kevin Sutherland	66	73	72	73	284	Bill Gross	62	68	67	65	262	-22
T-7	Phil Tataurangi	68	73	70	69	280	T-8	Ken Green	68	75	72	71	286	David Rivers	64	67	66	65	262	-24
T-10	Rod Pampling	70	68	70	73	281	T-8	Jeff Quigley	73	74	70	71	288	Frank Herringer	65	67	65	65	262	-26
T-10	Tim Clark	74	66	70	71	281	T-8	Dean Wilson	78	73	70	MC	na	Jack Uible	67	63	65	67	262	na
T-10	Rory Sabbatini	71	69	70	71	281	T-8	Dennis Paulson	72	71	77	MC	na	David Shaffer	66	63	65	66	260	na

2004 AT&T Pebble Beach National Pro-Am, February 5-8, 2004

	Professional	Rd1	Rd2	Rd3	PB	Total		Professional	Rd1	Rd2	Rd3	PB	Total	Amateur	Rd1	Rd2	Rd3	PB	Total	Help to Pro
1	Vijay Singh	67	68	68	69	272	1	Jerry Kelly	71	72	70	73	286	Robert Halmi, Jr.	65	64	61	64	254	-32
2	Jeff Maggert	71	68	67	69	275	2	Vijay Singh	67	68	68	69	272	Teddy Forstmann	66	62	62	66	256	-16
3	Phil Mickelson	68	68	71	69	276	T-3	David Edwards	74	68	72	73	287	John McCoy	67	60	65	67	259	-28
T-4	Arron Oberholser	69	67	67	76	279	T-3	Jesper Parnevik	70	67	73	70	280	George Lopez	70	61	64	64	259	-21
T-4	Mike Weir	73	70	66	70	279	T-3	Vaughn Taylor	70	73	73	MC	na	Reno Cruz	64	63	69	63	259	na
T-4	K.J. Choi	67	70	71	71	279	T-6	Tom Carter	75	71	78	MC	224	Jim Simmons	64	63	69	64	260	na
T-7	Jesper Parnevik	70	67	73	70	280	T-6	Steve Elkington	72	72	72	MC	na	Donald Lucas	63	67	66	64	260	na
T-7	Mark Hensby	70	67	73	70	280	T-6	Mike Heinen	74	73	81	MC	na	Bob Berg	64	63	66	67	260	na
T-7	Tom Pernice, Jr.	67	68	73	72	280	T-9	Casey Martin	71	74	71	MC	na	Scott DeSano	62	70	63	66	261	na
T-10	4-way tie					281	T-9	Mike Weir	73	70	66	70	279	George Roberts	68	66	62	65	261	-18

2005 AT&T Pebble Beach National Pro-Am, February 7-13, 2005

	Professional	Rd1	Rd2	Rd3	PB	Total		Professional	Rd1	Rd2	Rd3	PB	Total	Amateur	Rd1	Rd2	Rd3	PB	Total	Help to Pro
1	Phil Mickelson	62	67	67	73	269	1	Joel Kreibel	72	70	68	70	280	Barry McCollam	63	63	63	64	253	-27
2	Mike Weir	66	67	73	67	273	T2	Richard S. Johnson	68	69	70	76	283	Bob Halloran	64	63	64	66	257	-26
3	Greg Owen	67	69	67	72	275	T2	Jay Delsing	70	71	74	MC	na	Doug Kintzinger	58	65	66	68	257	na
T4	Paul Goydos	67	68	70	71	276	4	Scott Simpson	72	72	74	MC	na	Bill Murray	63	65	63	67	258	na
T4	Tim Clark	67	71	67	71	276	5	Jason Allred	74	71	79	MC	na	Carson Daly	62	67	64	66	259	na
T6	Darren Clarke	70	66	70	71	277	6	Tim Clark	67	71	67	71	276	Michael Bolton	62	66	66	66	260	-16
T6	Arron Oberholser	71	66	69	71	277	T7	Dickey Pride	66	71	72	74	283	Phillip Purcell	65	64	65	67	261	-22
8	Graeme McDowell	68	69	70	71	278	T7	Phil Mickelson	62	67	67	73	269	Steve Lyons	61	63	66	71	261	-8
T9	Davis Love III	65	72	71	71	279	T9	Darren Clarke	70	66	70	71	277	Andrew Chandler	66	62	66	68	262	-15
T9	Jeff Sluman	71	66	69	73	279	T9	Brad Faxon	78	67	73	MC	na	Tom Ryan	68	60	66	68	262	na
							T9	Nick Watney	69	73	71	MC	na	Lisa Fernandez	66	65	64	67	262	na

2006 AT&T Pebble Beach National Pro-Am, February 6-12, 2006

	Professional	Rd1	Rd2	Rd3	PB	Total		Professional	Rd1	Rd2	Rd3	PB	Total	Amateur	Rd1	Rd2	Rd3	PB	Total	Help to Pro
1	Arron Oberholser	65	68	66	72	271	T-1	Arron Oberholser	65	68	66	72	271	Michael McCallister	59	65	63	68	255	-16
2	Rory Sabbatini	69	69	68	70	276	T-1	Hunter Mahan	68	73	67	73	281	Alan Heuer	60	66	63	66	255	-26
T3	Jonathan Byrd	69	65	74	69	277	T-3	Tim Clark	66	71	70	73	280	Michael Bolton	63	64	64	65	256	-24
T3	Mike Weir	63	67	69	78	277	T-3	Paul McGinley	71	68	71	70	280	Dermot Desmond	67	63	64	62	256	-24
T5	Craig Barlow	69	68	72	69	278	T-5	J.P. Hayes	70	73	73	MC	na	Scott DeSano	62	66	65	65	258	na
T5	Daniel Chopra	71	67	69	71	278	T-5	Duffy Waldorf	69	73	70	71	283	Jim Hoak	65	66	62	65	258	-25
T7	Vijay Singh	68	71	72	68	279	T-5	Shane Bertch	72	70	70	72	284	Richard Stricklen	66	64	64	64	258	-26
T7	Tom Lehman	72	65	72	70	279	8	Brian Davis (PB)	66	72	68	73	279	Ronald Turner	58	64	66	71	259	-20
T7	Brian Davis	66	72	68	73	279	T-9	Greg Kraft	67	72	75	MC	na	Mike Donnelly	58	67	67	68	260	na
T7	Luke Donald	62	72	71	74	279	T-9	Fredrik Jacobson	67	67	74	77	285	Bill Walters	65	63	65	67	260	-25
T7	Nick Watney	65	71	70	73	279	T-11	Brad Faxon	68	71	74	78	291	Tom Ryan	63	66	67	69	265	-26
							T-11	Will MacKenzie	70	69	70	74	283	Jim Orr	64	65	66		195	-88
							T-11	Mike Weir	63	67	69	78	277	George Roberts	62	64	67	72	265	-12

2007 AT&T Pebble Beach National Pro-Am, February 5-11, 2007

	Professional	Rd1	Rd2	Rd3	PB	Total		Professional	Rd1	Rd2	Rd3	PB	Total	Amateur	Rd1	Rd2	Rd3	PB	Total	Help to Pro
1	Phil Mickelson	65	67	70	66	268	1	Phil Mickelson	65	67	70	66	268	Harry You	60	62	66	61	249	-19
2	Kevin Sutherland	72	63	67	71	273	2	Tom Watson	70	68	72	71	281	Michael Watson	65	62	66	60	253	-28
3	John Mallinger	65	70	68	71	274	3	Greg Owen	68	70	71	67	276	Harris Barton	62	66	66	60	254	-22
T-4	Greg Owen	68	70	71	67	276	4	Jason Dufner	70	72	74	MC	na	Christopher Molumphy	65	64	66	61	256	na
T-4	Davis Love III	70	67	70	69	276	5	Bo Van Pelt	72	68	71	68	279	Blake Bozman	65	65	67	62	259	-20
T-6	Matt Kuchar	72	69	70	66	277	T-6	Brett Quigley	70	72	70	70	282	Frank Herringer	67	65	63	65	260	-22
T-6	Jim Furyk	67	65	76	69	277	T-6	Craig Kanada	68	69	71	73	281	Louis Welch	66	63	65	66	260	-21
T-6	Corey Pavin	68	72	67	70	277	T-6	J.B. Holmes	76	66	68	70	280	David Novak	71	62	64	63	260	-20
T-9	Ted Purdy	73	70	68	67	278	T-6	John Mallinger	65	70	68	71	274	Kerry Gordon	60	68	67	65	260	-14
T-9	Ryan Armour	68	71	72	67	278	10	Kevin Sutherland	72	63	67	71	273	Bill Gross	67	60	66	68	261	-12

2008 AT&T Pebble Beach National Pro-Am, February 9-15, 2008

	Professional	Rd1	Rd2	Rd3	PB	Total			Professional	Rd1	Rd2	Rd3	PB	Total	Team Score: Amateur	Rd1	Rd2	Rd3	PB	Total	Help to Pro
1	Steve Lowery	69	71	70	68	278	*	1	Fredrik Jacobson	73	67	70	74	284	Bill Walters	65	62	62	61	250	-34
2	Vijay Singh	70	70	67	71	278		2	D.A. Points	68	73	70	73	284	Peter Watzka	64	69	66	61	260	-24
T3	Dudley Hart	69	70	68	72	279		T3	Tim Clark	73	74	72	MC	na	Michael Bolton	64	67	67	63	261	na
T3	John Mallinger	67	74	73	65	279		T3	Parker McLachin	70	70	74	70	284	James E. Rohr	64	61	69	67	261	-23
T3	Corey Pavin	73	69	71	66	279		T3	Greg Owen	73	77	68	MC	na	Harris Barton	67	67	63	64	261	na
6	Jason Day	69	70	71	70	280		6	Tom Scherrer	70	75	72	MC	na	Ed Hirlihy	70	61	66	65	262	na
T7	Dustin Johnson	73	68	68	73	282		T7	Chris Riley	73	68	72	72	285	Jeff Britton	66	62	69	66	263	-22
T7	Nicholas Thompson	69	69	74	70	282		T7	Jay Williamson	68	71	72	75	286	Scott McNealy	64	65	66	68	263	-23
T9	Brent Geiberger	69	73	71	70	283		T7	Y.E. Yang	69	73	68	73	283	Jeffrey Donovan	67	64	67	65	263	-20
T9	Jason Gore	70	74	69	70	283		T10	Dudley Hart	69	70	68	72	279	Jeremy Jacobs	65	68	66	65	264	-15
T9	Joe Ogilvie	74	69	70	70	283		T10	Nicholas Thompson	69	69	74	70	282	Andy Hunter	66	64	69	65	264	-18
T9	Tag Ridings	73	71	68	71	283															
T9	Y.E. Yang	69	73	68	73	283															

* Lowery won on first play-off hole (No. 18) with a seven-foot birdie putt

2009 AT&T Pebble Beach National Pro-Am, February 9-15, 2009

	Professional	Rd1	Rd2	Rd3	PB	Total			Professional	Rd1	Rd2	Rd3	PB	Total	Team Score: Amateur	Rd1	Rd2	Rd3	PB	Total	Help to Pro
1	Dustin Johnson	65	69	67	-	201		T-1	Dustin Johnson	65	69	67	-	201	Joe Rice	63	67	63	-	193	-8
2	Mike Weir	67	69	69	-	205		T-1	Chris Stroud	69	69	70	-	208	Ron Christman	63	63	67	-	193	-15
3	Retief Goosen	68	64	74	-	206		3	Aron Price	68	69	75	-	212	Brian Tyler	66	62	66	-	194	-18
T-4	Bob Estes	68	72	67	-	207		T-4	Shigeki Maruyama	69	73	67	-	209	Reuben Richards, Jr.	65	68	62	-	195	-14
T-4	Mark Calcavecchia	67	69	71	-	207		T-4	Mike Weir	67	69	69	-	205	George Roberts	63	66	66	-	195	-10
T-6	D.J. Trahan	67	73	68	-	208		T-6	Mark Calcavecchia	67	69	71	-	207	Kenny Roberts	64	66	66	-	196	-11
T-6	Kevin Chappell	68	72	68	-	208		T-6	Kevin Chappell	68	72	68	-	208	Chris O'Donnell	66	67	63	-	196	-12
T-6	Bill Lunde	67	70	71	-	208		T-6	Robert Garigus	65	71	77	-	213	Brian Greenspun	63	66	67	-	196	-17
T-6	Chris Stroud	69	69	70	-	208		T-6	Jay Williamson	70	75	68	-	213	Scott McNealy	64	66	66	-	196	-17
T-10	4-way tie					209		T-10	7-way tie											197	

NOTES

CHAPTER 1

1. Colvin, Sidney, ed., *The Letters of Robert Louis Stevenson*, Charles Scribner's Sons, New York, 1905, p. 173.
2. Stevenson, Robert Louis. *Old Pacific Capitol*, (1880).
3. Hotel Del Monte Souvenir Booklet.
4. *A Piney Paradise*, Lucy Nealy McLane, Academy Library Guild, Fresno, CA, 1958. p. 34.
5. *A Piney Paradise*, Lucy Nealy McLane, Academy Library Guild, Fresno, CA, 1958. p. 40.
6. *Monterey Argus*, Saturday, September 29, 1888.
7. *A Piney Paradise*, Lucy Nealy McLane, Academy Library Guild, Fresno, CA, 1958. p. 134.
8. Morse, Samuel Finley Brown (1885–1969), unpublished memoirs.
9. February 27, 1919 letter to William W. Carson of San Francisco.

CHAPTER 2

10. Mackenzie, Alister, *The Spirit of St. Andrews*, p.170, Sleeping Bear Press, Chelsea, MI, 1995.
11. "Monterey Peninsula Country Club (Shore)" by Adam Brady, February 19, 2009 http://www.linksmagazine.com/golf_courses/united_states/california/monterey_peninsula_country_club.aspx
12. Mackenzie, p. 54.
13. Morse.
14. "Creating Poppy Hills," by Robert Trent Jones II, NCGA News, October 1984.

CHAPTER 3

15. *Los Angeles Times* (1886-Current File); Sep 15, 1911; ProQuest Historical Newspapers Los Angeles Times (1881–1986), pg. III4.
16. This was 1 under women's par of 77. For instance, the 15th played as a par-5 for the ladies.

CHAPTER 4

17. *Monterey Herald*, John Hallisey, August 30, 1981.

CHAPTER 5

18. *World of Professional Golf–1972*, Mark McCormick, p. 44.
19. *Monterey Herald*, June 12, 1972, "Host Pro Discusses His Links," U.S. Open supplement, pp. 24-25.
20. Ibid., p.5, and McCormack, p.65.
21. Nicklaus had now won two U.S. Amateurs (1959 and '61); three U.S. Opens (1962, '67 and '72); four Masters (1963, '65, '66 and '72); two PGAs (1963 and '71); and two British Opens (1966 and '70).
22. *Golf Digest*, "Read My Mind As I Play The Open," Tom Watson with Nick Seitz, February 1983, p. 48.

INDEX